TAO I

TAO I

The Way of All Life

Dr. & Master Zhi Gang Sha

ATRIA BOOKS
New York   London   Toronto   Sydney

Heaven's Library
Toronto

ATRIA BOOKS

A Division of Simon & Schuster, Inc.   Toronto, ON
1230 Avenue of the Americas
New York, NY 10020

The information contained in this book is intended to be educational and not for diagnosis, prescription, or treatment of any health disorder whatsoever. This information should not replace consultation with a competent healthcare professional. The content of the book is intended to be used as an adjunct to a rational and responsible healthcare program prescribed by a healthcare practitioner. The author and publisher are in no way liable for any misuse of the material.

First Atria Books hardcover edition May 2010

ATRIA BOOKS and colophon are trademarks of Simon & Schuster, Inc.

For information about special discounts for bulk purchases, please contact Simon & Schuster Special Sales at 1-866-506-1949 or business@simonandschuster.com.

The Simon & Schuster Speakers Bureau can bring authors to your live event. For more information or to book an event, contact the Simon & Schuster Speakers Bureau at 1-866-248-3049 or visit our website at www.simonspeakers.com.

Manufactured in the United States of America

10   9   8   7   6   5   4   3   2   1

Library of Congress Cataloging-in-Publication Data

Sha, Zhi Gang.
    Tao I : the way of all life / Zhi Gang Sha —1st Atria Books hardcover ed.
       p.   cm.
    Includes index.
    1. Spiritual life.   2. Spiritual healing.   3. Taoism—Miscellanea.   I. Title.
    BL624.S4757   2010
    204'.4—dc22   2010004343

ISBN 978-1-4391-9581-9
ISBN 978-1-4391-9651-9 (ebook)

Contents

Soul Power Series   xi

How to Receive the Divine Soul Downloads Offered
     in the Books of the Soul Power Series   xxv

     • What to Expect After You Receive Divine Soul
     Downloads   xxvii

Foreword to the Soul Power Series by
     Dr. Michael Bernard Beckwith   xxix

How to Read This Book   xxxi

List of Divine Soul Downloads   xxxv

List of Figures   xxxvii

Introduction   xxxix

1: *Important Wisdom of Tao*   *1*

     • What Is Tao?   2

     • The Significance of Studying and Practicing Tao   28

     • The Steps to Reach Tao   30

     • Summary of Tao Training   41

2: Tao I Text   **59**

o 道可道   Tao Ke Tao   65
o 非常道   Fei Chang Tao   65
o 大无外   Da Wu Wai   76
o 小无内   Xiao Wu Nei   77
o 无方圆   Wu Fang Yuan   82
o 无形象   Wu Xing Xiang   82
o 无时空   Wu Shi Kong   85
o 顺道昌   Shun Tao Chang   85
o 逆道亡   Ni Tao Wang   87
o 道生一   Tao Sheng Yi   92
o 天一真水   Tian Yi Zhen Shui   94
o 金津玉液   Jin Jin Yu Ye   94
o 咽入丹田   Yan Ru Dan Tian   95
o 一生二   Yi Sheng Er   97
o 道丹道神   Tao Dan Tao Shen   99
o 服务人类   Fu Wu Ren Lei   101
o 服务万灵   Fu Wu Wan Ling   105
o 服务地球   Fu Wu Di Qiu   106
o 服务宇宙   Fu Wu Yu Zhou   108
o 治愈百病   Zhi Yu Bai Bing   109
o 预防百病   Yu Fang Bai Bing   116
o 返老还童   Fan Lao Huan Tong   122
o 长寿永生   Chang Shou Yong Sheng   134
o 和谐人类   He Xie Ren Lei   135
o 道业昌盛   Tao Ye Chang Sheng   137
o 功德圆满   Gong De Yuan Man   154
o 万灵融合   Wan Ling Rong He   160
o 丹神养肾   Dan Shen Yang Shen   167
o 二生三   Er Sheng San   168

o 三万物	San Wan Wu	168
o 天地人	Tian Di Ren	169
o 神气精	Shen Qi Jing	170
o 肾生精	Shen Sheng Jing	175
o 精生髓	Jing Sheng Sui	176
o 髓充脑	Sui Chong Nao	177
o 脑神明	Nao Shen Ming	178
o 炼精化气	Lian Jing Hua Qi	180
o 炼气化神	Lian Qi Hua Shen	182
o 炼神还虚	Lian Shen Huan Xu	183
o 炼虚还道	Lian Xu Huan Tao	185
o 合道中	He Tao Zhong	188
o 无穷尽	Wu Qiong Jin	188
o 道灵宫	Tao Ling Gong	190
o 信息雪山	Xin Xi Xue Shan	194
o 灵语言	Ling Yu Yan	196
o 灵信通	Ling Xin Tong	209
o 灵歌舞	Ling Ge Wu	232
o 灵敲打	Ling Qiao Da	248
o 灵草药	Ling Cao Yao	265
o 灵针灸	Ling Zhen Jiu	294
o 灵按摩	Ling An Mo	301
o 灵治疗	Ling Zhi Liao	303
o 灵预防	Ling Yu Fang	319
o 灵转化	Ling Zhuan Hua	323
o 灵圆满	Ling Yuan Man	328
o 灵智慧	Ling Zhi Hui	331
o 灵潜能	Ling Qian Neng	333
o 换灵脑身	Huan Ling Nao Shen	335
o 服务三界	Fu Wu San Jie	339

o 灵光普照　Ling Guang Pu Zhao 340

o 万物更新　Wan Wu Geng Xin 343

o 誓为公仆　Shi Wei Gong Pu 349

o 世代服务　Shi Dai Fu Wu 355

o 灵光圣世　Ling Guang Sheng Shi 358

o 创新纪元　Chuang Xin Ji Yuan 358

o 道道道　Tao Tao Tao 361

o 道定得　Tao Ding De 364

o 道慧明　Tao Hui Ming 364

o 道喜在　Tao Xi Zai 367

o 道体生　Tao Ti Sheng 369

o 道圆满　Tao Yuan Man 372

o 道合真　Tao He Zhen 373

o 道果成　Tao Guo Cheng 375

o 道神通　Tao Shen Tong 377

o 道法自然　Tao Fa Zi Ran 379

• Conclusion 382

3: Jin Dan—Tao Practice in Daily Life 387

• What Is Jin Dan? 387

• The Power and Significance of Jin Dan 389

• How to Build Your Jin Dan 390

• Divine Jin Dan and Tao Jin Dan 397

• Sacred Jin Dan Mantras for Daily Practice 399

  1. Morning Practice Upon Waking Up—
金丹醒神　Jin Dan Xing Shen 401

  2. Practice Before Meals—
金丹进谷　Jin Dan Jin Gu 402

  3. Practice After Meals—
金丹化谷　Jin Dan Hua Gu 404

4. Practice to Heal Your Liver and Wood Element—
金丹舒肝 Jin Dan Shu Gan and
金丹治木 Jin Dan Zhi Mu   406

5. Practice to Heal Your Heart and Fire Element—
金丹养心 Jin Dan Yang Xin and
金丹治火 Jin Dan Zhi Huo   408

6. Practice to Heal Your Spleen and Earth Element—
金丹健脾 Jin Dan Jian Pi and
金丹治土 Jin Dan Zhi Tu   410

7. Practice to Heal Your Lungs and Metal Element—
金丹宣肺 Jin Dan Xuan Fei and
金丹治金 Jin Dan Zhi Jin   413

8. Practice to Heal Your Kidneys and Water Element—
金丹壮肾 Jin Dan Zhuang Shen and
金丹治水 Jin Dan Zhi Shui   415

9. Evening Practice Before Going to Sleep—
金丹睡眠 Jin Dan Shui Mian   417

10. Practice to Boost Energy Anytime—
金丹能量 Jin Dan Neng Liang   419

11. Practice to Self-Heal Anytime—
金丹治量 Jin Dan Zhi Liao   420

12. Practice to Prevent Sickness Anytime—
金丹预防 Jin Dan Yu Fang   422

13. Practice to Prolong Life Anytime—
金丹长寿 Jin Dan Chang Shou   423

14. Practice to Transform Every Aspect of
Your Life Anytime—
金丹转化 Jin Dan Zhuan Hua   425

15. Practice to Enlighten Your Soul, Heart, Mind,
and Body Anytime—
金丹圆满 Jin Dan Yuan Man   426

Conclusion   431
Acknowledgments   435
A Special Gift   439
Index   443
Other Books of the Soul Power Series   463

Soul Power Series

THE PURPOSE OF life is to serve. I have committed my life to this purpose. Service is my life mission.

My total life mission is to transform the consciousness of humanity and all souls in all universes, and enlighten them, in order to create love, peace, and harmony for humanity, Mother Earth, and all universes. This mission includes three empowerments.

My first empowerment is to teach *universal service* to empower people to be unconditional universal servants. The message of universal service is:

> *I serve humanity and all universes unconditionally.*
> *You serve humanity and all universes unconditionally.*
> *Together we serve humanity and all souls in all universes unconditionally.*

My second empowerment is to teach *healing* to empower people to heal themselves and heal others. The message of healing is:

I have the power to heal myself.
You have the power to heal yourself.
Together we have the power to heal the world.

My third empowerment is to teach *the power of soul,* which includes soul secrets, wisdom, knowledge, and practices, and to transmit Divine Soul Power to empower people to transform every aspect of their lives and enlighten their souls, hearts, minds, and bodies.

The message of Soul Power is:

> *I have the Soul Power to transform my consciousness and every aspect of my life and enlighten my soul, heart, mind, and body.*
> *You have the Soul Power to transform your consciousness and every aspect of your life and enlighten your soul, heart, mind, and body.*
> *Together we have the Soul Power to transform consciousness and every aspect of all life and enlighten humanity and all souls.*

To teach the power of soul is my most important empowerment. It is the key for my total life mission. The power of soul is the key for transforming physical life and spiritual life. It is the key for transforming and enlightening humanity and every soul in all universes.

The beginning of the twenty-first century is the transition period into a new era for humanity, Mother Earth, and all universes. This era is named the Soul Light Era. The Soul Light Era began on August 8, 2003. It will last fifteen thousand years. Natural disasters—including tsunamis, hurricanes, cyclones, earthquakes,

floods, tornados, hail, blizzards, fires, drought, extreme tempera-
tures, famine, and disease—political, religious, and ethnic wars,
terrorism, proliferation of nuclear weapons, economic challenges,
pollution, vanishing plant and animal species, and other such up-
heavals are part of this transition. In addition, millions of people
are suffering from depression, anxiety, fear, anger, and worry. They
suffer from pain, chronic conditions, and life-threatening illnesses.
Humanity needs help. The consciousness of humanity needs to be
transformed. The suffering of humanity needs to be removed.

The books of the Soul Power Series are brought to you by
Heaven's Library and Atria Books. They reveal soul secrets and
teach soul wisdom, soul knowledge, and soul practices for your
daily life. The power of soul can heal, prevent illness, rejuvenate,
prolong life, and transform consciousness and every aspect of life,
including relationships and finances. The power of soul is vital to
serving humanity and Mother Earth during this transition period. The power of soul will awaken and transform the consciousness of humanity and all souls.

In the twentieth century and for centuries before, *mind over
matter* played a vital role in healing, rejuvenation, and life transformation. In the Soul Light Era, *soul over matter*—Soul Power—
will play *the* vital role to heal, rejuvenate, and transform all life.

There are countless souls on Mother Earth—souls of human
beings, souls of animals, souls of other living things, and souls of
inanimate things. *Everyone and everything has a soul.*

Every soul has its own frequency and power. Jesus had miraculous healing power. We have heard many heart-touching stories
of lives saved by Guan Yin's[1] compassion. Mother Mary's love has

---

1 Guan Yin is known as the Bodhisattva of Compassion and, in the West, as the Goddess of
Mercy.

created many heart-moving stories. All of these great souls were given Divine Soul Power to serve humanity. In all of the world's great religions and spiritual traditions, including Buddhism, Taoism, Christianity, Judaism, Hinduism, Islam, and more, there are similar accounts of great spiritual healing and blessing power.

I honor every religion and every spiritual tradition. However, I am not teaching religion. I am teaching Soul Power, which includes soul secrets, soul wisdom, soul knowledge, and soul practices. Your soul has the power to heal, rejuvenate, and transform life. An animal's soul has the power to heal, rejuvenate, and transform life. The souls of the sun, the moon, an ocean, a tree, and a mountain have the power to heal, rejuvenate, and transform life. The souls of healing angels, ascended masters, holy saints, Taoist saints, Hindu saints, buddhas, and other high-level spiritual beings have great Soul Power to heal, rejuvenate, and transform life.

Every soul has its own standing. Spiritual standing, or soul standing, has countless layers. Soul Power also has layers. Not every soul can perform miracles like Jesus, Guan Yin, and Mother Mary. Soul Power depends on the soul's spiritual standing in Heaven. The higher a soul stands in Heaven, the more Soul Power that soul is given by the Divine. Jesus, Guan Yin, and Mother Mary all have a very high spiritual standing.

Who determines a soul's spiritual standing? Who gives the appropriate Soul Power to a soul? Who decides the direction for humanity, Mother Earth, and all universes? The top leader of the spiritual world is the decision maker. This top leader is the Divine. The Divine is the creator and manifester of all universes.

In the Soul Light Era, all souls will join as one and align their consciousness with divine consciousness. At this historic time, the Divine has decided to transmit divine soul treasures to humanity and all souls to help humanity and all souls go through Mother Earth's transition.

Let me share two personal stories with you to explain how I reached this understanding.

First, in April 2003, I held a Power Healing workshop for about one hundred people at Land of Medicine Buddha, a retreat center in Soquel, California. As I was teaching, the Divine appeared. I told the students, "The Divine is here. Could you give me a moment?" I knelt and bowed down to the floor to honor the Divine. (At age six, I was taught to bow down to my tai chi masters. At age ten, I bowed down to my qi gong masters. At age twelve, I bowed down to my kung fu masters. Being Chinese, I learned this courtesy throughout my childhood.) I explained to the students, "Please understand that this is the way I honor the Divine, my spiritual fathers, and my spiritual mothers. Now I will have a conversation with the Divine."

I began by saying silently, "Dear Divine, I am very honored you are here."

The Divine, who was in front of me above my head, replied, "Zhi Gang, I come today to pass a spiritual law to you."

I said, "I am honored to receive this spiritual law."

The Divine continued, "This spiritual law is named the Universal Law of Universal Service. It is one of the highest spiritual laws in the universe. It applies to the spiritual world and the physical world."

The Divine pointed to the Divine. "I am a universal servant." The Divine pointed to me. "You are a universal servant." The Divine swept a hand in front of the Divine. "Everyone and everything is a universal servant. A universal servant offers universal service unconditionally. Universal service includes universal love, forgiveness, peace, healing, blessing, harmony, and enlightenment. *If one offers a little service, one receives a little blessing from the universe and from me. If one offers more service, one receives more blessing. If one offers unconditional service, one receives unlimited blessing."*

The Divine paused for a moment before continuing. "There is another kind of service, which is unpleasant service. Unpleasant service includes killing, harming, taking advantage of others, cheating, stealing, complaining, and more. If one offers a little unpleasant service, one learns little lessons from the universe and from me. If one offers more unpleasant service, one learns more lessons. If one offers huge unpleasant service, one learns huge lessons."

I asked, "What kinds of lessons could one learn?"

The Divine replied, "The lessons include sickness, accidents, injuries, financial challenges, broken relationships, emotional imbalances, mental confusion, and any kind of disorder in one's life." The Divine emphasized, "This is how the universe operates. This is one of my most important spiritual laws for all souls in the universe to follow."

After the Divine delivered this universal law, I immediately made a silent vow to the Divine:

> *Dear Divine,*
>
> *I am extremely honored to receive your Law of Universal Service. I make a vow to you, to all humanity, and to all souls in all universes that I will be an unconditional universal servant. I will give my total GOLD* [gratitude, obedience, loyalty, devotion] *to you and to serving you. I am honored to be your servant and a servant of all humanity and all souls.*

Hearing this, the Divine smiled and left.

My second story happened three months later, in July 2003, while I was holding a Soul Study workshop near Toronto. The Divine came again. I again explained to my students that the Divine had appeared, and asked them to wait a moment while I bowed down 108 times and listened to the Divine's message. On this occasion, the Divine told me, "Zhi Gang, I come today to choose you as my direct servant, vehicle, and channel."

I was deeply moved and said to the Divine, "I am honored. What does it mean to be your direct servant, vehicle, and channel?"

The Divine replied, "When you offer healing and blessing to others, call me. I will come instantly to offer my healing and blessing to them."

I was deeply touched and replied, "Thank you so much for choosing me as your direct servant."

The Divine continued, "I can offer my healing and blessing by transmitting my permanent healing and blessing treasures."

I asked, "How do you do this?"

The Divine answered, "Select a person and I will give you a demonstration."

I asked for a volunteer with serious health challenges. A man named Walter raised his hand. He stood up and explained that he had liver cancer, with a two-by-three-centimeter malignant tumor that had just been diagnosed from a biopsy.

Then I asked the Divine, "Please bless Walter. Please show me how you transmit your permanent treasures." Immediately, I saw the Divine send a beam of light from the Divine's heart to Walter's liver. The beam shot into his liver, where it turned into a golden light ball that instantly started spinning. Walter's entire liver shone with beautiful golden light.

The Divine asked me, "Do you understand what software is?"

I was surprised by this question but replied, "I do not understand much about computers. I just know that software is a computer program. I have heard about accounting software, office software, and graphic design software."

"Yes," the Divine said. "Software is a program. Because you asked me to, I transmitted, or downloaded, my Soul Software for Liver to Walter. It is one of my permanent healing and blessing treasures. You asked me. I did the job. This is what it means for you to be my chosen direct servant and channel."

I was astonished. Excited, inspired, and humbled, I said to the Divine, "I am so honored to be your direct servant. How blessed I am to be chosen." Almost speechless, I asked the Divine, "Why did you choose me?"

"I chose you," said the Divine, "because you have served humanity for more than one thousand lifetimes. You have been very committed to serving my mission through all of your lifetimes. I am choosing you in this life to be my direct servant. You will transmit countless permanent healing and blessing treasures from me to humanity and all souls. This is the honor I give to you now."

I was moved to tears. I immediately bowed down 108 times again and made a silent vow:

Dear Divine,

I cannot bow down to you enough for the honor you have given to me. No words can express my greatest gratitude. How blessed I am to be your direct servant to download your permanent healing and blessing treasures to humanity and all souls! Humanity and all souls will receive your huge blessings through my service as your direct

*servant. I give my total life to you and to humanity. I will
accomplish your tasks. I will be a pure servant to humanity and all souls.*

I bowed again. Then I asked the Divine, "How should Walter
use his Soul Software?"

"Walter must spend time to practice with my Soul Software,"
said the Divine. "Tell him that simply to receive my Soul Software does not mean he will recover. He must practice with this
treasure every day to restore his health, step by step."

I asked, "How should he practice?"

The Divine gave me this guidance: "Tell Walter to : *Divine
Liver Soul Software heals me. Divine Liver Soul Software heals me.
Divine Liver Soul Software heals me. Divine Liver Soul Software
heals me.*"

I asked, "For how long should Walter chant?"

The Divine answered, "At least two hours a day. The longer
he practices, the better. If Walter does this, he could recover in
three to six months."

I shared this information with Walter, who was excited and
deeply moved. Walter said, "I will practice two hours or more
each day."

Finally I asked the Divine, "How does the Soul Software
work?"

The Divine replied, "My Soul Software is a golden healing
ball that rotates and clears energy and spiritual blockages in Walter's liver."

I again bowed to the Divine 108 times. Then I stood up and

offered three Soul Softwares to every participant in the workshop as divine gifts. Upon seeing this, the Divine smiled and left.

Walter immediately began to practice as directed for at least two hours every day. Two and a half months later, a CT scan and MRI showed that his liver cancer had completely disappeared. At the end of 2006 I met Walter again at a signing in Toronto for my book *Soul Mind Body Medicine.* In May 2008 Walter attended one of my events at the Unity Church of Truth in Toronto. On both occasions Walter told me that there was still no sign of cancer in his liver. For nearly five years his Divine Soul Download healed his liver cancer. He was very grateful to the Divine.

This major event of being chosen as a direct divine servant happened in July 2003. As I mentioned, a new era for Mother Earth and all universes, the Soul Light Era, began on August 8, 2003. The timing may look like a coincidence but I believe there could be an underlying spiritual reason. Since July 2003 I have offered divine transmissions to humanity almost every day. I have offered more than ten divine transmissions to all souls in all universes.

I share this story with you to introduce the power of divine transmissions or Divine Soul Downloads. Now let me share the commitment that I made in *Soul Wisdom,* the first book of my Soul Power Series, and that I have renewed in every one of my books since:

From now on, I will offer Divine Soul Downloads in every book I write.

Divine Soul Downloads are permanent divine healing and blessing treasures for transforming your life. There is an ancient saying: *If you want to know if a pear is sweet, taste it.* If you want to know the power of Divine Soul Downloads, experience it.

Divine Soul Downloads carry divine frequency with divine

love, forgiveness, compassion, and light. Divine frequency transforms the frequency of all life. Divine love melts all blockages, including soul, mind, and body blockages, and transforms all life. Divine forgiveness brings inner peace and inner joy. Divine compassion boosts energy, stamina, vitality, and immunity. Divine light heals, prevents sickness, rejuvenates, and prolongs life.

A Divine Soul Download is a new soul created from the heart of the Divine. The Divine Soul Download transmitted to Walter was a Soul Software. Since then, I have transmitted several other types of Divine Soul Downloads, including Divine Soul Herbs, Divine Soul Acupuncture, Divine Soul Operation, and Divine Soul Mind Body Transplants.

A Divine Soul Transplant is a new divine soul of an organ, a part of the body, a bodily system, cells, DNA, RNA, the smallest matter in cells, or the spaces between cells. When it is transmitted, it replaces the recipient's original soul of the organ, part of the body, system, cells, cell units, DNA, RNA, smallest matter in cells, or spaces between cells. A new divine soul can also replace the soul of a home or a business. A new divine soul can be transmitted to a pet, a mountain, a city, or a country to replace their original souls. A new divine soul can even replace the soul of Mother Earth.

A Divine Mind Transplant is also a light being created by the Divine. It carries divine consciousness to replace original consciousness of the recipient's system, organ, part of the body, cells, cell units, DNA, RNA, smallest matter, or spaces.

A Divine Body Transplant is another light being created by the Divine. This light being carries divine energy and divine tiny matter to replace original energy and tiny matter of the recipient's system, organ, part of the body, cells, cell units, DNA, RNA, smallest matter, or spaces.

Everyone and everything has a soul. The Divine can download any soul you can conceive of. These Divine Soul Downloads are permanent divine healing, blessing, and life-transformation treasures. They can transform the lives of anyone and anything. Because the Divine created these divine soul treasures, they carry Divine Soul Power, which is the greatest Soul Power among all souls. All souls in the highest layers of Heaven will support and assist Divine Soul Downloads. Divine Soul Downloads are the crown jewel of Soul Power.

Divine Soul Downloads are divine presence. The more Divine Soul Downloads you receive, the faster your soul, heart, mind, and body will be transformed. The more Divine Soul Downloads your home or business receives and the more Divine Soul Downloads a city or country receives, the faster their souls, hearts, minds, and bodies will be transformed.

In the Soul Light Era, the evolution of humanity will be created by Divine Soul Power. Soul Power will transform humanity. Soul Power will transform animals. Soul Power will transform nature and the environment. Soul Power will assume the leading role in every field of human endeavor. Humanity will deeply understand that *the soul is the boss.*

Soul Power, including soul secrets, soul wisdom, soul knowledge, and soul practices, will transform every aspect of human life. Soul Power will transform every aspect of organizations and societies. Soul Power will transform cities, countries, Mother Earth, all planets, stars, galaxies, and all universes. Divine Soul Power, including Divine Soul Downloads, will lead this transformation.

I am honored to have been chosen as a divine servant to offer Divine Soul Downloads to humanity, to relationships, to homes, to businesses, to pets, to cities, to countries, and more. In the last few years I have already transmitted countless divine souls to humanity and to all universes. I repeat to you now: *I will offer Divine Soul Downloads within each and every book of the Soul Power Series.* Clear instructions on how to receive these Divine Soul Downloads will be provided in the next section, "How to Receive the Divine Soul Downloads Offered in the Books of the Soul Power Series," as well as on the appropriate pages of each book.

I am a servant of humanity. I am a servant of the universe. I am a servant of the Divine. I am extremely honored to be a servant of all souls. I commit my total life and being as an unconditional universal servant.

I will continue to offer Divine Soul Downloads for my entire life. I will offer more and more Divine Soul Downloads to every soul. I will offer Divine Soul Downloads for every aspect of life for every soul.

I am honored to be a servant of Divine Soul Downloads.

Human beings, organizations, cities, and countries will receive more and more Divine Soul Downloads, which can transform every aspect of their lives and enlighten their souls, hearts, minds, and bodies. The Soul Light Era will shine Soul Power. The books in the Soul Power Series will spread Divine Soul Downloads, together with Soul Power—soul secrets, soul wisdom, soul knowledge, and soul practices—to serve humanity, Mother Earth, and all universes. The Soul Power Series is a pure servant for humanity and all souls. The Soul Power Series is honored to be a Total GOLD[2] servant of the Divine, humanity, and all souls.

The final goal of the Soul Light Era is to join every soul as one in love, peace, and harmony. This means that the consciousness

---

2 Total GOLD means total gratitude, total obedience, total loyalty, and total devotion to the Divine.

of every soul will be totally aligned with divine consciousness. There will be difficulties and challenges on the path to this final goal. Together we will overcome them. We call all souls of humanity and all souls in all universes to offer unconditional universal service, including universal love, forgiveness, peace, healing, blessing, harmony, and enlightenment. The more we offer unconditional universal service, the faster we will achieve this goal.

The Divine gives his heart to us. The Divine gives his love to us. The Divine gives Divine Soul Downloads to us. Our hearts meld with the Divine's heart. Our souls meld with the Divine's soul. Our consciousnesses align with the Divine's consciousness. We will join hearts and souls together to create love, peace, and harmony for humanity, Mother Earth, and all universes.

> *I love my heart and soul*
> *I love all humanity*
> *Join hearts and souls together*
> *Love, peace and harmony*
> *Love, peace and harmony*

Love all humanity. Love all souls. Thank all humanity. Thank all souls.

Thank you. Thank you. Thank you.

Zhi Gang Sha

How to Receive the Divine Soul Downloads Offered in the Books of the Soul Power Series

$\mathcal{T}$HE BOOKS OF the Soul Power Series are unique. For the first time in history, the Divine is downloading the Divine's soul treasures to readers as they read these books. Every book in the Soul Power Series will include Divine Soul Downloads that have been preprogrammed. When you read the appropriate paragraphs and pause for a minute, divine gifts will be transmitted to your soul.

In April 2005 the Divine told me to "leave Divine Soul Downloads to history." I thought, "A human being's life is limited. Even if I live a long, long life, I will go back to Heaven one day. How can I leave Divine Soul Downloads to history?"

In the beginning of 2008, as I was editing the paperback edition of *Soul Wisdom*, the Divine suddenly told me: "Zhi Gang, offer my downloads within this book." The Divine said, "I will preprogram my downloads in the book. Any reader can receive them as he or she reads the special pages." At the moment the

Divine gave me this direction, I understood how I could leave Divine Soul Downloads to history.

Preprogrammed Divine Soul Downloads are permanently stored within this book and every book in the Soul Power Series. If people read this book thousands of years from now, they will still receive the Divine Soul Downloads. As long as this book exists and is read, readers will receive the Divine Soul Downloads.

Allow me to explain further. The Divine has placed a permanent blessing within certain paragraphs in these books. These blessings allow you to receive Divine Soul Downloads as permanent gifts to your soul. Because these divine treasures reside with your soul, you can access them twenty-four hours a day—as often as you like, wherever you are—for healing, blessing, and life transformation.

It is very easy to receive the Divine Soul Downloads in these books. After you read the special paragraphs where they are preprogrammed, close your eyes. Receive the special download. It is also easy to apply these divine treasures. After you receive a Divine Soul Download, I will immediately show you how to apply it for healing, blessing, and life transformation.

You have free will. If you are not ready to receive a Divine Soul Download, simply say *I am not ready to receive this gift*. You can then continue to read the special download paragraphs, but you will not receive the gifts they contain. The Divine does not offer Divine Soul Downloads to those who are not ready or not willing to receive the Divine's treasures. However, the moment you are ready, you can simply go back to the relevant paragraphs and tell the Divine *I am ready*. You will then receive the stored special download when you reread the paragraphs.

※

The Divine has agreed to offer specific Divine Soul Downloads in these books to all readers who are willing to receive them. The Divine has unlimited treasures. However, you can receive only the ones designated in these pages. Please do not ask for different or additional gifts. It will not work.

After receiving and practicing with the Divine Soul Downloads in these books, you could experience remarkable healing results in your physical, emotional, mental, and spiritual bodies. You could receive incredible blessings for your love relationships and other relationships. You could receive financial blessings and all kinds of other blessings.

Divine Soul Downloads are unlimited. There can be a Divine Soul Download for anything that exists in the physical world. The reason for this is very simple. *Everything has a soul.* A house has a soul. The Divine can download a soul to your house that can transform its energy. The Divine can download a soul to your business that can transform your business. If you are wearing a ring, that ring has a soul. If the Divine downloads a new divine soul to your ring, you can ask the divine soul in your ring to offer divine healing and blessing.

I am honored to have been chosen as a servant of humanity and the Divine to offer Divine Soul Downloads. For the rest of my life, I will continue to offer Divine Soul Downloads. I will offer more and more of them. I will offer Divine Soul Downloads for every aspect of every life.

I am honored to be a servant of Divine Soul Downloads.

What to Expect After You Receive Divine Soul Downloads

Divine Soul Downloads are new souls created from the heart of the Divine. When these souls are transmitted, you may feel a strong vibration. For example, you could feel warm or excited. Your body could shake a little. If you are not sensitive, you may not feel anything. Advanced spiritual beings with an open Third Eye can actually see a huge golden, rainbow, purple, or crystal light soul enter your body.

These divine souls are your yin companions[3] for life. They will stay with your soul forever. Even after your physical life ends, these divine treasures will continue to accompany your soul into your next life and all of your future lives. In these books, I will teach you how to invoke these divine souls anytime, anywhere to give you divine healing or blessing in this life. You also can invoke these souls to leave your body to offer divine healing or blessing to others. These divine souls have extraordinary abilities to heal, bless, and transform. If you develop advanced spiritual abilities in your next life, you will discover that you have these divine souls with you. Then you will be able to invoke these divine souls in the same way in your future lifetimes to heal, bless, and transform every aspect of your life.

It is a great honor to have a divine soul downloaded to your own soul. The divine soul is a pure soul without bad karma. The divine soul carries divine healing and blessing abilities. The download does not have any side effects. You are given love and light with divine frequency. You are given divine abilities to serve yourself and others. Therefore, humanity is extremely honored that the Divine is offering his downloads. I am extremely honored to be a servant of the Divine, of you, of all humanity, and of all souls to offer Divine Soul Downloads. I cannot thank the Divine enough. I cannot thank you, all humanity, and all souls enough for the opportunity to serve.

Thank you. Thank you. Thank you.

---

3 A yang companion is a physical being, such as a family member, friend, or pet. A yin companion is a soul companion without a physical form, such as your spiritual fathers and mothers in Heaven.

Foreword to the
Soul Power Series

$\mathcal{J}$ HAVE ADMIRED DR. Zhi Gang Sha's work for some years
now. In fact, I clearly remember the first time I heard him
describe his soul healing system, Soul Mind Body Medicine.
I knew immediately that I wanted to support this gifted healer
and his mission, so I introduced him to my spiritual community
at Agape. Ever since, it has been my joy to witness how those who
apply his teachings and techniques experience increased energy,
joy, harmony, and peace in their lives.

Dr. Sha's techniques awaken the healing power already present in all of us, empowering us to put our overall well-being in
our own hands. His explanation of energy and message, and how
they link consciousness, mind, body, and spirit, forms a dynamic
information network in language that is easy to understand and,
more important, to apply.

Dr. Sha's time-tested results have proven to thousands of students and readers that healing energies and messages exist within

specific sounds, movements, and affirmative perceptions. Weaving in his own personal experiences, Dr. Sha's theories and practices of working directly with the life-force energy and spirit are practical, holistic, and profound. His recognition that Soul Power is most important for every aspect of life is vital to meeting the challenges of twenty-first-century living.

The worldwide representative of his renowned teacher, Dr. Zhi Chen Guo, one of the greatest qi gong masters and healers in the world, Dr. Sha is himself a master of ancient disciplines such as tai chi, qi gong, kung fu, the *I Ching,* and feng shui. He has blended the soul of his culture's natural healing methods with his training as a Western physician, and generously offers his wisdom to us through the books in his Soul Power Series. His contribution to those in the healing professions is undeniable, and the way in which he empowers his readers to understand themselves, their feelings, and the connection between their bodies, minds, and spirits is his gift to the world.

Through his Soul Power Series, Dr. Sha guides the reader into a consciousness of healing not only of body, mind, and spirit, but also of the heart. I consider his healing path to be a universal spiritual practice, a journey into genuine transformation. His professional integrity and compassionate heart are at the root of his being a servant of humankind, and my heartfelt wish for his readers is that they accept his invitation to awaken the power of the soul and realize the natural beauty of their existence.

Dr. Michael Bernard Beckwith
Founder, Agape International Spiritual Center

How to Read This Book

*I*N EVERY BOOK of my Soul Power Series, I reveal soul secrets and teach soul wisdom, soul knowledge, and soul practices. Secret and sacred wisdom and knowledge are important. *Practice is even more important.* Since ancient times, serious Buddhist, Taoist, qi gong, and kung fu practitioners have spent hours and hours a day in practice. Their dedication empowers them to develop and transform their frequency, their consciousness, and their purification further and further. In the modern world, successful professionals in every field similarly spend hours a day for months and years in practice. Their commitment empowers them to develop and transform their power and abilities further and further.

Every book in my Soul Power Series offers new approaches to healing, rejuvenation, and life transformation. Along with the teachings of sacred wisdom and knowledge, I also offer Divine Soul Downloads as a servant, vehicle, and channel of the Divine. I am honored to serve you through these books. However, *the most important service offered in these books is the practices.* In this book I lead you in many practices. If you spend four or five minutes to do each practice, I fully understand that it will take you some time to finish all of them. Do a few practices today. Tomorrow do another few practices. Do a few more the day after tomorrow. The practices are vital. If you do not do them, how can you experience their power and benefits? If you do not experience their power and benefits, how can you fully understand and absorb the teaching?

For this particular book, *Tao I: The Way of All Life*, the practices are even more important than for the previous books of my Soul Power Series. This book reveals even simpler, even more powerful, and even more profound soul secrets, wisdom, knowledge, and *practical techniques* than my previous books. The practices give you and every reader even more effective ways to heal, prevent sickness, rejuvenate, prolong life, and transform every aspect of life, including relationships and finances, as well as to enlighten soul, heart, mind, and body. If you do not do the practices, this book will be only a theoretical exercise for you. You may find it interesting, even fascinating, but you will not receive the tremendous potential benefits for every aspect of your life.

The CD enclosed with this book is to lead you and guide you in some of the basic aspects of the practices. For those of you who seriously need or desire healing, rejuvenation, and transformation, and for the serious Tao student and practitioner, *the audio version of this book* (available in a boxed set of CDs) *is an essential companion to this print version* that you have in your hands. In the audio version of this book, I lead you and guide you in all of the vital Tao practices in depth and deliver additional blessings for your healing, prevention of sickness, rejuvenation, longevity, transformation, enlightenment, and Tao journeys.

My message to you is that as you read this book, make sure you do not miss the practices. Use the enclosed CD and the audio version of this book as essential practice guides and aids that could significantly boost and accelerate the results you obtain. I deliberately guide you in this book and lead you in the audio version of this book to do spiritual practices using the power of soul for healing, prevention of sickness, rejuvenation, prolonging life, and transforming every aspect of life, including relationships and finances. Reading this book and, even more, practicing with the audio version of this book, are like being at a workshop with me. When you go to a workshop and the teacher leads you in a meditation or practice, you do not run off to do something else, do you?

Do not rush through this book. Do every practice that I ask you to do. You will receive ten, fifty, a hundred times the benefit that you would receive if you simply read through the book quickly. To receive Divine Soul Downloads does not mean you automatically receive their benefits. You must invoke them and practice to experience and receive divine healing and blessing. Remember also that going through this book just once is not enough. My advanced students go through my books many times. Every time they read and do the practices, they reach more and more "aha!" moments. They receive more and more remarkable healing, purification, and life transformation results.

These are important messages for you to remember as you read this book. I wish each of you will receive great healing, rejuvenation, purification, and life transformation by doing the practices in this book, especially by doing them with me in the audio version. Receive the benefits of *soul over matter,* which is the power of soul. Receive the benefits of Divine Soul Power and Tao Power.

Practice. Practice. Practice.
Experience. Experience. Experience.
Benefit. Benefit. Benefit.
Hao! Hao! Hao!
Thank you. Thank you. Thank you.

List of Divine Soul Downloads

Chapter Two

1. Divine Soul Transplant of Divine Love, 162
2. Divine Mind Transplant of Divine Love, 162
3. Divine Body Transplant of Divine Love, 162
4. Divine Soul Transplant of Divine Forgiveness, 162
5. Divine Mind Transplant of Divine Forgiveness, 162
6. Divine Body Transplant of Divine Forgiveness, 163
7. Divine Soul Transplant of Divine Compassion, 163
8. Divine Mind Transplant of Divine Compassion, 163
9. Divine Body Transplant of Divine Compassion, 163
10. Divine Soul Transplant of Divine Light, 163
11. Divine Mind Transplant of Divine Light, 163
12. Divine Body Transplant of Divine Light, 163
13. Tao Soul Herb Bo He Soul Transplant, 269
14. Tao Soul Herb Bo He Mind Transplant, 269
15. Tao Soul Herb Bo He Body Transplant, 269
16. Tao Soul Herb Sheng Mai Ya Soul Transplant, 280

17. Tao Soul Herb Sheng Mai Ya Mind Transplant, 280
18. Tao Soul Herb Sheng Mai Ya Body Transplant, 280
19. Tao Soul Herb Chao Bai Zhu Soul Transplant, 284
20. Tao Soul Herb Chao Bai Zhu Mind Transplant, 284
21. Tao Soul Herb Chao Bai Zhu Body Transplant, 284
22. Tao Soul Herb Shi Chang Pu Soul Transplant, 287
23. Tao Soul Herb Shi Chang Pu Mind Transplant, 287
24. Tao Soul Herb Shi Chang Pu Body Transplant, 287
25. Tao Soul Herb Sheng Huai Shan Soul Transplant, 290
26. Tao Soul Herb Sheng Huai Shan Mind Transplant, 290
27. Tao Soul Herb Sheng Huai Shan Body Transplant, 290
28. Divine Soul Transplant of Kidneys, 336
29. Divine Mind Transplant of Kidneys, 336
30. Divine Body Transplant of Kidneys, 337

List of Figures

1. Normal creation and reverse creation of Tao, 19
2. Yin-yang symbol, 79
3. The sacred divine code 3396815 stimulates many areas of the body, 198
4. Lotus Hands Body Power position, 220

Introduction

MILLIONS OF PEOPLE in history have studied Tao (pronounced *dow*) and continue to study Tao. People who have not studied Tao, and even people who have studied Tao, may think that Tao is very sacred, mysterious, and hard to understand. They may know that it is very profound, ancient, and sacred philosophy, wisdom, and practices. They may relate Tao with *Tao Te Jing* (pronounced *dow duh jing*), the great classic, world-renowned philosophy book by Lao Zi (pronounced *lao dz*), who is considered to be the founder of Taoism. They may relate Tao with images of saints and sages with long, completely white hair and yet with perfectly smooth skin and baby faces, full of youthful vitality and flexibility. They may relate Tao to secret practices for energy, rejuvenation, longevity, and even immortality. They may relate Tao to fairy-tale stories about saints who could fly, disappear, and move instantly from one place to another without a vehicle.

Tao is a sacred word. Many people dream of studying Tao but they do not know how to do it. It is very difficult to move deeply into the study of Tao, because Tao is sacred and secret teaching. In history, a Tao master would pass the true secrets to only a few chosen disciples, maybe even just one disciple.

I am honored to be the sole chosen 373rd-generation lineage holder of Peng Zu (pronounced *pung zoo*), the teacher of Lao Zi. In Chinese history, Peng Zu is renowned as the "long-life star" who lived to the age of eight hundred eighty. I have also been chosen as a disciple and worldwide representative of Dr. and Master Zhi Chen Guo, a spiritual leader, my most beloved spiritual father, one of the leading qi gong masters in the world, and the founder of Zhi Neng Medicine and Body Space Medicine. I am also very honored to have been chosen as the holder of two other major Taoist lineages. As humble servants, my two masters of these lineages do not permit me to reveal their names.

I am extremely honored to be a chosen servant, vehicle, and channel of the Divine. In December 2008, the Divine gave me the new *Tao I* text that is a major teaching and focus of this book. The Divine told me that he will give me at least three new Tao texts very quickly. Therefore, I am planning to publish *Tao II* and *Tao III* within the next two years, releasing one major Tao book a year. These Tao teachings are new divine Tao teachings at the present time. They contain the key essence of the ancient Tao wisdom, but there are many profound new divine teachings for the Soul Light Era, the fifteen-thousand-year-long era that started on August 8, 2003.

This is the message the Divine gave to me when he delivered the *Tao I* text in December 2008:

> *Dear my son Zhi Gang,*
> *I am revealing to you the new Tao text for the Soul Light Era. You were chosen by your physical teachers and*

*masters as a major ancient Tao lineage holder. In July
2003, I chose you as my servant, vehicle, and channel.
Dear my son, I am guiding you now to teach new divine
sacred Tao wisdom, knowledge, and practices. You will
continue to share the essence of ancient Taoist wisdom,
knowledge, and practices, but now you will focus on sharing my direct divine teaching of new Tao wisdom, knowledge, and practices with humanity. You will teach Tao,
The Way of All Life. Yes, you will still share the essence of
traditional Taoism, but you will not be teaching Taoism.
You must let all of your students and readers know this.
You are not moving away from or changing the topic of the
Soul Power Series. New Tao teaching is advanced teaching
about the soul. It is further teaching of the Soul Power
Series.*

I am extremely honored to be the divine servant to offer new
divine Tao teaching to humanity. I am also extremely honored to
be a chosen Taoist lineage holder. I am eternally grateful for all of
my masters, including my physical masters and Heaven's saints,
for their teaching, blessing, and transformation.

In this book, I will share the essence of ancient Taoist sacred wisdom, knowledge, and practices for healing, rejuvenation, and life transformation, as well as new divine teaching
and Tao wisdom for the Soul Light Era. Now, the Divine has
specially chosen me to share divine Tao sacred wisdom, knowledge, and practical treasures with you and humanity. How
blessed I am to be a servant of you, humanity, and the Divine.

Divine sacred teaching is extremely simple, powerful, and
profound. I am extremely honored to bring this teaching directly

from the Divine to humanity. I am very honored to be an unconditional universal servant for humanity and all souls. I cannot honor the Divine enough for choosing me as a servant. I am blessed. I am your humble servant. I cannot serve you, humanity, and all souls enough.

Important Wisdom of Tao

MANY BEINGS HAVE strived to reach Tao. Taoists strive to reach Tao. All spiritual beings in all realms may not use the same words, but they all strive to reach Tao, for Tao is the source of all universes and ultimate oneness. Many spiritual beings strive to reach this oneness with God, with the Divine. In their hearts and souls, they also wish to reach this oneness with Tao. When this oneness is achieved, one's physical journey and one's spiritual journey are highly accomplished.

We are in a special time of transition. Humanity and Mother Earth are facing great challenges. At this historic time, the Divine and Tao are bringing new sacred Tao secrets, wisdom, knowledge, and practical techniques to humanity. I am honored to be a chosen servant and vehicle of the Divine and Tao to bring these gifts to you and humanity in this book and future books. They will empower you and many others to study, understand, practice, and reach Tao with the simplest and most powerful wisdom and practices.

What Is Tao?

Tao is The Way. Tao is the source of all universes. Tao is the universal principles and laws. Millions of people in history have searched for Tao, studied Tao, and practiced Tao, but only a very small number of people in history have accomplished and reached the goal of Tao. I will explain this goal later in this chapter.

First let me explain the profound wisdom of a few important sentences from Lao Zi's classic, *Tao Te Jing*. From this wisdom, I will reveal the new divine sacred philosophy, wisdom, knowledge, and practices.

TAO SHENG YI (TAO CREATES ONE)

"Tao" (pronounced *dow*) means *the source of all universes—emptiness, nothingness, The Way of all life.* "Sheng" (pronounced *shung*) means *creates.* "Yi" (pronounced *yee*) means *one.* Therefore, "Tao sheng yi" means *Tao creates One.* Tao creates countless universes. Countless universes are one. One is unity. In fact, we can think that Tao *is* One, One *is* Tao.

YI SHENG ER (ONE CREATES TWO)

"Er" (pronounced *ur*) means *two.* Therefore, "Yi sheng er" means *One creates Two.* Two is Heaven and Earth. Heaven and Earth are yang and yin.

A man and a woman have intercourse to produce a baby. Man is yang. Woman is yin. Yin and yang combine to produce a new baby. Heaven is yang. Mother Earth is yin. Heaven and Earth interconnect to produce new souls and to produce all things in all universes.

ER SHENG SAN (TWO CREATES THREE)

"San" (pronounced *sahn*) means *three*. Therefore, "Er sheng san" means *Two creates Three*. One plus Two is Three. Tao is One. Yang and Yin are two. Tao plus Yang and Yin (Heaven and Earth) are three.

SAN SHENG WAN WU (THREE CREATES ALL THINGS)

"Wan" (pronounced *wahn*) means *ten thousand*. In Chinese, "ten thousand" represents *all* or *every*. "Wu" (pronounced *woo*) means *thing*. Therefore, "San sheng wan wu" means *Three creates all things*. Three is Tao plus Yang and Yin.

NORMAL CREATION AND REVERSE CREATION

Now I will reveal the most important divine sacred philosophy, wisdom, knowledge, and practices of the two kinds of creation. One kind is normal creation. The other is reverse creation. These two creations can guide all life, including a human being's energy, vitality, stamina, healing, prevention of sickness, rejuvenation, transformation of relationships and finances, enlightenment, scientific study, and all occupations, as well as all nature.

Normal Creation

The process of normal creation is:

Tao sheng yi. Yi sheng er. Er sheng san. San sheng wan wu.

TAO → One → Two → Three → all things
creates

Tao creates One. One creates Two. Two creates Three. Three creates all things. This direction is normal creation or *shun sheng* in Chinese. "Shun" (pronounced *shwun*) literally means *normal*. "Sheng" (pronounced *shung*) means *creation*.

Reverse Creation

The process of reverse creation is:

Wan wu gui (pronounced *gway*) san. San gui er. Er gui yi. Yi gui Tao.

all things → Three → Two → One → TAO
return to

All things return to Three. Three returns to Two. Two returns to One. One returns to Tao. This direction is reverse creation or *ni sheng* in Chinese. "Ni" (pronounced *nee*) means *reverse*. "Sheng" again means *creation*.

For example, there is a very important teaching of Tao:

Fan lao huan tong

"Fan" (pronounced *fahn*) means *return*. "Lao" (pronounced *lao,* rhymes with *now*) means *old age*. "Huan" (pronounced *hwahn*) means *back to*. "Tong" (pronounced *tawng*) means *baby*. Therefore, "fan lao huan tong" means:

Return old age to the health and purity of a baby.

This process is an example of reverse creation or *ni sheng*. Everyone desires *fan lao huan tong*. There are many secret wisdoms and practices to accomplish and reach *fan lao huan tong*.

What is the simplest way and the most powerful way to reach *fan lao huan tong*? The Divine and Tao showed me this way. I am very honored to begin sharing it with humanity later in this book.

This book is the sixth in my Soul Power Series. The first five books are:

- *Soul Wisdom: Practical Soul Treasures to Transform Your Life*
- *Soul Communication: Opening Your Spiritual Channels for Success and Fulfillment*
- *The Power of Soul: The Way to Heal, Rejuvenate, Transform, and Enlighten All Life*
- *Divine Soul Songs: Sacred Practical Treasures to Heal, Rejuvenate, and Transform You, Humanity, Mother Earth, and All Universes*
- *Divine Soul Mind Body Healing and Transmission System: The Divine Way to Heal You, Humanity, Mother Earth, and All Universes*

These five books can be summarized in one sentence:

Soul Power and the Divine Soul Mind Body Healing and Transmission System can heal, prevent sickness, rejuvenate, prolong life, and transform every aspect of life, including relationships and finances, as well as enlighten soul, heart, mind, and body, for you, your loved ones, humanity, Mother Earth, and all universes.

The techniques I share in the Soul Power Series are simple, practical, powerful, and effective. I am not changing the direction of my teaching in this book. Tao teaching is *advanced* soul teaching. Tao teaching makes soul teaching even more direct, more simple, more practical, more powerful, and more profound. I am an unconditional universal servant. I am honored to share new Tao teaching and more from the Divine with humanity and all souls in all universes.

Normal creation and reverse creation are both important. Let me give you an example of each. Conventional modern medicine focuses more on normal creation (*shun sheng*). It studies and researches the human systems, then the organs, then the cells, then the DNA and RNA, and then the components of DNA and RNA. Conventional modern medical research moves toward smaller and smaller aspects of the body. This movement is endless.

Traditional Chinese medicine focuses more on reverse creation (*ni sheng*). In traditional Chinese medicine, diagnosis and treatment can identify and address many sicknesses. A single person could have many unhealthy organs and symptoms and signs. However, traditional Chinese medicine also summarizes all sicknesses in one sentence:

All sickness is due to an imbalance of yin and yang.

Yin and yang are two. To balance yin and yang is to return to one. To return to one is to return to Tao. In one sentence:

To heal is to return to Tao.

Tao includes everything. Therefore, Tao includes normal creation and reverse creation. Western medicine moves in the direction of normal creation. Traditional Chinese medicine moves in the direction of reverse creation. In order to serve humanity's health better, it is vital to combine Western medicine and traditional Chinese medicine. Expanding the concept, combining all modalities of conventional medicine and all modalities of complementary and alternative medicine is vital. Tao wisdom has guided us to realize this.

Tao can be divided into Da Tao and Xiao Tao. "Da" (pronounced *dah*) means *big*. "Xiao" (pronounced *shee-ow*) means *small*. Da Tao (Big Tao) is the universal principles and laws. Xiao Tao (Small Tao) means the principles and laws in every aspect of life.

There is a renowned ancient spiritual teaching:

Shun tao zhe chang

Follow Tao, flourish.

"Shun" literally means *follow*. Tao is The Way. "Zhe" means *the person*. "Chang" means *flourishes*. Therefore, "Shun tao zhe chang" (pronounced *shwun dow juh chahng*) literally means *one who follows the Tao will flourish*.

Ni tao zhe wang

Go against Tao, end.

"Ni" means *go against*. "Wang" means *finish* or *die*. Therefore, "Ni tao zhe wang" (pronounced *nee dow juh wahng*) literally means *one who goes against the Tao will be blocked, finished, end, or die*.

For example, consider the Xiao Tao (Small Tao) of weather. The four seasons is the Tao of weather. The four seasons follow Tao. To follow Tao means that in the winter, people need to wear winter clothing. In some countries and cities, the temperature in winter can drop to −40° C. Imagine wearing a light summer

T-shirt in this weather. The extremely cold temperature can kill that person easily. One *must* wear enough warm clothes in this kind of weather. It does not matter who you are. It does not matter whether you are a kind person or a selfish person. Tao treats every person the same, because Tao is universal principles and laws that everyone must follow. You must wear warm winter clothes in that kind of winter weather. Otherwise, you could lose your life easily. All of this means that everyone must follow the Tao of weather.

In the opposite direction, the temperature in a very hot country or city can climb higher than +40° C. If one wears a heavy winter overcoat and long underwear in this weather, the heat could easily kill this person. One *must* follow the Tao of weather.

There is a Xiao Tao of eating. Eat healthy food. Eat regularly. Do not eat too much, especially before sleeping. Many people on Mother Earth do not follow the Tao of eating, which are eating principles. The Tao of eating is so simple but many people ignore it. If you do not follow the Tao of eating, it will affect your health. It will affect your longevity. When people become very sick, they could regret the way they have eaten but it could be too late.

A renowned Japanese doctor wrote a book in which he recommended that we chew every mouthful of food thirty to forty times. He explains the many benefits of doing this. People do believe that chewing food more thoroughly is better, but how many people actually do this simple practice? This is the Tao of eating.

There is a Xiao Tao of sleeping. Sleep enough. Make sure you have good, quality sleep. In ancient times, when the sun set, people were guided to rest. When the sun rose, people were guided to get up. In modern times, many scientific studies have shown how going to sleep earlier can benefit the endocrine system, nervous system, and all systems. Many people on Mother Earth have the problem that they do not follow the Tao of sleep.

There is a Xiao Tao of work. There is a Xiao Tao of business. If you do not follow the Tao of business, you will not be successful. There are business principles to follow. This is the Tao of business.

These examples tell us that Tao is in every aspect of our life. They also tell us that Tao is simple. Tao can benefit our lives tremendously. What is important is that we have to *follow* Tao. Do it! Follow Tao, flourish. Do not follow Tao, blockages.

Scientists have made a great contribution with their research and findings. Remember the normal creation of Tao: Tao creates One. One creates Two. Two creates Three. Three creates all things. This process is endless.

In many cases, scientific study follows this direction. Physicists try to find the smallest things in the universe. Biologists study a human being at the cell level, then move to the DNA and RNA level, and then research even tinier levels.

One very important principle of Tao is that you cannot find the smallest things in the universe. Not too long ago, physicists thought quarks and leptons were the smallest particles of matter. More recently, physicists have developed String Theory, where "strings" are the smallest particles of matter. But, in fact, there is no way for scientists to discover the smallest things in the universe. The new Tao texts that I have received include this phrase:

Xiao wu nei

Smaller than smallest

"Xiao" (pronounced *shee-yow*) means *small.* "Wu" (pronounced *woo*) means *no.* "Nei" (pronounced *nay*) means *inside.* "Xiao wu nei" can be translated as *smaller than smallest.* I will explain this further in chapter 2.

The more you study details, the more you could forget the unity of the whole picture. The whole picture is One or Tao. For example, to study DNA and RNA very well, deeper and deeper, and to study the smallest things in the cells, deeper and deeper, is great. But you may forget that DNA, RNA, and the smallest things inside the cells are part of the whole body. If the condition of the whole body changes, the condition of the DNA and RNA could follow. Therefore, to study microscopic details is important, but to study the macro conditions at the same time is also important. In fact, in many cases, to study the macro conditions is *more* important. Tao includes micro and macro conditions.

In summary, normal creation and reverse creation can guide scientific study and every aspect of life. Each can be explained in a one-sentence secret:

Normal creation is to go from the macro to the micro.

Reverse creation is to go from the micro to the macro.

The essence of normal creation and reverse creation can be summarized in the following diagram:

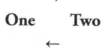

and in two sentences:

The process of normal creation moves from One to Two. The process of reverse creation returns from Two to One. This is the highest philosophy to transform everything in the universe.

I will use cancer as an example. Millions of people suffer and die from cancer. The World Health Organization recently reported that the number of deaths annually from cancer exceeds the number of deaths from AIDS and malaria combined. Cancer is not an epidemic, but it is widespread.

Cancer cells reproduce rapidly. Cellular reproduction is to divide from one to two at the DNA level. Then each of them will subdivide from one to two quickly again. This follows normal creation. Conventional modern medicine uses surgery, chemotherapy, and radiation to kill cancer cells and stop DNA subdivision.

The Divine guided me to the wisdom that Tao has two creations. One can divide into two. Two can join together as one. According to Tao wisdom, it is possible for cancer cells to return to normal cells. This is reverse creation. The healing approaches of conventional modern medicine, various types of complementary and alternative medicine, and energy and spiritual healings have all helped some cancer cases recover. But from Tao wisdom, we must know that it is possible for cancer cells to return to normal cells. This is the reverse creation of Tao. This is guidance from the Divine, from Tao. We need to have more understanding and experience of cancer healing and recovery using this wisdom.

Many spiritual seekers have studied with many masters, have read hundreds of books, and learned a multitude of techniques. They may think they have learned a lot. They may be very happy they know so many techniques. But they may not realize that:

Da Tao zhi jian

"Da" means *big.* Tao is The Way. "Zhi" (pronounced *jr*) means *extremely.* "Jian" (pronounced *jyen*) means "simple." Therefore, "Da Tao zhi jian" means *The Big Way is extremely simple.*

Some people may think they are great because they know

many secrets, wisdoms, and techniques in spiritual study or other aspects of life. They do not realize *Da Tao zhi jian*. They do not realize that every aspect of life can be guided by the process of normal creation and the process of reverse creation. They do not understand or realize the Tao of their whole life. They may not even find the Xiao Tao (Small Tao) in a single part of their life.

Many times I have seen that the more one learns and the more techniques one knows, the more confused one could be. The Big Way, the truth is very simple, very easy to learn, and very powerful.

Take healing, for example. **The Tao of healing is to balance yin and yang.** To balance yin and yang is to return two to one. This is to find the Tao of healing.

Rejuvenation is another example. **The Tao of rejuvenation is to reach *fan lao huan tong*.** If you know how to reach *fan lao huan tong*, then you have found the Tao of rejuvenation.

Every aspect of life has its Xiao Tao or Small Tao. To study and to practice Tao is to find Tao in every aspect of life. Then, follow Tao for that aspect of life. That aspect of your life will flourish.

Apply Tao wisdom to realize and follow the Xiao Tao of different aspects of your life. Then find the Tao of your entire life. One day you may reach an "aha!" moment. You may realize that the Tao of one's physical life is to offer service to others, to make others healthier and happier. This service benefits one's soul journey. The physical journey is limited. The soul journey is forever. Then you could realize the Tao of one's physical journey in one sentence:

The Tao of one's physical journey
is to serve one's soul journey.

Move this teaching further: What is the Tao of one's soul journey? One day you could have another "aha!" moment. The Tao of one's soul journey is to uplift your soul standing to the divine realm. Why? If one's soul reaches the divine realm, that soul will stop reincarnation. That soul will continue to serve humanity and all souls in all universes in the soul form, but not in a physical form as a human being anymore. To summarize in one sentence:

**The Tao of one's soul journey
is to stop reincarnation.**

Move this teaching even further: What is the Tao of humanity? Another day you could receive another "aha!" moment. Mother Earth is in a transition period. All kinds of natural disasters, conflicts, challenges, sicknesses, and other sufferings of humanity are the purification process of humanity. The "aha!" moment would be the realization that the Tao of humanity can be summarized in one sentence:

**The Tao of humanity is to join together
in love, peace, and harmony.**

Continue to move the teaching even further: What is the Tao of all souls in all universes? There are imbalances and disharmonies in the Soul World and in all layers of Heaven. As on Earth, so in Heaven. The Tao of all souls in all universes can be summarized in one sentence:

**The Tao of all souls in all universes
is to reach *wan ling rong he*.**

"Wan" literally means *ten thousand*. It represents *all* or *every*. "Ling" means *soul*. "Rong he" means *join as one*. Therefore, "Wan ling rong he" (pronounced *wahn ling rawng huh*) means *all souls join as one*.

⁕

I have used one-sentence secrets to summarize the Tao of healing, the Tao of rejuvenation, the Tao of one's physical journey, and the Tao of one's soul journey. These Taos belong to Xiao Tao. I have also used one-sentence secrets to summarize the Tao of humanity and the Tao of all souls in all universes. These Taos belong to Da Tao.

It does not matter whether a Tao belongs to Xiao Tao or Da Tao. All Taos and Tao itself can be summarized in one sentence:

Tao creates all things and all things return to Tao.

This is normal creation and reverse creation. This is the philosophy of Tao, which is the philosophy of all things in all universes.

NEW DIVINE SACRED TAO PRACTICE FOR
NORMAL CREATION AND REVERSE CREATION

In December 2009, I led a Tao Retreat in Frankfurt, Germany. Suddenly, the Divine told me: *Zhi Gang, teach people to sing a Tao Song of Normal Creation and Reverse Creation*. I only had time to teach the students the *Tao Song of Normal Creation*. I am releasing both parts to humanity now. You can listen to me singing them on track 1 of the enclosed CD.

Tao Song of Normal Creation

The lyrics of the Tao Song of Normal Creation and their pronunciation are:

道生一	*Tao sheng yi*	*dow shung yee*
一生二	*Yi sheng er*	*yee shung ur*
二生三	*Er sheng san*	*ur shung sahn*
三生万物	*San sheng wan wu*	*sahn shung wahn woo*

As explained at the beginning of this chapter, this means:

Tao creates One
One creates Two
Two creates Three
Three creates all things

TAO → One → Two → Three → all things
     creates

To sing or chant this Tao Song is to receive healing and blessing directly from the power of Tao (the source of all universes, The Way of all life).

To sing or chant this Tao Song is to receive healing and blessing directly from the power of One (unity of all universes).

To sing or chant this Tao Song is to receive healing and blessing directly from the power of Two (Heaven and Earth, Yang and Yin).

To sing or chant this Tao Song is to receive healing and blessing directly from the power of Three (Tao, Heaven, and Earth).

To sing or chant this Tao Song is to receive healing and
   blessing directly from the power of Wan Wu (all things
   in all universes).
To sing or chant this Tao Song is to experience normal
   creation of Tao. This is how Heaven, Earth, and countless universes were created by Tao.

I would like every reader to realize that the Tao Song of Normal Creation carries power beyond any comprehension and any
words.

Tao Song of Reverse Creation

The lyrics of the Tao Song of Reverse Creation and their pronunciation are:

万物归三	*Wan wu gui san*	*wahn woo gway sahn*
三归二	*San gui er*	*sahn gway ur*
二归一	*Er gui yi*	*ur gway yee*
一归道	*Yi gui Tao*	*yee gway dow*
道法自然	*Tao fa zi ran*	*dow fah dz rahn*
道法自然	*Tao fa zi ran*	*dow fah dz rahn*
道法自然	*Tao fa zi ran*	*dow fah dz rahn*

all things → Three → Two → One → TAO
        return to

"Gui" means *returns to*.
   "Wan wu gui san" means *All things in all universes return to
Three*.
   "San gui er" means *Three returns to Two*.
   "Er gui yi" means *Two returns to One*.

"Yi gui Tao" means *One returns to Tao.*

Tao is The Way, the universal principles and laws. "Fa" (pronounced *fah*) means *universal methods.* "Zi ran" (pronounced *dz rahn*) means *to be natural.* "Tao fa zi ran" can be translated as *Follow Nature's Way.*

To sing or chant the Tao Song of Reverse Creation is also to receive healing and blessing from all things in all universes, from Three (Tao, Heaven, Earth), from Two (Yang and Yin), from One (unity of all universes), and from Tao (the source of all universes and The Way of all life).

To sing or chant this Tao Song is to experience the power of reverse creation of Tao.

To sing or chant this Tao Song is to purify your soul, heart, mind, and body deeply.

To sing or chant this Tao Song is to heal and rejuvenate you, your loved ones, all humanity, Mother Earth, and all universes.

To sing or chant this Tao Song is especially to reach *fan lao huan tong* (transform old age to the health and purity of a baby).

The power of this Tao Song is unexplainable and unimaginable. I always teach: *If you want to know if a pear is sweet, taste it.* If you want to know if the Tao Song of Reverse Creation is powerful, experience it.

Tao Song of Normal Creation and Reverse Creation

道生一	*Tao sheng yi*	*dow shung yee*
一生二	*Yi sheng er*	*yee shung ur*
二生三	*Er sheng san*	*ur shung sahn*
三生万物	*San sheng wan wu*	*sahn shung wahn woo*
万物归三	*Wan wu gui san*	*wahn woo gway sahn*
三归二	*San gui er*	*sahn gway ur*

二归一	*Er gui yi*	*ur gway yee*
一归道	*Yi gui Tao*	*yee gway dow*
道法自然	*Tao fa zi ran*	*dow fah dz rahn*
道法自然	*Tao fa zi ran*	*dow fah dz rahn*
道法自然	*Tao fa zi ran*	*dow fah dz rahn*

TAO ➜ One ➜ Two ➜ Three ➜ all things
creates

all things ➜ Three ➜ Two ➜ One ➜ TAO
return to

THE SIGNIFICANCE AND POWER OF NORMAL CREATION AND REVERSE CREATION OF TAO

Normal creation of Tao is how all universes are created. Reverse creation of Tao is how all universes will return to Tao.

Tao is the permanent universal principles and laws. Tao creates all universes. All universes will return to Tao. This circle is constant. Tao continues to create Heaven, Earth, and all universes. At the same time, Heaven, Earth, and all universes are returning to Tao.

Tao has created countless Heavens and Earths, and countless planets, stars, galaxies, and universes. Countless planets, stars, galaxies, and universes are returning to Tao. Humanity stays in its own Heaven and Earth. This Heaven and this Earth are very tiny specks within all Heavens and all Earths in all universes. In the Tao text explained in chapter 2, there is this phrase:

Da wu wai

"Da" (pronounced *dah*) means *big*. "Wu" (pronounced *woo*) means *no*. "Wai" (pronounced *wye*) means *outside*. "Da wu wai" can be translated *as big without boundary* or *bigger than the biggest*. Tao cannot be measured. Tao has no limits.

The normal creation and the reverse creation of Tao are constantly taking place. In history, we understand that some cities and countries have disappeared. New cities and countries are created during Mother Earth's changes. In fact, at this moment, I received spiritual guidance and the wisdom again that Mother Earth herself has disappeared many times before, and that a new Mother Earth has always been created afterward. It is the same for other planets, stars, galaxies, and universes. This is the circle of normal creation and reverse creation of Tao.

Normal creation and reverse creation of Tao can be summarized in one sentence:

The universal law of reincarnation is that normal creation and reverse creation of Tao create all universes, and all universes return to Tao.

This can be summarized in a diagram:

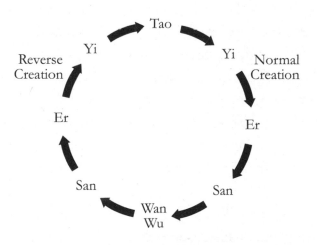

Figure 1. Normal creation and reverse creation of Tao

There is ancient renowned spiritual wisdom that also expresses this universal law of reincarnation:

Zhong wei shi, shi wei zhong

"Zhong" (pronounced *jawng*) means *end*. "Wei" (pronounced *way*) means *is*. "Shi" (pronounced *shr*) means *beginning*. Therefore, "Zhong wei shi, shi wei zhong" means:

An ending is a beginning. A beginning is an ending.

This is one of the highest philosophies. I will use a human being's life to explain it further.

When a human being's physical life ends, his or her soul leaves the physical body. This is the beginning of the soul's next life. This is *Zhong wei shi,* an ending is a beginning.

Generally speaking, the soul will reincarnate to its next physical life as a human being again. When the soul enters its next physical body, we know that this physical body will end in about one hundred years. *Shi wei zhong,* a beginning is an ending, tells us that to see the beginning of physical life is to understand that this life is limited. Its ending is in front of you.

Let me use a star as another example. Stars are created from Tao. Stars disappear. New stars are created.

All things, including Heaven and Earth, are created by Tao. Heaven and Earth are not permanent. Tao has created countless Heavens and Earths. Countless Heavens and Earths will return to Tao. Heaven, Earth, or a star could take billions, even countless years to return to Tao. In every moment, within the universes, new planets, stars, galaxies, and universes are being created. At the same time, they are all returning to Tao, disappearing, and turning to emptiness and nothingness. In one sentence:

The process of Tao creating all universes and all universes returning to Tao is the highest philosophy and truth of existence.

This process is the universal natural principles, laws, and rules. There is another renowned statement to express this process:

Zi sheng zi mie

"Zi" (pronounced *dz*) means *yourself.* "Sheng" (pronounced *shung*) means *produce.* "Mie" (pronounced *myeh*) means *end* or *die.* Therefore, "Zi sheng zi mie" can be translated as *your creation produces your own ending.* Think about a human being's life, from the first breath at birth to the last breath when physical life ends. Think about a star from its newborn state to its disappearance. This is the rule of Tao.

Why is a human being's life limited? A star, the sun, the moon, Heaven, and Earth could have long, long lives, but they cannot live forever because they are in the yin yang world, which belongs to Two in the normal creation of Tao.

Remember the normal creation of Tao:

Tao sheng yi (One)
Yi sheng er (Two)
Er sheng san (Three)
San sheng wan wu (all things in all universes)

Er is Two, Heaven and Earth, yang and yin. Mother Earth and humanity are in the yin yang world. Anything in the yin yang world will follow *Zi sheng zi mie. Zi sheng zi mie* is a rule in the yin yang world. It is also a rule of Tao because Tao created yin and yang.

Why does a human being need to do Xiu Lian or purification practice? "Xiu" (pronounced *sheo*) means *purification*. "Lian" (pronounced *lyen*) means *practice*. Every practice to purify our souls, hearts, minds, and bodies is a practice to advance our spiritual journeys. Therefore, Xiu Lian is the totality of one's spiritual journey.

This book teaches Xiu Tao. "Xiu Tao" means *to practice Tao and reach Tao*. Xiu Tao is one of the highest kinds of Xiu Lian. The final goal of Xiu Tao is to go beyond yin and yang, to return to One, which is to return to Tao. If you can truly reach Tao, you will no longer be controlled by the rules of the yin yang world. There is another renowned ancient spiritual statement:

Chao chu yin yang, tiao chu san jie, tuo chu wu xing

"Chao chu" (pronounced *chow choo*) means *go beyond*. "Yin yang" means *yin yang world*. "Tiao chu" (pronounced *tee-yow choo*) means *jump out of*. "San jie" (pronounced *sahn jyeh*) means *Heaven, Earth, and human being*. "Tuo chu" (pronounced *twaw choo*) means *escape from control*. "Wu xing" (pronounced *woo shing*) means *Five Elements world, including Wood, Fire, Earth, Metal, and Water*. Therefore, "Chao chu yin yang, tiao chu san jie, tuo chu wu xing" means *go beyond the yin yang world, jump out from the control of Heaven, Earth, and human being, and escape the control of the Five Elements world*. To do this is to reach Tao.

When you truly reach Tao and meld with Tao, you will reach this Tao condition, which is to be out of the control of yin yang, Heaven, Earth, human beings, and Five Elements. This means you have reached the level of Tao saints, who are Tao servants who have the abilities to harmonize all universes. You meld with Tao as one. You become Tao. Because Tao is permanent, your life becomes permanent. This reveals how immortality is attainable. This is exactly the Tao training that the Divine and Tao asked me to offer. We are doing Xiu Tao together in order to reach Tao and become Tao. I will explain the process of Tao training a little later in this chapter.

To become Tao and meld with Tao takes the greatest effort from a Total GOLD servant. In the teaching of the Soul Power Series, GOLD means *gratitude, obedience, loyalty, and devotion.* Total GOLD means total GOLD to the Divine, Tao, humanity, and all souls. To be a Total GOLD servant is to be an unconditional servant to the Divine, Tao, humanity, and all souls. A Total GOLD servant can be summarized in one sentence:

A Total GOLD servant is a servant who offers unconditional universal service, including unconditional love, forgiveness, peace, healing, blessing, harmony, and enlightenment, to the Divine, Tao, humanity, and all souls in all universes.

To be a Total GOLD servant is to accomplish the purpose of one's physical journey and one's spiritual journey. This purpose is expressed in another one-sentence secret:

The purpose of one's physical journey and spiritual journey is to serve others in order to make others healthier and happier.

TWO WAYS TO RETURN TO TAO

Tao creates everyone and everything in all universes. Everyone and everything is the son or daughter of Tao. We come from Tao and return to Tao. There are two ways to return to Tao.

The first way to return to Tao is through the normal path of life for most human beings as explained above: *Zi sheng zi mie*. A human being's life normally follows this process:

Birth → Growth → Maturity → Aging → Death

This is *Zi sheng zi mie*, as I explained in the previous section. This is a rule of the yin yang world. It is a rule of Tao.

The other way to return to Tao is the way of Xiu Tao. When you do Xiu Tao, the process of your life could be different:

Birth → Growth → Maturity
→ Aging → Fan Lao Huan Tong
(transform old age to the health and purity of a baby)
→ Stay in the baby state for long, long life
→ Immortality

If you do Xiu Tao in middle age, say at the age of thirty or forty, the process of your life could be like this:

Birth → Growth → Maturity → Transform
middle age to the baby state → Stay in the baby
state for long, long life → Immortality

If you do Xiu Tao as a child or a teenager, the process of your life could be like this:

**Birth → Growth → Transform your youth
to the baby state → Stay in the baby state
for long, long life → Immortality**

Knowing the two ways to return to Tao is vital wisdom for a human being's life. The first way to return to Tao is the yin-yang rule. Because the yin yang world is limited, a human being's life is limited. The second way to return to Tao is the Tao way. Tao is unlimited. Therefore, a human being's life can be unlimited. This is the highest philosophy for immortality. This is exactly the direction of our Tao training.

I will reveal one of the highest divine secrets here. To return to Tao is to meld with Tao. The most important wisdom is that Tao is permanent. Tao does not change. Tao will not change. Tao continuously creates everything and everything continuously returns to Tao.

My divine Tao training program will last ten years or more. The last step of this training is to become a Tao saint, who is a Tao servant. A Tao servant is one who completely melds with Tao. A Tao servant is one who returns completely to the emptiness and nothingness of the Tao condition. Such a person could then live a long, long life that is beyond comprehension. This is the direction for immortality.

Five thousand years ago, *The Yellow Emperor's Internal Classic,* the authoritative text of traditional Chinese medicine, stated:

Shang Gu Zhen Ren
"Shang gu" (pronounced *shahng goo*) means *far* or *distant ancient.* "Zhen ren" (pronounced *jun wren*) means *saints who melded with Tao.* "Shang gu zhen ren" means *the saints who melded with Tao in distant ancient times.*

Ti Xie Tian Di

"Ti xie" (pronounced *tee shyeh*) means *completely connect and meld*. "Tian" (pronounced *tyen*) means *Heaven*. "Di" (pronounced *dee*) means *Earth*. "Ti xie tian di" means *completely connected and melded with Heaven and Earth*.

Ba Wo Yin Yang

"Ba wo" (pronounced *bah waw*) means *master*. "Yin yang" means the *yin yang world*. "Ba wo yin yang" means *mastered yin and yang*.

Hu Xi Jing Qi

"Hu xi" (pronounced *hoo shee*) means *breathe and receive nourishment*. "Jing qi" (pronounced *jing chee*) means *the essence of the universe*. "Hu xi jing qi" means *breathed and received nourishment from the essence of the universe*.

Du Li Shou Shen

"Du li" (pronounced *doo lee*) means *do by yourself.* "Shou shen" (pronounced *sho shun*) means *focus your soul, heart, and mind*. "Du li shou shen" means *concentrate and focus on your soul, heart, and mind*.

Jing Shen Nei Shou

"Jing shen" (pronounced *jing shun*) means *mind*. "Nei" (pronounced *nay*) means *internal*. "Shou" means *concentration* or *focus*. "Jing shen nei shou" means *use your mind to concentrate or focus inside your body*.

Ji Rou Ruo Yi

"Ji rou" (pronounced *jee roe*) means *muscles and tissues*. "Ruo yi" (pronounced *rwaw yee*) means *meld with the soul, heart, and mind as one.* "Ji rou ruo yi" means *meld soul, heart, mind, and body as one.*

Shou Bi Tian Di

"Shou" means *long life.* "Bi" means *just like.* "Tian" means *Heaven.* "Di" means *Earth.* "Shou bi tian di" (pronounced *sho bee tyen dee*) means *life is as long as Heaven's and Earth's.*

Wu You Zhong Shi

"Wu you" means *no.* "Zhong shi" means *ending.* "Wu you zhong shi" (pronounced *woo yo jawng shr*) means *physical life has no ending.*

In summary, these statements can be translated as:

Saints who melded with Tao in distant ancient times completely connected and melded with Heaven and Earth. They mastered yin and yang. They breathed and received nourishment from the essence of the universe.

Concentrate and focus on your soul, heart, and mind. Use your mind to focus inside your body. Meld soul, heart, mind, and body as one. Life is as long as Heaven's and Earth's. Physical life has no ending.

These renowned statements in *The Yellow Emperor's Internal Classic* have revealed and explained the qualities of an immortal being.

Normal creation and reverse creation of Tao have unlimited benefits for humanity and everything in the universe. They are the highest universal principles, laws, and rules.

Apply normal creation and reverse creation of Tao to understand humanity, Mother Earth, and all universes.

Apply normal and reverse creation of Tao for healing, preventing sickness, rejuvenating, prolonging life, and transforming every aspect of life, including relationships and finances.

Apply normal and reverse creation of Tao to move in the direction of immortality.

Apply normal and reverse creation of Tao to help humanity pass this difficult transition period for humanity and Mother Earth.

Apply normal and reverse creation of Tao in order to create love, peace, and harmony for humanity, Mother Earth, and all universes.

Apply normal and reverse creation of Tao to create a new evolution for humanity and everything in all universes.

Study Tao.

Practice Tao.

Reach Tao.

Meld with Tao.

A new humanity is coming.

A new world is coming.

A new universe is coming.

The Significance of Studying and Practicing Tao

To study and practice Tao has unlimited benefits. These benefits are:

- To learn and realize that Tao is The Way of all life
- To apply Tao to transform all life
- To learn and realize that Tao is the source of all universes
- To apply Tao to transform all universes
- To learn and realize that Tao is the universal principles and laws that everyone and everything must follow
- To learn and realize the universal principles and laws

in order to truly understand: "Follow Tao, flourish. Go against Tao, finish or end."

- To apply Tao to flourish in every aspect of life
- To learn and realize normal creation and reverse creation
- To apply normal creation and reverse creation to guide and transform every aspect of your life
- To learn and apply Tao for healing
- To learn and apply Tao for prevention of illness
- To learn and apply Tao for rejuvenation (*fan lao huan tong*)
- To learn and apply Tao for prolonging life
- To learn and apply Tao for immortality
- To learn and apply Tao for transforming relationships
- To learn and apply Tao for transforming finances
- To learn and apply Tao for enlightening the soul
- To learn and apply Tao for enlightening the mind
- To learn and apply Tao for enlightening the body
- To learn and apply Tao for the evolution of human beings
- To learn and apply Tao for developing the potential powers of the soul, including soul wisdom, intelligence, and abilities to transform all life
- To learn and apply Tao for developing the potential powers of the mind, including mind wisdom, intelligence, and abilities to transform all life
- To learn and apply Tao for developing the potential powers of the body, including body wisdom, intelligence, and abilities to transform all life
- To learn and apply Tao for developing extraordinary saints' abilities

- To learn and apply Tao to become a Total GOLD unconditional universal servant and a Tao servant

The Steps to Reach Tao

To study and practice Tao is to move to Tao. To reach Tao, there are five major steps:

1. Remove all sicknesses.
2. *Fan lao huan tong* (transform old age to the health and purity of a baby; to reach *fan lao huan tong* is to become a human saint or servant).
3. Become a Mother Earth saint or servant.
4. Become a Heaven saint or servant.
5. Become a Tao saint or servant.

I will explain each of these in depth.

Step 1. Transform all sicknesses in the physical, emotional, mental, and spiritual bodies to health.

A human being can have imbalances in the physical, emotional, mental, and spiritual bodies. To reach Tao, the first step is to remove all sicknesses in the physical, emotional, mental, and spiritual bodies. In order to remove all sicknesses, there are a few vital substeps:

- Produce *Tian Yi Zhen Shui* (Heaven's unique sacred liquid)

    "Tian" means *Heaven*. "Yi" means *singular* or *unique*. "Zhen" means *sacred*. "Shui" means *liquid* or *water*. "Tian Yi Zhen Shui" (pronounced *tyen yee jun shway*) means *Heaven's unique sacred liquid.* A practitioner will produce this Heaven's unique sacred and true liquid during Tao practice. Where is this sacred and true liquid produced? It is produced in Heaven and poured into your brain to emerge through your palate and into your mouth. I will explain and lead you in the sacred practice to produce Tian Yi Zhen Shui in chapter 3. Tian Yi Zhen Shui comes from the essence of Heaven through practicing Tao. This liquid is named *Heaven's sacred liquid.*

- Produce *Jin Jin Yu Ye* (Golden liquid, jade liquid)

   The first "jin" in this phrase means *golden.* The second "jin" is a different Chinese word that means *liquid.* "Yu" means *jade.* "Ye" is another word for *liquid.* "Jin Jin Yu Ye" (pronounced *jeen jeen yü yuh*) means *golden liquid, jade liquid.* Golden and jade express the importance of these liquids. These liquids emerge inside one's mouth. There are two acupuncture points under the tongue at the root or base of the tongue. These two acupuncture points are named *Jin Jin* and *Yu Ye.* These two acupuncture points are like the source of a mountain spring.

   How is Jin Jin Yu Ye produced? There are another two acupuncture points on the soles of the feet named Yong Quan (Kidney Meridian 1), just behind the balls of the feet. The essence of Mother Earth enters through the two Yong Quan points on both feet, then goes up through the legs and body to the Jin Jin and Yu Ye acupuncture points under the tongue. The golden liquid, jade liquid then flows out from these two acupuncture points.

Jin Jin Yu Ye is the essence of Mother Earth. This gold liquid, jade liquid is named *Earth's sacred liquid*.

- *Yan Ru Dan Tian* (Swallow Heaven's sacred liquid [Tian Yi Zhen Shui] and Earth's sacred liquid [Jin Jin Yu Ye] into the Lower Dan Tian)

"Yan" (pronounced *yahn*) means *swallow*. "Ru" (pronounced *roo*) means *goes into*. "Dan Tian" (pronounced *dahn tyen*) is the Lower Dan Tian, a foundational energy center of the body. Located in the lower abdomen, the Lower Dan Tian is the life force and life source for a human being. It carries the force and source of energy, vitality, stamina, immunity, healing, prevention of sickness, rejuvenation, longevity, and immortality, as well as for soul, mind, and body enlightenment and advanced soul, mind, and body enlightenment.

The purpose of swallowing Heaven's sacred liquid and Earth's sacred liquid is to build a Jin Dan (Golden Dan) in your lower abdomen.

- *Shen Qi Jing He Yi* (Join all souls, energies, and matter in the whole body as one)

"Shen" (pronounced *shun*) represents all of one's souls, including the body soul and the souls of all systems, organs, cells, cell units, DNA, RNA, smallest matter, and spaces in the body. "Qi" (pronounced *chee*) represents all energy within all systems, organs, cells, cell units, DNA, RNA, smallest matter, and spaces in the body. "Jing" represents all matter within all systems, organs, cells, cell units, DNA, RNA, smallest matter, and spaces in the body. "He yi" (pronounced *huh yee*) means *join as one*.

All sicknesses are due to disunity or separation of Shen Qi Jing. To join Shen Qi Jing as one is to heal all sicknesses in the physical, emotional, mental, and spiritual bodies. There are layers of joining Shen Qi Jing as one. The more complete the unity of Shen Qi Jing one achieves, the more complete the healing that will occur.

- Jin Dan Lian Cheng (Form the Golden Dan)

    "Jin" means *golden*. "Dan" means *light ball*. "Lian" means *cook*. "Cheng" means *accomplished*. To join Shen Qi Jing as one is to build the Jin Dan. To swallow Heaven's sacred liquid and Earth's sacred liquid (Tian Yi Zhen Shui and Jin Jin Yu Ye) is to nourish and build the Jin Dan with the essence of energy and the essence of matter from Heaven and Earth. "Jin Dan Lian Cheng" (pronounced *jeen dahn lyen chung*) means *form the golden dan*. The Jin Dan is the key to remove all sicknesses and to make you younger and younger until you reach *fan lao huan tong*.

- Bai Bing Xiao Chu (Remove all sicknesses)

    "Bai" (pronounced *bye*) means *one hundred*. "Bing" means *sickness*. "Bai bing" represents all sicknesses. "Xiao chu" (pronounced *shee-yow choo*) means *remove*. Therefore, "Bai Bing Xiao Chu" means *remove all sicknesses*.

After forming the Jin Dan, one has gained the energy, vitality, stamina, and immunity to self-heal. The Jin Dan can promote qi flow in all of the meridians. The Jin Dan can also promote qi flow in all of the spaces between organs and between cells.

The Jin Dan has layers. Different layers of Jin Dan have different frequencies and vibrations with different levels of power to heal, rejuvenate, and prolong life. When you turn on your Jin Dan, qi will flow automatically in all parts of the body. The Jin Dan has the power to remove your soul blockages, which are bad karma, little by little. The Jin Dan also has the power to remove energy and matter blockages.

Because the Jin Dan can remove soul, mind, and body blockages for the various systems, organs, cells, and parts of the body, it is the most important treasure for a Xiu Tao practitioner. Apply the Jin Dan for healing all kinds of sicknesses of the physical, emotional, mental, and spiritual bodies. All sicknesses could be removed quickly.

This is Tao healing for humanity. This Tao teaching is available now. Grab this Tao training and these practices to remove all sicknesses of your physical, emotional, mental, and spiritual bodies.

Step 2. Fan Lao Huan Tong (transform old age to the health and purity of a baby) to become a human saint (servant).

"Fan" means *return*. "Lao" means *old age*. "Huan" means *back to*. "Tong" means *baby*. To return to the health and purity of a baby is to become a human saint (servant). To become a human saint is to gain divine abilities to serve humanity, including healing, preventing sickness, rejuvenating, prolonging life, and transforming every aspect of life, including relationships and finances, as well as enlightening the soul, heart, mind, and body of humanity. A human saint is a Total GOLD (gratitude, obedience, loyalty, and devotion to the Divine) unconditional universal servant.

Throughout history, millions of people have studied and practiced Tao. One of the most profound secrets and practices of Tao is to accomplish *fan lao huan tong*. Fan Lao Huan Tong is a sacred phrase. Spiritual practitioners dream of reaching this condition. Millions of people in history have heard about Fan Lao Huan Tong and desire to reach this state, but very few people have truly accomplished it. The Divine guided me to offer sacred Tao teachings and practices to humanity to show humanity how to truly reach *fan lao huan tong*.

To truly reach *fan lao huan tong,* there are three key steps:

- Ming Xin Jian Xing (Enlighten your heart to see your true self)

  "Ming" means *enlighten.* "Xin" (pronounced *sheen*) means *heart.* "Jian" (pronounced *jyen*) means *see.* "Xing" (pronounced *shing*) means *true self.* In Tao teaching, one's true self is named Yuan Shen (pronounced *ywen shun*). "Yuan" means *original.* "Shen" means *soul.* In other books of the Soul Power Series, I have shared many secrets and much wisdom and knowledge about the body soul. The body soul is Yuan Shen, as I taught in *The Power of Soul,* the third book of the Soul Power Series.

  When a woman and a man have intercourse, at the moment the sperm and egg connect, Tao responds. Tao will send Yuan Shen, one's original soul, to the embryo. Yuan Shen comes from Tao. Tao is One. One creates Two. Two is Yuan Jing (original matter) and Yuan Qi (original qi). In fact, Yuan Shen creates Yuan Jing and Yuan Qi. Yuan Jing and Yuan Qi are yin and yang. Yuan Shen plus Yuan Jing and Yuan Qi are three. Three creates all things.

Every system has a soul. Every organ has a soul. Every cell has a soul. Every cell unit has a soul. Every DNA and RNA has a soul. Yuan Shen, Yuan Jing, and Yuan Qi are three. These three will produce all souls for all systems, organs, cells, cell units, DNA, RNA, smallest matter inside the cells, and spaces between the cells.

The body soul is the boss of a human being. Listen to the guidance of this boss and your life can be smooth, happy, and successful. Ignore this boss or go against this boss, and life could be full of struggles. Many people do not know that your own soul could be the biggest blockage in your life. If your body soul or Yuan Shen is not happy, if it does not feel well, all kinds of challenges will follow because your boss got lost. Heal your body soul first, then healing of the souls, minds, and bodies of all systems, organs, cells, cell units, DNA, RNA, smallest matter, and spaces between the cells will follow.

I have shared one-sentence secrets in all of the books of my Soul Power Series. In one sentence, the key to soul healing is:

Heal the soul first; then healing of the mind and body will follow.

Every soul in every part of the body has the Soul Power to heal, rejuvenate, prolong life, and transform life. Yuan Shen, one's body soul, is of course the most important soul for a person. For most people, this soul is hidden. The majority of humanity cannot see this soul. It may take many years, even many life-times, of dedicated Xiu Lian in order to be able to see your Yuan Shen or body soul.

By doing Xiu Lian or Xiu Tao, one can reach *ming xin jian xing* (pronounced *ming sheen jyen shing*), which is to enlighten one's heart in order to see the Yuan Shen that was hidden within the heart.

To see one's Yuan Shen is to reach soul enlighten-ment. To reach soul enlightenment is the first step on one's enlightenment journey. The second step is to reach mind enlightenment, which is to enlighten one's consciousness. The third step is to reach body enlightenment, which is to enlighten the energy and matter of one's body in order to reach immortality.

After reaching soul, mind, and body enlighten-ment, one is truly rejuvenated. This one moves in the direction of *fan lao huan tong*, which means to return the old age condition to the baby condition. To reach *fan lao huan tong*, one becomes a human saint, which is a special servant. This special servant will gain ex-traordinary abilities to help others, to heal them, and to make them joyful.

- Xiu Lian Ying Er (Xiu Lian Baby or Soul Baby)

    As I have explained, "Xiu lian" (pronounced *sheo lyen*) means *purification practice,* and it represents the totality of the spiritual journey. "Ying er" (pro-nounced *ying ur*) means *baby.* A Xiu Lian Baby is a Soul Baby. It is not a physical baby.

    Receiving a Xiu Lian Baby is the second major step to reach *fan lao huan tong.* A Soul Baby is created by the Divine, who transmits it to the recipient's abdomen. A Soul Baby carries divine frequency, vibration, and consciousness. This Soul Baby has a higher spiritual standing in Heaven than the recipient's body soul. This Soul Baby will join as one with the original soul to uplift the person's spiritual standing.

How does one receive such a Soul Baby? How does one nourish, feed, and grow this Soul Baby? How does this Soul Baby join with one's original body soul? Where does this Soul Baby join with one's original soul?

For the Xiu Lian Baby, there are many sacred teachings and practices that I will share in future Tao books. This is absolutely a divine secret: achieve advanced soul enlightenment and *fan lao huan tong* to become a human saint (servant).

- Bi Gu Jing Hua (Fasting to purify)

"Bi gu" (pronounced *bee goo*) means *to fast*. "Jing hua" (pronounced *jing hwah*) means *purification and transformation*.

To study and practice Tao, there are special ways to fast. The most special way is a divine way. The divine way makes fasting so much easier. It accelerates all of the purification processes—soul, heart, mind, and body. There is spiritual guidance and important principles to follow. These will also be shared in detail in my future Tao books.

To reach *fan lao huan tong* is the signal of the human saint. Saints are high-level servants. Saints are given divine abilities to help humanity heal, rejuvenate, and transform. The Divine asked me to offer Tao training to help Tao practitioners reach *fan lao huan tong.* I am honored to be a chosen servant to share the top secrets from the Divine in order to offer Tao training to practitioners to empower them to reach *fan lao huan tong.*

Step 3. Become a Mother Earth saint (servant).

A saint is a servant. There are different layers of saints in Heaven and on Mother Earth. All saints in history are great servants. They are given divine abilities to serve humanity and all souls. To become a Mother Earth saint is to gain divine abilities to harmonize Mother Earth. This layer of saint can reduce natural disasters and other imbalances of Mother Earth. Fairy-tale stories in history, such as stopping storms and transforming natural disasters, can be performed by this layer of saints.

This is a very high-level saint. Since creation, fewer than one hundred saints have reached this layer. The Divine told me that in the fifteen thousand years of the Soul Light Era, the Divine will produce more than two hundred Mother Earth saints.

Step 4. Become a Heaven saint (servant).

A Heaven saint is given the divine abilities to harmonize Heaven. There are countless layers of Heaven. There are countless abilities. There are not enough words to explain the power of a Heaven saint. A Heaven saint can transform and restructure Heaven.

Since creation, fewer than fifty saints have reached the layer of Heaven saint. The Divine told me that in the fifteen thousand years of the Soul Light Era, the Divine will produce more than one hundred Heaven saints.

Step 5. Become a Tao saint (servant).

A Tao saint is given the divine abilities to harmonize all universes. There are countless universes. One universe includes countless galaxies, stars, and planets. A Tao saint is a universal servant who applies divine abilities to transform all universes.

Since creation, fewer than twenty saints have reached the layer of Tao saint. The Divine told me that in the fifteen thousand years of the Soul Light Era, the Divine will produce more than fifty Tao saints.

To become a human saint, Mother Earth saint, Heaven saint, and Tao saint is to become a pure, unconditional servant to harmonize and transform humanity, Mother Earth, Heaven, and all universes. From a human saint to a Mother Earth saint to a Heaven saint to a Tao saint, divine abilities uplift higher and higher. The power is beyond words and comprehension.

I am extremely honored to be a servant of humanity and all souls, as well as a servant of the Divine. I am honored to reveal these highest divine secrets to the public. I am just a servant and vehicle to offer the teaching that the Divine has given me.

This secret divine Tao wisdom, knowledge, and practices are available now. I cannot honor the Divine enough for choosing me as a vehicle and vessel for humanity and all souls to make this sacred and secret divine Tao teaching and practices available.

I am extremely honored and humbled to be a servant of you, humanity, and all souls. I am also extremely honored to be a teacher to share divine Tao teaching and practices with humanity.

Divine Tao teaching is extremely simple.

It is powerful.

It is healing.

It is rejuvenating.

It is life transforming.
It is enlightening.
It is serving.
The purpose of life is to serve. To study and practice Tao is to reach *fan lao huan tong* and become a divine servant for humanity.

> *I love my heart and soul*
> *I love all humanity*
> *Join hearts and souls together*
> *Love, peace and harmony*
> *Love, peace and harmony*

Summary of Tao Training

I have explained the five major steps of divine Tao training:

1. Remove all kinds of sickness.
2. *Fan lao huan tong* (become a human saint or servant).
3. Become a Mother Earth saint or servant.
4. Become a Heaven saint or servant.
5. Become a Tao saint or servant.

I would like to emphasize that to study and practice Tao (do Xiu Tao) until finally reaching Tao will take at least ten years. In ancient times, it took fifty to seventy years of serious practice to reach Tao. Now, at the dawn of the Soul Light Era, the time required to reach Tao could be significantly shorter because:

- The Divine has cleared and will specially clear total personal, ancestral, and relationship karma, as well as curses and negative memories, for chosen Tao practitioners. Since July 2003, I have offered Divine Karma Cleansing of total personal, ancestral, relationship, and other karma for thousands of people worldwide. This divine service on a major group basis ended in December 2009.

In the future I and possibly my Worldwide Representatives will offer total personal, ancestral, and relationship karma cleansing only in private sessions for life-threatening and other very serious conditions. In order to reach Tao, advanced Tao practitioners must request and receive special approval from Divine Guidance to receive total personal, ancestral, and relationship karma cleansing in a private consultation. I and some of my Worldwide Representatives will continue to offer Divine Karma Cleansing for sickness karma, relationship karma between two people, financial karma, business karma, and residential karma to the public.

I shared this one-sentence secret about karma in *The Power of Soul*, the authoritative book of my Soul Power Series:

Karma is the root cause of success and failure in every aspect of life.

Anyone could carry significant bad karma from his or her hundreds or thousands of lifetimes. Bad karma is the mistakes a person has made by harming others. Bad karma will seriously block a person's spiritual journey and physical journey. It is very hard for a person who carries significant bad karma to be committed as a pure servant for humanity and all souls.

In my teaching, a pure servant is a Total GOLD servant (gratitude, obedience, loyalty, devotion). If one is not a pure servant, it is very hard to progress in Tao training. A Tao practitioner cannot reach Tao without seriously purifying soul, heart, mind, and body. A serious Tao practitioner must build a light body in order to reach *fan lao huan tong* and move further.

Just to accomplish *fan lao huan tong*, the second of five steps to reach Tao, is not easy. Although millions of people in history on the Tao practice journey have wished to achieve *fan lao huan tong*, not many have done it. Think about yourself, whatever your age may be. To transform old age or even middle age to the health and purity of a baby is not easy, but it is possible. How? It takes a lot of personal effort to purify soul, heart, mind, and body.

In history, there have been thousands of approaches to spiritual practice on Mother Earth. What is the best way for spiritual practice? In one sentence:

The best spiritual practice is to offer total GOLD service to humanity and all souls.

Offering total GOLD service to humanity and all souls is the best way to purify your soul, heart, mind, and body.

Total Divine Karma Cleansing for the Tao practitioner will speed his or her journey to reach Tao beyond comprehension. Bad karma will block your purification, healing, and rejuvenation. It would be very difficult to reach *fan lao huan tong*. It is the greatest honor that the Divine is willing to continue to clear personal, ancestral, and relationship karma for ready Tao practitioners. We are extremely blessed.

- *Divine and Tao Soul Mind Body Transplants can save people thirty to fifty years of Xiu Tao practice.* The Soul Mind Body Transplants now available have never been given to the public. I will present and explain some of the more important ones:

  o Divine and Tao *Tian Yi Zhen Shui* Soul Mind Body Transplants

    "Tian" means *Heaven*. "Yi" means *one*. "Zhen" means *sacred*. "Shui" means *water* or *liquid*. "Tian yi zhen shui" means *Heaven's unique sacred liquid*.

    Divine and Tao *Tian Yi Zhen Shui* means the Divine and Tao offer a direct channel from Heaven to deliver Heaven's sacred liquid to your body. The significance is that the Divine and Tao offer Heaven's nutrients to nourish and transform the Tao practitioner's soul, heart, mind, and body.

  o Divine and Tao *Jin Jin Yu Ye* Soul Mind Body Transplants

    The first "Jin" means *gold*. The second "Jin" means *liquid*. "Yu" means *jade*. "Ye" means *liq-

uid. This gold liquid, jade liquid is *Mother Earth's sacred liquid.*

Divine and Tao *Jin Jin Yu Ye* (pronounced *jeen jeen yü yuh*) means the Divine and Tao offer a direct channel from Mother Earth to deliver Mother Earth's sacred liquid to your body. The significance is that the Divine and Tao offer Mother Earth's nutrients to nourish and transform the Tao practitioner's soul, heart, mind, and body.

o Divine and Tao *Shen Qi Jing He Yi* Soul Mind Body Transplants

"Shen" means *souls, including the souls of the body, systems, organs, cells, cell units, DNA, RNA, smallest matter inside the cells, and spaces between cells.* "Qi" means *vital energy or life force of the body, systems, organs, and cells.* "Jing" means *matter of the body, systems, organs, and cells.* "He yi" means *join as one.*

Divine and Tao *Shen Qi Jing He Yi* (pronounced *shun chee jing huh yee*) means Divine and Tao create and transmit Divine and Tao souls, energy, and matter to you. The significance is that these Divine and Tao souls, energy, and matter will transform the frequency and vibration of the souls, energy, and matter of your body, systems, organs, cells, cell units, DNA, and RNA to Divine and Tao frequency and vibration. It will speed the process of your *fan lao huan tong* beyond words and comprehension.

o Divine and Tao *Tian Di Ren He Yi* Soul Mind Body Transplants

"Tian" means *Heaven*. "Di" means *Mother Earth*. "Ren" means *human being*. "He yi" means *join as one*. "Tian di ren he yi" is pronounced *tyen dee wren huh yee*.

Divine and Tao *Tian Di Ren He Yi* Soul Mind Body Transplants means that the Divine and Tao gather the soul, energy, and matter of Heaven, Earth, and human being and transmit them to your body. Heaven, Earth, and human being are named San Jie (pronounced *sahn jyeh*) in Chinese. "San" means *three*. "Jie" means *level*. The significance is that the Divine and Tao will gather the essence of San Jie to nourish and transform your soul, heart, mind, and body. This is beyond imagination.

o Divine and Tao *Jin Dan* Soul Mind Body Transplants

Divine and Tao *Jin Dan* Soul Mind Body Transplants means that the Divine and Tao create a golden light ball, which is a Jin Dan, and transmit it to your lower abdomen. Divine Jin Dan and Tao Jin Dan are among the most powerful divine and Tao treasures for healing all aspects of the physical, emotional, mental, and spiritual bodies. They are also the most important Divine and Tao treasures for prevention of sickness, rejuvenation, and prolonging life. These are vital treasures for *fan lao huan tong*.

o Divine and Tao *Bi Gu* Soul Mind Body Transplants

Divine and Tao *Bi Gu* Soul Mind Body Transplants means that the Divine and Tao download permanent divine and Tao essential nutrients, including vitamins, minerals, amino acids, proteins, and divine liquid to the Tao practitioner. The significance is that after receiving these divine treasures, the Tao practitioner can do a special fasting practice (Bi Gu) to purify soul, heart, mind, and body. The main purpose of divine and Tao Bi Gu is to build a divine and Tao light body.

To reach *fan lao huan tong* and to gain divine abilities as a human saint, Mother Earth saint, Heaven saint, and Tao saint, the Tao practitioner *must* build a divine and Tao light body. The divine and Tao light body is essential to attain extraordinary saint's abilities.

o Divine and Tao *Tuo Tai Huan Gu* Soul Mind Body Transplants

Tuo Tai Huan Gu (pronounced *twaw tye hwahn goo*) is a special Tao Xiu Lian term. "Tuo Tai" means *transform a human baby to a saint baby*. "Huan Gu" means *transform human bones to saint's bones*. "Tuo tai huan gu" can be translated as *completely change your systems, organs, and cells from human to saint*.

Divine and Tao *Tuo Tai Huan Gu* Soul Mind Body Transplants means the Divine and Tao will offer Soul Mind Body Transplants for your entire body, from head to toe, skin to bone, including all systems, organs, cells, cell units, DNA, RNA, smallest matter inside the cells, and spaces between the cells.

The significance is that the soul, mind, and body of all of you, from head to toe, skin to bone, will be transformed to divine and Tao soul, mind, and body. We cannot comprehend enough how blessed we are that the Divine and Tao are willing to offer this kind of transmission to Tao practitioners.

o Tao *Baby* Soul Mind Body Transplants

A father and mother create a physical baby. A Tao Baby is a Soul Baby, not a physical baby. A Tao Baby is a special divine soul that the Tao creates and transmits to a Tao practitioner's lower abdomen. The purpose of the Tao Baby is to further advance the spiritual development of an advanced spiritual being.

A Tao Baby carries Tao frequency and a very high spiritual standing that will transform the frequency of the entire being of the receiving Tao practitioner, as well as uplift the Tao practitioner's soul standing in the spiritual world. In future Tao books, I will explain how a Tao Baby grows within one's body.

The Tao Baby is one of the top secrets in ancient Xiu Lian practice. Since creation, Tao has offered the Tao Baby only to the highest spiritual leaders on Mother Earth. Until now, Tao has never offered the Tao Baby to the general public.

Now Tao has chosen to offer the Tao Baby to humanity at this historic period of Mother Earth's transition.

I would like everyone to know that this Tao opportunity is rare. People understand that timing is important for every success. The person who can catch the right time is the luckiest one. The Tao Baby is a very advanced spiritual treasure from Tao. I am honored to be a chosen servant to offer this priceless Tao treasure for totally dedicated and totally committed spiritual beings to reach advanced soul enlightenment. To receive the Tao Baby is advanced soul enlightenment. There are not enough words to express the greatest honor of receiving a Tao Baby.

o Tao *Nectar* Soul Mind Body Transplants

A human baby needs mother's milk, cow's milk, or other special nutrients. A Tao Baby also needs special milk or food to be nourished and grow.

Tao Nectar is a permanent Tao treasure of Tao milk and Tao nutrients to feed and grow the Tao Baby. This is one of the highest secrets of Xiu Tao. We are honored that Tao offers this treasure to Tao practitioners.

o Tao *Fan Lao Huan Tong* Soul Mind Body Transplants

"Fan" means *transform and go backward.* "Lao" means *old age.* "Huan" means *to.* "Tong" means *baby.* As explained before, "Fan lao huan tong" means *transform the condition of old*

*age to the health and purity of the baby's condi-
tion.*

Tao *Fan Lao Huan Tong* Soul Mind Body
Transplants means Tao creates three light beings:
Tao *Fan Lao Huan Tong* Soul Transplant, Tao
Fan Lao Huan Tong Mind Transplant, and Tao
Fan Lao Huan Tong Body Transplant.

The Tao *Fan Lao Huan Tong* Soul Transplant
is a Tao light being that will transform the receiving Tao practitioner's soul to a Tao Fan Lao Huan
Tong soul.

The Tao *Fan Lao Huan Tong* Mind Transplant is a Tao light being that carries Tao Fan Lao
Huan Tong consciousness to transform the Tao
practitioner's consciousness to Tao consciousness.

The Tao *Fan Lao Huan Tong* Body Transplant
is a Tao light being that carries Tao Fan Lao Huan
Tong energy and tiny matter that will transform
the Tao practitioner's energy and matter to Tao
energy and matter.

At this moment on Sunday, January 3, 2010,
the Tao Committee is telling me that Tao has
never offered Tao *Fan Lao Huan Tong* Soul Mind
Body Transplants to anyone on Mother Earth.
The Tao Committee is also telling me that at my
Tao retreat that begins on May 7, 2010, ready
ones will receive this one of the greatest honors
for a spiritual being. We are extremely honored
to wait for that special moment. These treasures
will speed your *fan lao huan tong* journey beyond

words. Only with these treasures and serious practice can we achieve *fan lao huan tong*. These treasures carry Tao power beyond any words and thoughts to help recipients reach *fan lao huan tong*.

- *The Divine and Tao are releasing the most powerful techniques and practices for Tao practitioners.* These practices will accelerate the transformation of every Tao practitioner beyond comprehension. Remember, *Da Tao zhi jian*—The Big Way is extremely simple. The most important practical techniques that I am sharing with you and every reader are to sing Tao Songs, Divine Soul Songs, and your own Soul Songs and to Soul Dance.

   Tao Songs are Soul Songs given by Tao, just as Divine Soul Songs are given by the Divine. Tao Songs and Divine Soul Songs carry Tao and divine frequency, which can transform your frequency from head to toe, skin to bone. They can also transform the frequencies of your emotional body, mental body, and spiritual body.

   I have offered Divine Soul Mind Body Transplants as divine gifts in every book of my Soul Power Series. This book is the sixth in the series. In it, I will again offer Divine Soul Mind Body Transplants. I will also offer Tao Soul Mind Body Transplants for the first time. My Worldwide Representatives and I also offer Divine Soul Mind Body Transplants in our workshops, retreats, and private consultations. We also offer several Divine Soul Mind Body Transplants as gifts in our regular Sunday Divine Blessings teleconferences. I have further offered many Divine Soul Mind Body Transplants as gifts on my Facebook page ("Dr. Sha"). Therefore, your Soul Song already carries some divine frequencies that can transform not only your frequency, but also the frequency of those who receive your Soul Song.

To sing your own Soul Songs and to Soul Dance is a Tao yin-yang practice. To sing your Soul Songs is Tao yin practice. To Soul Dance is Tao yang practice. Soul Song and Soul Dance are a yin-yang pair. Soul Song is yin. Soul Dance is yang.

Yin and yang can always be subdivided further. Therefore, Soul Song can be divided into yin and yang. This is the nature of yin and yang; they can be subdivided endlessly. If you sing a Soul Song in a gentle, soft, and tender voice, that is yin Soul Song. If you sing a Soul Song in an exciting, strong, and powerful voice, that is yang Soul Song.

Soul Dance can also be divided into yin and yang. If you dance in a fast and vigorous way, that is yang Soul Dance. If you dance in a slow and gentle way, that is yin Soul Dance.

To sing Soul Songs and do Soul Dance is the divine way and Tao way to heal, prevent sickness, rejuvenate, and transform every aspect of your life, including relationships and finances. Soul Song and Soul Dance can open your heart and soul to receive blessings from the Divine, Tao, Source, and every saint, buddha, healing angel, ascended master, guru, lama, and all kinds of spiritual fathers and mothers in all layers of Heaven. You also can receive blessings from Mother Earth and the countless planets, stars, galaxies, and universes.

Beginning in 2010, my Worldwide Representatives and I, as well as hundreds of my Divine Master Teachers and Healers and Master Teachers and Healers, are offering Soul Song and Soul Dance Concerts for Healing and Rejuvenation worldwide. We also gather thousands of people in dozens of Power of Soul groups worldwide to sing Soul Songs and to Soul Dance regularly.

On my Facebook page, I have already received hundreds of heart-touching and moving stories about Soul Song and Soul Dance. I welcome you to read them. These stories can absolutely inspire you to sing Soul Songs and to Soul Dance.

In order to serve humanity further, I created a special Soul Song and Soul Dance Healer Certification Training program in early 2010. People from anywhere in the world can receive the majority of this training online. I welcome you to join this training. To become a Soul Song and Soul Dance Healer is to gain divine and Tao healing power to be a pure servant to make others happier and healthier. As part of the training, each Soul Song and Soul Dance Healer will receive about three hundred major permanent Divine Soul Mind Body Transplants to empower him or her to carry divine healing power to serve humanity, Mother Earth, and all souls in all universes.

I will reveal, teach, and lead you in Tao techniques and practices in chapter 3 of this book. Chapter 2 will cover the new, sacred

Tao texts that I received in late 2008. They contain many soul secrets, wisdom, and knowledge, as well as practical techniques. I made my commitment many years ago that in every book I write and every teleconference, workshop, Soul Song and Soul Dance Concert, and retreat I teach, I will emphasize practices. Wisdom and practices are also a yin-yang pair. Students, teachers, and practitioners need both of them. Practice is vital for healing, rejuvenation, and life transformation.

With the Divine and Tao Soul Downloads described above and the newly revealed Tao techniques and practices, a serious Tao practitioner can now reach *fan lao huan tong* in about four years instead of thirty to fifty years. To reach *fan lao huan tong* is step 2 of Tao training. I will fully explain steps 3, 4, and 5 of the Tao training program in future Tao books.

It is very important to realize that everyone and everything in the universe is a son or daughter of Tao. Tao creates everything. If one understands this, then one can realize that our lives belong to Tao. The purpose of life is to serve Tao and to accomplish the mission of Tao.

The mission of Tao is to harmonize humanity, Mother Earth, Heaven, and all universes. The more one serves humanity, Mother Earth, Heaven, and all universes, the more one receives blessings from Tao. Tao frequency and vibration will transform the frequency and vibration of our Shen Qi Jing. It takes time to transform the Shen Qi Jing of every part of the body to Tao frequency and vibration. We have to increase the quantity of Tao's Shen Qi Jing in our bodies in order to completely transform to the quality of Tao. When you reach Tao, the frequency of your whole body, including all systems, organs, and cells, will have been completely transformed to Tao frequency. Only then can you reach *fan lao huan tong*. Remember, to accomplish *fan lao huan tong* is only to accomplish step 2 of Tao training. To return and maintain your soul, mind, and body to the purity and health of the baby state is to move in the direction of immortality.

To reach immortality is to be a better servant. It is to balance humanity, Mother Earth, Heaven, and all universes. This is the final goal of studying and practicing Tao. To reach immortality is to become a Tao saint. The new divine Tao training will take at least ten years. That does not mean that you will be able to reach the Tao saint level in ten years; it could take much, much longer, but the direction of Tao training is very clear. Power is given from the Divine and Tao. Every Tao practitioner needs to practice seriously, dedicatedly, and persistently for healing, rejuvenation, purification, transformation, and enlightenment in every aspect of life.

To reach the level of a human saint, a Mother Earth saint, a Heaven saint, and a Tao saint is to gain divine and Tao abilities to be a better servant. During Tao training, Tao practitioners could gain amazing divine and Tao abilities beyond imagination. But remember my teaching: The more power you are given, the more divine and Tao abilities you receive for healing, rejuvenation, and life transformation, the more you should be a quiet and humble servant.

It will take a long, long time to reach the final goal of Tao. In order to do it, we must take good care of our health to serve Tao. We are the sons and daughters of Tao. We have to learn the Tao secrets, wisdom, knowledge, and especially the practical techniques or treasures to strengthen our health and balance our soul, heart, mind, and body. Balance ourselves first. Then balance our family. Then balance society. Then balance cities, countries, Mother Earth, and all universes.

Mother Earth is in a transition period. This means Mother

Earth is going through purification. Many natural disasters are occurring. Humanity is also suffering from sickness, depression, anxiety, fear, and many other imbalances on Mother Earth. At this historic moment, to study and practice Tao in order to balance humanity, Mother Earth, and all universes is important beyond any explanation. Join hearts and souls together on our Tao journey. Join hearts and souls together to reach Tao.

Let us sing the first Divine Soul Song that I received on September 10, 2005: *Love, Peace and Harmony*. You can listen to me on the enclosed CD:

> *Lu la lu la li*
> *Lu la lu la la li*
> *Lu la lu la li lu la*
> *Lu la li lu la*
> *Lu la li lu la*
>
> *I love my heart and soul*
> *I love all humanity*
> *Join hearts and souls together*
> *Love, peace and harmony*
> *Love, peace and harmony*

Now let us sing a Divine Soul Song that I received on December 26, 2009, *Divine Healing; Thank You, Divine*. Listen to me on the enclosed CD:

> *Lu ya yo-ou yi*
> *Lu ya yo-ou yi*
> *Lu ya yo-o-ou yi*

Lu ya yo-o-ou yi
Lu ya-a yo-ou yi-i-ya

Divine Healing
Divine Healing
Divine Healing
Divine Healing
Divine Healing

Thank you, Divine
Thank you, Divine
Thank you, Divine
Thank you, Divine
Thank you, Divine

2

Tao I Text

As I was meditating one morning in China in December 2008, the Divine told me: *Zhi Gang, I am giving you a new divine Tao text. You can share these teachings with humanity. This new text carries divine Tao sacred wisdom, knowledge, and practices.*

I was excited, moved, and touched. Below is the complete new divine Tao text that I received. I will give a one-sentence translation or explanation of every line, as well as a pronunciation guide. After that I will explain each line in detail. This text contains profound divine secrets, wisdom, knowledge, and practical techniques that you can learn and apply to benefit your physical journey, spiritual journey, and Tao journey. I am extremely honored that the Divine released this Tao text to me. I am grateful to have been chosen as a vehicle to share this Tao text with humanity.

道可道　　**Tao Ke Tao**　　　　　　*dow kuh dow*
Tao that can be explained by words or
comprehended by thoughts

非常道	**Fei Chang Tao**	*fay chahng dow*
	Is not the eternal Tao or true Tao	
大无外	**Da Wu Wai**	*dah woo wye*
	Bigger than Biggest	
小无内	**Xiao Wu Nei**	*shee-yow woo nay*
	Smaller than Smallest	
无方圆	**Wu Fang Yuan**	*woo fahng ywen*
	No Square, No Circle	
无形象	**Wu Xing Xiang**	*woo shing shyahng*
	No Shape, No Image	
无时空	**Wu Shi Kong**	*woo shr kawng*
	No Time, No Space	
顺道昌	**Shun Tao Chang**	*shwun dow chahng*
	Follow Tao, Flourish	
逆道亡	**Ni Tao Wang**	*nee dow wahng*
	Go against Tao, Finish	
道生一	**Tao Sheng Yi**	*dow shung yee*
	Tao creates One	
天一真水	**Tian Yi Zhen Shui**	*tyen yee jun shway*
	Heaven's unique sacred liquid	
金津玉液	**Jin Jin Yu Ye**	*jeen jeen yü yuh*
	Golden Liquid, Jade Liquid (Mother Earth's sacred liquid)	
咽入丹田	**Yan Ru Dan Tian**	*yahn roo dahn tyen*
	Swallow into the Lower Dan Tian	
一生二	**Yi Sheng Er**	*yee shung ur*
	One creates Two	
道丹道神	**Tao Dan Tao Shen**	*dow dahn dow shun*
	Tao Golden Light Ball, Tao Heart Soul	

服务人类	**Fu Wu Ren Lei**	*foo woo wren lay*
	Serve all humanity	
服务万灵	**Fu Wu Wan Ling**	*foo woo wahn ling*
	Serve all souls	
服务地球	**Fu Wu Di Qiu**	*foo woo dee cheo*
	Serve Mother Earth	
服务宇宙	**Fu Wu Yu Zhou**	*foo woo yü joe*
	Serve all universes	
治愈百病	**Zhi Yu Bai Bing**	*zhr yü bye bing*
	Heal all sickness	
预防百病	**Yu Fang Bai Bing**	*yü fahng bye bing*
	Prevent all sickness	
返老还童	**Fan Lao Huan Tong**	*fahn lao hwahn tawng*
	Return old age to the health and purity of a baby	
长寿永生	**Chang Shou Yong Sheng**	*chahng sho yawng shung*
	Long life, immortal	
和谐人类	**He Xie Ren Lei**	*huh shyeh wren lay*
	Harmonize all humanity	
道业昌盛	**Tao Ye Chang Sheng**	*dow yuh chahng shung*
	Tao career flourishes	
功德圆满	**Gong De Yuan Man**	*gawng duh ywen mahn*
	Serve unconditionally and gain complete virtue to reach full enlightenment	
万灵融合	**Wan Ling Rong He**	*wahn ling rawng huh*
	All souls join as one	
丹神养肾	**Dan Shen Yang Shen**	*dahn shun yahng shun*
	Tao Dan, Tao Shen nourish kidneys	

二生三	**Er Sheng San**	*ur shung sahn*
	Two creates Three	
三万物	**San Wan Wu**	*sahn wahn woo*
	Three creates all things	
天地人	**Tian Di Ren**	*tyen dee wren*
	Heaven, Earth, Human Being	
神气精	**Shen Qi Jing**	*shun chee jing*
	Soul Energy Matter	
肾生精	**Shen Sheng Jing**	*shun shung jing*
	Kidneys create Jing	
精生髓	**Jing Sheng Sui**	*jing shung sway*
	Jing creates spinal cord	
髓充脑	**Sui Chong Nao**	*sway chawng now*
	Spinal cord fills brain	
脑神明	**Nao Shen Ming**	*now shun ming*
	Mind reaches enlightenment	
炼精化气	**Lian Jing Hua Qi**	*lyen jing hwah chee*
	Transform Jing to Qi	
炼气化神	**Lian Qi Hua Shen**	*lyen chee hwah shun*
	Transform Qi to Shen	
炼神还虚	**Lian Shen Huan Xu**	*lyen shun hwahn shü*
	Transform and return Shen to Xu	
炼虚还道	**Lian Xu Huan Tao**	*lyen shü hwahn dow*
	Transform and return Xu to Tao	
合道中	**He Tao Zhong**	*huh dow jawng*
	Meld with Tao	
无穷尽	**Wu Qiong Jin**	*woo chyawng jeen*
	The benefits for all life are endless	
道灵宫	**Tao Ling Gong**	*dow ling gawng*
	Tao Soul Temple	

信息雪山	**Xin Xi Xue Shan**	*sheen shee shoo-eh shahn*
	Message Center, Snow Mountain	
灵语言	**Ling Yu Yan**	*ling yü yahn*
	Soul Language	
灵信通	**Ling Xin Tong**	*ling sheen tawng*
	Soul Communication	
灵歌舞	**Ling Ge Wu**	*ling guh woo*
	Soul Song, Soul Dance	
灵敲打	**Ling Qiao Da**	*ling chee-yow dah*
	Soul Tapping	
灵草药	**Ling Cao Yao**	*ling tsow yow*
	Soul Herbs	
灵针灸	**Ling Zhen Jiu**	*ling jun jeo*
	Soul Acupuncture	
灵按摩	**Ling An Mo**	*ling ahn maw*
	Soul Massage	
灵治疗	**Ling Zhi Liao**	*ling jr lee-ow*
	Soul Healing	
灵预防	**Ling Yu Fang**	*ling yü fahng*
	Soul Prevention of Illness	
灵转化	**Ling Zhuan Hua**	*ling jwahn hwah*
	Soul Transformation	
灵圆满	**Ling Yuan Man**	*ling ywen mahn*
	Soul Enlightenment	
灵智慧	**Ling Zhi Hui**	*ling jr hway*
	Soul Intelligence	
灵潜能	**Ling Qian Neng**	*ling chyen nung*
	Soul Potential	
换灵脑身	**Huan Ling Nao Shen**	*hwahn ling now shun*
	Soul Mind Body Transplant	

服务三界	**Fu Wu San Jie**	*foo woo sahn jyeh*
	Serve Heaven, Earth, and Human Being	
灵光普照	**Ling Guang Pu Zhao**	*ling gwahng poo jow*
	Shining Soul Light	
万物更新	**Wan Wu Geng Xin**	*wahn woo gung sheen*
	Everything is renewed	
誓为公仆	**Shi Wei Gong Pu**	*shr way gawng poo*
	Vow to be an unconditional universal servant	
世代服务	**Shi Dai Fu Wu**	*shr dye foo woo*
	Serve in all lives	
灵光圣世	**Ling Guang Sheng Shi**	*ling gwahng shung shr*
	Soul Light Era	
创新纪元	**Chuang Xin Ji Yuan**	*chwahng sheen jee ywen*
	Create a new era	
道道道	**Tao Tao Tao**	*dow dow dow*
	The Way, the Source, the Universal Principles and Laws	
道定得	**Tao Ding De**	*dow ding duh*
	Tao stillness	
道慧明	**Tao Hui Ming**	*dow hway ming*
	Tao intelligence, Tao realization	
道喜在	**Tao Xi Zai**	*dow shee dzye*
	Tao happiness and joy	
道体生	**Tao Ti Sheng**	*dow tee shung*
	Tao body is produced	
道圆满	**Tao Yuan Man**	*dow ywen mahn*
	Tao enlightenment	

道合真	**Tao He Zhen**	*dow huh jun*
	Meld with Tao and become a Tao saint (servant)	
道果成	**Tao Guo Cheng**	*dow gwaw chung*
	Tao harvest	
道神通	**Tao Shen Tong**	*dow shun tawng*
	Complete Tao saint abilities	
道法自然	**Tao Fa Zi Ran**	*dow fah dz rahn*
	Follow Nature's Way	

道可道, 非常道
Tao Ke Tao, Fei Chang Tao

Tao that can be explained by words or comprehended by thoughts is not the eternal Tao or true Tao

Tao is The Way. Tao is the source of all universes. Tao is the universal principles and laws. Without Tao, there would be no human beings, no Mother Earth, no universes.

Why do we need to study Tao? Because Tao creates everything in all universes. Tao guides every aspect of life. To study and practice Tao is to understand that every aspect of life has a Tao. To study and practice Tao is to bless every aspect of life.

For example, eating has a Tao. There is an ancient wisdom: *chi ba cheng bao.* (Eat only until you are eighty percent full.) "Chi" (pronounced *chee*) means *eat.* "Ba cheng" (pronounced *bah chung*) means *eighty percent.* "Bao" (pronounced *bow*, rhymes with *cow*) means *full.* This wisdom teaches us to eat the proper amount of food in order to benefit digestion and absorption.

Another ancient wisdom for eating is *chi su dan* (eat vegetables and less fat, oil, and salt). "Chi" (pronounced *chee*) again means *eat.* "Su" (pronounced *soo*) means *vegetables.* "Dan" (pronounced *dahn*) means *less fat, oil, and salt.* This simple statement has absolutely expressed and guided many to the Tao of eating for thousands of years. In modern times, there is much scientific research proving this wisdom. Millions of people follow this Tao principle of eating for their health.

Sleeping has a Tao. In ancient Tao teaching, *ri luo wo, ri chu qi.* (When the sun sets, sleep. When the sun rises, wake up.) This Tao of sleeping is so simple. Again, modern research has demonstrated that going to sleep earlier has many benefits for the endocrine system, circulatory system, and more. Unfortunately, millions of people on Mother Earth do not follow the Tao of sleeping.

The Tao of eating and the Tao of sleeping are examples of Xiao Tao (Small Tao). Every aspect of life has a Tao. For example, I have taught soul healing since 1993. The Divine guided me that the Tao of soul healing is the healing result. In order to spread soul healing to humanity, the Tao is to demonstrate great healing results.

Almost immediately after I began to teach soul healing, I started to realize the power of soul more and more deeply. I focused on self-healing in my teaching. Many good and even remarkable healing results quickly inspired me to travel worldwide to teach soul healing.

As I write this, I have been teaching soul healing worldwide for seventeen years. I have offered soul healing teaching to hundreds of thousands of people. There are thousands of heart-touching and moving stories of soul healing.

In 2008, I created the Soul Power Series. This is the sixth book in the series. All six have been published in a span of less than two years. The first five books are:

- *Soul Wisdom: Practical Soul Treasures to Transform Your Life*

- *Soul Communication: Opening Your Spiritual Channels for Success and Fulfillment*
- *The Power of Soul: The Way to Heal, Rejuvenate, Transform, and Enlighten All Life*
- *Divine Soul Songs: Sacred Practical Treasures to Heal, Rejuvenate, and Transform You, Humanity, Mother Earth, and All Universes*
- *Divine Soul Mind Body Healing and Transmission System: The Divine Way to Heal You, Humanity, Mother Earth, and All Universes*

The Soul Power Series has given humanity a complete soul system for soul healing, soul rejuvenation, and soul transformation of every aspect of life. Soul is the boss of one's life. *Heal and transform the soul first; then healing and transformation of every aspect of life will follow.*

Tao is the source of all universes. Tao creates One. In fact, Tao is One and One is Tao. One creates Two. Two is Heaven and Earth, yang and yin. Heaven and Earth interact to produce all souls and all things in all universes, but they all come from Tao.

To study and practice Tao is advanced soul study and practice. It is most important to understand that everything has a Tao. I explained above the Tao of eating, the Tao of sleeping, and the Tao of soul healing. In fact, there is a Tao for every aspect of your life. For example, business has a Tao. A relationship has a Tao. To realize the Tao in any aspect of life is to follow the spiritual principles and laws to ensure your success in that part of life.

Take healing as another example. How can all of a person's sicknesses in the physical, emotional, mental, and spiritual bodies be healed? What is the Tao of healing? To heal all sicknesses in these four bodies, the Tao of healing can be summarized in one sentence:

The Tao to heal all sickness is Shen Qi Jing He Yi.

Shen represents all souls in the whole body, including the souls of systems, organs, and cells. Qi represents all energies in the whole body, including the energies of systems, organs, and cells. Jing represents all matter in the whole body, including the matter of systems, organs, and cells. A person's physical, emotional, mental, and spiritual bodies are made of soul, energy, and matter. Any kind of sickness is due to an imbalance in and the separation of Shen Qi Jing. To join Shen Qi Jing as one is to balance the whole body. To join Shen Qi Jing as one is to return to Tao.

Remember the process of reverse creation of Tao that I shared in chapter 1:

all things → Three → Two → One → TAO
return to

Shen Qi Jing He Yi (pronounced *shun chee jing huh yee*) is to return to Tao. I am honored to share this highest divine secret to heal and transform all life. This highest secret can be summarized in one sentence:

To return to Tao is the solution for healing,
rejuvenating, transforming, and enlightening all life.

How can one apply Shen Qi Jing He Yi to heal all sicknesses? This is the way to do it. Apply the Four Power Techniques that I shared in my book *Power Healing*.[4]

---

4 *Power Healing: The Four Keys to Energizing Your Body, Mind and Spirit* (San Francisco: HarperSanFrancisco, 2002).

Body Power. Sit up straight. Put the tip of your tongue as close as you can to the roof of your mouth without touching it. Put one palm on your abdomen. Place your other palm over this hand.

Soul Power. Say *hello:*

> *Dear Divine, dear Tao, dear saints in Heaven, I am*
> *honored to invoke you to request healing for* _____
> (state your healing request silently or aloud).

Mind Power. Visualize the Jin Dan (golden light ball) rotating counterclockwise in your Lower Dan Tian, a foundational energy center located in your lower abdomen.

A renowned ancient Chinese statement about spiritual healing is:

Jin guang zhao ti, bai bing xiao chu

"Jin" means *golden.* "Guang" means *light.* "Zhao" means *shine.* "Ti" means *body.* "Bai" means *one hundred,* which represents *every* or *all.* "Bing" means *sickness.* "Xiao chu" means *to remove.* Therefore, "Jin guang zhao ti, bai bing xiao chu" (pronounced *jeen gwahng jow tee, bye bing shee-ow choo*) means:

Golden light shines; all sicknesses are removed.

Visualizing a golden light ball rotating counterclockwise in your Lower Dan Tian is absolutely one of the most important Tao healings for all sicknesses.

Sound Power. Sing or chant:

Shen Qi Jing He Yi
Shen Qi Jing He Yi
Shen Qi Jing He Yi
Shen Qi Jing He Yi
Shen Qi Jing He Yi
Shen Qi Jing He Yi
Shen Qi Jing He Yi . . .

Sing or chant for three minutes now. Remember, I explain in the beginning of every book of the Soul Power Series that when I ask you to spend time to practice, do not skip the practice. Three to five minutes of practice per time is vital for healing, rejuvenation, and life transformation. In fact, to heal chronic and life-threatening conditions, you must practice at least two hours per day in total.

My new teaching is that **the fastest way to heal is to sing or chant all the time**, either silently or aloud. Every moment of singing or chanting is healing and transforming. The more you sing or chant, the faster you could heal.

Shen Qi Jing He Yi is a mantra. This mantra is extremely powerful, beyond words and comprehension. Practice more and more. A great healing result is waiting for you.

Mother Earth is in a transition period, with many natural disasters, conflicts between nations and religions, communicable diseases and other sicknesses, wars, financial challenges, and all kinds of problems for humanity and Mother Earth. How can we apply Tao to serve humanity and Mother Earth at this critical historic period?

All problems in humanity, Mother Earth, and all universes are due to imbalance in and separation of Heaven, Earth, and human beings. To help humanity, Mother Earth, and all universes rebalance and reunite, I will share an extremely powerful Tao practice. This practice is so powerful that we cannot use any words and thoughts to explain or comprehend it. This Tao practice can be summarized in one sentence:

Tian Di Ren He Yi

"Tian" means *Heaven*. "Di" means *Mother Earth*. "Ren" means *human being*. "He yi" means *join as one*. Therefore, "Tian di ren he yi" (pronounced *tyen dee wren huh yee*) means *Heaven, Earth, and human being join as one*.

This is one of the highest philosophies of Tao. Tian Di Ren He Yi is Heaven, Earth, and human being returning to Tao. Remember that to return to Tao is the solution for everything in your life, the lives of your loved ones, the life of humanity, and the lives of all souls. In one sentence:

To return to Tao is the way of all life.

Spiritual practitioners throughout history often thought that philosophy is theoretical guidance, while practice is the practical exercise. They believed philosophy and practice are separate. In fact, the highest philosophy is the most powerful practice. They are the yin and yang of Tao. When you put them together, yin and yang join as one. Two returns to One. One returns to Tao.

Now let me share with you how to put Tian Di Ren He Yi, one of the highest philosophies in all universes, into practice. This is the way to do it. Apply the Four Power Techniques:

Body Power. Sit up straight. Put the tip of your tongue as close as you can to the roof of your mouth without touching it. Put one palm on your abdomen. Place your other palm over this hand.

Soul Power. Say *hello:*

> *Dear Divine, dear Tao, dear saints in Heaven, I am*
> *honored to invoke you to request healing for* _____
> (state your healing request silently or aloud).
> *I am very grateful.*

Mind Power. Visualize the Jin Dan (golden light ball) rotating counterclockwise in your Lower Dan Tian.

Sound Power. Sing or chant silently or aloud:

> *Tian Di Ren He Yi*
> *Tian Di Ren He Yi*
> *Tian Di Ren He Yi*
> *Tian Di Ren He Yi*
> *Tian Di Ren He Yi*
> *Tian Di Ren He Yi*
> *Tian Di Ren He Yi . . .*

Do it now for at least three minutes. The more you sing or chant, the faster you could heal.

This singing or chanting is also to serve humanity, Mother Earth, and all universes. The purpose of life is to serve. When you serve, the Divine and the Akashic Records record your service. You are given virtue, which is divine flowers. Divine flowers are spiritual currency that blesses every aspect of your lives, current and future.

To serve is to clear karma. When you serve, Heaven gives you virtue. Your karmic lessons are forgiven more and more. The more you serve, the more you are forgiven. In chapter 2 (on karma) of the authority book of my Soul Power Series, *The Power of Soul:*

The Way to Heal, Rejuvenate, Transform, and Enlighten All Life,
I shared the one-sentence secret of karma:

**Karma is the root cause of success and
failure in every aspect of life.**

This sentence is the Tao of karma. Karma is key for every aspect of life. If one has good karma, he or she will be blessed in his or her current life and future lives. If one has bad karma, he or she will learn lessons, which could be in every aspect of life, including health, relationships, and finances.

Tian Di Ren He Yi is one of the most important services for Mother Earth and beyond now. To practice Tian Di Ren He Yi is to give great service to humanity, Mother Earth, and all universes. The Divine and the Akashic Records will give huge amounts of virtue to bless those who offer unconditional service during this historic period. Therefore, to practice Tian Di Ren He Yi is the sacred Tao practice to clear your own bad karma to bless every aspect of your life, including healing, prevention of sickness, rejuvenation, prolonging life, transformation of relationships and finances, and enlightenment of soul, heart, mind, and body for yourself and your loved ones.

I would like to share one karma cleansing story. On Easter Sunday in 2006, I offered Divine Karma Cleansing to hundreds of people worldwide in a teleconference. Three weeks later I was doing a book signing event. A man came to me and said, "Master Sha, I received karma cleansing on Easter Sunday. The next day I was in a car accident. Why did this happen right after my karma was cleansed?"

I replied, "Close your eyes." I checked with the leaders of the Akashic Records. They showed me his Akashic Records book, which included the lessons he was supposed to learn due to his bad karma. It had been arranged for him to have a serious car accident, after which he would have suffered a stroke and gone into a vegetative state. Two and a half years after these events, he was to lose his life. The leaders of the Akashic Records told me to say "Congratulations!" to him.

I asked the man, "What kind of injury do you have from your accident?" He said, "A little whiplash." I told him what I saw and what I heard from the leaders of the Akashic Records. I said, "Congratulations. Instead of going into a vegetative state, the Divine Karma Cleansing transformed your condition to a slight whiplash."

This man instantly realized the truth of karma cleansing. He put his palms together in front of his chest and moved backward with gratitude and humility, saying, "I got it. I got it. I got it. Thank you. Thank you. Thank you."

This story is to share with you that Divine Karma Cleansing service is for saving life. Since July 2003, more than twenty thousand people worldwide have received Divine Karma Cleansing. There are many lifesaving stories among them. There are thousands of heart-touching and moving stories, including healing and transformation of liver cancer, lymphatic cancer, and other cancers, genetic sickness for newborn babies who were hopeless, as well as many chronic pain and other conditions for twenty, thirty, or more years. Thousands of people have been moved to tears from Divine Karma Cleansing and divine healing. I am honored to be a servant of humanity and the Divine to offer Divine Karma Cleansing and Divine Soul Mind Body Transplants for humanity. All credit goes back to Divine. I am a servant for humanity.

I share this story to let every reader know that karma is ex-

tremely important for one's life. To practice Tian Di Ren He Yi
is to self-clear bad karma, as well as to gain good karma. The
benefits are immeasurable. Let us practice Tian Di Ren He Yi together for three more minutes to serve humanity, Mother Earth,
and all universes.

Sing or chant with me now:

> *Tian Di Ren He Yi*
> *Tian Di Ren He Yi*
> *Tian Di Ren He Yi*
> *Tian Di Ren He Yi*
> *Tian Di Ren He Yi*
> *Tian Di Ren He Yi*
> *Tian Di Ren He Yi . . .*

Continue to sing or chant for three minutes. Stop reading and
put your mind in your lower abdomen. Visualize the Jin Dan
(golden light ball) rotating counterclockwise in your Lower Dan
Tian.

Tao is the source of all universes.

Tao is the way of all life.

Tao is the universal principles and laws.

Let us study Tao.

Let us practice Tao.

Apply Tao to transform every aspect of life.

Apply Tao to transform humanity.

Apply Tao to transform Mother Earth.

Apply Tao to transform all universes.

Hao. Hao. Hao.

Thank you. Thank you. Thank you.

大无外

Da Wu Wai

Bigger than Biggest

Tao is big without boundaries. Tao creates One. One creates Two. Two is Heaven and Earth, yang and yin. Two creates Three. Three includes Tao, yang, and yin. Three creates all things.

The universe is huge. Cosmologists have observed that the visible part of the universe extends fourteen billion light years from us. The speed of light is about 186,000 miles per second, which is more than 670,000,000 (six hundred seventy million) miles per hour. Therefore, the farthest stars and galaxies observed are about 14,000,000,000 × 670,000,000 × 24 × 365 miles away from us. If I multiply this number out, it is:

82,170,000,000,000,000,000,000,000 (82.17 sextillion) miles.

If the farthest visible stars are this far away, we can begin to imagine how big the universe is.

The founder of Buddhism, Shi Jia Mo Ni Fuo,[5] said, "One universe has three thousand big worlds. One big world has three thousand small worlds. A solar system is only one small world." From this statement of Shi Jia Mo Ni Fuo, we can also imagine how big the universe is.

Tao creates countless universes. Can we imagine how big Tao is?

Tao is emptiness and nothingness. Tao is the creator of all universes. Tao is the biggest without boundary. You cannot measure how big Tao is.

---

5 This is his name in Chinese. Other names include Shakyamuni, Siddhartha Gautama, and, simply, the Buddha.

Tao creates One. One is unity. Unity is endless. Use a human being as an example. A human being is unity. A human being is a small universe. There are many systems in the human body. Every system has many organs. Every organ has many cells. Take, for example, the central nervous system, which includes the brain and spinal cord. Scientists have determined that there are tens of billions of brain cells in the brain. In fact, there are millions and billions of cells in every organ. We do not know exactly how many cells are in a human body, but it has been estimated that there are more than 100,000,000,000,000 (one hundred trillion).

A human being is a son or daughter of Tao. A human being is like one molecule of Tao. There are about 6.8 billion human beings on Mother Earth. There could be other beings in other planets, stars, galaxies, and universes. Tao is endless.

In summary, Tao is the source and creator of all universes. Therefore, Tao is "Da wu wai" (pronounced *dah woo wye*), bigger than biggest.

小无内
Xiao Wu Nei

Smaller than Smallest

Scientists always try to discover the smallest components of the universe. Are they quarks, leptons, and gauge bosons that exist in four dimensions? Are they "strings" that exist in eleven dimensions? In fact, scientists will never be able to discover the smallest things in the universe because Tao is emptiness and nothingness. Tao is endless. Tao exists in any space and in any time. Tao includes the smallest things in the universe and Tao includes the biggest things in the universe because Tao is the creator of all things in all universes.

The Yellow Emperor's Internal Classic, the authoritative book of traditional Chinese medicine, states:

Qi ju zhe cheng xing, qi san zhe cheng feng

"Qi" means *energy.* "Ju" means *accumulation.* "Zhe" means *become.* "Cheng" means *form.* "Xing" means *shape.* "San" means *dissipate.* "Feng" means *wind.* Therefore, "Qi ju zhe cheng xing, qi san zhe cheng feng" (pronounced *chee jü juh chung shing, chee sahn juh chung fung*) means *energy accumulation forms a shape; energy dissipation is just like the wind flowing away.*

This wisdom explains the formation of any growth in the body, including cysts, benign tumors, and cancers. It also gives the healing solution for any such growths in terms of energy. This wisdom has guided traditional Chinese medicine for more than five thousand years.

Xing, shape, expresses a thing. A thing has form. It can be in the physical form or the soul form. It is definable, graspable, and observable. *San,* dissipation, becomes nothingness, which is Tao. Tao is not a thing. Tao is "no-thing." Tao has no form. Tao is everywhere. Tao is nowhere. Tao cannot be defined, grasped, or observed. A thing has limits and boundaries. Nothingness, Tao, has no limits, no boundaries.

Humans often try to use "a thing" to understand nothingness, but we can never fully understand and comprehend nothingness. Tao is nothingness. Tao has the smallest energy and smallest matter. These can form the smallest things that are beyond scientists' ability to measure. In history, scientists have always continued to discover smaller and smaller things. For example, there was a time when atoms were not known. Then, atoms were considered to be the smallest building blocks of matter. Scientists will continue further to discover smaller and smaller things.

Because the nature of Tao is nothingness, which is beyond endless and beyond infinite, scientific study and research can never discover the smallest things in the universe, nor the biggest things in the universe. This is the sacred and profound wisdom of Tao. It does not matter how many human beings try to use their limited minds to comprehend unlimited Tao. Human beings will never discover the smallest or the largest things in the universe.

We are in the yin yang world or realm. There is "somethingness," and there is nothingness. Wu ji (pronounced *woo jee*) is emptiness or nothingness. Tai chi (pronounced *tye chee*) is existence or "somethingness," which includes yin and yang.

Figure 2. Yin-yang symbol

People know and understand many things in the yin yang world, because yin yang is "something." But if this is all they know, their realization is limited. The highly developed spiritual being will go into the emptiness and nothingness condition, which is the Tao condition. If you can apply the Tao condition to see the world, you will see a completely different world than the one we think of normally. In one sentence:

Yin and Yang are Two, which is limited;
Tao is One, which is unlimited.

If you comprehend only things in the yin yang world, then you will not be able to understand the whole picture. From Tao to everything, from the macrocosm to the microcosm, is the normal creation of Tao. From everything back to Tao, from the microcosm to the macrocosm, is the reverse creation of Tao. To have a complete view of humanity, Mother Earth, and all universes, you must see both the normal creation and the reverse creation of Tao. If you truly understand these two creations fully, than you will understand the highest philosophy of Tao and you will be able to explain anything in the universe.

I repeat the processes of normal creation and reverse creation to emphasize them.

The process of **normal creation** is:

> **TAO → One → Two → Three → all things**
> **creates**

The process of **reverse creation** is:

> **all things → Three → Two → One → TAO**
> **return to**

Normal creation goes from the macrocosm to the microcosm. Reverse creation goes from the microcosm to the macrocosm.

Tao includes normal creation and reverse creation. Study and apply normal creation and reverse creation for every aspect of life. Then you will be able to remove all kinds of blockages in every aspect of life. This is *Shun Tao chang* (Follow Tao, flourish).

Tao is infinity, the source of all universes. Tao has unlimited sacred wisdom, knowledge, and practices. To study Tao and practice Tao is to have the potential of gaining unlimited power and abilities to serve humanity, Mother Earth, and all universes. Therefore, you may be able to understand further the power, wisdom, and abilities of the five major steps of divine Tao training that I introduced in chapter 1:

- Remove all sickness
- Become a human saint (servant)—*Fan lao huan tong*
- Become a Mother Earth saint (servant)
- Become a Heaven saint (servant)
- Become a Tao saint (servant)

To understand and deeply realize the nature of Tao, which is emptiness, nothingness, infinite, and endless, is vital in studying and practicing Tao.

One can gain unlimited wisdom by studying and practicing Tao.

One can gain unlimited power by studying and practicing Tao.

A human being's life is limited. To study Tao and to practice Tao is to reach Tao and meld with Tao. Human life can then go into the unlimited condition of Tao. Therefore, *fan lao huan tong* is possible. Long, long life is possible. Immortality is possible.

Tao is miraculous and profound.

Tao has unlimited wisdom, knowledge, and practices.

Tao has unlimited power.

Study Tao well.

Practice Tao well.

Reach Tao as early as possible.

I wish you great success in your Tao study and practice journey.

Tao is miraculous and profound.

无方圆
Wu Fang Yuan

No Square, No Circle

"Fang" means *square*. A square represents east, west, north, and south. These are two dimensions. "Yuan" means *circle* or *ball*. It includes east, west, north, south, center, up, and down. These are three dimensions. "Wu" means *no*. Therefore, "Wu fang yuan" (pronounced *woo fahng ywen*) means *no square, no circle*.

Tao has no shape and no dimensions, which means Tao has all dimensions. Tao has more than three dimensions. Tao is emptiness, nothingness, infinite, and endless. It holds all universes in all directions. Tao has countless dimensions.

无形象
Wu Xing Xiang

No Shape, No Image

"Xing xiang" (pronounced *shing shyahng*) means *shape* or *image*. Tao creates all universes. It is endless. It is nothingness. The universe is big without ending. As human beings, we do not know how big the universe is. Anything we can see is expressed by the Chinese word *you* (pronounced *yo*). "You" means *existence* or "*somethingness.*" Anything that we cannot see is expressed by the Chinese word *wu* (pronounced *woo*). "Wu" means *nothingness*. Nothingness is Tao. Wu creates You, but Wu and You are totally different conditions.

Scientists can see a lot. They can see very distant stars in the universe through electronic telescopes. They can see very small things through electronic microscopes. It is important to know that it does not matter how far away or big the things that scientists can see or discover are. It also does not matter how small the things scientists can see or discover are. All of these things are in existence, which is the world of You. What scientists and human beings cannot see or discover, what is bigger than biggest, smaller than smallest, farther than farthest, and nearer than nearest—all of these belong to the world of Wu.

Humans can see the world of You but, generally speaking, they cannot see the world of Wu. The world of You is limited. Humans belong to the world of You. Tao is Wu, nothingness and emptiness. Tao creates the world of You. The totality of what humanity can see and comprehend is a tiny speck of Tao. Only very highly developed spiritual beings can see or understand even some small parts of Wu. It has been impossible for any human being ever to understand the complete picture of Wu. To understand the complete picture of Wu is to completely meld with Tao. Tao is limitlessly big and limitlessly small. Tao has unlimited secrets, wisdom, knowledge, and practical techniques. Tao has unlimited power and abilities. It is not possible for anyone to see or completely understand all of Tao. Therefore, Tao has no shape, no image.

Humanity never can see the whole picture of Tao. We all know the story of the blind person touching an elephant. If the blind person touches the elephant's leg, he might say, "The elephant is like a column." If this blind person touches the elephant's side, he might say, "The elephant is like a big wall." Because the blind person cannot see the entire elephant, any conclusion and judgment he makes by touching only one part of the elephant will be limited. A blind person cannot grasp the whole picture from one touch.

Humanity sees the universe in exactly the same way the blind person "sees" the elephant. Humanity has limited wisdom and a limited view of the universe. Humanity can see limited small things and limited big things. To understand or even imagine the unlimited universe, much less the unlimited Tao, is very difficult with limited vision.

To study Tao and practice Tao in order to reach Tao is to go into deeper and deeper spiritual study and practice. There is unlimited wisdom and unlimited vision within the Tao. An advanced spiritual being with highly developed spiritual channels could see some part of the unlimited universes. An ordinary human being cannot see this view.

To practice Tao is to transform your own frequency to Tao frequency. To practice Tao is to transform your limited vision to infinite vision. To practice Tao is to transform limited wisdom, knowledge, and techniques to the unlimited wisdom, knowledge, and techniques of Tao.

Always remember to be a humble servant. If, after at least ten years, you accomplish all five steps of Tao training, if you reach the Tao saint/servant level, congratulations! This means you are melded with Tao. You are given Tao abilities to harmonize all universes. But do not think that you understand all of Tao or you have complete Tao power. Yes, the power and abilities of Tao saints are beyond any words and any comprehension. But the closer you get to complete Tao, the more you realize how difficult and how far this ultimate goal is. Always be a humble servant. In one sentence:

The higher the power an advanced spiritual being has received from Tao, the more humble this being should be.

无时空
Wu Shi Kong

No Time, No Space

"Shi" (pronounced *shr*) means *time*. "Kong" (pronounced *kawng*) means *space*. The universe consists of time and space. A human's life is limited. When one sees the lives of the sun and the moon, one may think the lives of the sun and the moon are unlimited in comparison to one's own life. In fact, the lives of the sun and the moon are also limited. The life of Tao is unlimited. This is because Tao creates Heaven and Earth. Tao creates the sun and the moon.

Tao creates all universes. It holds all time and all space. Tao is emptiness, nothingness, infinite. Tao has no beginning, no ending, no time, no space. Universes begin and end, but Tao exists forever. Tao has no age. Tao persists. Tao exists. Tao is endless. Tao is Tao.

顺道昌
Shun Tao Chang

Follow Tao, Flourish

"Shun" (pronounced *shwun*) means *follow*. "Chang" (pronounced *chahng*) means *flourish*. Tao is the universal laws and principles. Tao has Da Tao (Big Tao) and Xiao Tao (Small Tao). Big Tao is the universal principles and laws. Small Tao is the small principles and laws in every aspect of life, including eating, sleeping, relationships, business, and health.

Follow the Tao, flourish. Go against the Tao, end. Take business as an example. Business has principles, including leadership, infrastructure, financial control, marketing, teamwork, coordination, communication, love, peace, harmony, and more. Generally speaking, successful businesses are strong in these areas and qualities. If your business is not successful, find out which areas need improvement.

If a business follows business principles and has great quality in the above areas, the business could be very successful. If a business does not follow business principles and lacks good quality in these areas, the business will be blocked and will not be successful. This is the Tao of business.

Relationships have a Tao. If a person is kind, generous, loving, forgiving, and compassionate, he or she could have many sincere friends. If a person is selfish, greedy, and self-centered, he or she will find it very hard to have sincere friendships.

A person who follows the Tao of eating and sleeping, as well as the Tao of working, is likely to have good health. A person who eats unhealthy food, who eats too much, who does not sleep regularly or not enough, who works too much without rest and balance, is likely to be unhealthy and stressed, and have all kinds of emotional imbalances.

If the leader of a country does not follow the Tao of leadership—does not do things to benefit his or her citizens, does not have love, forgiveness, care, and compassion for them, does not establish good policies and programs for them, he or she could lose the citizens' support and lead the country in the wrong direction.

Tao is in every aspect of life. Follow the Tao in every aspect of life and life will flourish. If you have a blockage in some aspect of life, make sure that you find the Tao of that part of life and remove or transform the blockage by following the Tao of that part of life. You will be blessed and flourish. This is very simple Tao guidance, but it is very useful and practical guidance. If you can follow this guidance, you could transform the blocked and weak areas of your life quickly.

逆道亡

Ni Tao Wang

Go against Tao, Finish

"Ni" (pronounced *nee*) means *go against*. "Wang" (pronounced *wahng*) means *finish* or *end*.

Everyone has to eat and everyone should eat properly. This is to follow the Tao of eating. If a person does not eat, it would be hard to survive. Everyone has to drink and drink enough. This is to follow the Tao of drinking. If a person does not drink enough, that person's health could be deeply affected.

There is a Tao of emotions. Many people on Mother Earth have unbalanced emotions. I would like to share some very important spiritual wisdom about emotions that many people are not aware of. The specific issue is the emotion of being upset or angry. In fact, many people are upset or angry. When they are upset, they may yell, they may argue, but they do not know what they have lost.

I have shared some key aspects of this wisdom in some of my previous books. I would like to present this wisdom again because virtue is such a vital aspect of life, including a human being's life and the lives of all universes.

Virtue is the record of services in all of one's lifetimes. Virtue is expressed and given in the form of Heaven's flowers. There are two kinds of service and two kinds of virtue: good and bad. Good virtue is expressed in golden, rainbow, purple, crystal, and other brightly colored flowers. Bad virtue is expressed in black, dark, and gray flowers.

If a person offers good service, which includes love, forgiveness, care, compassion, generosity, kindness, integrity, and purity, to others in this life and in previous lifetimes, Heaven will give this person's soul good virtue with bright, colorful light flowers. If a person offers unpleasant services, which includes killing, harming, and taking advantage of others in this life and in previous lives, Heaven will give this person's soul black, dark, or gray flowers.

Good virtue gives one rewards in all aspects of life. These rewards include good health, a good marriage, good children, good relationships, good finances, and more. Good virtue can give one success in every aspect of life.

Bad virtue gives one lessons to learn. These lessons can include poor health, a poor marriage, challenges with children, financial difficulties, and other blockages in any aspects of life.

The consequences of virtue, good and bad, follow a divine universal spiritual law: karma. Millions of people deeply believe in karma. Some people may not believe in karma. Nobody is forced to believe in karma, but I am honored to share my insights. I not only believe deeply in karma, I have offered Divine Karma Cleansing since July 2003.

The Divine told me to share a one-sentence secret about karma in chapter 2 of my book *The Power of Soul:*

Karma is the root cause of success and failure in every aspect of life.

Through the mistakes we have made in this life and previous lives, we create our bad karma. This is a spiritual debt. We must pay a price for this spiritual debt by learning lessons in different aspects of life.

Divine Karma Cleansing works in this way. If the Divine clears your karma, all the souls that you have harmed in this life and previous lifetimes will be gathered in the Akashic Records. There, the Divine will pay your spiritual debt by offering the Divine's virtue to the souls you harmed. These souls' future lives will be blessed. Then, you will be forgiven. Because your spiritual debt has been paid, the disasters and lessons you were to learn are canceled on the spot. Only the Divine has the power to offer total karma cleansing in this way. I am extremely honored to be a chosen servant of the Divine to have offered Divine Karma Cleansing to humanity for more than six years. Thousands of heart-touching and moving stories have demonstrated to my eyes the amazing power of karma cleansing.

You can also self-clear your bad karma. There is only one way to self-clear karma: offer unconditional service to others. Make others happier and healthier. Offer this service unconditionally, which means without any expectation. In the books of my Soul Power Series, I have taught many ways to offer love, forgiveness, care, compassion, and kindness to others, to humanity, and to all souls in all universes. The more you serve, the faster you can self-clear bad karma. When you serve, Heaven gives you flowers. The lessons you were to receive due to your bad karma are canceled, little by little.

I have explained the essence of virtue and karma cleansing. The purpose is to emphasize the significance of your virtue and your karma for your life. It can be summarized in one sentence:

**For your good karma, receive blessings
and rewards from Heaven;
for your bad karma, learn lessons in
this life and your future lives.**

Now I will share a very important teaching for you and every reader. There is a renowned spiritual statement:

Huo shao gong te lin

"Huo" literally means *fire,* but here it refers to fiery behavior and emotions, such as being upset or angry, or yelling at others. "Shao" means *burn.* "Gong te" means *virtue.* "Lin" means *forest.* "Huo shao gong te lin" can be translated as *being upset or angry, or yelling at others is a fire to burn the forest of your good virtue* or simply *anger burns virtue.*

What happens when two people quarrel? When one yells at the other, this one is literally throwing virtue to the other. If the other person yells back, then the other person is throwing virtue right back. If you really understand this spiritual law, if you are really a high-level spiritual being, you can control your emotions and remain calm. When someone is upset with or angry at you, just relax and let the other person continue to yell. The more the person yells at you, the more virtue this person will lose. You will gain this person's virtue.

I have explained how important virtue is for one's spiritual journey and one's physical life. To lose virtue is to lose the most valuable asset not only for one's present life, but for all of one's lifetimes. To lose virtue is to lose spiritual standing. To lose virtue is to lose your yin money in the spiritual world. Remember my teaching. Virtue, which is spiritual currency or yin money, can transform into yang money, which is money in the physical world. To lose virtue is to lose spiritual money, just like losing physical money. To lose virtue is worse than losing physical money. To lose virtue could lead to many challenges in this lifetime and future lifetimes. Therefore, this profound and important spiritual teaching, *Huo shao gong te lin,* is to share with humanity not to be upset, not to be angry, not to yell, because you will lose your most important and valuable possession: virtue.

The Tao of forgiveness is very important for your virtue, your karma, and more. If everyone in a family were to apply total, unconditional forgiveness, there would be no quarreling, no fighting, no conflict in the family. If people were to apply forgiveness in society and between nations, there would be no war.

Spiritual teaching and practice are essential to bring love, peace, and harmony to humanity, Mother Earth, and all universes. If one cannot forgive, is upset, angry, or quarrelling, this one will lose virtue. Conflict between two countries is the same as conflict between two persons. Every action, behavior, and thought of a person, an organization, or a country is recorded in the Akashic Records. If a person, an organization, or a country serves well, good virtue is given. If a person, an organization, or a country harms and hurts, bad virtue is given.

Following Tao is very important for life. Being upset and angry, yelling, and fighting are not following Tao and you will lose virtue. Your life will be deeply, deeply affected. Sometimes you may not see the lessons right away, but they will come. They could come at any moment. They could come in this life and in many, many fiuture lives. This is how karma works.

Highly developed spiritual beings check their actions, behaviors, and thoughts at least three times a day, as Kong Zi (Confucius) taught. If they realize they did something wrong, they instantly do a spiritual practice to ask for forgiveness from the Divine and the souls they harmed; they sing or chant and give love to humanity and all souls. Because of their sincere apologies and requests for forgiveness, they can be forgiven very quickly by the Divine. They are blessed by the Divine with divine forgiveness to remove their negative actions, behaviors, and thoughts.

In this way and others, highly developed spiritual beings pay greatest attention to avoiding creating bad karma because they understand deeply that bad karma will block their spiritual journey and their physical journey. Bad karma could block every aspect of their lives. I have used the behaviors and emotions of being upset, angry, quarreling, and yelling as examples that one *must* follow the Tao of every aspect of life. These negative behaviors and emotions go against Tao. Therefore, a person who does these things could learn big lessons.

In fact, Mother Earth is a place to learn lessons. Every human being on Mother Earth is to learn some lessons. Follow Tao and practice Tao. You can literally avoid the lessons by clearing your own bad karma. The key to self-clear karma is to give unconditional service to others, to society, and to humanity.

Follow the Tao in every aspect of life and you will flourish. Go against the Tao in any aspect of life and all kinds of lessons could be given; all kinds of blockages will deeply affect your life.

道生一

Tao Sheng Yi

Tao creates One

Tao is the source of all universes. Tao is the creator.

Recall the process of normal creation:

> **TAO → One → Two → Three → all things**
> **creates**

All universes are endless. But compared with Tao, all universes are limited. Tao is unlimited. All universes are You (existence). Tao is Wu (nothingness).

One is unity. Countless universes are One. To understand One, to realize One, and to return to One is the most important practice for all things.

Reverse creation is also very important for all life. Normal creation and reverse creation are the highest philosophy of Tao to guide everything in countless universes.

Recall the process of reverse creation:

all things → Three → Two → One → TAO
return to

To heal is to reach one or reach Tao. Shen Qi Jing He Yi is to join all souls, all energy, and all matter in the whole body as one. To join Shen Qi Jing as one is to heal.

To heal humanity, Mother Earth, and Heaven is to join Heaven, Earth, and human beings as one. I shared Shen Qi Jing He Yi and Tian Di Ren He Yi in chapter 1. Later in this chapter, I will lead you to practice Shen Qi Jing He Yi and Tian Di Ren He Yi a lot. Just practicing Shen Qi Jing He Yi could heal all of your sicknesses in your physical, emotional, mental, and spiritual bodies very quickly. If more and more human beings were to practice Tian Di Ren He Yi, if more and more souls in all universes were to practice Tian Di Ren He Yi, Mother Earth's transition could pass very quickly. Love, peace, and harmony for humanity, Mother Earth, Heaven, and all universes could be achieved quickly.

天一真水

Tian Yi Zhen Shui

Heaven's unique sacred liquid

"Tian" means *Heaven*. "Yi" means *one*. "Zhen" means *sacred* or *true*. "Shui" means *water* or *liquid*. "Tian yi zhen shui" (pronounced *tyen yee jun shway*) means *Heaven's unique sacred liquid*.

Tao creates Heaven and Earth. When one practices Tao, Heaven blesses. Heaven will pour Heaven's liquid to the Tao practitioner's brain. This sacred liquid will then go through the palate into the mouth. This Heaven's sacred liquid carries Heaven's nutrients to nourish every cell of the body.

Later in this chapter, I will lead you to practice to receive Tian Yi Zhen Shui. This Heaven's unique sacred liquid will give you divine sacred healing and rejuvenation.

金津玉液

Jin Jin Yu Ye

Golden Liquid, Jade Liquid (Mother Earth's sacred liquid)

The first "Jin" means *golden*. The second "Jin" means *liquid*. "Yu" means *jade*. "Ye" is another word for *liquid*. "Jin jin yu ye" (pronounced *jeen jeen yü yuh*) means *golden liquid, jade liquid*. Golden and jade express the precious value of these liquids.

There are two acupuncture points under the tongue named Jin Jin and Yu Ye. These particular acupuncture points are actually two physical holes. They are like the source of a spring. Liquid will come out of these holes. This special sacred liquid carries the essence of Mother Earth.

Tao creates Mother Earth. When one practices Tao, Mother

Earth blesses. Mother Earth will send nutrients through the Jin Jin and Yu Ye acupuncture points under the tongue. The liquid emerging from these two holes is named Jin Jin Yu Ye, which is Mother Earth's sacred liquid. This Mother Earth's sacred liquid carries the nutrients of Mother Earth for healing and rejuvenation.

咽入丹田
Yan Ru Dan Tian

Swallow into the Lower Dan Tian

"Yan" means *swallow*. "Ru" means *go into*. "Dan Tian" refers to the *Lower Dan Tian*. "Yan ru dan tian" (pronounced *yahn roo dahn tyen*) means to swallow tian yi zhen shui (Heaven's sacred liquid) and jin jin yu ye (Mother Earth's sacred liquid) into the Lower Dan Tian.

Everybody understands the following. When the sun shines on the ocean or a lake, some water transforms to steam and rises toward Heaven, where it can accumulate and become clouds. This is Mother Earth's qi rising. Mother Earth's qi is named Di Qi. "Di" (pronounced *dee*) means *Mother Earth*. "Qi" (pronounced *chee*) is vital energy or life force. The clouds in Heaven will turn to rain and fall to Mother Earth. This is Heaven's qi falling. Heaven's qi is named Tian Qi. ("Tian" means *Heaven*.)

Two ancient statements express how Tian Qi and Di Qi move and exchange. This is a natural phenomenon. This is the Tao of Di Qi and Tian Qi to balance Heaven and Earth. These two statements are:

Di qi shang sheng (Mother Earth's qi rises)
Tian qi xia jiang (Heaven's qi falls)

"Shang sheng" means *rises*. "Xia jiang" means *falls*.

Mother Earth's qi rises and Heaven's qi falls. This is yin-yang exchange. *Di Qi* is yin. *Tian Qi* is yang. These exchanges are vital to balance the energies of Heaven and Earth. Di Qi and Tian Qi directly affect weather conditions on Mother Earth. This will affect the growth of crops. It will affect the spread of disease. *Di qi shang sheng* (pronounced *dee chee shahng shung*) and *Tian qi xia jiang* (pronounced *tyen chee shyah jyahng*) are vital to balance Heaven and Earth.

There is an ancient, renowned statement in spiritual teaching:

Tian ren he yi (Heaven and human being join as one)

"Tian" literally means *Heaven*. "Ren" means *a human being* or *humanity*. "He" means *join as*. "Yi" means *one*. "Tian ren he yi" (pronounced *tyen wren huh yee*) means *Heaven and human beings are one*.

Heaven is the big universe. A human being is the small universe. What the big universe has, the small universe has. In the big universe, there is *Di qi shang sheng, tian qi xia jiang*.

A human being is a small universe. In this small universe, there is also *Di qi shang sheng, tian qi xia jiang*. Within a human being, everything above the diaphragm belongs to *tian* (Heaven). Everything below the level of the navel belongs to *di* (Earth). The area between the diaphragm and the level of the navel belongs to *ren* (human being).

To swallow tian yi zhen shui and jin jin yu ye is *Tian qi xia jiang* within the body. When this Heaven's qi falls, the Di Qi automatically rises. This will adjust yin and yang inside the body. Tian Qi is yang. Di Qi is yin. To swallow this sacred liquid is *Tian qi xia jiang* inside the body. It will stimulate *Di qi shang sheng.* Yang, yin, Heaven, and Earth will automatically move in the direction of balance. The more you swallow these sacred liquids, the faster you will balance yang and yin, Heaven and Earth inside your body.

This technique is extremely simple and powerful for healing all kinds of sickness. I will lead every reader to practice Tao in chapter 3. Here I will share the first four sentences of a Tao Song with you as the first practical technique in this book:

Tao sheng yi (pronounced *dow shung yee*)
Tian yi zhen shui (pronounced *tyen yee jun shway*)
Jin jin yu ye (pronounced *jeen jeen yü yuh*)
Yan ru dan tian (pronounced *yahn roo dahn tyen*)

Sing or chant these four phrases again and again. Listen to me singing on the enclosed CD. When you sing or chant these four lines, tian yi zhun shui and jin jin yu ye will emerge in your mouth automatically and you will swallow them into the Lower Dan Tian.

一生二
Yi Sheng Er

One creates Two

"Yi sheng er" (pronounced *yee shung ur*) means *One creates Two.* Two is Heaven and Earth. Heaven is yang. Earth is yin. Two is the yin yang world.

Heaven and Earth, yang and yin, are very important for humanity, Mother Earth, and Heaven. They connect with every aspect of life for humanity, Mother Earth, and Heaven.

For example, to heal is to balance yin and yang. In the human body, the front side is yin, the back side is yang. The outside of the body is yang, the inside of the body is yin. The upper part of the body is yang, the lower part of the body is yin.

Five Elements is another very important theory from *The Yellow Emperor's Internal Classic,* the ancient authoritative book on traditional Chinese medicine and also a foundational book of Tao teaching. The paired yin-yang organs of the Wood element are the liver and gallbladder. The yin-yang organs of the Fire element are the heart and small intestine. The yin-yang organs of the Earth element are the spleen and stomach. The yin-yang organs of the Metal element are the lungs and large intestine. The yin-yang organs of the Water element are the kidneys and urinary bladder.

To balance the liver and gallbladder is to balance the Wood element. To balance the heart and small intestine is to balance the Fire element. To balance the spleen and stomach is to balance the Earth element. To balance the lungs and large intestine is to balance the Metal element. To balance the kidneys and urinary bladder is to balance the Water element. To balance the Five Elements together is to balance the whole body. To balance the whole body is to balance yin and yang. To balance yin and yang is to return to Tao. Remember the process of reverse creation: All things return to Three. Three returns to Two. Two returns to One and One returns to Tao.

There are unlimited benefits to balancing yin and yang:

- To balance yin and yang is the key to healing all sickness in traditional Chinese medicine.
- To balance yin and yang is to prevent sickness in traditional Chinese medicine.

- To balance yin and yang is to rejuvenate in Tao teaching.
- To balance yin and yang is to balance emotions.
- To balance yin and yang is to balance relationships.
- To balance yin and yang is to balance Heaven and Earth.
- To balance yin and yang is to bring love, peace, and harmony to humanity, Mother Earth, and all universes.

道丹道神
Tao Dan Tao Shen

Tao Golden Light Ball, Tao Heart Soul

Tao is the source of all universes. "Dan" (pronounced *dahn*) means *light ball*. "Tao Shen" (pronounced *dow shun*) means *soul of Tao's heart*. Tao Dan and Tao Shen carry Tao consciousness, Tao frequency, Tao vibration, and Tao power. When a Tao practitioner reaches a very advanced level, the Divine and Tao will offer Tao Dan and Tao Shen to special chosen ones.

The Divine told me to begin teaching Tao in December 2008. In June 2009, I started to offer Divine Downloads of Tao organs to advanced students in Germany. These Tao organs are so powerful that I hardly have the words to explain. The Divine and Tao directed me to offer Tao organs, which are Tao Soul Mind Body Transplants, to humanity starting in March 2010. I am extremely honored that the Divine and Tao have chosen me as their servant to offer their permanent Soul Mind Body Transplants. I am humbled and extremely grateful.

In history, only very rare saints have received Tao Dan and

Tao Shen. Tao practitioners who reach a very high level of soul enlightenment may apply to receive Tao Dan and Tao Shen. The Divine asked me to communicate with the Divine and Tao to check the readiness of each applicant to receive Tao Dan and Tao Shen. If they are ready, the Divine and Tao will prepare me to offer a special transmission of Tao Dan and Tao Shen. I am extremely honored to be a special servant and vehicle of the Divine and Tao to offer the special transmission of Tao Dan and Tao Shen to advanced soul enlightened beings.

Tao Dan and Tao Shen carry Tao power for healing, prevention of sickness, rejuvenation, prolonging life, transformation of every aspect of life, including relationships and finances, and soul, mind, and body enlightenment for humanity, Mother Earth, and all universes. The power of Tao Dan and Tao Shen cannot be explained by any words nor comprehended by any thoughts.

When I received Tao Dan and Tao Shen in December 2008, the Tao Dan or Tao light ball was huge—the size of the universe. It vibrated with such a tiny, refined frequency that my whole body was tingling gently and radiating light of many different colors. When I invoke and apply my Tao Dan to boost energy, stamina, and vitality or to heal others, the result is instant in most cases. As for my Tao Shen, the soul of Tao's heart, the love, forgiveness, compassion, and light that this soul carries are beyond explanation. Tao Shen has the power to remove one's soul, mind, and body blockages almost instantly.

After I received Tao Dan and Tao Shen, the Divine and Tao joined the Tao Dan and Tao Shen in my Lower Dan Tian as one. This combination of Tao Dan and Tao Shen brought a completely new frequency, vibration, and consciousness to my soul, mind, and body. After receiving Tao Dan and Tao Shen I was a completely new person. I cannot find the words to explain the profound transformation I experienced from head to toe and skin to bone. I am extremely grateful, but I do not have enough words to express my greatest gratitude to the Divine and Tao.

After Tao Dan and Tao Shen joined as one, I invoked them to offer service for humanity and all souls in all universes. The multiple-colored light from my lower abdomen radiated out to all universes. I could not see any ending through my Third Eye. Since then, any time I invoke and "turn on" my conjoined Tao Dan and Tao Shen, Tao light always radiates to all universes.

Tao Dan and Tao Shen have brought my frequency, vibration, and consciousness to the Tao level. My power for healing, rejuvenation, prolonging life, transforming relationships and finances, and enlightening soul, mind, and body for humanity has been uplifted so much that I cannot bow down enough for this honor. In fact, when the Divine and Tao transmitted Tao Dan and Tao Shen to me, the Divine and Tao held a special Heaven's conference for this event. I was humbled and speechless. I was moved to tears. I was extremely honored. I could never bow down enough for this greatest honor and blessing. I am preparing to offer Tao Dan and Tao Shen to the ready Tao practitioners in my ten-year Tao training program.

服务人类
Fu Wu Ren Lei

Serve all humanity

"Fu wu" (pronounced *foo woo*) means *serve*. "Ren lei" (pronounced *wren lay*) means *humanity*. There have been all kinds of spiritual beings, groups, and religions in history, including Buddhists, Taoists, Christian saints, healing angels, ascended masters, Hindus, Muslims, Jews, Hawaiian kahunas, ancient Egyptian priests, indigenous peoples, and many others. Every spiritual group offers many spiritual techniques to empower spiritual practitioners to purify their souls, hearts, and minds and to gain spiritual power to heal, serve, and transform the lives of others.

The founder of Buddhism, Shi Jia Mo Ni Fuo, taught eighty-four thousand methods of spiritual practice. Different levels of spiritual beings can receive different levels of spiritual teaching and training. Buddhist teaching has profound wisdom. Every spiritual group is unique with its own unique wisdom, knowledge, and techniques to move further on the spiritual journey.

Since creation, there have been countless Xiu Lian (spiritual) practices and techniques in all spiritual teachings. What is the *best* method to accomplish one's spiritual journey? The best method can be summarized in one sentence:

The best Xiu Lian is service.

To serve is the purpose of physical life. To serve is also the purpose of the soul journey. To serve is to make others happier and healthier. To serve is to transform relationships, finances, and every aspect of others' lives. To serve is to awaken and transform humanity to be pure servants of humanity and all souls in all universes.

When you serve, the Divine and Akashic Records give you virtue, which is spiritual flowers or spiritual currency. Virtue transforms every aspect of your physical, emotional, mental, and spiritual bodies. Virtue also transforms your relationships and finances, as well as uplifts your soul standing.

To uplift your soul standing in Heaven is to move your soul closer to the divine realm. If your soul can reach the divine realm, you will not have to reincarnate again. Your soul will still be very much available to serve. In fact, any soul that reaches the divine realm is given very special divine power and abilities for healing, rejuvenation, and transformation of every aspect of life. Invoke the souls who have reached the divine realm and ask them to give you a blessing. You could receive remarkable healing and life transformation results.

To serve is to self-clear karma. The more you serve, the more virtue you will receive from the Divine, Tao, and Heaven. This can transform every aspect of life.

The purpose of your physical life is to serve your soul life. The purpose of your soul life is to uplift your soul to the divine realm. It could take forty thousand lifetimes or more to reach the divine realm. To uplift your soul to the divine realm is to accomplish the ultimate goal of your soul journey. To uplift your soul standing in Heaven, step by step, you must serve more and more. There is no second way.

Remember the Universal Law of Universal Service: *Serve a little, receive a little blessing from the Divine. Serve more, receive more blessings from the Divine. Serve unconditionally, receive unlimited blessings from the Divine.* Service can be summarized in one sentence:

Service is the fastest way to uplift one's soul to the divine realm, as well as the best way to transform every aspect of one's life.

Serve. Serve. Serve.
Divine blessings. Divine blessings. Divine blessings.
Transform. Transform. Transform.
Enlighten. Enlighten. Enlighten.
Serve more. Serve more. Serve more.

More divine blessings. More divine blessings. More divine blessings.

Transform further. Transform further. Transform further.

Enlighten further. Enlighten further. Enlighten further.

The above mantra, *serve—divine blessings—transform—enlighten—serve more—more divine blessings—transform further—enlighten further,* is a positive feedback loop. The more service you offer to others, humanity, and all souls, the more blessings the Divine will give you, and the more life transformation and enlightenment of your soul, heart, mind, and body will happen.

Dear every reader, have you thought at this moment about what kind of service you have given to humanity and all souls? What kind of service you would like to offer in the future? The highest spiritual practice is to serve others. I emphasize the one-sentence secret:

The best Xiu Lian is service.

There are many ways to serve. You can do volunteer work, donate money to charity, teach, heal, sing or chant mantras, sing a Soul Song, or do a Soul Dance. For example, you can choose one Divine Soul Song and sing it repeatedly in your heart as much as you can, anywhere, anytime. The benefits are beyond any words. The moment you begin to sing or chant, you are serving. Singing or chanting is one of the highest and most important services we can offer on Mother Earth at this time.

In the spiritual journey, one must serve unconditionally. Let us join hearts and souls together to serve and to create love, peace, and harmony for humanity, Mother Earth, and all universes.

服务万灵
Fu Wu Wan Ling

Serve all souls

"Fu wu" (pronounced *foo woo*) means *serve*. "Wan" (pronounced *wahn*) literally means *ten thousand*; in Chinese, *wan* represents *all* or *every*. "Ling" means *soul*. So "wan ling" means *every soul of humanity and every soul of countless planets, stars, galaxies, and universes.*

There are about 6.8 billion people on Mother Earth now. Every human being has a soul. A human being has many systems, many organs, and billions of cells. Every system, every organ, and every cell has a soul. There are countless planets, stars, galaxies, and universes. Every planet, star, galaxy, and universe has a soul.

What is every soul's purpose? It is to be uplifted higher and higher in Heaven's realm. The divine realm is the highest realm. Souls on Mother Earth and in all universes desire to be uplifted to the divine realm. A soul that reaches the divine realm will stop reincarnation. Why does the soul desire to reach the divine realm? Because souls who reach the divine realm are given divine abilities to serve others. These divine abilities can transform other souls' lives instantly. To reach the divine realm is to be empowered with divine abilities to be a better servant.

To study and practice Tao is to serve all humanity and all souls in all universes. To serve all souls is to uplift one's soul standing to higher and higher layers of Heaven. Finally, one's soul standing can reach the divine realm to accomplish its journey and stop reincarnation.

In the Soul Light Era, the final goal of all souls can be summarized in one sentence:

The direction for all souls of all universes is to reach
***wan ling rong he* (all souls in all universes join as one).**

It will take a long time to reach this goal, but this is soul direction for all souls. To move in this direction is to serve all souls unconditionally.

服务地球
Fu Wu Di Qiu

Serve Mother Earth

"Fu wu" means *serve*. "Di qiu" (pronounced *dee cheo*) means *Earth*. Mother Earth is in a transition period. There are major challenges on Mother Earth, including many natural disasters. Mother Earth is out of balance. It is very urgent and very important to serve Mother Earth. A significant way to serve Mother Earth is to transform the consciousness of Mother Earth. How can we transform the consciousness of Mother Earth? Sing or chant a special sentence to Mother Earth. This sacred sentence is:

Tian Di Ren He Yi
(Heaven, Mother Earth, and human beings join as one.)

Sing or chant this as much as you can. Listen to me singing on the enclosed CD. If millions of people were to sing or chant this, it would definitely balance Mother Earth beyond comprehension. When you sing or chant *Tian di ren he yi,* you are offering the intention to balance and to create love, peace, and harmony for Heaven, Mother Earth, and human beings.

You are giving love to Mother Earth. Love melts all blockages and transforms all life.

You are giving forgiveness to Mother Earth. Forgiveness brings inner joy and inner peace.

You are giving compassion to Mother Earth. Compassion boosts energy, stamina, vitality, and immunity.

You are giving light to Mother Earth. Light heals, balances, and transforms Mother Earth.

You are bringing divine oneness to Mother Earth. You are bringing unity of Heaven, Mother Earth, and humanity to Mother Earth.

Also, as I taught earlier in this book, to sing or chant *Tian di ren he yi* is a major healing for all your sicknesses of the physical, emotional, mental, and spiritual bodies. The power of this simple practice is beyond words. But remember, *Da Tao zhi jian*— The Big Way is extremely simple. The most powerful and profound teachings and practices are the simplest teachings and practices.

Sing or chant:

Tian Di Ren He Yi
Tian Di Ren He Yi
Tian Di Ren He Yi
Tian Di Ren He Yi
Tian Di Ren He Yi
Tian Di Ren He Yi
Tian Di Ren He Yi . . .

Sing or chant for at least three to five minutes at a time, three to five times per day. There is no time limit for this singing or chanting. The more singing or chanting you do, the more blessing you offer Mother Earth, and the more blessing you can receive yourself.

服务宇宙
Fu Wu Yu Zhou

Serve all universes

"Fu wu" means *serve*. "Yu zhou" (pronounced *yü joe*) means *universes*. Through normal creation, Tao creates countless universes. In the Soul Light Era, the divine direction and Tao direction is to move in reverse creation, which is to join all things and all universes as one.

There is a special mantra to serve universes, *Universal Light*. For the melody, listen to me singing on the enclosed CD. Let us sing or chant now:

> *Universal Light*
> *Universal Light*
> *Universal Light*
> *Universal Light*
> *Universal Light*
> *Universal Light*
> *Universal Light* . . .

The moment you sing or chant *Universal Light*, Tao, the Divine, and all layers of Heaven and Earth will radiate light to you, to Mother Earth, and to all universes. If there were millions of people singing or chanting *Universal Light* together, imagine how much light would shine in the universe. One person singing or chanting is just like one light bulb shining. Millions of people singing or chanting are just like millions of light bulbs shining. Group singing or chanting has much more transformative power.

The Divine has taught me that singing or chanting is one of the most important services we can offer to Mother Earth and all universes in the Soul Light Era. I offered a Soul Song and Soul Music Concert in June 2009 in Germany with professional musicians, including a world-renowned opera singer. The audience was deeply moved. The audience gave the performers a long standing ovation. This is how much people loved the Soul Songs and Soul Music.

Many years ago, the Divine told me that millions of people singing or chanting together will be the solution to remove pollution. Singing or chanting at this level will transform the consciousness of humanity and all souls in all universes.

To sing or chant is to remove soul, mind, and body blockages from all universes.

To sing or chant is to purify the soul, heart, mind, and body of all universes.

To sing or chant is to transform the negative mind-sets, attitudes, beliefs, and behaviors, as well as attachment and ego, of humanity and all souls.

To sing or chant is to transform and enlighten all life.

To sing or chant is to serve humanity, Mother Earth, and all universes.

治愈百病
Zhi Yu Bai Bing

Heal all sickness

"Zhi yu" means *heal* or *cure*. "Bai" means *one hundred*. In Chinese, one hundred represents *all* or *every*. "Bing" means *sickness*. "Bai bing" means *all sicknesses in the physical, emotional, mental, and spiritual bodies*. Therefore, "Zhi yu bai bing" (pronounced *jr yü bye bing*) means *heal all sickness*.

A human being has physical, emotional, mental, and spiritual bodies. All kinds of sicknesses in any of these bodies are due to soul, mind, and body blockages. Two of my previous books, *Soul Mind Body Medicine: A Complete Soul Healing System for Optimum Health and Vitality*[6] and *Divine Soul Mind Body Healing and Transmission System: The Divine Way to Heal You, Humanity, Mother Earth, and All Universes*,[7] explain this teaching in depth.

The first step in studying and practicing Tao is to heal. In chapter 3, I will teach several practical techniques for healing your physical, emotional, mental, and spiritual bodies. Now I am releasing a new Tao secret for self-healing all kinds of sicknesses. Apply the Four Power Techniques that I shared in *Soul Mind Body Medicine*:

- Body Power
- Soul Power
- Sound Power
- Mind Power

Body Power. Sit up straight. Put the tip of your tongue as close as you can to the roof of your mouth without touching it. Put both palms on your lower abdomen, one palm over the other hand. Males, put your left palm on your lower abdomen and your right palm over your left hand. Females, put your right palm on the lower abdomen and your left palm over your right hand.

Soul Power. Say *hello*:

---

6 *Soul Mind Body Medicine: A Complete Soul Healing System for Optimum Health and Vitality* (Novato, California: New World Library, 2006).

7 *Divine Soul Mind Body Healing and Transmission System: The Divine Way to Heal You, Humanity, Mother Earth, and All Universes* (New York/Toronto: Heaven's Library/Atria Books, 2009).

> *Dear Divine, dear Tao, dear all universes, dear all of*
>   *my spiritual fathers and mothers in Heaven and in*
>   *the physical world,*
> *I love you.*
> *You have the power to heal me.*
> *Please heal and bless me.*
> *I am very grateful.*
> *Thank you.*

Sound Power. Sing or chant repeatedly (you can listen to me on the enclosed CD):

> *Tian Di Ren He Yi* (pronounced *tyen dee wren huh yee*)
> *Tian Di Ren He Yi*
> *Tian Di Ren He Yi*
> *Tian Di Ren He Yi*
> *Tian Di Ren He Yi*
> *Tian Di Ren He Yi*
> *Tian Di Ren He Yi* . . .

Sing or chant for at least three minutes per time. Do this practice at least three times per day. There is no time limit for this practice. The more times you sing or chant, and the longer you sing or chant per time, the better.

As I have shared earlier, "tian" means *Heaven.* "Di" means *Earth.* "Ren" means *human being.* "He" means *join as.* "Yi" means *one.* "Tian di ren he yi" means *Heaven, Earth, and human being join as one.*

All sicknesses in your physical, emotional, mental, and spiritual bodies are due to disharmony and imbalances of Heaven, Mother Earth, and human beings.

In ancient spiritual teaching, *tian* is the big universe, *ren* is the small universe. What the big universe has, the small universe also has. What the small universe has, the big universe also has. The big universe is within the small universe; that is, inside the body. The area above the diaphragm belongs to Heaven. The area between the level of the diaphragm and the level of the navel belongs to human beings. The area below the level of the navel belongs to Mother Earth.

Heaven's area (above the diaphragm) includes the lungs, heart, thyroid, brain, and more. The human being's area (between the diaphragm and the level of the navel) includes the liver, gallbladder, stomach, pancreas, spleen, and more. Mother Earth's area (below the level of the navel) includes the small intestine, large intestine, urinary bladder, kidneys, ovaries, uterus, sexual organs, and more.

To sing *Tian Di Ren He Yi* is to gather energy and light from Heaven, Earth, and human realms to your body, as well as to align all of your soul, energy, and matter in all of your major organs as one in your abdomen. The more you sing or chant, the more energy from Heaven, Earth, and human realms will gather in your Lower Dan Tian, It will also promote alignment of the soul, energy, and matter in every one of your systems, organs, and cells, from head to toe and skin to bone. This gathering of energies will help form your Jin Dan (golden light ball). "Jin" means *gold*. "Dan" means *light ball*. The Jin Dan is located in your lower abdomen. It is one of the most powerful treasures of the entire Tao training program.

Mind Power. Concentrate on your lower abdomen. All the soul, energy, and matter of your body join as one golden light ball that rotates counterclockwise in your lower abdomen. Continue to sing or chant with me:

Tian Di Ren He Yi
Tian Di Ren He Yi
Tian Di Ren He Yi
Tian Di Ren He Yi
Tian Di Ren He Yi
Tian Di Ren He Yi
Tian Di Ren He Yi . . .

This practice has power that could totally shock you. It can restore your health quickly beyond words. It can also boost your energy, stamina, and vitality quickly beyond belief. How does it work? *Tian Di Ren He Yi* is one of the major Tao mantras. When you sing or chant *Tian Di Ren He Yi,* the Divine, Tao, and all saints in all layers of Heaven, as well as all Mother Earth, all planets, stars, galaxies, and universes, will respond to your calling and bless you. Energy from Heaven and Earth will join as one with your energy in your lower abdomen. All you need to do is pay attention to building your Jin Dan, the golden light ball in your lower abdomen.

How do you build the Jin Dan? It is not easy. You have to sing or chant this Tao mantra, *Tian Di Ren He Yi,* a lot each day. Visualize a golden light ball accumulating and concentrating in your lower abdomen. The Jin Dan is a priceless, sacred divine and Tao treasure to heal all sicknesses in your physical, emotional, mental, and spiritual bodies. This treasure has not been explained enough to humanity. In history, this treasure has been delivered only to a very limited number of lineage holders. The Divine and Tao asked me to share with humanity how important the Jin Dan is for healing and rejuvenating humanity.

The Jin Dan is located just below the navel, in the upper part of one's Lower Dan Tian. In many of my other books, such as *Power Healing: The Four Keys to Energizing Your Body, Mind and Spirit* and *Soul Mind Body Medicine: A Complete Soul Healing System for Optimum Health and Vitality,* I have explained that the Lower Dan Tian is a foundational energy center that is key for immunity, stamina, vitality, and longevity. After you form a Jin Dan, energy will flow freely in all parts of the body. This will remove soul, mind, and body blockages to your healing, prevention of sickness, rejuvenation, prolongation of life, and transformation of every aspect of life, including relationships and finances.

The most important type of blockage is soul blockages, which are bad karma. To self-clear bad karma, one must serve. *Tian Di Ren He Yi* is one of the most powerful Tao mantras for offering service to humanity, Mother Earth, and all universes. The moment you sing or chant *Tian Di Ren He Yi,* Heaven will give you virtue to reward you for your service to humanity, Heaven, and Mother Earth. This virtue will reduce your karmic debt. Disasters and all other lessons you are to learn because of your bad karma can be reduced. The more you sing or chant, the more virtue you are given and the more the disasters and lessons created by your bad karma will be removed.

Before you build a Jin Dan, first sing or chant *Tian Di Ren He Yi* to self-clear your bad karma. Then you can build a Jin Dan step by step. Why does it take a long time to build a Jin Dan? The main reason is karmic issues. One must self-clear karma first; then formation of the Jin Dan will follow. In ancient times, it took practitioners thirty to fifty years to build a complete Jin

Dan. A person with heavy bad karma may not be able to build a complete Jin Dan in an entire lifetime, even with a lot of dedicated practice.

Now, at the dawn of the Soul Light Era, building a Jin Dan can be accelerated because the Divine and Tao are now offering Divine and Tao Jin Dan Downloads. These permanent divine treasures can literally save a practitioner thirty to fifty years of practice. It is similar to karma cleansing. A person with heavy bad karma could take fifty, seventy-five, or more than one hundred *lifetimes* to self-clear the bad karma. The Divine can clear one's total karma in seconds. From July 2003 through 2009, at the Divine's request, I offered Divine Karma Cleansing of total personal, ancestral, relationship, and other karma for thousands of people on Mother Earth. This divine service on a major group basis ended in December 2009. I cannot honor the Divine enough to be a servant to serve humanity in this special way.

The Divine has also asked me to download Divine Jin Dan and Tao Jin Dan to ready Tao practitioners and to those in serious need of healing. Divine Jin Dan and Tao Jin Dan could heal all sicknesses. For chronic and life-threatening conditions, it may take months or years to completely heal, but many "hopeless" cases could have hope of healing from the Divine Jin Dan and Tao Jin Dan. In one sentence:

The Divine Jin Dan and Tao Jin Dan are divine and Tao treasures to heal all sicknesses, prevent all sicknesses, and help humanity reach *fan lao huan tong* (transform and return old age to the health and purity of a baby).

I am extremely honored, grateful, and privileged.

预防百病
Yu Fang Bai Bing

Prevent all sickness

"Yu fang" means *prevent*. "Bai bing" means *one hundred sicknesses*, which indicates *all sicknesses*. Therefore, "Yu fang bai bing" (pronounced *yü fahng bye bing*) means *prevent all sickness*.

The Yellow Emperor's Internal Classic, the authoritative book of traditional Chinese medicine, states:

Shang gong zhi wei bing, bu zhi yi bing.

"Shang gong" means *the best doctor*. "Zhi" means *treat*. "Wei bing" means *before sickness happens*. "Bu" means *not*. "Yi bing" means *already sick*. "Shang gong zhi wei bing, bu zhi yi bing" (pronounced *shahng gawng jr way bing, boo jr yee bing*) can be translated as *the best doctor prevents people from becoming sick instead of treating them after they become sick*.

There are many approaches and techniques in conventional modern medicine, traditional Chinese medicine, and all healing modalities for preventing sickness. I honor all methods from all medical professionals and all healing modalities. I am honored to share a Tao secret for preventing all sickness.

This secret is to sing or chant:

> *Shen Qi Jing He Yi* (pronounced *shun chee jing huh yee*)
> *Shen Qi Jing He Yi*
> *Shen Qi Jing He Yi*
> *Shen Qi Jing He Yi*
> *Shen Qi Jing He Yi*

Shen Qi Jing He Yi
Shen Qi Jing He Yi . . .

Listen to me singing *Shen Qi Jing He Yi* on the enclosed CD.

I have already taught in this book that this sentence means: *All souls, energy, and matter join as one.*

"Shen" means all souls, including one's body soul and the souls of all systems, organs, cells, cell units, DNA, RNA, smallest matter inside the cells, and spaces between the cells.

"Qi" means energy, including the whole body's qi and the qi of all systems, organs, cells, cell units, DNA, RNA, smallest matter inside the cells, and spaces between the cells.

"Jing" means matter, including the whole body's matter and the matter of all systems, organs, cells, cell units, DNA, RNA, smallest matter inside the cells, and spaces between the cells.

"He" means *join.*

"Yi" means *one.*

"Shen qi jing he yi" means *a human being's souls, energy, and matter all join as one.*

Now sing or chant for three minutes:

Shen Qi Jing He Yi
Shen Qi Jing He Yi
Shen Qi Jing He Yi
Shen Qi Jing He Yi
Shen Qi Jing He Yi
Shen Qi Jing He Yi
Shen Qi Jing He Yi . . .

The moment you sing or chant *Shen Qi Jing He Yi*, you are aligning all of your souls, energy, and matter as one. Your body's immunity will be boosted instantly. Every time you sing or chant, you are preventing sickness. There is no time limit. This singing or chanting is not only for preventing sickness; this is also another sacred Tao mantra and practice to build a Jin Dan.

A Jin Dan is a divine or Tao treasure for preventing sickness. Every time you sing or chant *Shen Qi Jing He Yi,* you are forming a Jin Dan. The more you sing or chant, the faster you will build your Jin Dan. The more complete your Jin Dan, the stronger your immune system will be and the more sickness will be prevented.

You can sing or chant *Shen Qi Jing He Yi* silently or aloud. In fact, you can sing or chant this and any mantra anytime, anywhere, silently or aloud. *Shen Qi Jing He Yi* is also a major secret for healing all sicknesses. All sicknesses are due to the misalignment and imbalance of *Shen Qi Jing.* To join Shen Qi Jing as one is to totally align and balance Shen Qi Jing. Healing of any sickness can result. In one sentence:

Shen Qi Jing He Yi is one of the major divine treasures and Tao treasures to heal all sickness, to prevent all sickness, and to help humanity reach *fan lao huan tong*.

Shen Qi Jing He Yi and *Tian Di Ren He Yi* are two of the most important divine and Tao treasures for healing, prevention of sickness, and rejuvenation to reach *fan lao huan tong*, longevity, and immortality.

Tao is in daily life. To practice Tao is to practice Tao in every aspect of life. You may think you have no or very little time to sing or chant. This is not true. You have a lot of time for thinking, for your business, your relationships, and many other things. Why not spend some time to think about *Shen Qi Jing He Yi* and *Tian Di Ren He Yi*? In fact, the moment you think about *Shen Qi*

Jing He Yi and *Tian Di Ren He Yi,* you are receiving their benefits for healing, prevention of sickness, and rejuvenation.

If you really want to heal yourself, prevent sickness, and reach *fan lao huan tong,* you must spend time to practice. The Divine, Tao, and Heaven are most fair. They always reward those who have practiced sincerely and dedicatedly.

Right after you awaken, you can sing or chant silently:

> *Shen Qi Jing He Yi*
> *Shen Qi Jing He Yi*
> *Shen Qi Jing He Yi*
> *Shen Qi Jing He Yi*
> *Shen Qi Jing He Yi*
> *Shen Qi Jing He Yi*
> *Shen Qi Jing He Yi . . .*

Sing or chant for five minutes, then you can get up to begin your daily routine, but continue to sing or chant silently nonstop:

> *Shen Qi Jing He Yi*
> *Shen Qi Jing He Yi*
> *Shen Qi Jing He Yi*
> *Shen Qi Jing He Yi*
> *Shen Qi Jing He Yi*
> *Shen Qi Jing He Yi*
> *Shen Qi Jing He Yi . . .*

Before meals, sing or chant for two minutes while putting your attention on your lower abdomen. Silently ask the souls of your digestive system and your digestive organs to prepare for the intake of food. These two minutes are very important to prepare all the beneficial digestive fluids from the various organs of your digestive system. It will help you digest well and absorb well.

After eating, spend five minutes silently singing or chanting again:

Shen Qi Jing He Yi
Shen Qi Jing He Yi
Shen Qi Jing He Yi
Shen Qi Jing He Yi
Shen Qi Jing He Yi
Shen Qi Jing He Yi
Shen Qi Jing He Yi . . .

These five minutes will really help your digestion and absorption. When I studied with my Peng Zu lineage Master, Professor and Dr. De Hua Liu, I saw that he rotated his Jin Dan for digestion and absorption after each meal. The first time I observed him in this practice, I was surprised to hear a loud gurgling sound coming from his abdomen. After every meal he would always rotate his Jin Dan and every time I heard the same clear, strong sound come from his abdomen. That is how powerful his Jin Dan is. It took Master Liu his whole life to build his Jin Dan. Peng Zu, the founder of the lineage and the teacher of Lao Zi, downloads his Jin Dan only to his lineage. I was honored to receive this Jin Dan. Two of my Worldwide Representatives, Peter Hudoba and Shu Chin Hsu, follow me in the Peng Zu lineage. They both received this Jin Dan also.

Now the Divine has asked me to download his Jin Dan to chosen divine servants. As I outlined in chapter 1, I will offer a ten-year Tao training program with five major steps. In this Tao training program, Total GOLD servants to the Divine and Tao will make a total commitment to study and practice Tao. As they progress in the training, the Divine and Tao will check their readiness to receive a Divine Jin Dan and a Tao Jin Dan. I am thrilled and touched that the Divine and Tao are going to download their Jin Dans to chosen ones. There will be many chosen ones. It will not be like a traditional Taoist lineage in which only one or two lineage holders in each generation can receive the lineage's Jin Dan treasure. Also, there is a big difference between the Divine Jin Dan and the Tao Jin Dan and the Jin Dan of any lineage.

You can build your own Jin Dan by singing or chanting *Shen Qi Jing He Yi* or *Tian Di Ren He Yi,* as well as through other spiritual, energy, and physical exercises. To build a complete Jin Dan in this way, it usually takes at least thirty years of practicing for hours each day. How blessed we are that the Divine and Tao are ready to download their Jin Dans to chosen ones. We are extremely honored and blessed.

In conclusion, the Jin Dan can be summarized in one sentence:

Divine Jin Dan and Tao Jin Dan are divine and Tao treasures for prevention and healing of all sicknesses and for rejuvenation to reach *fan lao huan tong*.

In chapter 3, I will share and teach every reader more secret and sacred practices for forming a Jin Dan and applying the Jin Dan to heal and prevent all sicknesses and to rejuvenate soul, heart, mind, and body in order to reach *fan lao huan tong*.

Divine Jin Dan and Tao Jin Dan are divine and Tao treasures for all life.

返老还童

Fan Lao Huan Tong

Return old age to the health and purity of a baby

Fan lao huan tong is a statement from Taoist teaching. This state-ment is powerful because it indicates that age can be reversed. I remind you again about the process of reverse creation:

all things → Three → Two → One → TAO
    return to

Reverse creation reveals that *fan lao huan tong* is possible.

In yin-yang theory, which is used in traditional Chinese med-icine, everything can be divided into yin and yang. In particular, the body can be divided into yin and yang. This can be done in different ways. For example, the upper half of the body above the diaphragm belongs to yang; the lower half below the diaphragm belongs to yin. The outside of the body belongs to yang; the in-side of the body belongs to yin. The front side of the body belongs to yin; the back side of the body belongs to yang.

I am going to review the Five Elements theory in traditional Chinese medicine in order to prepare you for deeper teaching. In traditional Chinese medicine, the body is also divided into five elements: Wood, Fire, Earth, Metal, and Water. The Wood element includes the yin organ of the liver and its paired yang organ, the gallbladder. The Fire element includes the heart (yin) and small intestine (yang). The Earth element includes the spleen (yin) and stomach (yang). The Metal element includes the lungs (yin) and large intestine (yang). The Water element includes the kidneys (yin) and urinary bladder (yang).

In traditional Chinese medicine, each element is further divided within the body. For example, the Wood element includes not only the liver and gallbladder, but also the sense organ of the eyes, all tendons in the body, and anger in the emotional body.

I will expand this teaching further. Each organ has millions of cells. For example, the liver has millions of cells. This progression indicates the application of normal creation of Tao in traditional Chinese medicine. You can see clearly that the teaching of traditional Chinese medicine follows normal creation in its diagnosis. Each element has its own symptoms and signs for diagnosis. In this way, traditional Chinese medicine applies normal creation of Tao.

In conventional modern medicine, a human body has systems and organs. An organ consists of many cells. A cell consists of cell units, DNA, RNA, smallest matter inside the cells, and spaces between the cells. Sickness could occur at the level of a system, organ, cell, or DNA and RNA. In this way, conventional modern medicine follows normal creation.

However, in traditional Chinese medicine the essence of treatment follows reverse creation. All kinds of problems can be summarized as an imbalance of Five Elements and then further summarized as an imbalance of yin and yang. This follows reverse creation. The final healing in traditional Chinese medicine is to balance yin and yang. To balance yin and yang is to return to One. To return to One is to return to Tao. In this way, traditional Chinese medicine applies reverse creation as well as normal creation.

In my personal opinion, conventional modern medicine mainly applies normal creation of Tao. Conventional modern medicine divides the body into systems, organs, cells, cell units, DNA, and RNA. It goes deeper and deeper, smaller and smaller. This follows the principle of normal creation. I do not see that conventional modern medicine has used the wisdom of reverse creation of Tao to guide its healing approach.

To study, practice, and reach Tao is exactly to follow the direction of reverse creation. All things return to Three. Three returns to Two. Two returns to One. One returns to Tao. In traditional Chinese medicine, all cells of the body return to the Five Elements, then return to yin and yang, and finally return to One. To return to One is to return to Tao. Tao is emptiness. Tao is the source and creator of all universes. In summary, treatment in traditional Chinese medicine is to follow reverse creation.

The Yellow Emperor's Internal Classic, the ancient but still authoritative book of traditional Chinese medicine, states:

> *Shang gu zhen ren:* In distant ancient times (*shang gu*), the true saints (*zhen ren*)
>
> *Ti xie tian di:* Connected and melded (*ti xie*) with Heaven (*tian*) and Earth (*di*)
>
> *Ba wo yin yang:* Mastered (*ba wo*) yin and yang
>
> *Hu xi jing qi:* Breathed (*hu xi*) the essence of matter (*jing*) and energy (*qi*) from the universe
>
> *Jing shen nei shou:* And focused and concentrated within ("Jing shen" means *mind*; "nei" means *within*; "shou" means *concentration* or *focus*.)
>
> *Shou bi tian di:* Age (*shou*) is as long as Heaven's (*tian*) and Earth's (*di*)
>
> *Wu you zhong shi:* Physical life has no (*wu you*) end (*zhong shi*)

Fan lao huan tong is total rejuvenation for a human being. To transform old age to the purity and health of a baby is easy to say. It is difficult to do. This renowned statement first appeared thousands of years ago in Taoist teaching. Throughout history, millions of people have studied and practiced Tao, but only a very limited number of practitioners have reached Tao. To reach Tao is to become a saint of the highest level. As I explained in chapter 1, I am honored to offer five steps of Tao training to humanity to reach Tao. I am honored to be a servant to train four layers of saints:

- Human saint (servant)
- Mother Earth saint (servant)
- Heaven saint (servant)
- Tao saint (servant)

To be a saint is to be a servant. To be a saint you must be humble. This training is pure training. Nobody is allowed to gain ego, to even think, "How special I am." The moment you think you are special, you have gained ego. Your ego will affect your progress on your spiritual journey.

To be a saint is to gain divine abilities and Tao abilities to harmonize and bless humanity, Mother Earth, Heaven, and all universes. The Divine and Tao are ready to download their powers to chosen ones. To gain power and to gain abilities is to be a better servant.

I have shared in my teaching that there are so many spiritual groups and teachings in history, that it is difficult to count. There are all kinds of religions too. In every spiritual group and religion, there could be thousands of techniques and methods. What is the best method or best technique to fulfill one's spiritual journey? What is the best and fastest way to uplift your soul to the divine realm in order to stop reincarnation? What is the best way to gain divine power and abilities to be a divine servant to serve humanity, Mother Earth, and all souls? The answer to all of these questions can be summarized in one sentence:

Unconditional universal service with total GOLD
is the best and fastest way to fulfill one's spiritual
journey, and to gain divine power and abilities,
to be a divine servant for humanity, Mother
Earth, Heaven, and all souls in all universes.

My spiritual teaching can be summarized as unconditional total GOLD service, where G is *gratitude,* O is *obedience,* L is *loyalty,* and D is *devotion.* Total GOLD is to the Divine, Tao, humanity, and all souls. Unconditional total GOLD service means to serve without any condition, without expecting anything in return.

Total GOLD service is most important for one's spiritual journey. Total GOLD is the divine yardstick to determine how far and fast a spiritual being's spiritual journey will be. If one offers a little service, one will have little growth. If one offers more service, one will have more growth. If one offers unconditional total GOLD service, one can have unlimited growth.

Heaven and the Akashic Records record every soul's service. There is an ancient statement: *If you do not want people to know, do not do it.* Anything you do, good things and unpleasant things, is recorded. Heaven records your activities, behaviors, and even your thoughts. High-level purification is to purify your thoughts. How can you purify your thoughts? When you have an unpleasant thought, sincerely say, "Sorry, Divine. Please forgive me."

Kong Zi, known in the West as Confucius, said, "Yi ri san si." "Yi" means *one.* "Ri" means *day.* "San" means *three.* "Si" means *thinking.* "Yi ri san si" means *each day, reflect three times.* Check what you have done wrong in activities, behaviors, and especially thoughts. Did you have unpleasant, unhealthy thoughts? Did you have unpleasant activities and behavior? If so, connect with the Divine, Tao, and Heaven and say:

"Dear Divine, dear Tao, and dear Heaven, please forgive me." Then sing or chant:

Tian Di Ren He Yi
Tian Di Ren He Yi
Tian Di Ren He Yi
Tian Di Ren He Yi
Tian Di Ren He Yi
Tian Di Ren He Yi
Tian Di Ren He Yi . . .

Tian Di Ren He Yi is one of the most powerful Tao mantras to offer service to humanity, Mother Earth, Heaven, and all universes. This mantra is so powerful that it is beyond anyone's comprehension and words. There is no limitation on how long you can sing or chant this Tao mantra. You can sing or chant *Tian Di Ren He Yi* silently anytime, anywhere. Sing or chant this Tao mantra in your heart nonstop.

Many people have busy minds full of stress, struggles, and challenges. They want to transform every aspect of their lives. When they have struggles, many people turn even more to their minds. The more you use your mind, the more you may get lost because your mind could lead you in the wrong direction. It is important to connect with your soul and heart to receive guidance from them. Your soul and heart can guide you in the right direction to better solutions for every aspect of your life.

When you face any challenges or blockages, whether in health, relationships, or finances, to use your mind is not wrong. But do not forget spiritual guidance and practice. Do not forget the teaching that *the soul is the boss*. Realize that your soul is your boss.

Mother Earth and Heaven have souls. Every business has a soul. Every relationship has a soul. Do not forget the one-sentence secret for soul healing and more: *Heal the soul first; then healing of the mind and body will follow.*

When you sing or chant *Tian Di Ren He Yi*, it may appear that there is no connection to your health, relationships, and finances. Therefore, you may decide not to sing or chant this Tao mantra very much. That would be a pity. To explain why, let me share the true secret of this Tao mantra with you now.

To chant *Tian Di Ren He Yi* is to serve humanity and all souls. The moment you chant, Heaven knows right away. The Divine and Tao also know right away. They will all instantly give you virtue and bless your health, relationships, and finances. You do not need to ask for any blessings. All you need to do is give pure service for humanity and all souls by singing or chanting this Tao mantra.

I have shared the major spiritual secret of Say Hello Healing and Say Hello Blessing in my previous books, starting in 2002 with *Power Healing: The Four Keys to Energizing Your Body, Mind and Spirit*. This secret can be summarized in one sentence:

Say Hello Healing and Blessing is one of the most important soul secrets, wisdom, knowledge, and practical techniques for healing, preventing sickness, rejuvenating, prolonging life, and transforming every aspect of life, including relationships and finances.

Now is the time to share an even deeper one-sentence secret with you and humanity:

Only serve *without* asking.

Let me explain.

If you are a Total GOLD servant, you need to remember only to serve. When you serve, Heaven records your service, the saints see your service, the Divine sees your service, and Tao sees your service. They can see your life challenges better than you can yourself. They can see the health, relationship, financial, and other issues in your life. Because you are a Total GOLD servant, you do not need to ask for any blessing. You just serve. For example, you may be chanting:

Tian Di Ren He Yi

Tian Di Ren He Yi

Tian Di Ren He Yi

Tian Di Ren He Yi

Tian Di Ren He Yi

Tian Di Ren He Yi

Tian Di Ren He Yi . . .

When you chant *Tian Di Ren He Yi,* all saints, buddhas, healing angels, ascended masters, lamas, gurus, and all other kinds of spiritual fathers and mothers in all layers of Heaven, as well as the Divine and Tao, will all hear your chanting. They will come to you and join your chanting, spontaneously and willingly. You may not call them consciously. You are just serving. But they know you are serving. They are unconditional universal servants. They love unconditional servants on Mother Earth. They will join you without your calling them. They can see your life blockages. They will bless your life to remove your soul, mind, and body blockages in different parts of your life. The Divine or Tao could give you one *"waaaa!"* flash of light. Your troubles and blockages could be transformed instantly.

In the beginning of every book of the Soul Power Series, I share the Universal Law of Universal Service that the Divine gave me in April 2003 at the Land of Medicine Buddha in Soquel, California:

> *Serve a little, receive a little blessing from Heaven.*
> *Serve more, receive more blessing from Heaven.*
> *Serve unconditionally, receive unlimited blessing from*
>   *Heaven.*

Many people carry bad karma. Some people carry very heavy bad karma. If one carries heavy karma, clearing it takes many times more service than it would for a person who does not have heavy karma. Therefore, if you chant a little, if you serve for a few years, you may not notice any significant personal benefits from your service. It is vital for you and every reader to understand this. For some people, it may take thirty to fifty years of dedicated service before the benefits are evident. Therefore, some people do not believe that service can transform life.

I personally believe that service is the number one way to transform every aspect of life. If you do not see any transformation from your service, it may be because you carry heavy bad karma. To serve is to clear karma. To serve is to transform every aspect of life. The Divine at this moment is telling me this one-sentence secret:

To serve is to transform all life.

When you serve, many saints, all of your spiritual fathers and mothers in Heaven, the Divine, and Tao will bless you. They know your problems. How much they will bless you depends on how much you serve. Generally speaking, you have to clear your bad karma first. When you begin to serve, it is to clear your own bad karma. After your bad karma is cleansed, the blessings will follow.

Thousands of people worldwide have shared heart-touching and moving stories of their life transformation on my website and on my Facebook page. These people have done the practices. They have been singing, chanting, saying *hello,* invoking Divine Soul Mind Body Downloads, and using Soul Power in other ways. They demonstrate and confirm that great healing results and life transforming experiences are very attainable through these teachings. Sometimes, results are instant.

In one's spiritual journey, one could suddenly have an "aha!" moment. One "aha!" moment is to understand that life is to serve and that to serve is to transform every aspect of life. I have trained my advanced students to be unconditional Total GOLD servants. They have had this "aha!" moment. I wish every person on the spiritual journey can have this "aha!" moment as quickly as possible.

Even though I have taught Tao for less than one year, many of my advanced students have already received remarkable results for healing and rejuvenation. These results may not be typical, but they can be reached by everyone. But I must share an ancient spiritual secret that is important to understand the results you can achieve for healing, rejuvenation, and prolonging life:

Yang shou you xian, ji de zeng shou

"Yang" means *physical life.* "Shou" means *age.* "You" means *has.* "Xian" means *limitation.* "Ji" means *accumulate.* "De" means *virtue.* "Zeng" means *increase.* Therefore, "Yang shou you xian, ji de zeng shou" (pronounced *yahng sho yo shyen, jee duh dzung sho*) means *physical life is limited, but accumulating virtue through service prolongs physical life.*

Everyone's *yang shou* is different. Some people live for more than one hundred years. Some people live to the age of eight. Some people transition from physical life at age fifty. Some newborn babies cannot survive. Some fetuses cannot survive. The root cause of one's *yang shou* is karma.

The length of one's physical life is arranged in the Akashic Records, the place in Heaven where the lives of human beings, animals, and all souls are recorded. Reincarnation is arranged by the Akashic Records. How long a person stays on Mother Earth in a lifetime is decided by the Akashic Records according to your karma. If you have very advanced spiritual abilities and are given divine permission to access the Akashic Records, the leaders of the Akashic Records can then give you information about the length of one's life and more. (Not many people on Mother Earth can access information from the Akashic Records. You must be a high-level spiritual being who offers unconditional service to others. Then the Divine may choose you as a special servant and give you a Divine Order granting you access to information in the Akashic Records.)

I want to share a heart-touching story. A couple who belonged to a church in Los Angeles had twins, a boy and a girl. These twins suffered from an incurable and very serious genetic sickness. They were considered to be hopeless cases. The events coordinator of this church called me to ask if these twins' lives could be saved. I talked with the Divine, who showed me that these two babies had heavy karma. I asked the Divine to save them. The Divine responded, "Zhi Gang, offer my karma cleansing for them through the Akashic Records." I did. I offered Divine Karma Cleansing for these twins. They are both healthy now. I am speechless that the Divine saved these twins through Divine Karma Cleansing.

There is **only one way** to transform your *yang shou* (length of physical life) that has been arranged by the Akashic Records. Now is the time to share this secret and sacred wisdom with you and humanity. To reach *fan lao huan tong,* these steps are vital:

Step 1. Remove all kinds of karma, including personal, ancestral, and relationship karma, as well as curses and negative memories. Bad karma will absolutely block your *fan lao huan tong* because bad karma is the root blockage of every aspect of life.

Step 2. Follow the Tao, including Da Tao (Big Tao) and Xiao Tao (Small Tao). Da Tao is the universal laws and principles. Xiao Tao includes the Tao of eating, sleeping, and more. To have a regular life, including proper sleep, eating, and exercise, is vital to one's health.

Step 3. Do the yin yang Tao practice of Soul Song and Soul Dance. To chant the Tao Song and to do Soul Dance are very important practices for *fan lao huan tong.* They heal, prevent sickness, rejuvenate, and prolong life. In chapter 3, I will give you the vital practices for healing and *fan lao huan tong.*

Step 4. Serve unconditionally. This is the most important practice for *fan lao huan tong. Fan lao huan tong* is easy to say. It is very difficult to achieve, but it is possible. This book and my ten-year Tao training program are to lead Tao practitioners to achieve *fan lao huan tong.* I am looking forward to seeing many people worldwide move in this direction.

长寿永生
Chang Shou Yong Sheng

Long life, immortal

"Chang shou" (pronounced *chahng sho*) means *long life*. "Yong sheng" (pronounced *yawng shung*) means *immortal*. For the last few years, I have thought that if I could live to be one hundred years old, I could then write books about longevity. If I could live to be hundreds of years old, then at that time I could write a book about immortality.

However, the Divine told me, "Zhi Gang, you do not need to wait to be that age to write books about longevity and immortality because there are millions of seniors who need the wisdom and practical techniques right away. Millions of baby boomers are also waiting for this wisdom and these techniques."

The Divine guided me to lead a ten-year Tao training program, as I introduced in chapter 1. These ten years of Tao training consist of five steps. Step 1, remove all sicknesses of the physical, emotional, mental, and spiritual bodies, takes the first two years. How can a person live a long life with sickness? In chapter 3, I will explain in detail Tao practices to remove all sicknesses in the first two years of Tao training.

Step 2 is to practice to reach *fan lao huan tong*. If a Tao practitioner does not reach *fan lao huan tong*, it is hard to talk about longevity and even harder to talk about immortality.

To reach *fan lao huan tong* is vital for longevity and immortality. A Tao practitioner who reaches *fan lao huan tong* needs to continue to do Tao practice in order to maintain the health and purity of the baby state. Then, longevity is possible.

A Tao practitioner who attains longevity needs to continue to practice Tao in order to maintain the baby state with health and purity forever. Then immortality is possible.

To heal all sickness is to go through the process of reverse creation of Tao.

To reach *fan lao huan tong* is to go through the process of reverse creation of Tao.

To have longevity is to go through the process of rejuvenation of Tao.

To reach immortality is to completely meld with Tao.

和谐人类
He Xie Ren Lei

Harmonize all humanity

"He xie" means *harmonize.* "Ren lei" means *humanity.* "He xie ren lei" (pronounced *huh shyeh wren lay*) means *harmonize humanity.*

The steps of Tao training (remove all sicknesses, accomplish *fan lao huan tong* to become a human saint or servant, become a Mother Earth saint or servant, become a Heaven saint or servant, become a Tao saint or servant) are all to gain greater and greater divine and Tao abilities to serve.

Saints are servants. Different levels of saints are given different levels of power from the Divine and Tao to serve.

To reach *fan lao huan tong* is to become a human saint or servant. The Divine and Tao give this one the ability to serve and harmonize humanity, include healing, prevention of sickness, rejuvenation, transformation, and enlightenment for humanity.

To become a Mother Earth saint or servant is to receive divine and Tao abilities to harmonize everything on Mother Earth.

To become a Heaven saint or servant is to receive divine and Tao abilities to harmonize everything in Heaven.

To become a Tao saint or servant is to receive divine and Tao abilities to harmonize everything in all universes.

The purpose of Tao training can be summarized in one sentence:

Tao training is to gain divine and Tao abilities to serve humanity, Mother Earth, Heaven, and all universes.

I shared the following teaching in my authoritative book of the Soul Power Series, *The Power of Soul: The Way to Heal, Rejuvenate, Transform, and Enlighten All Life,* as well as earlier in this book. I want to emphasize this teaching again:

A human being has a physical journey and a soul journey; the purpose of both is to serve.

To serve is to heal.

To serve is to prevent sickness.

To serve is to purify soul, heart, mind, and body.

To serve is to clear bad karma and accumulate good karma.

To serve is to reach *fan lao huan tong*.

To serve is to transform relationships.

To serve is to transform finances.

To serve is to reach soul, heart, mind, and body enlightenment.

To serve is to create love, peace, and harmony for humanity, Mother Earth, and all universes.

To serve is to reach *wan ling rong he*.

道业昌盛

Tao Ye Chang Sheng

Tao career flourishes

Tao is The Way, the universal principles and laws. "Ye" means *career*. "Chang sheng" means *flourish*. "Tao ye chang sheng" (pronounced *dow yuh chahng shung*) means *Tao career flourishes*.

I explained earlier that Tao has Da Tao (Big Dao) and Xiao Tao (Small Dao). Da Tao is the universal laws and principles. Xiao Tao is Tao in every aspect of life.

For example, my Soul Power Series has a Xiao Tao. The Tao of the Soul Power Series is to produce benefits and results for people in healing, rejuvenation, and transformation in every aspect of life. If people experience transformation of their health, relationships, finances, and other aspects of life, they will then be motivated to study and practice the teachings of the Soul Power Series more. The Soul Power Series can be summarized in one sentence:

Soul can heal, prevent sickness, rejuvenate, prolong life, and transform every aspect of life, including relationships and finances, as well as enlighten your soul, heart, mind, and body.

The Soul Power Series is an unconditional universal servant. All of my books empower humanity to self-heal and self-transform every aspect of life. Therefore, the Tao, The Way of the Soul Power Series is to produce healing and life transformation for humanity.

Every aspect of life has a Tao. Earlier I explained the Tao of eating. Eat more vegetables. Eat more natural food. Eat less.

Generally speaking, eat only until you are eighty percent full. Never eat until you feel completely full. Let me share a Tao practice to prepare our digestive systems before eating and to promote good digestion and absorption after eating.

Apply the Four Power Techniques:

Body Power. Sit up straight. Put the tip of your tongue as close as you can to the roof of your mouth without touching it for a few seconds, and then relax your tongue. Put your right palm just above the navel and your left palm just below the navel.

Soul Power. Say *hello:*

> *Dear soul mind body of my digestive system, including my mouth, tongue, esophagus, stomach, small intestine, large intestine, liver, pancreas, and spleen* (in traditional Chinese medicine, the spleen is a key organ for the digestive system),
> *I love you.*
> *Prepare yourself for the intake of food.*
> *Do a good job.*
> *Thank you.*
> *Dear Tao Song,* Jin Dan Jin Gu,
> *I love you.*
> *You have the power to prepare my digestive system, including all of its organs and cells.*
> *Do a good job.*
> *Thank you.*

Mind Power. Visualize a bright, beautiful golden light ball rotating counterclockwise in your lower abdomen.

Sound Power. Sing or chant the Tao Song *Jin Dan Jin Gu* repeatedly. Listen to me singing on the enclosed CD. "Jin" means *gold*. "Dan" means *light ball*. The second "jin" means *go into*. "Gu" means *food*. "Jin dan jin gu" means your golden light ball is preparing your entire digestive system for eating.

Sing or chant:

> *Jin Dan Jin Gu* (pronounced *jeen dahn jeen goo*)
> *Jin Dan Jin Gu*
> *Jin Dan Jin Gu*
> *Jin Dan Jin Gu*
> *Jin Dan Jin Gu*
> *Jin Dan Jin Gu*
> *Jin Dan Jin Gu* . . .

Generally speaking, sing or chant for three to five minutes before each meal. The longer you chant, the better. If you can chant for ten minutes, wonderful! When you chant *Jin dan jin gu,* the golden light ball in your abdomen will radiate to your entire digestive system, including all of its organs, cells, DNA, and RNA, to prepare your digestive system to create digestive fluids and enzymes and for every organ and cell in your digestive system to function well.

When you sing or chant *Jin dan jin gu,* you may produce liquid (saliva) in your mouth. This is a very good and important signal. Swallow that liquid. This is sacred wisdom that tells you your digestive system is starting to prepare well for food intake.

Join me to sing or chant for three minutes now. At this moment, I am in the Love Peace Harmony Center at 6119 Andrus Road in Boulder, Colorado. About sixty of my top teachers from all over the world are listening to me flow this book. My assistant is typing. I will sing for three minutes with everyone here at the Love Peace Harmony Center. Afterward I will ask a few people to share their experiences.

When you chant, close your eyes. Put your mind in your stomach and lower abdomen. When enough liquid accumulates in your mouth, swallow it.

Let's sing now:

> *Jin Dan Jin Gu*
> *Jin Dan Jin Gu*
> *Jin Dan Jin Gu*
> *Jin Dan Jin Gu*
> *Jin Dan Jin Gu*
> *Jin Dan Jin Gu*
> *Jin Dan Jin Gu . . .*

> *Hao!*

"Hao" means *good, fine.*

After three minutes, I asked four people to share their experiences.

> *My name is David Lusch. I am from Fremont, California. When we began chanting, I saw Master Sha's Jin Dan expand out to the universe and nourish all of us. There was immediately a lot of saliva in my mouth. All of Heaven— many saints, buddhas, and angels—were sending golden light to create the saliva, as well as to nourish every part of my being.*
>
> *I also saw three ancient Taoist saints. One held a lantern and another held a staff. All three were very happy we*

were doing this chanting. I saw Peng Zu (the teacher of Lao Zi) on his mountain and he was very happy. I saw Guan Yin and she came to bless everybody. It was like a procession of saints, buddhas, and Taoist masters. They were marching in. They were singing and were marching to the beat as we chanted.

And there were Heaven's animals. The dragons and elephants came. I got happier and happier. I saw many of the saints and buddhas inside of myself. They were coming within me and, I am sure, within you to prepare for digestion and absorption. I could see the souls of my stomach, small intestine, and large intestine sitting in the full lotus position, chanting, and moving to the melody. Every soul within me was chanting and moving back and forth. They were so happy for this preparation for food intake because they would not have to work as hard.

They received soul nourishment and divine and Tao nourishment. The human activity of preparing to eat was transformed to a high-level spiritual Tao practice. I saw the yin-yang symbol in the room. The light was incredible. I am ready to eat. All of Heaven and Tao responded. The heavens had great joy that we were doing this practice and that it would be spread to humanity.

Thank you, Master Sha. Thank you, Divine. Thank you, Tao.

My name is Petra Herz. I come from Germany. This was an incredible experience. When we began to chant, I saw Heaven begin to open. I saw a lot of saints whose names I don't know. Ancient saints and buddhas were coming. They were so happy. I saw that my Jin Dan was immediately run-

ning to Master Sha's Jin Dan to be nourished. Everybody got a very nice lotus seat. We were blessed with a lot of wonderful flowers. We were nourished with golden liquid. My body was getting warm inside and very, very happy. I feel that everything inside of me was prepared for food intake. My whole digestive system received so much light, love, and flowers. I feel expanded, like my size got ten times bigger. I feel so grounded. I feel I prepared my body in a loving way. That is what I want every day for every meal.

My name is Linhu Zhu. I am from Atlanta, Georgia. This was an incredible feeling with a lot of love for my digestive system. I had a feeling that my stomach was not very happy because I had eaten something at dinner that was not very fresh. I feel like my hands sent a lot of warm energy to my stomach and gave healing to my stomach. Every time I chant, I will be very prepared for the food to come in, just like the mother is ready to feed the baby. Before, when I ate a meal I just wanted to get the job done. But this chanting brings a different aspect of the deep meaning of food.

My name is Jaylene Hamilton from Sudbury, Canada. When Master Sha said we would be chanting, the saliva started to come. I thought with this much saliva how was I going to chant? I then felt a beautiful presence and light come around me and in me. My body felt very peaceful and very loved. I still feel this light. I then began to feel this incredible heat as the light increased and the heat within my stomach and Lower Dan Tian began to expand. My body is feeling very blessed to have this practice because I usually eat quickly and am always in a hurry. I give my thanks quickly and then eat quickly so I can get back to work. My body said this is such a sacred time to be together and this practice is so simple. We have to allow ourselves and our souls to be connected to Tao in this way. I feel very humbled, very nourished, very loved, and so connected to our dear Master Sha and all souls. I think this will be the foundation of a great weight loss program. The love we feel will melt all blockages. Thank you for this teaching. I am very grateful.

There are many teachers here who would like to share their experiences. I chose these four. These are great experiences. They have realized the importance of this Tao practice. Two of them have explained that they usually do not take the time to eat properly, rushing to eat because they want to move to other tasks.

I am teaching that every aspect of life has a Tao. "Tao ye chang sheng" means *Tao career flourishes.* Follow the Tao of any aspect of life and that aspect of life will flourish. Follow the Tao of every aspect of life and your whole life will flourish. This is your Tao career.

Eating food properly and preparing the digestive system are very important for your health. Millions of people on Mother Earth have issues with their digestive system: mouth, gums, teeth, esophagus, stomach, liver, small intestine, large intestine, pancreas, and spleen. How many unhealthy conditions are connected with these organs? If everyone spent three minutes to prepare his or her digestive system to receive food with this simple yet powerful Tao practice, how many sicknesses of the digestive system could be prevented? As *The Yellow Emperor's Internal Classic* stated:

Shang gong zhi wei bing, bu zhi yi bing

As explained earlier in this chapter, this means *the best doctor prevents sickness instead of treating sickness.* This is such an important concept for Mother Earth in the Soul Light Era, the new fifteen-thousand-year era for Mother Earth and the universe that began on August 8, 2003. This precious wisdom was shared with humanity five thousand years ago. It has served millions of people in history.

I have studied conventional modern medicine (with an M.D. from China) and traditional Chinese medicine. I have studied tai chi, qi gong, kung fu, the *I Ching,* and feng shui, but I can say that the prevention wisdom in traditional Chinese medicine has not been been applied enough, even in China. Even less has it been applied enough in the West.

I am honored to be a universal servant for humanity and all souls to share this divine Tao practice with you and humanity.

Now let me share with you a secret and sacred Tao practice to help you digest and absorb food well *after* eating. Apply the Four Power Techniques:

Body Power. Sit up straight. Put the tip of your tongue as close as you can to the roof of your mouth without touching it for a few seconds, and then relax your tongue. Put your right palm above the navel and your left palm below the navel.

Soul Power. Say *hello:*

> *Dear my digestive system, including every organ, cell, cell unit, DNA, and RNA,*
> *I love you, honor you, and appreciate you.*
> *Please function well.*
> *Digest well.*

Absorb well.
Do a good job.
Thank you.
Dear Tao Song, Jin Dan Hua Gu,
I love you.
You have the power to help my digestive system digest
*   well and absorb well.*
Do a good job.
Thank you.

Mind Power. Visualize your Jin Dan (golden light ball in your lower abdomen) rotating counterclockwise.

Sound Power. Sing or chant the sacred Tao Song *Jin Dan Hua Gu* repeatedly. Listen to me singing on the enclosed CD.

Jin Dan Hua Gu (pronounced *jeen dahn hwah goo*)
Jin Dan Hua Gu
Jin Dan Hua Gu
Jin Dan Hua Gu
Jin Dan Hua Gu
Jin Dan Hua Gu
Jin Dan Hua Gu . . .

As explained in the previous Tao practice for food intake, "jin dan" means *golden light ball* and "gu" means *food*. "Hua" means *digest and absorb*.

I recommend you spend at least ten minutes doing this practice right after you finish a meal.

I will now sing with my teachers for ten minutes. Then I will ask several of them to share their experiences.

Let us chant now:

Jin Dan Hua Gu
Jin Dan Hua Gu
Jin Dan Hua Gu
Jin Dan Hua Gu
Jin Dan Hua Gu
Jin Dan Hua Gu
Jin Dan Hua Gu . . .

Hao!

We chanted for about ten minutes. I would like you to know that to chant *Jin Dan Jin Gu* and *Jin Dan Hua Gu* is not only to prepare for eating and to digest and absorb food well. To chant *Jin Dan Jin Gu* and *Jin Dan Hua Gu* is to build your light body. I will share more about the many incredible secrets of these Tao Song practices later.

I asked several of those present to share their experiences of the *Jin Dan Hua Gu* practice.

My name is Trevor Allen from Melbourne, Australia. There is a rejuvenation of every organ of my digestive system that is rejuvenating the rest of my body.

My name is G. K. Khoe. I am from Vancouver, Canada. During this exercise, I felt myself suddenly enclosed within a big ball that was constantly expanding. Then I lost all sense of where I am and who I am. I did not know what I was doing. The only thing I noticed was that saliva was pouring out and I continually had to swallow.

My name is Christopher Keehn from Monterey, California. That was a beautiful practice. Saliva started running immediately in my mouth. The intensity and luminosity of the light filled my entire body, not just the digestive tract.

My name is Susanne Kaiser. I am from North Carolina. In the first practice, when we were preparing to eat, I noticed energy flowing from the earth into my body, as well as the formation of saliva. The message I received was that Mother Earth was participating in this practice.

In the second practice for digestion and absorption, I noticed the energy was flowing in a different direction. Energy was coming down from Heaven in this process. We are supported by Heaven when we do this practice. Heaven sends energy to us and this is how the light body is built in each of our energy centers.

These two practices have to be done together. Mother Earth participates and Heaven participates. Their energies will integrate within our bodies. I feel deep gratitude. These practices are not only to serve our bodies, they are a service that we offer to all souls.

My name is Marcelo Celis. I am from Los Angeles, California. The insight that I received from this practice was that this is the way to build the light body. It does not matter so much what we eat, but that we do this practice. This is one of the most precious and special practices that have been brought to Mother Earth at this time, for all universes and all souls. When my hands were on my abdomen, they became warmer and warmer, and I had to move them away from my body. I expanded in a profound way. At first, I was chanting from my throat. I started to feel pain there, which reminded me to bring my awareness down to my Jin Dan. Immediately I started to perspire. Master Sha's teaching is to place our awareness in the Jin Dan. These two practices cannot be separated. They work together and they are in harmony. They have to be honored. They are among the most precious gifts that we have been given as humans at this time.

My name is Robyn Rice from Australia. As soon as I began chanting, I experienced the blockages in my body melting. It took only about a minute. I began to feel this amazing oneness and incredible light. I felt like I was in a totally different place. It was like a melding. I could feel the limitations from my mind just melt away, leading to complete unity with the universe. It was really beautiful.

My name is Patricia Smith. I am from Watsonville, California. As we started, there was this brilliant, vibrating golden light that looked like an opening in the heavens. Billions of souls started to pour out. This was not only my connection with the Divine, but also directly with Master Sha's Jin Dan. As these souls poured into my own Jin Dan, there was a vibration, an expansion, and a burst of brilliant light. If I were looking at it with my eyes open, it would have been blinding. I was literally disappearing. It was getting difficult to continue chanting. My whole body expanded and merged with Master Sha and the Divine's Jin Dan. I have been tired, but now my energy is elevated and I am alert. My entire Middle Jiao feels like it has been rejuvenated: liver, large and small intestines, spleen, and pancreas. An experience like this after each meal will make each person strong, focused, and better able to serve. Hao!

My name is David Lusch from Fremont, California. What I saw happening was that all of Heaven and Earth, the universe, all souls were participating in this practice, and there was incredible divine light and Tao light being sent down to us. We received many soul nutrients to nourish the souls of our organs, systems, cells, cell units, DNA, RNA, and tiniest matter. Negative memories and soul memories of unpleasant experiences with food and digestion and absorption were being cleared. Whole areas of our bodies became lighter, clearer, and better functioning.

All the light coming in was also nourishing our energy and matter, increasing their vibration and frequency. What came to me was that doing these practices while doing Bi Gu would make Bi Gu more effective because I would not feel as hungry. I feel very nourished and it seems that the food that I would eat would go further.

I mentioned earlier that to chant *Jin Dan Jin Gu* and *Jin Dan Hua Gu* is to build your light body. One of the most important purposes of the ten-year Tao training program that I described in chapter 1 is to build the light body. Why? Because the second step of Tao training is to teach and train Tao practitioners to reach *fan lao huan tong*, to transform old age to the purity and health of a baby.

Fan lao huan tong is an ancient Taoist term and goal. Millions of Tao practitioners in history have desired to reach *fan lao huan tong*, but not too many people have really achieved it.

Why has *fan lau huan tong* been so difficult to achieve? There are a few major reasons.

- Ancient Tao teaching has been kept very secret. The true secrets have not been shared widely. Historically, a great Tao master passes the true secrets to only one or two chosen lineage holders before transitioning from physical life.
- Tao teaching has had many complicated techniques and processes that many students lack the patience to learn and practice.
- The few great Tao practitioners who have reached the Tao and have gained great experience, wisdom, knowledge, and practical techniques are not willing to share with the public. They also keep what they have learned very secret. Tao wisdom, knowledge, and practical techniques are very powerful. Unfortunately, they have not been spread to humanity.

I personally honor all Tao masters and all spiritual masters in all realms. Thank you so much for the wisdom and knowledge that we have learned from all of you. We cannot honor you enough.

In this book and future Tao books, I am honored to share the secrets, wisdom, knowledge, and practical techniques that the Divine and Tao gave to me directly. I am honored to have open spiritual channels that allow me to receive the secrets, wisdom, knowledge, and practical techniques directly from the Divine and Tao. I do not need to study or prepare anything. I am not writing this book. I am flowing this book. What I hear from the Divine and Tao, I share on the spot.

There are unlimited secrets, wisdom, knowledge, and practical techniques from the Divine, Tao, and all of Heaven. There have been many millions of books on Mother Earth. There are countless books in Heaven. Heaven's books are named "tian shu." "Tian" means *Heaven.* "Shu" means *books.*

Open your spiritual channels in order to gain advanced spiritual abilities to read *tian shu.* To read Mother Earth's books is not enough. To read Heaven's books is the task of a highly developed spiritual being. I will teach my advanced teachers to read *tian shu.* This is my teaching: ask for the wisdom directly from Heaven, from the Divine, and from Tao.

There is a true secret, vital to the spiritual journey, that many spiritual beings may not be aware of. This true secret is to **offer service to humanity and all souls**. In the beginning of every book in my Soul Power Series, I mention the Universal Law of Universal Service. The Divine revealed this universal law in April 2003. Because it is so important, I repeat its essence:

> *Serve a little, receive a little blessing from the Divine and Heaven.*
> *Serve more, receive more blessing from the Divine and Heaven.*
> *Serve unconditionally, receive unlimited blessing from the Divine and Heaven.*

What is the best way for a spiritual being to do spiritual development? The best way is to **serve unconditionally**. Meditating, chanting, and other spiritual practices are important, but if you simply do these practices, you have not received the key for spiritual development. The key for spiritual development is to offer unconditional universal service. The best way to fulfill your spiritual journey is to serve unconditionally.

This is also the secret for highly developing your spiritual channels: offer unconditional universal service. Serve a little, open your spiritual channels a little. Serve more, develop more spiritual abilities. Serve unconditionally, develop unlimited spiritual abilities.

This highest secret for your spiritual channels is that what you can see in your Third Eye and what you can hear from the Divine and Heaven depend on how much unconditional service you are giving and how many tasks you are carrying for the divine mission.[8]

Serve unconditionally and you will be given bigger divine tasks. Accomplish your tasks and you will be given deeper Third Eye images. You will be given higher secrets, wisdom, knowledge, and practical techniques from the Divine and Heaven. The Divine and your spiritual fathers and mothers in Heaven decide what you can see and what you can hear, based on your service.

I have trained hundreds of students and teachers who can see spiritual Third Eye images and who can hear from and communicate with the Divine and Heaven. Often, when I offer a divine healing and blessing, I ask them to share their Third Eye images and the messages they receive from the Divine. Ten of my students and teachers may give you ten different images and messages. They are all correct. They are sharing spiritual images and messages from different perspectives and layers. The Divine and Heaven give each person different views and angles of the full picture and complete message.

---

8 The divine mission is to transform the consciousness of humanity and all souls, and enlighten them, in order to create love, peace, and harmony for humanity, Mother Earth, and all universes.

If you carry more divine tasks, if you serve unconditionally, then you will be given deeper images and messages. You will have deeper insights. You will be given more advanced and more simple techniques and wisdom.

In conclusion, the key to developing your spiritual channels can be summarized in one sentence:

To serve humanity and all souls unconditionally is to develop your highest spiritual abilities.

I am not saying that you do not need to do spiritual practices to develop your spiritual channels. These kinds of spiritual practices are important, but they are limited. If you forget to serve unconditionally, you will not gain higher levels of spiritual abilities. This is the Tao of opening spiritual channels. Follow this Tao, and you will develop advanced spiritual abilities. This is *Tao ye chang sheng* for opening spiritual channels.

The Tao practices of chanting *Jin Dan Jin Gu* and *Jin Dan Hua Gu* are the Tao of food intake and digestion and absorption. Following this Tao will prevent many sicknesses for millions of people worldwide. Follow this Tao and your health, your rejuvenation, and your longevity could receive remarkable benefits. This is *Tao ye chang sheng* for food intake and digestion and absorption.

I have shared a few examples of how to follow Tao and flourish. If you do not follow Tao, you could have many blockages. To realize Tao in every aspect of life is to find the true secrets, wisdom, and practical techniques for that aspect of life. Follow Tao and that part of life will flourish.

Can we find the Tao of the purpose of one's life? Some lawyers may think the purpose of their life is to be a good lawyer. Some doctors may think the purpose of their life is to be a good doctor. Some may think the purpose of their life is to be a good writer. Some may think that the purpose of their life is to be a good singer. Some may think that the purpose of their life is to be a good teacher. Some may think that the purpose of their life is to be a good scientist. Some may think that the purpose of their life is to be a good skater.

To be a good lawyer, doctor, writer, singer, teacher, scientist, skater, parent, spouse, or anything else takes study and practice. Anyone who can realize and follow the Tao of his or her profession could flourish in their career.

What is the Tao of all of professions? The Tao of all of them is to serve humanity. *To serve is the Tao of all professions.* How should one serve? Serve with love, forgiveness, compassion, and light. Serve with sincerity, honesty, and kindness. To follow these principles is to follow the Tao principle. Follow the Tao principle and your career will flourish.

功德圆满
Gong De Yuan Man

Serve unconditionally and gain complete virtue to reach full enlightenment

"Gong de" (pronounced *gawng duh*) means *virtue*. Virtue is spiritual currency in Heaven. Virtue is expressed as colored flowers—red, gold, rainbow, purple, crystal, and more—in your Akashic Record book.

How does a person receive spiritual virtue? You gain virtue by serving others to make them happier and healthier. You gain virtue by offering your unconditional love, forgiveness, compassion, kindness, and purity. The souls of the ones you serve are very appreciative and will give red dots to your soul. Ten red dots form a small red flower. Ten small red flowers form a big flower. Other colors of flowers "grow" in a similar way. When you make other people happy and appreciative, your soul receives virtue from their souls. In addition, when you serve others, whether they are human beings, animals, trees, cities, countries, or the environment, Heaven will place flowers in your book in the Akashic Records. At the same time, flowers come directly to your soul.

The Divine made a spiritual law: to serve is to receive virtue. Virtue blesses one's spiritual journey and physical journey. If one has a virtue deposit in Heaven's virtue bank, that virtue is spiritual currency that could transform to physical money on Mother Earth. If one has financial challenges on Mother Earth and does not have enough virtue in Heaven's virtue bank, it is very difficult for this one to gain physical money.

Virtue has much more important value for your spiritual upliftment. If one accumulates a lot of virtue in Heaven's virtue bank, this one's soul will be uplifted higher and higher in Heaven.

There are millions of people on their spiritual journey. Why do you need a spiritual journey? What is the final goal of the spiritual journey? The final goal of the spiritual journey is to uplift your soul standing to the divine realm, where the Divine stays. Why does a soul need to go to the divine realm? If your soul reaches the divine realm, your soul stops reincarnation. You do not need to become a human being anymore. You will serve in soul form, just like the Divine and the saints in the divine realm. When you call the Divine and saints in the divine realm, they will come to bless you in soul form. After their blessing, they return to the divine realm. They do not become a human being anymore. They serve you and humanity in soul form.

It is very important to know that even if one's soul reaches the divine realm, this soul can continue to be uplifted further, because there are even higher layers of Heaven's realms. In fact, there are unlimited realms in Heaven. Therefore, one's soul standing can be uplifted without limit. But always, only service can uplift one's soul standing.

Why does a person need to be uplifted to the divine realm? To stop reincarnation is one of the greatest benefits. Also, to be uplifted to the divine realm is to be given divine abilities to be a better servant. Think about a human's life. Compare it to the lives of the saints in Heaven and to the life of the Divine. One day, you will have an "aha!" moment. This "aha!" moment is "Wow! I got it!" The higher one's soul's standing, the greater the divine abilities one is given.

The purpose of physical life and spiritual life is to serve. It does not matter what kind of job you are doing. Doing any job is to serve others. To serve is to make others happier and healthier. If you make others unhappy and upset, that is not the kind of service I am talking about. I am talking about offering your love, forgiveness, compassion, and kindness. The most important values in a human being's life and in a soul's life are to be happier and healthier.

The Divine's service is to make humanity and all souls happier and healthier. The Divine has divine abilities to serve. Saints have saints' abilities to serve. A human has human abilities to serve. To serve is to gain higher abilities. The most important thing for anyone's spiritual journey is to serve humanity and all souls unconditionally. To serve unconditionally is to serve without expecting anything in return. It is to give completely. Do not expect any return. To give and expect something in return is not unconditional universal service.

Some people say, "I do not have time to serve. I am too busy."

Here is some very clear spiritual wisdom. If you do not have time to serve, you will not gain virtue. If you do not gain virtue, your spiritual development cannot advance. In my workshops, I have had quite a few people tell me that they have served a lot, have done volunteer work for many years, and do a lot of kind things for others. Yet they still have major struggles in their health, relationships, and finances. They say, "We serve a lot, and our life still has so many challenges. How can we believe that service can benefit and transform life?" My answer to them is:

If you think you have served a lot and your life still has so many challenges, think about what your life might be like if you had not served a lot. Your life could be much worse. Because you have served a lot, you have been given a lot of virtue already. Why does your life still have so many challenges? You could have very heavy bad karma. In your previous lifetimes and this lifetime, you could have made a lot of mistakes, or your ancestors could have made a lot of mistakes. The mistakes you made, such as killing, harming, or taking advantage of others, lying, cheating, and stealing, are your spiritual debts to others. These debts must be repaid. You may need to offer a lot more service to gain enough virtue to repay your karmic debts. If you continue to serve more and more, if you really can offer unconditional universal service, your life could see very significant transformation.

I have shared this vital wisdom about karma many times in all of my books. One of the most important teachings is to sing Divine Soul Songs to self-clear bad karma and transform every aspect of your life, including health, relationships, and finances. When you chant, you give love, forgiveness, compassion, and light to others, humanity, Mother Earth, and all universes. You will receive virtue from them and from Heaven's virtue bank. Singing Divine Soul Songs is service. Singing a little is not enough, especially if you have heavy bad karma. You need to sing a lot.

When a person has bad karma, the bad karma will deeply affect this person's thinking. This kind of person may find it very difficult to believe in karma issues. They do not believe that chanting can clear bad karma. They do not believe that chanting can transform health, relationships, and finances. Therefore, spiritual teaching can be given only to the ready ones. Advanced spiritual teaching can only be given to even fewer.

What is advanced spiritual teaching? It is very simple. Advanced spiritual teaching is to be an unconditional universal servant. To be an unconditional universal servant is easy to say and difficult to do. *Do I have time to offer some service? Do I have time to offer more service? Do I have time to offer unconditional universal service?* To progress on your spiritual journey is to show the Divine, Tao, and Heaven how much service you want to give. You do your job; Heaven will record it. You serve; Heaven will reward you.

Whatever your belief system and spiritual practices, spiritual development can be summarized in one sentence:

The spiritual journey is the journey to serve others, humanity, Mother Earth, and all universes, in order to create love, peace, and harmony for humanity, Mother Earth, and all universes.

I have just explained "gong de" or virtue. "Yuan man" means *enlightenment.* "Gong de yuan man" (pronounced *gawng duh ywen mahn*) can be translated as *serve unconditionally and gain complete virtue to reach full enlightenment.*

To serve is to gain virtue. To gain virtue is to have your soul standing in Heaven uplifted. Heaven has layers. To reach the divine realm requires a lot of virtue. A spiritiual being could take forty to fifty *thousand* lifetimes of good service in order to reach the divine realm. This is how difficult it is for a spiritual being to reach the divine realm. There are millions and billions of spiritual beings in history who have served very hard and continue to serve very hard because reaching the divine realm is the final goal of a soul.

There are many challenges in one's spiritual journey: health, relationships, finances, and other issues. To progress on your spiritual journey, you must purify your soul, heart, mind, and body. You must remove the soul, mind, body blockages in your health, relationships, finances, and other issues. You must share your love, forgiveness, compassion, and light to humanity, Mother Earth, and all universes. There is no second way to fulfill your spiritual journey. To reach *gong de yuan man* is to reach full enlightenment.

A dedicated spiritual being will remove all kinds of blockages on the spiritual journey and truly trust and believe that service is the way to uplift soul standing and reach the divine realm. To serve the divine mission unconditionally is to take a rocket up through Heaven.

I wish that you and every spiritual being will deeply understand that the only way to fulfill your spiritual journey is to serve. There is no second way. The Divine has said this very clearly.

To serve a little is to receive a little blessing and develop your spiritual journey a little.

To serve more is to receive more blessing and develop your spiritual journey more.

To serve unconditionally is to receive unlimited blessing and develop your spiritual journey fully in order to reach *gong de yuan man.*

To reach *gong de yuan man* is to reach full enlightenment.

Enlightenment includes soul enlightenment, mind enlightenment, and body enlightenment. Enlighten your soul first, then enlighten your mind. Finally, enlighten your body. Each step is more difficult than the previous one.

I encourage you to learn more by studying the chapter on soul enlightenment in the authority book of my Soul Power Series, *The Power of Soul: The Way to Heal, Rejuvenate, Transform, and Enlighten All Life*. Then, join my Worldwide Representatives and me at a Soul Healing and Enlightenment Retreat to receive a Divine Order to enlighten your soul.

万灵融合
Wan Ling Rong He

All souls join as one

"Wan" means *ten thousand*, which in Chinese represents *all* or *every*. "Ling" means *soul*. "Rong he" means *join as one*. The Soul Light Era started on August 8, 2003 and will last fifteen thousand years. What is the final goal of this era? It is to reach *wan ling rong he* (pronounced *wahn ling rawng huh*), all souls joining as one.

The Soul World has a Light Side and a Dark Side. The Light Side includes buddhas, saints, healing angels, ascended masters, gurus, lamas, and all kinds of spiritual fathers and mothers in all layers of Heaven. The Dark Side includes demons, monsters, and ghosts.

All souls joining as one means that all souls on the Light Side and the Dark Side join as one. This is not easy at all. To meld them together requires unconditional love, forgiveness, compassion, and light. Think about it. The Light Side and Dark Side are opposites. Selflessness and selfishness are a pair of opposites. Selfishness is the Dark Side. Selflessness is the Light Side. To meld them together is difficult. Conflict and harmony, war and peace are also pairs of opposites. Conflict is the Dark Side. Harmony is the Light Side. To meld them as one is not easy.

Wan ling rong he is to meld all of the Light Side and all of the Dark Side as one. It will take the greatest effort of all humanity and all souls to achieve this final goal in the Soul Light Era. How can we achieve this goal? Apply divine love, forgiveness, compassion, and light.

Divine love melts all blockages and transforms all life.

Divine forgiveness brings inner joy and inner peace.

Divine compassion boosts energy, stamina, vitality, and immunity.

Divine light heals, prevents sickness, and transforms every aspect of life, including relationships and finances.

Let us do a practice to meld the Light Side and the Dark Side. Chant:

> *Divine love, divine forgiveness, divine compassion,*
>   *and divine light meld the Light Side and Dark*
>   *Side. Thank you.*
> *Divine love, divine forgiveness, divine compassion,*
>   *and divine light meld the Light Side and Dark*
>   *Side. Thank you.*
> *Divine love, divine forgiveness, divine compassion,*
>   *and divine light meld the Light Side and Dark*
>   *Side. Thank you.*
> *Divine love, divine forgiveness, divine compassion,*
>   *and divine light meld the Light Side and Dark*
>   *Side. Thank you.*
> *Divine love, divine forgiveness, divine compassion,*
>   *and divine light meld the Light Side and Dark*
>   *Side. Thank you.*

Divine love, divine forgiveness, divine compassion,
   and divine light meld the Light Side and Dark
   Side. Thank you.
Divine love, divine forgiveness, divine compassion,
   and divine light meld the Light Side and Dark
   Side. Thank you . . .

Now I will offer Divine Soul Mind Body Transplants of Divine Love, Divine Forgiveness, Divine Compassion, and Divine Light as divine gifts to every reader.

Sit up straight. Put the tip of your tongue close to the roof of your mouth without touching it. Put both palms on your lower abdomen.

Sit quietly for two minutes. Open your heart and soul to receive these permanent divine treasures that will be downloaded to your soul.

Divine Soul Transplant of Divine Love
Transmission!

Divine Mind Transplant of Divine Love
Transmission!

Divine Body Transplant of Divine Love
Transmission!

Divine Soul Transplant of Divine Forgiveness
Transmission!

Divine Mind Transplant of Divine Forgiveness
Transmission!

Divine Body Transplant of Divine Forgiveness Transmission!

Divine Soul Transplant of Divine Compassion Transmission!

Divine Mind Transplant of Divine Compassion Transmission!

Divine Body Transplant of Divine Compassion Transmission!

Divine Soul Transplant of Divine Light Transmission!

Divine Mind Transplant of Divine Light Transmission!

Divine Body Transplant of Divine Light Transmission!

Hao! Hao! Hao!
Thank you. Thank you. Thank you.
You are very blessed.
Join the twelve Soul Mind Body Transplants together as one.

Hei ya ya you! Hei ya ya you! Ya ya you you you! (This is Soul Language to send a Divine Order to join these twelve divine souls you have just received as one.)

You are extremely blessed beyond words. We cannot honor the Divine enough.

Let us practice with these new divine treasures now.

Soul Power. Say *hello:*

> *Dear Divine Love Soul Mind Body Transplants, Divine Forgiveness Soul Mind Body Transplants, Divine Compassion Soul Mind Body Transplants, and Divine Light Soul Mind Body Transplants,*
> *I love you, honor you, and appreciate you.*
> *Please turn on to serve wan ling rong he.*
> *Thank you.*

Sound Power. Chant:

> *Divine Love, Forgiveness, Compassion, and Light Soul Mind Body Transplants bring wan ling rong he.*
> *Thank you.*
> *Divine Love, Forgiveness, Compassion, and Light Soul Mind Body Transplants bring wan ling rong he.*
> *Thank you.*
> *Divine Love, Forgiveness, Compassion, and Light Soul Mind Body Transplants bring wan ling rong he.*
> *Thank you.*
> *Divine Love, Forgiveness, Compassion, and Light Soul Mind Body Transplants bring wan ling rong he.*
> *Thank you.*
> *Divine Love, Forgiveness, Compassion, and Light Soul Mind Body Transplants bring wan ling rong he.*
> *Thank you.*
> *Divine Love, Forgiveness, Compassion, and Light Soul Mind Body Transplants bring wan ling rong he.*
> *Thank you.*

Divine Love, Forgiveness, Compassion, and Light Soul
Mind Body Transplants bring wan ling rong he.
Thank you . . .

This is one of the most powerful chants that you can do to offer divine service to humanity, Mother Earth, and all universes. You are assisting all souls to join as one. Every moment you chant this mantra, virtue (divine flowers) is given to your book in the Akashic Records and to your soul.

Chant a little, receive few flowers.
Chant more, receive more flowers.
Chant nonstop, receive unlimited flowers.

The more people chant this mantra, the faster *wan ling rong he* could be achieved. This is one of the most important services that we can offer. It is powerful because the twelve permanent divine treasures that the Divine downloaded to your soul have unlimited power to remove soul, mind, and body blockages in order to bring *wan ling rong he* in the Soul Light Era.

We thank you, Divine, for your generosity. To receive divine treasures does not mean that *wan ling rong he* is achieved. We have to do our part. We have to invoke our divine treasures and chant. To chant is to serve. To chant is to bring *wang ling rong he*.

Let us join hearts and souls together to chant this mantra again:

Divine Love, Forgiveness, Compassion, and Light Soul
Mind Body Transplants bring wan ling rong he.
Divine Love, Forgiveness, Compassion, and Light Soul
Mind Body Transplants bring wan ling rong he.

Divine Love, Forgiveness, Compassion, and Light Soul
  Mind Body Transplants bring wan ling rong he.
Divine Love, Forgiveness, Compassion, and Light Soul
  Mind Body Transplants bring wan ling rong he.
Divine Love, Forgiveness, Compassion, and Light Soul
  Mind Body Transplants bring wan ling rong he.
Divine Love, Forgiveness, Compassion, and Light Soul
  Mind Body Transplants bring wan ling rong he.
Divine Love, Forgiveness, Compassion, and Light Soul
  Mind Body Transplants bring wan ling rong he . . .

Chant more and more to be an unconditional universal servant. I wish *wang ling rong he* can come to all universes as soon as possible.

Let us chant for two minutes more. Stand up. Chant:

Divine Love, Forgiveness, Compassion, and Light Soul
  Mind Body Transplants bring wan ling rong he.
Divine Love, Forgiveness, Compassion, and Light Soul
  Mind Body Transplants bring wan ling rong he.
Divine Love, Forgiveness, Compassion, and Light Soul
  Mind Body Transplants bring wan ling rong he.
Divine Love, Forgiveness, Compassion, and Light Soul
  Mind Body Transplants bring wan ling rong he.
Divine Love, Forgiveness, Compassion, and Light Soul
  Mind Body Transplants bring wan ling rong he.
Divine Love, Forgiveness, Compassion, and Light Soul
  Mind Body Transplants bring wan ling rong he.
Divine Love, Forgiveness, Compassion, and Light Soul
  Mind Body Transplants bring wan ling rong he . . .

Hao!

丹神养肾

Dan Shen Yang Shen

Tao Dan, Tao Shen nourish kidneys

"Dan" means *Tao Dan,* which is the Tao light ball. "Shen" means *Tao Shen,* which is the heart of Tao.

Tao Dan and Tao Shen carry Tao power to heal, boost energy, stamina, vitality, and immunity, prevent sickness, rejuvenate soul, heart, mind, and body, and transform every aspect of life, including relationships and finances.

There is a simple practice that anybody can do. Chant:

> *Dan Shen Yang Shen* (pronounced *dahn shun yahng*
>   *shun*)
> *Dan Shen Yang Shen*
> *Dan Shen Yang Shen*
> *Dan Shen Yang Shen*
> *Dan Shen Yang Shen*
> *Dan Shen Yang Shen*
> *Dan Shen Yang Shen . . .*

"Yang" means *nourish*. The second "shen" means *kidneys*. Therefore, "Dan shen yang shen" means *Tao Dan and Tao Shen nourish kidneys*. You can absolutely chant *Dan Shen Yang Shen* to transform the quality of your kidneys. Let us chant now:

> *Dan Shen Yang Shen* (pronounced *dahn shun yahng*
>   *shun*)
> *Dan Shen Yang Shen*
> *Dan Shen Yang Shen*
> *Dan Shen Yang Shen*
> *Dan Shen Yang Shen*

Dan Shen Yang Shen
Dan Shen Yang Shen . . .

In Tao teaching, the kidneys are a vital organ because they produce *jing*. Jing is matter for the whole body. You will learn much deeper wisdom about this from later parts of the Tao text.

二生三

Er Sheng San

Two creates Three

"Er" means *two*. Two is Heaven and Mother Earth. Heaven is yang. Mother Earth is yin. "Sheng" means *creates*. "San" means *three*. "Er sheng san" (pronounced *ur shung sahn*) means *Two creates Three*.

What is Three in Tao teaching? Tao plus yin and yang are Three.

We have learned that in normal creation of Tao, Tao creates One. One creates Two. Two creates Three. Three creates all things.

三万物

San Wan Wu

Three creates all things

"San" means *three*. "Wan wu" means *ten thousand things,* which represents everything in all universes. "San wan wu" (pronounced *sahn wahn woo*) means *Tao, yin, and yang create all things in all universes.*

A man and a woman together create a baby. Heaven and Earth interact to create a soul. Tao, yin, and yang, which are Three, create all things in countless universes.

天地人
Tian Di Ren

Heaven, Earth, Human Being

"Tian" means *Heaven*. "Di" means *Mother Earth*. "Ren" means *human being*.

In Tao teaching, to gather soul, energy, and matter from Heaven, Earth, and human being together to your body is to build your Jin Dan golden light ball. Jin Dan is the Tao secret for all healing, rejuvenation, longevity, and further to immortality.

Earlier in this chapter I shared the sacred sentence and powerful Tao chant, *Tian Di Ren He Yi*—Heaven, Earth, and human being join as one.

To chant Tian Di Ren He Yi (pronounced *tyen dee wren huh yee*) is to bring the soul, energy, and matter of Heaven, Earth, and human being to you, to build your Jin Dan. Listen to me singing on the enclosed CD.

Let us chant now:

Tian Di Ren He Yi
Tian Di Ren He Yi
Tian Di Ren He Yi
Tian Di Ren He Yi
Tian Di Ren He Yi
Tian Di Ren He Yi
Tian Di Ren He Yi . . .

Chant for at least three minutes. There is no time limit. The more you chant, the more benefits you will receive.

神气精
Shen Qi Jing

Soul Energy Matter

One of the most important traditional Tao teachings is Jing Qi Shen (pronounced *jing chee shun*). This has been taught for thousands of years. When I received this Tao text, the Divine and Tao changed the order to Shen Qi Jing.

Jing is matter. It represents all of the matter in the body, including all systems, organs, cells, cell units, DNA, RNA, smallest matter inside the cells, and spaces between the cells. In traditional Tao practice, there are many techniques for producing jing and transforming jing to higher frequencies and purity. The frequencies and purities of jing are unlimited. Serious Tao practitioners devote their whole life to producing and improving the quality of jing.

Qi is energy. It represents all of the energy in the body, including the energies of all systems, organs, cells, cell units, DNA, RNA, smallest matter inside the cells, and spaces between the cells.

Everything is made of matter. Energy is tiny matter. Like jing, qi or energy also has different frequencies and layers of power. Since ancient times, serious Tao practitioners have practiced developing and refining their qi for hours each day.

There are four important times in the day for Tao practitioners to practice:

- 11:00 PM–1:00 AM, which is named Zi time (pronounced *dz*)
- 5:00 AM–7:00 AM, which is named Mao time (pronounced *mow*, rhymes with *now*)

- 11:00 AM–1:00 PM, which is named Wu time (pronounced *woo*)
- 5:00 PM–7:00 PM, which is named You time (pronounced *yo*)

Why are these four time periods important?

Zi time (11:00 PM–1:00 AM) is the gallbladder meridian's time. During these two hours, the energy of the gallbladder is most active. This is also the most yin time of the day. From this time, yang increases more and more, while yin decreases more and more. Therefore, this is a time of yin-yang exchange. All of these factors make Zi time a vital time for energy and spiritual practice.

Mao time (5:00 AM–7:00 AM) is the large intestine meridian's time. During these two hours, the energy of the large intestine is most active. It is early morning, sunrise time. It is the time when the sun and much of nature offer the most pleasant energy. Many Tao practitioners do special practices while facing the sun when it is just beginning to rise. They receive remarkable nourishment. They could increase the frequency and purity of their qi and jing significantly. The frequency and purity of one's qi (energy) and jing (matter) directly affect one's power for healing, preventing sickness, rejuvenating, and prolonging life.

Wu time (11:00 AM–1:00 PM) is the heart meridian's time. During these two hours, the energy of the heart meridian is most active. This is the most yang time of the day. From this time yang will decrease, while yin will increase. This is the other time (with Zi time) of yin-yang exchange. Practicing during times of yin-yang exchange is powerful for healing and rejuvenation.

You time (5:00 PM–7:00 PM) is the kidney meridian's time. During these two hours, the energy of the kidney meridian is most active. In Tao teaching and in traditional Chinese medicine, the kidneys produce jing. The kidneys are in charge of water metabolism. The kidneys store the essence of matter and connect with all of the bones in the body. Tao practice has paid great attention to You time because the kidneys produce the most jing in this time. Therefore, it is a vital time for improving the quality of your jing.

Shen represents all souls in the body, including the body soul and the souls of all systems, organs, cells, cell units, DNA, RNA, smallest matter inside the cells, and spaces between the cells.

Matter is inside the cells. When cells contract, matter vibrates and transforms to energy outside the cells. When cells expand, energy outside the cells vibrates and transforms into matter inside the cells. This transformation between matter inside the cells and energy outside the cells is constant.

Matter and energy are both carriers of message. Message is soul. Matter carries soul. Energy carries soul. A human being has a soul. A system has a soul. An organ has a soul. A cell has a soul. DNA and RNA have souls.

A human being has countless souls. An organ could have billions of souls and more, because every cell, every cell unit, every DNA, every RNA, and every space has a soul.

A human being has a complete soul system. In fact, an animal also has a soul system. Anything and everything in all universes has a soul system.

In ancient Tao teaching and practice, the three words Jing Qi Shen summarize all of the matter, energies, and souls of a being. The purpose of all of the energy and spiritual practices in Tao training is to purify and increase the frequency and vibration of matter, energies, and souls. There are so many powerful stories in history of high-level Tao masters' remarkable abilities for healing, rejuvenation, and longevity. Ancient Tao teaching has many powerful secrets, wisdom, knowledge, and practical techniques.

When I received the Tao text for this book, the Divine and Tao told me to change the order from Jing Qi Shen to Shen Qi Jing. There are divine and Tao secrets within this change of order. In ancient Tao practice, one must do a lot of movement, such as ·tai chi and qi gong, chanting, and meditation to create matter, boost energy, and transform the soul.

Now, in the Soul Power Series, I offer teaching of Shen Qi Jing for the Soul Light Era. The new way to create matter, boost energy, and transform the soul is to start from the soul. In July 2003, the Divine chose me as a servant to transmit divine souls, minds, and bodies of systems, organs, cells, cell units, DNA, RNA, smallest matter inside the cells, and spaces between the cells. This means that the Divine, and now Tao also, offer transmissions or "downloads" of Soul Mind Body Transplants. A Soul Transplant changes an original soul. A Mind Transplant changes a consciousness. A Body Transplant changes energy and matter. After the Divine or Tao downloads Soul Mind Body Transplants to your system, organ, or cells, you no longer have the original system, organ, or cells.

Divine and Tao Soul Mind Body Transplants of systems, organs, and cells carry divine frequency and vibration to transform the frequency and vibration of the original systems, organs, and cells. Divine Mind Transplants transform the consciousness of the original systems, organs, and cells. Divine Body Transplants transform the energy and tiny matter of the original systems, organs, and cells.

Shen Qi Jing signifies the Divine's and Tao's new way for a Tao practitioner to create matter, boost energy, and transform the soul. Divine and Tao Soul Mind Body Transplants are the divine and Tao way for our time. I was extremely fortunate, blessed, and honored to be a chosen one in July 2003 to offer Soul Mind

Body Transplants. In the last seven years I have offered countless Divine and Tao Soul Mind Body Transplants to humanity, pets, and more.

The new way is extremely simple. How can you create matter, boost energy, and transform the soul? This is the way:

Soul Power. Say *hello:*

> *Dear Shen Qi Jing of my whole body, all systems, organs, cells, cell units, DNA, RNA, smallest matter inside the cells, and spaces between the cells,*
> *I love you, honor you, and appreciate you.*
> *You have the power to transform yourselves.*
> *You have the power to uplift your frequency and vibration in order to heal, rejuvenate, and prolong life.*
> *Do a good job.*
> *Thank you.*

Sound Power. Then sing or chant silently or aloud:

> *Shen Qi Jing He Yi* (pronounced *shun chee jing huh yee*)
> *Shen Qi Jing He Yi*
> *Shen Qi Jing He Yi*
> *Shen Qi Jing He Yi*
> *Shen Qi Jing He Yi*
> *Shen Qi Jing He Yi*
> *Shen Qi Jing He Yi . . .*

I taught you this sentence of the Tao text earlier. It means *Shen Qi Jing join as one.* Chant or sing now for three minutes. You can sing with me on the enclosed CD. In fact, chanting or singing this mantra is one of the most important Tao practices for your daily life. To join all souls, all energy, all matter in the body, all systems, all organs, and all cells as one is a sacred practice. It is one of the most powerful practices for boosting energy, stamina, vitality, and immunity. It is also one of the most powerful techniques for self-healing all of your sicknesses, including your physical, emotional, mental, and spiritual bodies. There is no time limit to how much you can chant. The more you chant, the more benefits you could receive.

肾生精

Shen Sheng Jing

Kidneys create Jing

"Shen" means *kidneys*. "Sheng" means *create*. "Jing" means *matter*. Therefore, "Shen sheng jing" means *kidneys create matter*. This matter is for the whole body. Therefore, to strengthen the kidneys is one of the most important secrets for boosting energy, vitality, stamina, and immunity, and for healing, preventing sickness, rejuvenating, and transforming all life.

How can you strengthen your kidneys? Tao practice has many techniques to boost kidney power. One of the most powerful practices is to simply chant *Shen Sheng Jing:*

> *Shen Sheng Jing* (pronounced *shun shung jing*)
> *Shen Sheng Jing*
> *Shen Sheng Jing*
> *Shen Sheng Jing*
> *Shen Sheng Jing*
> *Shen Sheng Jing*
> *Shen Sheng Jing . . .*

Chant for at least three minutes, sliently or aloud, but you need to chant a lot. You can chant anywhere, anytime. The more you chant, the stronger your kidneys will become. The more you chant, the more you will rejuvenate. The more you chant, the more you will prolong your life.

精生髓

Jing Sheng Sui

Jing creates spinal cord

"Jing" means *matter*. "Sheng" means *creates*. "Sui" (pronounced *sway*) means *spinal cord*. Therefore, "Jing sheng sui" means *matter creates spinal cord*.

In Tao teaching and in traditional Chinese medicine, the kidneys produce jing. Jing creates sui. To have strong kidneys is to have strong jing. To have strong jing is to have strong sui. In traditional Chinese medicine, sui includes bone marrow and the spinal cord. They are all interconnected.

Jing goes through two invisible energy holes in the tailbone into the spinal cord to nourish the spinal cord. This is how *jing sheng sui* happens.

Chant *Jing Sheng Sui* to strengthen your jing, your bone marrow, your spinal cord, and beyond. Let us chant now for three minutes:

> *Jing Sheng Sui* (pronounced *jing shung sway*)
> *Jing Sheng Sui*
> *Jing Sheng Sui*
> *Jing Sheng Sui*
> *Jing Sheng Sui*
> *Jing Sheng Sui*
> *Jing Sheng Sui* . . .

Remember to chant a lot. For this kind of practice there is no limit. Chant for your whole life. Chant every day. Chant every moment. The more you chant, the more your healing, rejuvenation, and longevity will benefit.

髓充脑

Sui Chong Nao

Spinal cord fills brain

"Sui" means *spinal cord.* "Chong" means *fill.* "Nao" means *brain.* Therefore, "Sui chong nao" (pronounced *sway chawhng now*) means *spinal cord fills the brain.* In modern anatomy, the brain and spinal cord belong to the central nervous system. In traditional Chinese medicine and Tao teaching, the spinal cord nourishes or "fills" the brain and the brain is the sea of bone marrow. This is a matter connection and an energy connection.

The practice is again simple. Directly chant *Sui Chong Nao* as a mantra.

I have shared a one-sentence secret about Sound Power and chanting mantras:

You *are* the mantra.

What you chant is what you become. What you chant is what will happen. How does it work? I will explain further as we go through more of the Tao text.

Let us chant together now for three minutes to strengthen our spinal cords and nourish our brains:

Sui Chong Nao (pronounced *sway chawhng now*)
Sui Chong Nao

Sui Chong Nao
Sui Chong Nao
Sui Chong Nao
Sui Chong Nao
Sui Chong Nao . . .

Always practice for at least three to five minutes per time. The more you practice, the better. You cannot do this practice too much. In fact, you cannot do it enough. We understand how important the spinal cord and brain are. We need to do this practice a lot. The more you practice, the faster you could heal and rejuvenate.

脑神明
Nao Shen Ming

Mind reaches enlightenment

"Nao" means *brain*. "Shen ming" means *enlightenment*. "Nao shen ming" (pronounced *now shun ming*) is to reach *mind enlightenment*. This is very powerful Tao teaching. In order to reach mind enlightenment, one of the secrets is to chant *Nao Shen Ming*.

Let us chant:

Nao Shen Ming
Nao Shen Ming
Nao Shen Ming
Nao Shen Ming
Nao Shen Ming
Nao Shen Ming
Nao Shen Ming . . .

Chant three to five minutes per time. The longer, the better.
We have learned:

Shen Sheng Jing: Kidneys produce jing
Jing Sheng Sui: Jing creates spinal cord
Sui Chong Nao: Spinal cord fills and nourishes the
    brain
Nao Shen Ming: Reach mind enlightenment

In fact, they are interconnected, one step at a time. They form
a chain reaction. Put them together to chant now:

Shen Sheng Jing (pronounced *shun shung jing*)
Jing Sheng Sui (pronounced *jing shung sway*)
Sui Chong Nao (pronounced *sway chawhng now*)
Nao Shen Ming (pronounced *now shun ming*)

Shen Sheng Jing
Jing Sheng Sui
Sui Chong Nao
Nao Shen Ming

Shen Sheng Jing
Jing Sheng Sui
Sui Chong Nao
Nao Shen Ming

Shen Sheng Jing
Jing Sheng Sui
Sui Chong Nao
Nao Shen Ming

Shen Sheng Jing
Jing Sheng Sui
Sui Chong Nao
Nao Shen Ming

Shen Sheng Jing
Jing Sheng Sui
Sui Chong Nao
Nao Shen Ming

Shen Sheng Jing
Jing Sheng Sui
Sui Chong Nao
Nao Shen Ming . . .

Chant or sing a lot. The more you chant, the better.

炼精化气
Lian Jing Hua Qi

Transform Jing to Qi

"Lian" means *practice*. "Jing" means *matter*. "Hua" means *transform*. "Qi" means *energy*. Energy is tiny matter. As I explained earlier in this chapter, matter inside the cells is constantly transforming to energy outside the cells, and energy outside the cells is constantly transforming back to matter inside the cells.

"Lian jing hua qi" (pronounced *lyen jing hwah chee*) means *transform jing to qi*. It is another ancient Tao term that is very important. It teaches Tao practitioners that they have to increase the frequency and purity of their matter and energy. In ancient Tao teaching, there are many sacred practices to accomplish *lian jing hua qi*. I have benefited greatly from these teachings and practices, but now there is a new way to transform jing to qi. We will use the Four Power Techniques:

Body Power. Sit up straight. Put the tip of your tongue as close as you can to the roof of your mouth without touching it for a few seconds, and then relax your tongue. Put both palms on your lower abdomen.

Soul Power. Say *hello*:

> *Dear soul mind body of Lian Jing Hua Qi,*
> *I love you.*
> *You are a great Tao teaching.*
> *We are honored to have a new way to do Lian Jing*
>   *Hua Qi.*
> *The new way is to chant Lian Jing Hua Qi.*
> *Thank you.*

How does it work? To chant *Lian Jing Hua Qi* is to give a Soul Order. Soul is the boss. Your body's matter will transform to energy automatically. The frequency of your matter and energy will be further transformed all of the time. The more you practice, the more transformation will occur, and the more power you will gain in your jing and your qi.

Mind Power. Visualize golden light in your entire body, from head to toe and skin to bone.

Sound Power. Chant repeatedly:

Lian Jing Hua Qi
Lian Jing Hua Qi
Lian Jing Hua Qi
Lian Jing Hua Qi
Lian Jing Hua Qi
Lian Jing Hua Qi
Lian Jing Hua Qi . . .

Chant for at least three to five minutes. The longer and the more often you chant, the better. Chanting *Lian Jing Hua Qi* is one of the most important daily Tao practices. There is no time limit for this chanting.

炼气化神
Lian Qi Hua Shen

Transform Qi to Shen

"Lian" means *practice*. "Qi" means *energy*. "Hua" means *transform*. "Shen" means *souls*. "Lian qi hua shen" (pronounced *lyen chee hwah shun*) means *transform qi to soul*. Why does ancient Tao teaching seek to transform energy to soul? Because soul has higher frequency. To transform qi to shen is to increase the frequency of energy to the soul level. Our new practice uses the Four Power Techniques:

Body Power. Sit up straight. Put the tip of your tongue as close as you can to the roof of your mouth without touching it for a few seconds, and then relax your tongue. Put both palms on your lower abdomen.

Soul Power. Say *hello:*

Dear soul mind body of Lian Qi Hua Shen,
I love you.
You have the power to transform Qi to Shen.
Do a good job.
I am extremely honored.
Thank you.

Mind Power. Visualize golden light in your entire body, from head to toe and skin to bone.

Sound Power. Chant:

Lian Qi Hua Shen
Lian Qi Hua Shen
Lian Qi Hua Shen
Lian Qi Hua Shen
Lian Qi Hua Shen
Lian Qi Hua Shen
Lian Qi Hua Shen . . .

Chant for at least three to five minutes. The longer you chant, the better. Chanting *Lian Qi Hua Shen* is another one of the most important daily Tao practices. There is no time limit for this chanting.

炼神还虚
Lian Shen Huan Xu

Transform and return Shen to Xu

"Lian" means *practice*. "Shen" means *souls*. "Huan" means *return*. "Xu" means *emptiness*. "Lian shen huan xu" (pronounced *lyen shun hwahn shü*) means *return shen to emptiness*.

After Lian Qi Hua Shen (the previous line, step, and practice), energy reaches the soul level. The next step is Lian Shen Huan Xu. The next layer for the soul is the empty layer.

The important secret I want everybody to know is that Lian Shen Huan Xu happens in the heart. The heart is where this step is accomplished. The Divine and Tao just released this secret to me.

Throughout history, millions of people have studied Tao. Many masters and practitioners have offered many explanations about the processes of Lian Jing Hua Qi, Lian Qi Hua Shen, Lian Shen Huan Xu, and the next line, Lian Xu Huan Tao. The secret has always been where these four steps of transformation occur in the body. I am honored that the Divine and Tao have released major sacred wisdom to me for this book.

Lian Jing Hua Qi happens in the kidneys. Lian Qi Hua Shen happens in the Zhong Gong (pronounced *jawng gawng*), the area above the navel. Lian Shen Huan Xu happens in the heart.

Now let us extend the Tao practice and chant:

> *Lian Jing Hua Qi* (pronounced *lyen jing hwah chee*)
> *Lian Qi Hua Shen* (pronounced *lyen chee hwah shun*)
> *Lian Shen Huan Xu* (pronounced *lyen shun
>   hwahn shü*)
>
> *Lian Jing Hua Qi*
> *Lian Qi Hua Shen*
> *Lian Shen Huan Xu*
>
> *Lian Jing Hua Qi*
> *Lian Qi Hua Shen*
> *Lian Shen Huan Xu*

Lian Jing Hua Qi
Lian Qi Hua Shen
Lian Shen Huan Xu

Lian Jing Hua Qi
Lian Qi Hua Shen
Lian Shen Huan Xu

Lian Jing Hua Qi
Lian Qi Hua Shen
Lian Shen Huan Xu

Lian Jing Hua Qi
Lian Qi Hua Shen
Lian Shen Huan Xu . . .

What is happening when you chant these three lines? Matter transforms into energy in the kidneys. Then the energy will be uplifted to the soul level in the Zhong Gong. Finally, the souls will go into the emptiness condition in the heart. These are vital secrets that the Divine and Tao are releasing in this book. Practice more. The benefits are beyond anyone's comprehension. This will serve humanity in a major way for healing and rejuvenation.

炼虚还道
Lian Xu Huan Tao

Transform and return Xu to Tao

"Lian" means *practice.* "Xu" means *emptiness.* "Huan" means *return.* Tao is The Way. "Lian xu huan Tao" (pronounced *lyen shü hwahn dow*) means *transform and return emptiness to Tao.*

Reaching emptiness happens in the heart. Returning to Tao happens in the brain. Tao is emptiness. Xu is emptiness also. Xu happens in the heart. Tao happens in the brain. The wisdom is that emptiness has layers. To reach Xu is to reach emptiness, but not complete emptiness. Tao is complete emptiness. To transform Xu to Tao is to reach complete emptiness.

The sacred practice is to chant *Lian Xu Huan Tao* in order to reach Tao. Chant with me now for three minutes:

> *Lian Xu Huan Tao*
> *Lian Xu Huan Tao*
> *Lian Xu Huan Tao*
> *Lian Xu Huan Tao*
> *Lian Xu Huan Tao*
> *Lian Xu Huan Tao*
> *Lian Xu Huan Tao* . . .

Chant for at least three to five minutes per time. The more you chant, the better.

Now we can do all four steps of transformation together, from Jing to Qi to Shen to Xu to Tao as one. To chant all four steps together is one of the most important daily Tao practices. Just by chanting these four Tao mantras, you could receive remarkable healing, rejuvenation, and longevity.

Chant now:

> *Lian Jing Hua Qi* (pronounced *lyen jing hwah chee*)
> *Lian Qi Hua Shen* (pronounced *lyen chee hwah shun*)
> *Lian Shen Huan Xu* (pronounced *lyen shun hwahn shü*)
> *Lian Xu Huan Tao* (pronounced *lyen shü hwahn dow*)

Lian Jing Hua Qi
Lian Qi Hua Shen
Lian Shen Huan Xu
Lian Xu Huan Tao

Lian Jing Hua Qi
Lian Qi Hua Shen
Lian Shen Huan Xu
Lian Xu Huan Tao

Lian Jing Hua Qi
Lian Qi Hua Shen
Lian Shen Huan Xu
Lian Xu Huan Tao

Lian Jing Hua Qi
Lian Qi Hua Shen
Lian Shen Huan Xu
Lian Xu Huan Tao

Lian Jing Hua Qi
Lian Qi Hua Shen
Lian Shen Huan Xu
Lian Xu Huan Tao

Lian Jing Hua Qi
Lian Qi Hua Shen
Lian Shen Huan Xu
Lian Xu Huan Tao . . .

Practice for three to five minutes each time. The more you practice, the better. These are very important practices to make you younger. The more you chant, the more you will rejuvenate yourself. This is absolutely one of the sacred practices in the *Tao I* teaching.

合道中

He Tao Zhong

Meld with Tao

"He" means *join as*. Tao is The Way. "Zhong" means *middle* or *center* or *within*. "He Tao zhong" (pronounced *huh dow jawng*) means *completely meld with Tao*.

When your Jing Qi Shen Xu Tao all join as one, you have reached He Tao Zhong. All matter, all energy, all souls meld with Tao. When you meld with Tao:

You will heal all sickness.

You will prevent all sickness.

You will rejuvenate.

You will reach *fan lao huan tong*.

You will prolong your life.

You will move in the direction of immortality.

无穷尽

Wu Qiong Jin

The benefits for all life are endless

"Wu" means *no*. "Qiong jin" means *ending*. "Wu qiong jin" (pronounced *woo chyawng jeen*) means that when you reach and meld with Tao, the benefits are endless.

In ancient Tao books, Tao saints are described as having white hair and baby faces. They have incredible vitality, stamina, immunity, and flexibility. Their Jing Qi Shen have joined as one.

Their wisdom is beyond comprehension. There are many "fairy-tale" stories about these Tao saints.

In the new ten-year Tao training program that I explained in chapter 1, advanced Tao practitioners could gain abilities that are very hard to comprehend. They will be given power from the Divine and Tao to be better servants for humanity, Mother Earth, and all universes.

This is an exciting time. The Tao practices, Tao training, and Tao opportunity are in front of you. I welcome you. Do the Tao practices well. Participate in the Tao training well. Remember to practice a lot. Practice with me using the audio version of this book. Purify your soul, heart, mind, and body. Prepare yourself for the five steps of Tao training. I am honored to share the Divine's and Tao's new secrets, wisdom, knowledge, and practical techniques, together with the essence of ancient Tao teaching and practice. Tao practitioners are blessed to have new divine and Tao opportunities to:

- Heal completely
- Reach *fan lao huan tong* (become a human saint or servant)
- Become a Mother Earth saint or servant
- Become a Heaven saint or servant
- Become a Tao saint or servant

I welcome you to join my Tao training program to benefit all of your life.

道灵宫

Tao Ling Gong

Tao Soul Temple

Tao is The Way. "Ling" means *soul*. "Gong" means *temple*. There-fore, "Tao ling gong" (pronounced *dow ling gawng*) means *Tao soul temple*. In a human being's body, there is a very important place that is located between the heart and the Message Center.

The Message Center, also known as the heart chakra, is a fist-sized energy center located in the center of your chest, behind the sternum. The Message Center is very important for develop-ing soul communication abilities and for healing. It is also the love center, forgiveness center, karma center, emotional center, life transformation center, soul enlightenment center, and more. Clearing blockages from your Message Center and opening and developing your Message Center are key to your ability to com-municate with your own soul and other souls.

The special area between the Message Center and the heart (i.e., just to the left of the Message Center) is named Ling Gong, which means *soul temple*.

At the moment your mother gave birth to you and you cried for the first time, the Akashic Records sent a special soul to your Ling Gong. This soul is named Tian Ming. "Tian" means *Heaven*. "Ming" means *order*. Tian Ming is a special soul that Heaven sends to your Ling Gong to literally guide your whole life. Your Tian Ming also records all of your life experiences, in-cluding your activities, behaviors, and thoughts. Tian Ming re-ports all of your life experiences to the Akashic Records.

Every human being has Tian Ming. Tian Ming carries your heavenly responsibilities in this life. If you follow Tian Ming's order and guidance, your life flourishes. If you go against your Tian Ming's order and guidance, your life could have huge challenges.

Why do I release this one of the highest divine soul secrets to humanity? The purpose is to let humanity know that each of us is literally under Heaven's guidance, even if you do not realize it. It is very important to know this. The best way to receive benefits from this teaching is to open your spiritual channels. If your spiritual channels are open, you can directly communicate with your Tian Ming to understand your true life purpose, especially to know what you should do to accomplish Heaven's tasks for your entire life.

The majority of humanity does not know about Tian Ming. I am teaching the Soul Power Series. I am teaching Tao. I release this secret to let you know there is a special spiritual way to open your spiritual channels so that you can directly receive guidance from your Tian Ming. Your life can then flourish much more.

Tian Ming resides in the Ling Gong. It carries your true life purpose. Tian Ming guides you to do exactly what the Divine, Tao, and Heaven want you to do. Tian Ming has all kinds of power for healing, preventing sickness, rejuvenating, prolonging life, and transforming every aspect of life.

The Divine and Tao are releasing Ling Gong wisdom to give everyone a highest secret for healing, rejuvenating, and transforming all life. Why is it called the Tao Ling Gong? Because the Ling Gong is the Tao place for a human being. Tao is the creator. The Ling Gong has power beyond comprehension. Let me share with you two sacred practices to transform your life.

First, let us apply the Ling Gong for healing. Use the Four Power Techniques:

Body Power. Sit up straight. Put the tip of your tongue as close as you can to the roof of your mouth without touching it for a few seconds, and then relax your tongue. Put one palm over your Ling Gong. Put your other palm over any part of your body that needs healing.

Soul Power. Say *hello:*

> *Dear soul mind body of my Ling Gong,*
> *Dear soul mind body of my Tian Ming,*
> *I love you.*
> *You have the power to heal* _____ (make your
>   request for healing).
> *Thank you.*

Mind Power. Visualize golden light in the area for which you requested healing, or in your entire body.

Sound Power. Chant repeatedly, silently or aloud:

> *Tian Ming heals me. Thank you.*
> *Tian Ming heals me. Thank you.*
> *Tian Ming heals me. Thank you.*
> *Tian Ming heals me. Thank you.*
> *Tian Ming heals me. Thank you.*
> *Tian Ming heals me. Thank you.*
> *Tian Ming heals me. Thank you . . .*

Practice for at least three to five minutes per time. The longer and the more often you practice, the better. The results could shock you. If you receive incredible results quickly, do not be surprised. This divine and Tao secret has never before been released to humanity. I am honored to be your servant to share this secret.

Second, let us apply the Ling Gong for life transformation:

Body Power. Sit up straight. Put the tip of your tongue as close as you can to the roof of your mouth without touching it for a few seconds, and then relax your tongue. Put one palm over your Ling Gong. Put your other palm over your Message Center.

Soul Power. Say *hello:*

> *Dear soul mind body of my Ling Gong,*
> *Dear soul mind body of my Tian Ming,*
> *I love you.*
> *You have the power to transform _____*
>   (make your request for transformation).
> *Thank you.*

Mind Power. Visualize golden light in your entire body (and, if you requested transformation of a relationship, for example, golden light radiating between you and the other person).

Sound Power. Chant repeatedly, silently or aloud:

> *Tian Ming transforms _____* (repeat your
>   request). *Thank you.*
> *Tian Ming transforms _____. Thank you.*
> *Tian Ming transforms _____. Thank you.*
> *Tian Ming transforms _____. Thank you.*

Tian Ming transforms _____. *Thank you.*
Tian Ming transforms _____. *Thank you.*
Tian Ming transforms _____. *Thank you . . .*

Practice for at least three to five minutes per time. The longer and the more often you practice, the better.

信息雪山
Xin Xi Xue Shan

Message Center, Snow Mountain

"Xin xi" (pronounced *sheen shee*) means *Message Center.* "Xue shan" (pronounced *shooeh shahn*) means *Snow Mountain.* I explained the location and the significance of the Message Center earlier in this chapter. The Snow Mountain Area is a foundational energy center at the base of the spine in front of the tailbone. It is known to yogis as the kundalini, to Taoists as the Golden Urn, and to traditional Chinese medicine practitioners as the Ming Men Area, which means the Gate of Life. These are two of the most important energy centers in the body for boosting energy, stamina, vitality, and immunity, as well as for developing your intelligence and opening your spiritual channels.

In ancient Tao teaching, there are two special practices, named Ming Gong (pronounced *ming gawng*) and Xing Gong (pronounced *shing gawng*). Ming Gong is to develop the body's foundational energy. Ming Gong is to increase and purify your energy, vitality, stamina, and immunity to rejuvenate and prolong your life. The sacred area for Ming Gong is the Snow Mountain Area. Xing Gong is to develop intelligence and open your spiritual channels. The sacred area for Xing Gong is the Message Center. Within Ming Gong and Xing Gong, there are many specific techniques and practices in ancient Tao teaching. I honor them all.

I will now share with you a new practice for Ming Gong and Xing Gong together. We will again apply the Four Power Techniques:

Body Power. Sit up straight. Put the tip of your tongue as close as you can to the roof of your mouth without touching it for a few seconds, and then relax your tongue. Put your right fist on your Message Center. Put your left fist on the Snow Mountain Area. Tap both areas continuously.

Soul Power. Say *hello:*

> *Dear soul mind body of my Message Center and Snow*
>   *Mountain Area,*
> *I love you.*
> *You have the power to boost my energy, stamina, vitality, and immunity, to rejuvenate me and prolong my*
>   *life, to develop my intelligence, and to open all of*
>   *my spiritual channels.*
> *Do a good job.*
> *Thank you.*

Mind Power. Visualize golden light shining in your Message Center and Snow Mountain Area.

Sound Power. Chant repeatedly, silently or aloud:

> *Develop Snow Mountain and Message Center.*
> *Develop Snow Mountain and Message Center.*

Develop Snow Mountain and Message Center.
Develop Snow Mountain and Message Center.
Develop Snow Mountain and Message Center.
Develop Snow Mountain and Message Center.
Develop Snow Mountain and Message Center . . .

Chant at least three to five minutes per time. The more you do this practice, the better.

Imagine, this simple practice can develop your Ming Gong and Xing Gong together. To develop your energy, stamina, vitality, immunity, to rejuvenate and prolong your life, to develop your intelligence, and to develop all of your spiritual channels is to completely transform your life. It may be too simple to believe. We are extremely honored that the Divine and Tao have released this secret in the Tao text.

灵语言
Ling Yu Yan

Soul Language

"Ling" means *soul*. "Yu yan" means *language*. So, "Ling yu yan" (pronounced *yü yahn*) means *Soul Language*.

The first book in my Soul Power Series, *Soul Wisdom: Practical Soul Treasures to Transform Your Life*, begins with its most extensive section, several chapters on Soul Language. Soul Language is the language of your soul. There are thousands of languages on Mother Earth. There is only one Soul Language for all of humanity and for all souls in all universes. Let me share the essence of Soul Language secrets, wisdom, knowledge, and practical techniques. This essence can be summarized as *what, why, how*, and *apply:*

- What is Soul Language? (I have just explained this.)
- Why do we need to learn Soul Language?
- How can we develop Soul Language?
- How can we apply Soul Language for healing, rejuvenation, and life transformation?

I learned Soul Language from my most beloved spiritual father, Dr. and Master Zhi Chen Guo, in 1993. I started to teach Soul Language to my students in 1996. Why do we need to learn Soul Language?

Soul Language carries soul frequency and vibration with love, forgiveness, compassion, and light. Soul Language has power beyond words. With Soul Language, you can:

- Heal yourself and heal others, as well as do group healing and remote healing.
- Prevent sickness in the physical, emotional, mental, and spiritual bodies.
- Rejuvenate your soul, heart, mind, and body.
- Transform every aspect of your life, including relationships and finances.

How can you develop your Soul Language?

There is a sacred divine code, 3396815, that we invoke in Chinese, *San San Jiu Liu Ba Yao Wu,* pronounced *sahn sahn jeo leo bah yow woo.* Each number in this code is also a vibrational healing sound. "San" is *three* in Chinese. This number sound stimulates cellular vibration in the chest and lungs. "Jiu" is *nine. Jiu* vibrates the cells in the lower abdomen. "Liu" is *six.* This number sound stimulates cellular vibration in the ribs and sides of the body. "Ba" is the number *eight* in Chinese. It stimulates the cells in and around the navel. "Yao" is one form of the number *one* in Chinese. This number sound vibrates the cells in the brain and the entire head. "Wu" means *five*. Wu stimulates the cells in the stomach, spleen, and mid-abdomen.

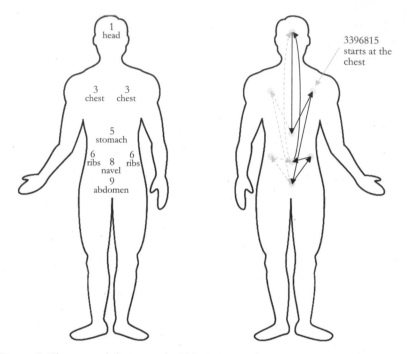

Figure 3. The sacred divine code 3396815 stimulates many areas of the body

San San Jiu Liu Ba Yao Wu is the sacred divine code for bringing out your Soul Language. The technique is extremely simple. It can be summarized in one sentence:

Chant *San San Jiu Liu Ba Yao Wu* as fast as you can to bring out your Soul Language.

Let's do it now. Apply the Four Power Techniques:

Body Power. Sit up straight or stand. Put the tip of your tongue as close as you can to the roof of your mouth without touching it for a few seconds, and then relax your tongue. Put your left palm over your Message Center. Put your right hand in the traditional prayer position, with fingers pointing upward. This is called the Soul Light Era Prayer Position. It is a special signal and connection with Heaven for the Soul Light Era.

Soul Power. Say *hello:*

> *Dear soul mind body of my Message Center,*
> *Dear soul mind body of San San Jiu Liu Ba Yao Wu,*
> *I love you.*
> *You have the power to bring out my Soul Language.*
> *Do a good job.*
> *Thank you.*

Sound Power. Chant out loud as fast as you can:

> *San San Jiu Liu Ba Yao Wu* (pronounced *sahn sahn*
>   *jeo leo bah yow woo*)
> *San San Jiu Liu Ba Yao Wu*
> *San San Jiu Liu Ba Yao Wu*
> *San San Jiu Liu Ba Yao Wu*
> *San San Jiu Liu Ba Yao Wu*
> *San San Jiu Liu Ba Yao Wu*
> *San San Jiu Liu Ba Yao Wu . . .*

When you chant as fast as you can, suddenly a special voice may come out. This special voice could be strange, funny, even shocking if you have never heard Soul Language before. It may be melodic. It may be like clicking sounds. It may be repetitive, for example, "yayayayayayaya . . ." or "ee-ee-ee-ee-ee . . ." or "yoyoyoyoyoyoyoyoyo . . ." or "ahahahahahahahah . . ." Do not have any expectations. Everyone's Soul Language sounds different. Just enjoy your special voice—your soul voice. If your Soul Language does not come out right away, practice more. Let go of wanting or trying to pronounce the sacred divine code correctly. It may take several times or several days of practice to bring out your Soul Language.

You could be very excited after you bring out your Soul Language. You may wonder, "Am I really speaking Soul Language?" This is the way to check. Stop the special voice. Then go back to chanting *San San Jiu Liu Ba Yao Wu* again as fast as you can. In a very short time, your special voice could flow out again. Then you will know that you are really speaking your Soul Language.

Soul Language can be translated into English, French, German, Chinese, and any other language you know. Soul Language is a universal language. More than ten years ago, I was teaching a few advanced students in Toronto. I spoke Soul Language and asked four of my students to translate my Soul Language into English, Spanish, German, and Chinese, respectively, at the same time. Another student spoke English and German fluently. After a few minutes, she exclaimed, "This is amazing! When Master Sha spoke Soul Language, I heard the translation in German and English and they have the same meaning!" In fact, all of my students gave the same translation in their native languages.

This story gives you an idea of why Soul Language is the universal language. It can be translated into any language you know on Mother Earth. One day, I will teach a workshop or retreat without speaking English or Chinese. I will only speak Soul Language. People from all nations around the world who can translate

Soul Language will be able to attend and understand the teaching without physical translators. Isn't that exciting? It will take some time to achieve this goal, but one day it will be achieved. Soul Language will contribute so much to humanity that it is beyond words.

Today, when there is an international conference at, for example, the United Nations, there are many translators to translate the speakers into various languages. One day millions of people on Mother Earth will open their spiritual channels to bring out their Soul Language and to translate Soul Language. We can have workshops, retreats, and conferences where the speaker speaks only Soul Language, and thousands and perhaps millions of people worldwide will be able to understand. That would be fascinating, miraculous, and profound.

There is a story I would like one of my Worldwide Representatives, Marilyn Smith, to share with you now. It is a great example of how Soul Language can be used for communication between two people who speak different languages.

The week before leaving Taiwan to return to California, I visited a Taoist temple with two students from Taipei. As we were going to a special part of the temple, we met two of the Taoist teachers who were outside having a lunch snack. The two students introduced me and explained a little about what I had been teaching. One of the students explained that I could speak and translate Soul Language.

The male Taoist teacher pointed to the other teacher and said, "So can she." He added, "In fact, she can translate as she speaks Soul Language." Our student pointed to me and said, "So can she." At that point, the woman Taoist teacher began to speak to me in Soul Language and I responded to what she was saying. We had a complete conversation in Soul Language.

The topic was the turmoil that exists at this time on Mother Earth and the responses to that turmoil. Those who were sitting at the table were quite amazed. The two students who brought me were also quite amazed. They kept saying, "She"—meaning the Taoist teacher—"does not speak any English." Then they pointed to me and said, "She does not speak any Chinese, and they just had a conversation." It was quite amazing, and all of those who were present were quite surprised.

The woman Taoist teacher was delighted. She had met someone she could converse with using Soul Language. In fact, she was so delighted that she accompanied us to the car, even though it was raining. This was a wonderful experience of using Soul Language to communicate with a person whose language you do not know.

Soul Language is the pure soul voice. If your spiritual channels are open, you will understand its meaning. If your spiritual channels are not open, you will not understand its meaning. Soul Language translation is one of the most important spiritual communication abilities. The first two books in my Soul Power Series, *Soul Wisdom: Practical Soul Treasures to Transform Your Life* and *Soul Communication: Opening Your Spiritual Channels for Success and Fulfillment,* have extensive teachings on how to open your spiritual channels and translate Soul Language.

Your Soul Language may have just come out. You could be fascinated to know what your soul is saying. You cannot wait to translate your Soul Language. You really want to open your spiritual channels. Read my other books. Join the Open Spiritual

Channels classes that I, my Worldwide Representatives, and certified Divine Master Teachers and Healers offer. Your spiritual journey could move further. You could gain deeper spiritual wisdom after you open your spiritual channels.

Some of you may have just brought out your Soul Language after a few minutes of practice. If your Soul Language did not come out, practice again. You may need to practice a few times to bring out your Soul Language. You may need to practice a few times a day for a few days to bring out your Soul Language. Be patient. Practice more. Generally speaking, your Soul Language will flow out quickly.

After bringing out your Soul Language, you can apply Soul Language for healing, rejuvenation, and life transformation. Let us first apply Soul Language for healing. Use the Four Power Techniques:

Body Power. Sit up straight or stand. Put the tip of your tongue as close as you can to the roof of your mouth without touching it for a few seconds, and then relax your tongue. Put your left palm over your Message Center. Put your right hand in the traditional prayer position, with fingers pointing upward. (Recall this is the Soul Light Era Prayer Position.)

Soul Power. Say *hello:*

> *Dear soul mind body of my Soul Language,*
> *I love you.*
> *Please heal my* _____ (make your healing
>   request).
> *Do a good job.*
> *Thank you.*

Mind Power. Visualize golden light shining in the organ or part of the body for which you requested healing.

Sound Power. Chant as quickly as possible.

> San San Jiu Liu Ba Yao Wu (pronounced *sahn sahn*
>   *jeo leo bah yow woo*)
> San San Jiu Liu Ba Yao Wu
> San San Jiu Liu Ba Yao Wu
> San San Jiu Liu Ba Yao Wu
> San San Jiu Liu Ba Yao Wu
> San San Jiu Liu Ba Yao Wu
> San San Jiu Liu Ba Yao Wu . . .

When your Soul Language comes out, continue to chant your Soul Language for three to five minutes. The more often and the longer you practice, the better.

You could be very surprised by the healing results after a few short minutes of practice. Practice more to restore your health as quickly as possible. If you do not feel any results right away, it does not mean that Soul Language does not work for healing. Practice more to receive the benefits as soon as possible.

Now let us apply Soul Language for rejuvenation. Use the Four Power Techniques:

Body Power. Sit up straight or stand. Put the tip of your tongue as close as you can to the roof of your mouth without touching it for a few seconds, and then relax your tongue. Put your left palm over your Message Center. Put your right hand in the traditional prayer position, with fingers pointing upward.

Soul Power. Say *hello:*

> *Dear soul mind body of my Soul Language,*
> *I love you.*
> *Please rejuvenate my soul, heart, mind, and body.*
> *Do a good job.*
> *Thank you.*

Mind Power. Visualize golden light shining in your soul, heart, mind, and body for rejuvenation.

Sound Power. Chant as quickly as possible:

> *San San Jiu Liu Ba Yao Wu*
> *San San Jiu Liu Ba Yao Wu*
> *San San Jiu Liu Ba Yao Wu*
> *San San Jiu Liu Ba Yao Wu*
> *San San Jiu Liu Ba Yao Wu*
> *San San Jiu Liu Ba Yao Wu*
> *San San Jiu Liu Ba Yao Wu . . .*

When your Soul Language comes out, continue to chant your Soul Language for three to five minutes. The more often and the longer you practice, the better.

Next, apply Soul Language to transform a relationship. Use the Four Power Techniques:

Body Power. Sit up straight. Put the tip of your tongue as close as you can to the roof of your mouth without touching it for a few seconds, and then relax your tongue. Put your left palm over your

Message Center. Put your right hand in the traditional prayer position, with fingers pointing upward.

Mind Power. Visualize golden light shining and connecting you and the other person.

Soul Power. Say *hello:*

> *Dear soul mind body of* _____ (name the
>   other person),
> *Dear soul mind body of my Soul Language,*
> *I love you, honor you, and appreciate you.*
> *Please heal and transform the relationship between me*
>   *and* _____ (name the person).
> *Do a good job.*
> *I am very grateful.*
> *Thank you.*

Sound Power. Chant as quickly as possible:

> *San San Jiu Liu Ba Yao Wu*
> *San San Jiu Liu Ba Yao Wu*
> *San San Jiu Liu Ba Yao Wu*
> *San San Jiu Liu Ba Yao Wu*
> *San San Jiu Liu Ba Yao Wu*
> *San San Jiu Liu Ba Yao Wu*
> *San San Jiu Liu Ba Yao Wu . . .*

When your Soul Language comes out, continue to chant Soul Language for three to five minutes. The more you practice, the better.

How simply you could transform a relationship with this powerful practice! Now let us apply Soul Language to transform your finances. At this time, early 2010, humanity and Mother Earth have many financial challenges. Soul Language can do wonders to boost your finances. Why? Because Soul Language carries soul frequency with love, forgiveness, compassion, and light. Soul frequency can transform the frequency of your business and finances. Love melts all blockages and transforms your business and finances. Forgiveness brings inner peace and inner joy to you, your whole business team, your customers, and your partners. Compassion boosts energy, stamina, and vitality for you and your business team. Light heals the challenges facing your business team, prevents future difficulties, and transforms all challenging issues in your business and finances.

To apply Soul Language to transform your finances, use the Four Power Techniques:

Body Power. Sit up straight. Put the tip of your tongue as close as you can to the roof of your mouth without touching it for a few seconds, and then relax your tongue. Put your left palm over your Message Center and your right hand in the traditional prayer position, with fingers pointing upward. (This is the Soul Light Era Prayer Position.)

Soul Power. Say *hello:*

> *Dear soul mind body of my business or finances* (name the business),
> *Dear soul mind body of my Soul Language,*
> *I love you.*

You have the power to transform my business and my
   finances.
Do a good job.
I am very grateful.
Thank you.

Mind Power. Visualize golden light shining in your business and your finances.

Sound Power. Chant as quickly as possible, until your Soul Language comes out:

   San San Jiu Liu Ba Yao Wu
   San San Jiu Liu Ba Yao Wu
   San San Jiu Liu Ba Yao Wu
   San San Jiu Liu Ba Yao Wu
   San San Jiu Liu Ba Yao Wu
   San San Jiu Liu Ba Yao Wu
   San San Jiu Liu Ba Yao Wu . . .

After your Soul Language comes out, continue to chant Soul Language for at least three to five minutes. The more you practice, the better.

Soul Language is the soul's voice. Now we are in the Soul Light Era. The Soul Light Era will shine Soul Language. Soul Language is a major treasure for transforming all life in the Soul Light Era.

Apply Soul Language to transform your health.

Apply Soul Language to rejuvenate your soul, heart, mind, and body.

Apply Soul Language to transform your relationships.

Apply Soul Language to transform your business and finances.

Apply Soul Language to transform your family.

Apply Soul Language to transform your organization.

Apply Soul Language to transform a city.

Apply Soul Language to transform a country.

Apply Soul Language to transform Mother Earth.

Apply Soul Language to transform all universes.

Apply Soul Language to bring love, peace, and harmony to humanity, Mother Earth, and all universes.

灵信通

Ling Xin Tong

Soul Communication

"Ling" means *soul*. "Xin" means *message*. "Tong" means *communicate well*. "Ling xin tong" (pronounced *ling sheen tawng*) means *soul communication*.

As I explained earlier in this chapter, a human being has a soul system, including a body soul, the souls of systems, organs, cells, cell units, DNA, RNA, smallest matter inside the cells, and spaces between the cells. A human brain has billions of cells. This means that a brain has billions of cell souls. Each cell has many cell units and uncountable smallest matter. This means there are billions and many more souls of cell units and smallest matter in a single cell.

If there are billions of souls within a single cell, can we imagine how many souls there are in one's body? Every organ has millions or billions of cells. It is impossible to count how many cells there are in one's body.

The important wisdom is that *all the souls in one's body communicate with one another*. Many people have not realized the wisdom that souls communicate on their own all the time. Souls communicate with the mind. Souls communicate with the body. If there is great balance in communication among one's soul, mind, and body, one is likely to be healthy. If there are communication blockages or disharmonies among one's soul, mind, and body, one's health could be affected instantly.

In the Soul Power Series, one of the foundational wisdoms for healing can be summarized in one sentence:

**Heal the soul first; then healing of the
mind and body will follow.**

In all of my books, I share with humanity how to do soul healing. I have shared many soul healing techniques. There are hundreds of thousands of heart-touching and moving stories worldwide from people who applied soul healing techniques to heal themselves and to heal others. I welcome you to read these stories on my Facebook page ("Dr. Sha"), and on the storyboard on my website (www.DrSha.com). There are thousands of heart-touching and moving stories and experiences from the application of many different soul healing techniques, including singing Soul Songs, listening to my Soul Songs, Soul Dance, Soul Operation, Say Hello Healing, offering others remote soul healing, and more. These stories could inspire you deeply. You could really want to learn more and try to self-heal and to help others heal. These stories touch me deeply. I am honored and grateful to share soul healing with humanity.

Let me share another major one-sentence secret now:

**If the soul of a person becomes sick, then
sickness of the mind and body will follow.**

A human being has many layers of souls. If the soul of a cell gets sick, sickness of that cell will follow. If the soul of an organ gets sick, sickness of that organ will follow. If the soul of a system gets sick, sickness of that system will follow. If a body soul gets sick, sickness of the person will follow.

I offered an important teaching in the first chapter, "Soul Basics," of the authority book of my Soul Power Series, *The Power of Soul: The Way to Heal, Rejuvenate, Transform, and Enlighten All Life:* **The soul is a golden light being.** A body soul is a golden light being. The soul of a system, organ, or cell is also a golden light being. They differ in size. A body soul is larger than a system soul, which is larger than an organ soul, which in turn is larger than a cell soul.

How can one tell if a soul is sick? A spiritual being with advanced spiritual abilities can see souls with an open Third Eye. I have trained hundreds of students worldwide who can see these golden light beings. In my travels worldwide since 1992, I have held hundreds of workshops and retreats. I have met quite a few people with open Third Eyes who are not my students.

If one can see the golden light being, one can also see changes in the golden light being's color. The color can change from gold to gray or dark. The golden light being can look tired, weak, or sad. The golden light being can look angry. If the golden light being's appearance changes in any of these ways, that tells you that the golden light being is sick, whether it is the soul of a person, a system, an organ, or a cell.

When a soul is sick, it does not mean that the body is already sick. Before conventional medicine can diagnose a liver sickness, for example, the soul of the liver changes first. How? The color of the soul changes. A healthy soul of the liver is vibrant, full of light, and gold in color. An unhealthy soul of the liver could be gray or dark. The size of the soul will also change if it is unwell. It will shrink and look weak and tired. However, even if you can see that a person's liver soul has changed in color and looks tired, that person could still have completely normal liver function. A medical checkup may not reveal any symptoms or signs of a liver condition.

A few months later, though, or possibly even one or two years later, that person could have a medically verifiable liver condition. This tells us that:

**The soul of an organ gets sick first; then
sickness of the organ will follow.**

All of my books have shared with the humanity that the soul can heal and transform all life. This is *soul over matter*.

The important wisdom to learn now is that when a soul gets sick, sickness of the body, system, organ, or cell will follow. Earlier I shared the foundational wisdom of soul healing: *Heal the soul first; then healing of the mind and body will follow*. If we know this wisdom, how do we prevent soul sickness? The one-sentence secret for preventing soul sickness is:

To communicate with your souls is to prevent sickness.

Everything has a soul, including our organs, systems, cells, cell units, DNA, RNA, smallest matter in the cells, and spaces between the cells. Everything has consciousness also. Everyone and everything is a universal servant. Each of these souls loves to serve. All we have to do is ask! This is the way to do it. Apply the Four Power Techniques to do soul communication in order to prevent soul sickness:

Body Power. Sit up straight. Put the tip of your tongue as close as you can to the roof of your mouth without touching it. We can use soul communication to request healing, rejuvenation, and transformation, and to receive wisdom from the highest spiritual beings. As I explained earlier in this chapter, the Message Center (heart chakra) is very important for developing soul communication abilities and for healing.

Soul Power. Say *hello:*

> *Dear souls of my body, systems, organs, cells, cell units,*
>   *DNA, RNA, smallest matter inside the cells, and*
>   *spaces between the cells,*
> *I love you, honor you, and appreciate you.*
> *You have the power to prevent sickness in my body, sys-*
>   *tems, organs, cells, cell units, DNA, RNA, smallest*
>   *matter inside the cells, and spaces between the cells.*
> *Do a good job.*
> *Thank you.*

Mind Power. Visualize golden light vibrating in your entire body, from head to toe, skin to bone.

Sound Power. Chant repeatedly:

> *Souls of my body, systems, organs, cells, cell units,*
>   *DNA, RNA, smallest matter inside the cells, and*
>   *spaces between the cells, heal yourselves and prevent*
>   *sickness. Thank you.*
> *Souls of my body, systems, organs, cells, cell units,*
>   *DNA, RNA, smallest matter inside the cells, and*

spaces between the cells, heal yourselves and prevent
sickness. Thank you.
Souls of my body, systems, organs, cells, cell units,
    DNA, RNA, smallest matter inside the cells, and
    spaces between the cells, heal yourselves and prevent
    sickness. Thank you.
Souls of my body, systems, organs, cells, cell units,
    DNA, RNA, smallest matter inside the cells, and
    spaces between the cells, heal yourselves and prevent
    sickness. Thank you.
Souls of my body, systems, organs, cells, cell units,
    DNA, RNA, smallest matter inside the cells, and
    spaces between the cells, heal yourselves and prevent
    sickness. Thank you.
Souls of my body, systems, organs, cells, cell units,
    DNA, RNA, smallest matter inside the cells, and
    spaces between the cells, heal yourselves and prevent
    sickness. Thank you.
Souls of my body, systems, organs, cells, cell units,
    DNA, RNA, smallest matter inside the cells, and
    spaces between the cells, heal yourselves and prevent
    sickness. Thank you. . . .

Hao!

Chant for three to five minutes per time. The longer and the
more often you chant, the better.

In some of my previous books, I shared a powerful ancient
one-sentence healing secret that is extremely simple:

Jin guang zhao ti, bai bing xiao chu

"Jin" means *gold*. "Guang" means *light*. "Zhao" means *shines*. "Ti" means *body*. "Bai" means *one hundred,* which in Chinese represents *all* or *everything* or *everyone*. "Bing" means *sicknesses*. "Xiao chu" means *remove*.

Therefore, "Jin guang zhao ti, bai bing xiao chu" (pronounced *jeen gwahng jow tee, bye bing shee-ow choo*) means *golden light shines, all sickness disappears*. Why is golden light so powerful that it can remove all sickness? Because golden light is spiritual light. This ancient statement has been one of the key spiritual wisdoms for healing for thousands of years. Many people in history have heard this statement. They have treated this statement as theory and wisdom, but they have not applied this wisdom enough to heal sicknesses.

How do you apply this wisdom for healing all sickness? This is the way I am offering and sharing with you and humanity. The way is so simple. My teaching is simple and practical, and it works. The simplest technique is the best technique. I have shared this wisdom with you in this book. This can be summarized in one sentence:

Da Tao zhi jian

"Da" means *big*. Tao is The Way. "Zhi" means *extremely*. "Jian" means *simple*. Therefore, "Da Tao zhi jian" means *The Big Way is extremely simple*. Many people on Mother Earth look for complicated answers. They believe that solving problems, spiritual development, and healing require a complicated process, wisdom, or knowledge. They have not realized that the truth is extremely simple. If you have not found the truth in one aspect of life, it is very difficult to flourish in that aspect of your life. Every aspect of life has truth. The truth of that aspect of life is the Xiao

Tao (Small Tao) of that aspect of life. "Da Tao" means *Big Tao*. Da Tao is The Way of all life and all universes.

Da Tao zhi jian: *The Big Way is extremely simple*. If you understand Da Tao zhi jian, apply Da Tao zhi jian to benefit your healing. How do you apply Da Tao zhi jian for healing all sickness? This is the way to do it. Apply the Four Power Techniques:

Body Power. Sit up straight. Put the tip of your tongue as close as you can to the roof of your mouth without touching it. Put one fist on your Message Center. Put the other fist on your Snow Mountain Area, the area of your lower back just above the tailbone. Tap both areas simultaneously.

Soul Power. Say *hello:*

> *Dear soul mind body of* Jin Guang Zhao Ti, Bai Bing
>   Xiao Chu,
> *I love you, honor you, and appreciate you.*
> *You have the power to heal all of my sicknesses.*
> *Do a good job!*
> *I am so honored that you can heal all of my sicknesses.*
> *Thank you.*

Sound Power. Chant repeatedly, silently or aloud:

> *Jin Guang Zhao Ti, Bai Bing Xiao Chu* (pronounced
>   *jeen gwahng jow tee, bye bing shee-ow choo*)
> *Jin Guang Zhao Ti, Bai Bing Xiao Chu*
> *Jin Guang Zhao Ti, Bai Bing Xiao Chu*
> *Jin Guang Zhao Ti, Bai Bing Xiao Chu*
> *Jin Guang Zhao Ti, Bai Bing Xiao Chu*

Jin Guang Zhao Ti, Bai Bing Xiao Chu
Jin Guang Zhao Ti, Bai Bing Xiao Chu . . .

Hao!

Chant for three to five minutes per time. The longer and the more often you chant, the better. In fact, if you were to chant *Jin Guang Zhao Ti, Bai Bing Xiao Chu* silently in your heart nonstop, you would hardly believe the healing results.

Now let me lead you to sing this sacred Tao healing mantra:

Jin Guang Zhao Ti, Bai Bing Xiao Chu
Jin Guang Zhao Ti, Bai Bing Xiao Chu
Jin Guang Zhao Ti, Bai Bing Xiao Chu
Jin Guang Zhao Ti, Bai Bing Xiao Chu
Jin Guang Zhao Ti, Bai Bing Xiao Chu
Jin Guang Zhao Ti, Bai Bing Xiao Chu
Jin Guang Zhao Ti, Bai Bing Xiao Chu . . .

Sing at least three to five minutes per time. The longer you sing, and the more often, the better. You can sing silently or aloud.

Now I am releasing another major secret for healing all sickness. Three secrets for spiritual and energy healing have been applied since ancient times. These three secrets are:

- **Kou Mi.** "Kou" means *mouth*. "Mi" means *secret*. "Kou mi" (pronounced *koe mee*) means *mouth secret*. "Mouth secret" means chanting healing mantras. There have been many major mantras in history. In my book, *Power Healing: The Four Keys to Energizing*

Your Body, Mind and Spirit, I shared a few of the most important mantras for humanity. They include:

o **Ling Guang Pu Zhao.** "Ling" means *soul.* "Guang" means *light.* "Pu" means *widely.* "Zhao" means *shining.* "Ling Guang Pu Zhao" (pronounced *ling gwahng poo jow*) means *shining soul light.*

o **Na Mo A Mi Tuo Fuo.** "Na mo" means *respect and honor.* "A Mi Tuo Fuo," is the Chinese name of the buddha who leads the Pure Land. He is more commonly called Amitabha. Na Mo A Mi Tuo Fuo (pronounced *nah moe ah mee twaw fwaw*) is one of the most popular mantras in history. It has been chanted by millions of people. It is a powerful mantra for purifying soul, heart, mind, and body.

o **Weng Ma Ni Ba Ma Hong.** Pronounced *wung mah nee bah mah hawhng,* this is the six-word enlightenment mantra of Guan Yin, the Bodhisattva of Compassion. Guan Yin's new name in the Soul Light Era is Ling Hui Sheng Shi (pronounced *ling hway shung shr*). "Ling" means *soul.* "Hui" means *intelligence.* "Sheng" means *saint.* "Shi" means *servant.* So, "Ling Hui Sheng Shi" means *soul intelligence saint servant.*

o **Weng Ar Hong.** This is one of the most powerful Tibetan healing mantras, vibrating all the major areas and organs of the body to promote the flow of qi.

o **3396815 (San San Jiu Liu Ba Yao Wu).** This sacred divine code was given to my beloved spiritual father, Master Zhi Chen Guo, by the Divine about 35 years ago. Pronounced *sahn sahn jeo leo bah yow woo,* it is the code to unlock one's Soul Language and more.

- o **God's Light.** This mantra was given to me by the Divine as I was writing my book *Power Healing.* That was divine creation on the spot.

- **Shen Mi.** "Shen" means *body.* "Mi" means *secret.* "Shen mi" refers to *secret body and hand positions for healing.* These body secrets include special positions while lying down, sitting, or standing. Hand secrets include mudras, the One Hand Near, One Hand Far Body Power secret, the One Hand Healing method, and many more.

- **Yi Mi.** "Yi" means *thinking.* "Mi" means *secret.* "Yi mi" means *thinking secret.* This refers to focusing the mind, using concentration, intention, and visualization for healing.

Many healing modalities apply one of these techniques. For example, there are modalities that use sound, that use specific body or hand positions, or that use creative visualization. What makes this soul healing system unique is that it applies all three techniques simultaneously.

Ancient spiritual teaching is "San mi he yi." "San" means *three.* "Mi" means *secret.* "He" means *to join as.* "Yi" means *one.* "San mi he yi" (pronounced *sahn mee huh yee*) means to *join Kou Mi, Shen Mi, and Yi Mi as one to do spiritual and energy practice for healing.* San mi he yi is very important.

Let me give an example to show you how to apply San Mi together to open your Third Eye:

Shen Mi (Body Power). Sit up straight. Put the tip of your tongue as close as you can to the roof of your mouth without touching it. Put both palms in lotus hands position as follows. Place your hands in front of your Message Center in the center of your chest. Gently touch the heels of your hands together, gently touch your thumbs together, and gently touch your little fingers together. Open all of your fingers, as though you were holding a beautiful lotus flower. See figure 4.

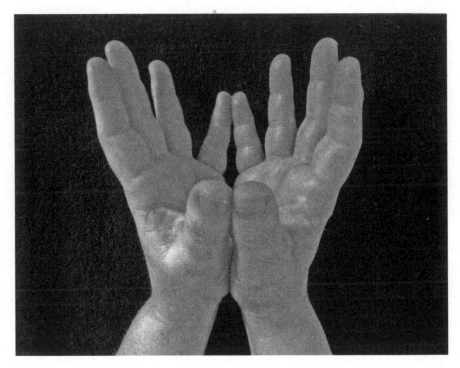

Figure 4. Lotus Hands Body Power position

Yi Mi (Mind Power). Visualize golden light shining in your Third Eye, which is located in the center of your head, in the area of the pineal gland.

Kou Mi (Sound Power). Sing or chant:

> *Weng Ma Ni Ba Ma Hong*
> *Weng Ma Ni Ba Ma Hong*
> *Weng Ma Ni Ba Ma Hong*
> *Weng Ma Ni Ba Ma Hong*
> *Weng Ma Ni Ba Ma Hong*
> *Weng Ma Ni Ba Ma Hong*
> *Weng Ma Ni Ba Ma Hong . . .*

Chant for at least three to five minutes per time; the longer, the better. To open your Third Eye you need to chant a lot, for thirty minutes or more per time.

Let us practice together now.

Sit up straight with both palms in the "lotus hands" position as described above. Close your eyes. Visualize golden light shining in your Third Eye and sing or chant:

> *Weng Ma Ni Ba Ma Hong*
> *Weng Ma Ni Ba Ma Hong*
> *Weng Ma Ni Ba Ma Hong*
> *Weng Ma Ni Ba Ma Hong*
> *Weng Ma Ni Ba Ma Hong*
> *Weng Ma Ni Ba Ma Hong*
> *Weng Ma Ni Ba Ma Hong . . .*

Chant much more to receive great benefits for opening your Third Eye.

To open your Third Eye, you need great foundational energy. Many spiritual beings with an open Third Eye are constantly tired because they do not have enough foundational energy. Let me show you how to apply San Mi to boost your foundational energy, stamina, vitality, and immunity:

Shen Mi (Body Power). Stand with your feet shoulder width apart. Bend your knees slightly. Put both palms on your lower abdomen, just below your navel. Remember the one-sentence secret of Body Power:

Where you put your hands is where energy goes.

Therefore, this position helps to move energy to the Lower Dan Tian to build your Jin Dan, your golden light ball. As I explained earlier in this chapter, Jin Dan is one of the greatest treasures in all of Tao training in history.

Yi Mi (Mind Power). Visualize a golden light ball forming in your lower abdomen. This is your Jin Dan. Visualize light from Heaven and Earth pouring into your Jin Dan and Lower Dan Tian.

Kou Mi (Sound Power). Sing or chant repeatedly:

Weng Ma Ni Ba Ma Hong
Weng Ma Ni Ba Ma Hong
Weng Ma Ni Ba Ma Hong
Weng Ma Ni Ba Ma Hong
Weng Ma Ni Ba Ma Hong
Weng Ma Ni Ba Ma Hong
Weng Ma Ni Ba Ma Hong . . .

Sing or chant for at least three to five minutes per time. Chant as long as you can; the longer, the better. Chanting this mantra has great benefits for spiritual and energy development. The more you chant, the more benefits you could receive. If you do this practice for thirty minutes, you will definitely understand the power of applying San Mi (Body Power, Sound Power, and Mind Power) together.

Hao!
Thank you. Thank you. Thank you.

The mantras I have given you in this section are powerful universal servants for humanity. You can chant any of these mantras to achieve different results. In the first practice, we chanted *Weng Ma Ni Ba Ma Hong* to open the Third Eye. In the second practice, we chanted *Weng Ma Ni Ba Ma Hong* to build the Jin Dan, which builds foundational energy, stamina, vitality, and immunity, and which in turn also benefits healing, rejuvenation, and longevity.

We applied the same Kou Mi (Sound Power), that is, we chanted the same mantra, in both practices. The difference was in the Shen Mi (Body Power). In the first practice, we moved energy toward the Third Eye. In the second practice, we moved energy toward the lower abdomen. These illustrate how to use different hand positions to achieve different results.

We also used different Yi Mi (Mind Power). We focused our mind on the Third Eye in the first practice but on the lower abdomen in the second practice. Remember the one-sentence secret of Mind Power:

**Where you focus your mind is where
you boost energy and heal.**

Therefore, to focus your mind on different areas of the body is to achieve different results. You can achieve great results from each of these two practices using the same mantra, but you must vary the Mind Power and Body Power to align with the goal of the practice.

I use these two practices to explain San Mi He Yi. To apply one secret is powerful. To apply all three secrets together is much more powerful. Therefore, in ancient Buddhism, Taoism, Confucianism, qi gong, and other spiritual and energy practices, the greatest secret is to apply San Mi simultaneously to develop energy, vitality, immunity, and stamina, and to heal, rejuvenate, and prolong your life.

Now let me release another major secret to you and all humanity. How can you heal all sickness? I will give you another way to heal all kinds of sickness.

There are thousands, hundreds of thousands, or millions of secrets, wisdom, knowledge, and practical techniques in spiritual and energy practice. There is no way to learn all of them. An entire lifetime would not be enough. However, there is a secret way to gather the essence of all of the secrets, wisdom, knowledge, and practical techniques together to heal, rejuvenate, and prolong life. I am honored to share this wisdom with you.

Everything has a soul, mind, and body. I have taught this wisdom since *Power Healing: The Four Keys to Energizing Your Body, Mind and Spirit* was published in 2002. I teach this wisdom in every book of my Soul Power Series and in all of my workshops and retreats worldwide. Use this wisdom to gather all of the secrets, wisdom, knowledge, and practical techniques in history to heal all sickness:

Soul Power. Say *hello:*

Dear all San Mi in history,
I love you, honor you, and appreciate you.
You have unlimited power, secrets, wisdom, knowledge,
    and practical techniques for healing and rejuvena-
    tion.
Please heal my _____ (state your request).
Do a good job.
I am extremely grateful.
Thank you.

Mind Power. Visualize golden light vibrating in your entire body, from head to toe, skin to bone.

Sound Power. Chant silently or aloud:

All San Mi heal my _____ (state your re-
    quest). *Thank you.*
All San Mi heal my _____ (state your re-
    quest). *Thank you.*
All San Mi heal my _____ (state your re-
    quest). *Thank you.*
All San Mi heal my _____ (state your re-
    quest). *Thank you.*
All San Mi heal my _____ (state your re-
    quest). *Thank you.*
All San Mi heal my _____ (state your re-
    quest). *Thank you.*
All San Mi heal my _____ (state your re-
    quest). *Thank you . . .*

For example, if you have knee pain, chant:

All San Mi heal my knees. Thank you.
All San Mi heal my knees. Thank you.
All San Mi heal my knees. Thank you.
All San Mi heal my knees. Thank you.
All San Mi heal my knees. Thank you.
All San Mi heal my knees. Thank you.
All San Mi heal my knees. Thank you . . .

Invoking "All San Mi" gathers all secrets, wisdom, knowledge, and practical techniques since ancient times. As you can imagine, there is unlimited power in San Mi. You are calling the soul, mind, and body of San Mi, which means you are gathering all spiritual and healing power to heal you. This is the *power of soul.*

You can also chant like this:

All San Mi heal all of my sicknesses. Thank you.
All San Mi heal all of my sicknesses. Thank you.
All San Mi heal all of my sicknesses. Thank you.
All San Mi heal all of my sicknesses. Thank you.
All San Mi heal all of my sicknesses. Thank you.
All San Mi heal all of my sicknesses. Thank you.
All San Mi heal all of my sicknesses. Thank you . . .

As with all the practices, chant three to five minutes per time. The longer and the more often you chant, the better. The power of this mantra is beyond imagination. Practice more and you will gain much deeper understanding. You could experience profound transformation. You could have many "aha!" moments during your practice.

In fact, this sacred and secret practice can be summarized in one brief sentence:

San Mi heals me.

Alternatively, it can be summarized in one sentence with a few more details:

San Mi heals, prevents sickness, rejuvenates, prolongs life, and transforms every aspect of life, including relationships and finances, and also enlightens soul, heart, mind, and body.

Repeat this chant as much as you can. You cannot imagine enough the benefits that you could receive from this secret practice. Do you love this simple practice?

Always remember to express gratitude when and after you practice. You are invoking the souls of very high spiritual beings and other unconditional universal servants to assist your healing, rejuvenation, prolongation of life, and transformation. Your gratitude moves Heaven, and you will be blessed more.

When my book *Power Healing: The Four Keys to Energizing Your Body, Mind and Spirit* was published, the Divine guided me to summarize the soul healing techniques for self-healing and healing of others, including remote healing techniques, by teaching the Four Power Techniques. They are Body Power, Sound Power, Mind Power, and Soul Power. I have shared the Four Power Techniques in all of my books since.

Body Power refers to special body or hand positions for healing and boosting energy. Body Power and Shen Mi are different names for the same thing. Sound Power is Kou Mi in ancient practice, and refers to chanting mantras for healing, boosting energy, and transforming relationships and finances. Sound Power and Kou Mi are the same thing. Mind Power is to apply creative visualization for healing and life transformation. Mind Power is Yi Mi in ancient practice. They are the same thing, but with different names.

In my book *Power Healing,* the Divine guided me to share with humanity another healing technique which is the single most important healing technique. This healing technique is named Soul Power. It applies the power of inner souls and outer souls for self-healing, healing others, boosting energy, stamina, vitality, and immunity, rejuvenating, and prolonging life.

Inner souls include the souls of your body's systems, organs, cells, cell units, DNA, RNA, smallest matter inside the cells, and spaces between the cells. Outer souls include the souls of nature and the souls of spiritual fathers and mothers in Heaven and all universes. Other outer souls are the souls of mountains and oceans, the souls of the sun, the moon, the Big Dipper, and the souls of countless stars, planets, galaxies, and universes. Soul Power applies the power of both inner and outer souls for healing, rejuvenation, and life transformation.

Spiritual fathers and mothers include the souls of healing angels, ascended masters, holy saints, Taoist saints, ancient saints, buddhas, lamas, gurus, Hawaiian kahunas, and all spiritual fathers and mothers on Mother Earth and in all layers of Heaven.

Soul Power includes countless souls. Remember that applying Soul Power includes invoking the souls of the Divine and Tao. The Divine and Tao are creators who carry power and abilities beyond any words, comprehension, or imagination.

Now I will reveal another top secret to heal all sickness. This is the way to do it:

Soul Power. Say *hello:*

> *Dear soul mind body of all Four Power Techniques,*
> *I love you, honor you, and appreciate you.*
> *Please heal all of my sicknesses.*
> *I am extremely grateful.*
> *Thank you very much.*

Sound Power. Chant repeatedly, silently or aloud:

> *Four Power Techniques heal all of my sicknesses.*
>   *Thank you.*
> *Four Power Techniques heal all of my sicknesses.*
>   *Thank you.*
> *Four Power Techniques heal all of my sicknesses.*
>   *Thank you.*
> *Four Power Techniques heal all of my sicknesses.*
>   *Thank you.*
> *Four Power Techniques heal all of my sicknesses.*
>   *Thank you.*
> *Four Power Techniques heal all of my sicknesses.*
>   *Thank you.*
> *Four Power Techniques heal all of my sicknesses.*
>   *Thank you . . .*

> *Hao!*

Chant three to five minutes per time, three to five times per day. The longer you chant, and the more often you chant, the better. The power of this chanting is beyond words. Remember this one-sentence secret:

Four Power Techniques heal all of my sicknesses; thank you.

This one-sentence secret includes all power in all universes and from all kinds of spiritual fathers and mothers, including the Divine. This is because it includes Soul Power, and everything has a soul. Human beings cannot comprehend enough the power of this practice.

Let me expand on this divine and Tao sacred and secret practice further. This one-sentence practice could be:

Four Power Techniques heal, prevent sickness, rejuvenate, prolong life, and transform every aspect of life, including relationships and finances, as well as enlighten soul, heart, mind, and body for me, my loved ones, humanity, Mother Earth, and all universes; thank you all.

The power of this practice is beyond words. How profound! Did you get a big "aha!" moment just now? Did you have a big "wow!" moment? Did you say, "I got it! I really got it! I understand the power of applying the Four Power Techniques together!"?

Chant this one-sentence secret as much as you can. The moment you have time to chant, do it. To chant this one-sentence divine and Tao sacred and secret practice is to offer service to yourself, your loved ones, humanity, Mother Earth, and all universes. Thank you, Divine. Thank you, Tao.

Practice a little, receive a little healing, blessing, and life transformation, and understand a little.

Practice more, receive more healing, blessing, and life transformation, and understand more.

Practice as much as you can or nonstop, receive unlimited healing, blessing, and life transformation, and understand deeper and deeper.

If you practice like this, one day you will receive a big "aha!" moment. You could have exciting realizations—"wow!" moments—such as:

> *Wow! I cannot believe how simple it is to heal myself.*
> *Wow! Wow! I cannot believe how simple it is to become*
> *   younger.*
> *Wow! Wow! Wow! I cannot believe how simple it is to*
> *   transform my relationships.*
> *Wow! Wow! Wow! Wow! I cannot believe how simple it*
> *   is transform my finances.*
> *Wow! Wow! Wow! Wow! Wow! I cannot believe how*
> *   simple it is to transform humanity, Mother Earth,*
> *   and all universes.*

This is one of the greatest secret and sacred practices. It is the Da Tao zhi jian practice: *The Big Way is extremely simple.*

Practice more.

Receive more benefits.

Express your gratitude.

Serve yourself and your loved ones.

Serve humanity.

Serve Mother Earth.

Serve all universes.

> *I love my heart and soul*
> *I love all humanity*

Join hearts and souls together
Love, peace and harmony
Love, peace and harmony

Hao! Hao! Hao!
Thank you. Thank you. Thank you.

灵歌舞
Ling Ge Wu

Soul Song, Soul Dance

"Ling" means *soul*. "Ge" means *song*. "Wu" means *dance*. Therefore, "Ling ge wu" (pronounced *ling guh woo*) means *Soul Song,
Soul Dance*.

The first book in my Soul Power Series, *Soul Wisdom: Practical Soul Treasures to Transform Your Life,* includes deep teachings
on Soul Song and Soul Dance. These teachings include how to
bring out your Soul Language and Soul Song and how to do Soul
Dance for energy boosting, healing, rejuvenation, prolonging life,
and transformation of every aspect of life. The fourth book in my
Soul Power Series, *Divine Soul Songs: Sacred Practical Treasures to
Heal, Rejuvenate, and Transform You, Humanity, Mother Earth,
and All Universes,* teaches eight major Divine Soul Songs to help
you and humanity heal, rejuvenate, prolong life, and transform
all aspects of life.

I have received thousands of heart-touching and moving stories on my website (www.DrSha.com) and on my Facebook page
("Dr. Sha") about the healing and life-transforming results people have received from Soul Song and Soul Dance. Soul Song and
Soul Dance are treasures for humanity and all universes.

Let me share the essence of the teachings for Soul Song, Soul

Dance, and Divine Soul Songs now. My teaching is straightforward. The simplest teaching is the best teaching. My teaching has four parts: *What, Why, How, Apply*.

Soul Song

What. What is Soul Song? Soul Song is **the song of one's soul**.

Why. Why do people need to learn Soul Song? What are the benefits of singing Soul Song?

- To sing Soul Song is to boost energy, stamina, vitality, and immunity.
- To sing Soul Song is to heal yourself and heal others, including remotely.
- To sing Soul Song is to transform your relationships.
- To sing Soul Song is to transform your finances.
- To sing Soul Song is to purify your soul, heart, mind, and body.
- To sing Soul Song is to enlighten your soul, heart, mind, and body.
- To sing Soul Song is to serve humanity by offering love, forgiveness, compassion, and light.
- To sing Soul Song is to serve Mother Earth by offering love, forgiveness, compassion, and light.
- To sing Soul Song is to serve all universes by offering love, forgiveness, compassion, and light.

How. How does Soul Song work? How does one bring out his or her Soul Song? Soul Song works because:

- Soul Song carries soul frequency and vibration, which can transform the frequency and vibration of your body, systems, organs, cells, cell units, DNA, RNA, smallest matter inside the cells, and spaces between the cells.
- Soul Song carries love, which melts all blockages and transforms all aspects of life.
- Soul Song carries forgiveness, which brings inner joy and inner peace.
- Soul Song carries compassion, which boosts energy, stamina, vitality, and immunity.
- Soul Song carries light, which heals, prevents sickness, rejuvenates, prolongs life, and transforms every aspect of life, including relationships and finances, as well as enlightens one's soul, heart, mind, and body.
- Soul Song is an unconditional universal servant to bring love, peace, and harmony to humanity, Mother Earth, and all universes.

Now let me explain how to bring out your Soul Song.

In the previous Tao text, *Ling Yu Yan* (Soul Language), you learned how to bring out your Soul Language and how to apply Soul Language for healing, rejuvenation, and life transformation. You may have already spoken your Soul Language and experienced its healing and blessing.

Soul Song is a further development of your Soul Language. After you have brought out your Soul Language, it is very easy to transform your Soul Language to Soul Song. Use the Four Power Techniques. The Divine showed me the Four Power Techniques in 2002. Since then, the Divine has guided me continuously to apply the Four Power Techniques for all healing, energy boosting, rejuvenation, and life transformation.

Let us apply the Four Power Techniques to bring out your Soul Song now:

Body Power. Sit up straight. Put the tip of your tongue as close as you can to the roof of your mouth without touching it. Place your left palm over your Message Center and your right hand in the traditional prayer position in front of your left hand.

Soul Power. Say *hello*:

> *Dear soul mind body of my Message Center, I love you.*
>   *You are the Soul Language center.*
> *Dear soul mind body of my Soul Song Channel* (starts
>   from the Hui Yin area [the perineum], goes up
>   through the seven soul houses to the top of your
>   head, then moves down behind the nose and into
>   the mouth),
> *Dear soul mind body of my Soul Language,*
> *I love you, honor you, and appreciate you.*
> *You have the power to bring out my Soul Song.*
> *Dear my beloved Message Center and my Soul Song*
>   *Channel, could you transform my Soul Language to*
>   *Soul Song?*
> *When I speak my Soul Language, let me turn to sing-*
>   *ing my Soul Language.*
> *Do a good job!*
> *I am very grateful.*
> *Thank you.*

Sound Power. Chant the sacred number code mantra 3396815, *San San Jiu Liu Ba Yao Wu* (pronounced *sahn sahn jeo leo bah* *yow woo*) very quickly. When your Soul Language comes out, instantly turn to singing your Soul Language. Congratulations! That is your Soul Song.

Soul Song is the further development of your Soul Language. As with Soul Language, everybody's Soul Song is unique. It may sound foreign, ancient, even otherworldly. It may have beautiful, complex melodies and rhythms. It may have simple, repetitive patterns. Have no expectations. Your Soul Song is perfect because it is *yours*. Everyone's Soul Song is perfect.

Practice Soul Song more and more. Your Soul Song could change all the time. Every time your Soul Song changes, your frequency and vibration are changing.

Apply. Soul Song can be applied to boost energy, heal, prevent sickness, rejuvenate soul, heart, mind, and body, and transform every aspect of life, including relationships and finances, as well as enlighten your soul, heart, mind, and body.

I will give a few examples of applying Soul Song for healing, prevention of sickness, rejuvenation, and life transformation. The practices are flexible. You can use the same wisdom and same "formulas" to apply Soul Song to transform any aspect of your life. We will always use the Four Power Techniques.

APPLY SOUL SONG TO SELF-HEAL

Body Power. Sit up straight. Put the tip of your tongue as close as you can to the roof of your mouth without touching it. Put your left palm over your Message Center (heart chakra). Put your right hand in the traditional prayer position, with fingers pointing upward. This is the Soul Light Era Prayer Position.

Soul Power. Say *hello:*

Dear soul mind body of my Soul Song,
I love you, honor you, and appreciate you.
Please heal my _____ (make your request).
Do a good job!
I am very grateful.
Thank you.

Mind Power. Visualize golden light shining in the area for which you requested healing.

Sound Power. Sing your Soul Song.

Open your heart and soul and sing your Soul Song now. Sing three to five minutes per time for healing. The longer and the more often you sing, the better. For chronic or life-threatening conditions, sing two hours or more per day. You can sing Soul Song several times throughout the day for a total of two hours or more.

APPLY SOUL SONG TO PREVENT SICKNESS

Body Power. Sit up straight. Put the tip of your tongue as close as you can to the roof of your mouth without touching it. Put your hands in the Soul Light Era Prayer Position.

Soul Power. Say *hello:*

Dear soul mind body of my Soul Song,
I love you, honor you, and appreciate you.
Please prevent all sickness in my physical, emotional,
*   mental, and spiritual bodies.*
Do a good job!
I am very grateful.
Thank you.

Mind Power. Visualize golden light shining in your entire body, from head to toe, skin to bone. Remember the wisdom: *Golden light shines; all sickness disappears.*

Sound Power. Sing your Soul Song.

Open your heart and soul and sing your Soul Song now. Sing for three to five minutes per time for prevention of sickness. The longer and the more often you sing, the better. For chronic or life-threatening conditions, sing two hours or more per day. You can sing Soul Song several times throughout the day for a total of two hours or more.

You could experience amazing results from applying the Four Power Techniques with your Soul Song for healing and preventing sickness.

APPLY SOUL SONG TO REJUVENATE
SOUL, HEART, MIND, AND BODY

Body Power. Sit up straight. Put the tip of your tongue as close as you can to the roof of your mouth without touching it. Put your hands in the Soul Light Era Prayer Position.

Soul Power. Say *hello:*

> *Dear soul mind body of my Soul Song,*
> *I love you, honor you, and appreciate you.*
> *Please rejuvenate my soul, heart, mind, and body.*
> *Do a good job!*
> *I am very grateful.*
> *Thank you.*

Mind Power. Visualize golden light shining in your entire body from head to toe, skin to bone.

Sound Power. Sing your Soul Song.

Sing your Soul Song now for three to five minutes to rejuvenate your soul, heart, mind, and body. The longer and the more often you sing, the better. If you have a chronic or life-threatening condition, sing two hours or more per day. You can sing Soul Song several times throughout the day for a total of two hours or more.

APPLY SOUL SONG TO TRANSFORM RELATIONSHIPS

Body Power. Sit up straight. Put the tip of your tongue as close as you can to the roof of your mouth without touching it. Put your hands in the Soul Light Era Prayer Position.

Soul Power. Say *hello:*

> *Dear soul mind body of* _____ (name the
>   person with whom you want to transform your
>   relationship),
> *Dear soul mind body of my Soul Song,*
> *I love you, honor you, and appreciate you.*
> *Please transform the relationship between* _____
>   (name the person) *and me.*
> *Do a good job!*
> *I am very grateful.*
> *Thank you.*

Mind Power. Visualize golden light shining between the other person and you.

Sound Power. Sing your Soul Song.

Sing your Soul Song now for three to five minutes to transform your relationship. The longer and the more often you sing, the better.

APPLY SOUL SONG TO TRANSFORM FINANCES OR A BUSINESS

Body Power. Sit up straight. Put the tip of your tongue as close as you can to the roof of your mouth without touching it. Put your hands in the Soul Light Era Prayer Position.

Soul Power. Say *hello:*

> *Dear soul mind body of my finances* (alternatively, name your business),
> *Dear soul mind body of my Soul Song,*
> *I love you, honor you, and appreciate you.*
> *Please transform my finances* (or *business*).
> *Do a good job!*
> *I am very grateful.*
> *Thank you.*

Mind Power. Visualize golden light shining in your entire business and finances.

Sound Power. Sing your Soul Song.

Sing your Soul Song now for three to five minutes to transform your finances. The longer and the more often you sing, the better.

⚹

Follow the same formula to apply Soul Song to transform any aspect of your life. Soul Song has power beyond words. I have recorded many Soul Songs for Healing and Rejuvenation. They are available from my website, www.DrSha.com, and from many Internet vendors. The Divine showed me that millions and billions of people in the Soul Light Era will sing Soul Songs for healing, prevention of sickness, rejuvenation, and transformation of every aspect of life. I call you to become a Soul Song Singer. Open your Soul Song Channel more and more. Practice every day. Sing a Soul Song for yourself, your loved ones, humanity, Mother Earth, and all universes.

Soul Dance

What. What is Soul Dance? Soul Dance is **soul-guided dance**.

Why. Why do people need to do Soul Dance?

- To Soul Dance is to boost energy, stamina, vitality, and immunity.
- To Soul Dance is to self-heal and heal others, including remotely.
- To Soul Dance is to transform your relationships.
- To Soul Dance is to transform your finances.
- To Soul Dance is to purify your soul, heart, mind, and body.
- To Soul Dance is to enlighten your soul, heart, mind, and body.
- To Soul Dance is to serve humanity by offering love, forgiveness, compassion, and light through your Soul Dance.

- To Soul Dance is to serve Mother Earth by offering love, forgiveness, compassion, and light through your Soul Dance.
- To Soul Dance is to serve all universes by offering love, forgiveness, compassion, and light through your Soul Dance.

How. How does Soul Dance work? How does one bring out his or her Soul Dance? Soul Dance works because:

- Soul Dance carries soul frequency and vibration, which can transform the frequency and vibration of your body, systems, organs, cells, cell units, DNA, RNA, smallest matter inside the cells, and spaces between the cells.
- Soul Dance carries love, which melts all blockages and transforms all life.
- Soul Dance carries forgiveness, which brings inner joy and inner peace.
- Soul Dance carries compassion, which boosts energy, stamina, vitality, and immunity.
- Soul Dance carries light, which heals, prevents sickness, rejuvenates, prolongs life, and transforms every aspect of life, including relationships and finances, as well as enlightens one's soul, heart, mind, and body.
- Soul Dance is an unconditional universal servant to bring love, peace, and harmony to humanity, Mother Earth, and all universes.

Now let me teach you how to bring out your Soul Dance. Apply the Four Power Techniques:

Body Power. Stand with your legs shoulder width apart. Put the tip of your tongue as close as you can to the roof of your mouth without touching it. Bend your knees slightly.

Soul Power. Say *hello:*

> *Dear soul mind body of myself,*
> *I love you, honor you, and appreciate you.*
> *You have the power to bring out my Soul Dance.*
> *Do a good job!*
> *Thank you.*
> *Dear my beloved soul,*
> *Please guide my legs, arms, and body to do Soul Dance*
>   *by following soul music.*
> *Do a good job!*
> *I am extremely grateful.*
> *Thank you.*

Listen to a Soul Song, to Soul Dance music, to a Soul Symphony, or to any appropriate spiritual music.

Mind Power. Visualize golden light shining in your entire body, from head to toe, skin to bone.

Sound Power. Sing or chant the Divine Soul Song *Happy Happy Happy.* Listen to me singing it in Soul Language, English, and Chinese on the enclosed CD.

> *Hei ya ya ya ya ya yo-ou yi*
> *Hei ya ya ya ya ya yo-ou yi*
> *Hei ya ya ya ya ya-a you yi*

Hei ya yo-ou-ou yi
Hei ya-a yo-ou yi-i ya

Happy happy happy ha-ap-py
Happy happy happy ha-ap-py
Happy happy happy-y hap-py
Happy ha-a-ap-py
Hap-py-y ha-ap-py-y-y

Kuai le kuai le kuai le kuai-ai le
Kuai le kuai le kuai le kuai-ai le
Kuai le kuai le kuai le-e kuai le
Kuai le kuai-ai-ai le
Kuai le-e kuai-ai le-e-e

Body Power. Do Soul Dance for five minutes to a half hour or more. The longer you practice, the more benefits you could receive.

※

The Divine has guided me to create a Soul Song and Soul Dance movement on Mother Earth. We have hundreds of Soul Song and Soul Dance Healers, Soul Song Singers, and Soul Dancers worldwide. The Divine has further guided me to create Soul Song and Soul Dance Concerts, workshops, retreats, and a Certification Training Program for Soul Song and Soul Dance Healers worldwide.

Why are Soul Song and Soul Dance so special? Because they carry divine frequency and vibration with divine love, forgiveness, compassion, and light. Soul Song and Soul Dance are divine treasures for humanity to transform all life, including relationships, finances, and every aspect of life.

The most important values in a human being's life are to be healthy and happy. Soul Song and Soul Dance can bring health and happiness to humanity, Mother Earth, and all universes.

Chanting, chanting, chanting
Divine chanting is healing
Chanting, chanting, chanting
Divine chanting is rejuvenating

Singing, singing, singing
Divine singing is transforming
Singing, singing, singing
Divine singing is enlightening

Humanity is waiting for divine chanting
All souls are waiting for divine singing
Divine chanting removes all blockages
Divine singing brings inner joy

Divine is chanting and singing
Humanity and all souls are nourishing
Humanity and all souls are chanting and singing
World love peace and harmony are coming
World love peace and harmony are coming
World love peace and harmony are coming

Apply. Soul Dance can be applied to boost energy, heal, prevent sickness, rejuvenate your soul, heart, mind, and body, and transform every aspect of life, including relationships and finances, as well as enlighten your soul, heart, mind, and body.

Therefore, I will give a few examples of applying Soul Dance.

We will use the Four Power Techniques. You can adapt the wisdom and "formula" in these examples to transform any aspect of your life through your Soul Dance.

APPLY SOUL DANCE TO SELF-HEAL

Body Power. Stand with your legs shoulder-width apart. Put the tip of your tongue as close as you can to the roof of your mouth without touching it. Bend your knees slightly.

Soul Power. Say *hello:*

> *Dear soul mind body of my Soul Dance,*
> *I love you, honor you, and appreciate you.*
> *Dear my soul,*
> *I love you, honor you, and appreciate you.*
> *Please guide my Soul Dance to heal my _____*
>   (make your request).
> *Do a good job!*
> *I am very grateful.*
> *Thank you.*

Mind Power. Visualize golden light shining in the area for which you requested healing.

Body Power. Do Soul Dance.
    Generally speaking, do Soul Dance for three to five minutes per time for healing. The longer and the more often you do Soul Dance, the better. For chronic or life-threatening conditions, Soul Dance for at least two hours. You can do Soul Dance several times throughout the day for a total of two hours or more.

APPLY SOUL DANCE TO REJUVENATE YOUR
SOUL, HEART, MIND, AND BODY

Body Power. Stand with your legs shoulder width apart. Put the tip of your tongue as close as you can to the roof of your mouth without touching it. Bend your knees slightly.

Soul Power. Say *hello:*

> *Dear soul mind body of my Soul Dance,*
> *I love you, honor you, and appreciate you.*
> *Dear my soul,*
> *I love you, honor you, and appreciate you.*
> *Please guide my Soul Dance to rejuvenate my soul,*
>   *heart, mind, and body.*
> *Do a good job!*
> *I am very grateful.*
> *Thank you.*

Mind Power. Visualize golden light shining in your entire body, from head to toe, skin to bone.

Body Power. Do Soul Dance.

Do Soul Dance for three to five minutes per time for rejuvenation. The longer and the more often you do Soul Dance, the better. For chronic or life-threatening conditions, Soul Dance at least two hours per day. You can do Soul Dance several times throughout the day for a total of two hours or more.

Soul Song and Soul Dance are practical divine treasures for humanity to transform their health, relationships, finances, and every aspect of life. They are practical, simple to learn, and powerful.

Practice Soul Song and Soul Dance more and more to benefit every aspect of your life.

灵敲打

Ling Qiao Da

Soul Tapping

"Ling means *soul*. "Qiao da" means *tapping*. "Ling qiao da" (pronounced *ling chee-yow dah*) means *Soul Tapping*.

Everybody understands tapping. When a baby is crying, the mother gently pats or taps the baby and says, "Baby, I love you. Calm down." If a child falls down and is crying, the mother holds the child, taps gently, and says, "Everything will be fine." Think about this kind of tapping by a mother to her baby or child. You can understand that the mother is giving love to the child.

Soul Tapping is not ordinary tapping. Soul Tapping includes tapping the soul, as well as tapping the body. Soul Tapping is divine wisdom and a practical technique that the Divine and Tao asked me to share with humanity. This profound wisdom and technique are so simple.

Now I am going to explain the *what, why, how,* and *application* of Soul Tapping.

What. There are two kinds of Soul Tapping. The first is Soul Self-Tapping—tapping your own soul and body to boost energy and self-heal. The second is Soul Tapping of others to offer them remote healing.

Why. Why should one learn Soul Tapping? Soul Tapping can heal the soul very quickly with divine love, forgiveness, compassion, and light. *Heal the soul first; then healing of the mind and body will follow.*

How. How do you do Soul Tapping? With the Four Power Techniques!

Body Power. Sit with your back free and clear or, better, stand with your legs shoulder width apart. Put the tip of your tongue as close as you can to the roof of your mouth without touching it. If you are sitting, keep your feet flat on the floor. If you are standing, bend your knees slightly. Make a fist with each hand. Put your right fist on your Message Center. Put your left fist on your Snow Mountain Area, on your lower back slightly above the tailbone.

Soul Power. Say *hello:*

> *Dear soul mind body of my Message Center and Snow*
> *   Mountain Area,*
> *I love you.*
> *You have the power to heal my* _____ (make
>   your request).
> *Do a good job.*
> *I am very grateful.*
> *Thank you.*

Mind Power. Visualize golden light shining in the organ or area for which you requested healing.

Body Power. Use your fists to tap your Message Center and your Snow Mountain Area simultaneously.

Sound Power. Chant repeatedly, silently or aloud:

> *Soul Tapping heals me. Thank you.*
> *Soul Tapping heals me. Thank you.*
> *Soul Tapping heals me. Thank you.*
> *Soul Tapping heals me. Thank you.*
> *Soul Tapping heals me. Thank you.*
> *Soul Tapping heals me. Thank you.*
> *Soul Tapping heals me. Thank you . . .*

Tap for at least three to five minutes per time. The longer you tap and the more often you tap, the better.

One area you are tapping in this practice is the Message Center. The Message Center is the soul healing center, the emotional center, the love, forgiveness, compassion, and light center, the karma center, the soul communication center, the life transformation center, and the soul enlightenment center. The Message Center has incredible power beyond comprehension. For soul healing, the Message Center is absolutely vital.

The Message Center is near the heart. Tapping the Message Center also strengthens the functions of the heart. The heart is in charge of blood circulation. The heart is vital for healing and for every aspect of life. The heart is the key for intelligence because the heart houses the mind and soul. Therefore, if you have a brain issue, healing the heart is vital. This is ancient wisdom of traditional Chinese medicine.

Many people think that intelligence comes from the brain, which is correct from the viewpoint of modern science. But they may not realize that to increase intelligence, the heart is the key. In traditional Chinese medicine, intelligence comes from the heart.

There are several different intelligences: intelligence of the mind, intelligence of the heart, and intelligence of the soul. Generally speaking, people have not had great awareness of the intelligence of the heart. People have very little awareness of the intelligence of the soul. In the future, I will write a book about developing all of one's intelligences, including the intelligences of soul, heart, mind, and body.

The other area you are tapping in this practice is the Snow Mountain Area. The Snow Mountain area is one of the two key foundational centers for energy, stamina, vitality, and immunity. (The Lower Dan Tian, described in chapter 1, is the other.) The Snow Mountain Area is also the key for rejuvenation and longevity. To tap on the Snow Mountain Area is to strengthen your kidneys. Because the kidneys produce Jing, the essence of matter for the whole body, the kidneys are vital for health, energy, rejuvenation, and longevity.

A human being's life can be divided into physical life and soul life. Physical life is limited. A person who can live to be one hundred years old is considered to be very blessed. How many people can live to be two hundred years old? And, in history, there are a few very rare people who lived beyond the age of two hundred. My Tao lineage founder, Peng Zu, the teacher of Lao Zi, lived to the age of eight hundred eighty. In the Peng Zu Tao lineage that I am very honored to hold, there have been several masters who lived for two hundred to four hundred years.

The founder of tai chi lived for about four hundred fifty years. The sacred Tao writings describe one Tao master who lived for more than fifteen hundred years. A sacred Buddhist book describes one Buddhist father who lived for more than twelve hundred years. I know that this is very difficult to believe. Is it really possible to live to such ages?

I am flowing this book in the Love Peace Harmony Center in Boulder, Colorado. I am with about sixty of my top teachers and healers. They are listening to my flow and watching my assistant type my flow.

When you have highly developed spiritual channels and become a true channel to communicate with the Divine, you can ask the Divine to explain almost anything to you. At this moment, I will communicate with the Divine. I am asking, "Dear Divine, for the masters whom I just discussed and who are recorded as living long, long lives—eight hundred, twelve hundred, even fifteen hundred years—is this really possible? I am honored to hear from you."

I will ask one of my Worldwide Representatives, Marilyn Smith, to flow the answer to my question from the Divine. She is not using her logical mind at all.

Marilyn's flow:

I am the Divine. My most beloved, it is absolutely possible for a human being to live to these ages. This will be extremely difficult for many to believe. The way that most people on Mother Earth live their lives at this time makes it impossible for them to reach these ages. However, there have been people throughout the history of Mother Earth who have lived very extraordinary lives. They have done practices that have put them in great alignment with me, my frequency and vibration, my love, forgiveness, compassion, light, and so much more. They have lived their lives as unconditional universal servants.

All of this made it possible for them to transform. That process of transformation brought about changes on the physical level that made it possible for them to reach very old age. So my response is "Yes, it is possible." However, those who reach very old age, such as the ones you referred to, must live lives of complete commitment. They must live lives of alignment with me. They must do practices and this must become their way of life. There will be no separation between their daily life and their life of practice. All becomes one and all becomes aligned with me. We become one. This is how some have reached what seem to be unbelievable ages. Thank you for this question and for this opportunity to give this teaching to my beloved sons and daughters worldwide. I am your loving Divine.

Thank you, Marilyn, for your direct soul communication with the Divine. Direct soul communication is to hear directly from the Divine and flow out the Divine's words. This is one of the communication techniques I have taught to my students worldwide.

Now I would like to ask Tao a question: "Dear beloved Tao, is it possible for a person to live to be hundreds of years old or more than a thousand years old? How can it happen?"

I am asking another one of my Worldwide Representatives, Francisco Quintero, to do a direct communication with Tao to answer my question. I have trained Marilyn and Francisco and thousands of students worldwide. Now I have more than ten Worldwide Representatives. I have about five hundred Master Teachers and Healers worldwide. My top teachers are pure soul communication channels. I have trained them well. They can communicate directly with the Divine and Tao. They can hear their teachings or see their images very clearly. The second book of my Soul Power Series, *Soul Communication: Opening Your Spiritual Channels for Success and Fulfillment,* teaches how to open four major spiritual channels (Soul Language Channel, Direct Soul Commmunication Channel, Third Eye Channel, Direct Knowing Channel).

Marilyn just now used her Direct Soul Communication Channel. I am going to ask Francisco to use his Third Eye Channel to answer my questions to Tao. I am asking Tao to show images to Francisco's Third Eye. I would like Tao to show Francisco the rare top saints or servants since creation who have stayed on Mother Earth as physical beings for hundreds and thousands of years. I am singing Soul Song for three minutes to ask Tao to show these special saints who have lived hundreds and thousands of years on Mother Earth as a human being to Francisco's Third Eye and to every one of my advanced teachers' Third Eyes.

Francisco, please share.

The images the Tao has shown me of those who have lived to be hundreds and thousands of years old were quite remarkable. Many of these people had powerful Jin Dans that were filled with divine light. This was the foundation for their lives. Each of them also had been incredibly blessed by the Divine for all of their major organs and systems.

The soul of every organ and system was replaced with a divine soul. The divine souls nourished their lives for long, long periods. Each of them also received divine nectar, vitamins, and minerals from Heaven to support and nourish their long lives. Each of them chanted sacred mantras to live a long life. They would chant these mantras not only for thirty minutes or one hour, but would make this chanting part of their entire day. They would chant twenty-four hours a day. This is how they were able to extend their lives for such long periods of time.

My other top teachers, do you have anything else to share? Petra Herz from Germany is another of my Worldwide Representatives. She would like to share her Third Eye images.

I was very impressed to see all these different saints and buddhas from different continents. I can summarize all of the specific things I saw.

I saw that all of them really have a light body. Their souls were very light and shining and they were all nourished by the Divine. All of them had a very big Jin Dan and a big belly.

All of these people were doing service for the Divine, including chanting for the whole day. They all have different secrets from the Tao, Christian, and other realms, but all were chanting nonstop.

Thank you for your sharing. Is there anyone else who would like to share their Third Eye images?

Yes, this is Worldwide Representative David Lusch.

I saw that many of these masters sat in the meditation position during the night and did practice. They did not sleep very much, if at all. Many humans do spiritual practice as part of their life. Spiritual practice for these masters is their life. Everything they were doing followed Tao, from walking to sitting to eating to talking—everything. It was their life.

I also saw that some masters started with the tantric practices of male and female exchanging yin and yang. But then they evolved to a practice that they did within themselves, and they did not have to do the male-female practice anymore.

I also saw a master with the extraordinary ability to fly off of a mountain. This is the additional information that I wanted to share.

Worldwide Representative Lynne Nusyna:

I was privileged to see a divine being, a most beautiful female master who has been soul chanting, soul singing, and soul dancing for many thousands of years. She continues to do this to this day. She is the inspiration and guiding force for soul singing and soul dancing coming to Mother Earth.

Worldwide Representative Patricia Smith:

The huge light bodies of these masters are very, very obvious. I saw several masters in various settings. One image that was very sharp was the master tending large gardens. These masters are in perfect alignment with the Divine and the universal energies. They avoid the energies and circumstances that would bring them out of alignment. Everything in their environment is brought into alignment. In particular, this garden is lush and abundant. Herbs and plants that would nurture the Earth come out of this garden. Another quality of these masters is this continuous flow of energy and light within their own bodies that not only keeps them in alignment, but affects the entire environment around them. These masters inhabit not just one place, but places all over the world.

Ellen Logan:

What I saw were these beautiful souls, very light and golden in color. They were standing initially in a circle and then became an oval shape. Their light bodies would then be absorbed into the Tao and then come back—a rebirth. They were bigger. This was a process of absorbing into the Tao and then coming back.

Thank you all for sharing. I am asking Tao to give me a short flow.

Dear my beloved daughters and sons, this is Ultimate Tao. I am delighted to answer Zhi Gang's question. My answer is "yes." To live a long life is absolutely possible.

Zhi Gang is a chosen servant to share the teaching directly from the Divine and Tao. In this book, he shares the normal creation of Tao and the reverse creation of Tao. You have learnd that the process of normal creation is:

Tao creates One. One creates Two. Two creates Three. Three creates all things.

The process of reverse creation is:

All things return to Three. Three returns to Two. Two returns to One. One returns to Tao.

Since creation, there have been rare Tao saints who have lived more than one thousand or two thousand years. In fact, there are immortals on Mother Earth. These top Tao saints do not need to appear to the public anymore.

In the teaching of The Yellow Emperor's Internal Classic, **Ju zhe cheng xing, san zhe cheng feng.** *This can be interpreted in different ways.*

In terms of an energy view, Ju zhe cheng xing, san zhe cheng feng means "energy accumulates to form a shape; energy dissipates just like wind flowing away." This wisdom explains how any growth, including cysts, tumors, and cancer, forms inside the body and how to heal them. Energy accumulates to form cysts, tumors, and cancer. Dissipate this energy and cysts, tumors, and cancer will disappear, just like wind flowing away.

In terms of saints' abilities, Ju zhe cheng xing, san zhe cheng feng can be interpreted in this way: A high-level saint who melds with Tao gains Tao abilities. This level of saint can gather energy and matter to their souls to assume a human shape. Their souls also have the ability to dissipate this energy and matter on the spot.

Dear my daughters and my sons, it may be very hard to believe this. You do not need to believe. I am your beloved Ultimate Tao. This secret is released for my beloved Tao practitioners. This is to tell you that it was already released five thousand years ago as Ju zhe cheng xing, san zhe cheng feng in The Yellow Emperor's Internal Classic. *Now Zhi Gang is releasing this explanation at a deeper level through my teaching as your beloved Ultimate Tao. You are loved and blessed to receive this teaching. This teaching is also to tell you that Zhi Gang is my chosen Tao servant to offer Tao training to humanity. This is training for immortality.*

You have heard the flows and images of Marilyn, Francisco, Petra, David, Lynne, Patricia, and Ellen. They have explained to you how these highest saints have been transformed with their light bodies and Jin Dan, and how they practice Tao in daily life. The wisdom of reverse creation has given you theoretical guidance on how you too can meld with

Tao. You have been given the process. Zhi Gang will offer my teaching and divine teaching to humanity one step at a time for reaching Tao.

To summarize to my beloved daughters and sons world-wide, these are my words to you, to all humanity, and to all saints. In one sentence:

To meld with Tao is to reach immortality.

Tao teaching is sacred and secret teaching. You may have heard about many fairytale stories throughout history. Tao teaching from Zhi Gang is this kind of teaching. Zhi Gang has received the honor and authority to pass these sacred teachings and practices from the Divine and Tao to human-ity and all souls.

Zhi Gang offers teaching that is extremely simple. It may be too simple to believe. Zhi Gang's teaching is to let you ex-perience Da Tao zhi jian—The Big Way is extremely simple. You are blessed. I am willing to give chosen Tao practitioners special blessings in order to assist them to meld with Tao. You are extremely blessed.

I am your beloved Ultimate Tao.

I and all of my top teachers bowed to the Divine and Ultimate Tao after this flow. We cannot bow down enough for the Divine and Tao to release such sacred and secret teachings and practices to humanity. We are extremely honored beyond imagination. We are honored to study Tao, practice Tao, and finally meld with Tao. To meld with Tao is to be a Tao servant who has Tao and divine abilities to serve humanity and all souls. We are extremely honored.

Apply. You can apply Soul Tapping to heal, prevent sickness, rejuvenate soul, heart, mind, and body, prolong life, transform relationships and finances, and enlighten your soul, heart, mind, and body. Use the Four Power Techniques:

Body Power. Sit with your back free and clear or, better, stand with your legs shoulder-width apart. Put the tip of your tongue as close as you can to the roof of your mouth without touching it. If you are sitting, keep your feet flat on the floor. If you are standing, bend your knees slightly. Put your right fist on your Message Center. Put your left fist on your Snow Mountain Area. Start Soul Tapping those areas now.

Soul Power. Say *hello:*

> *Dear Divine, dear Tao, dear all universes, dear my*
> *Message Center and dear my Snow Mountain Area,*
> *I love you, honor you, and appreciate you all.*
> *You have the power to heal, prevent sickness, rejuvenate,*
> *prolong life, transform my relationships and finances,*
> *and enlighten my soul, heart, mind, and body.*
> *I am extremely honored and appreciative.*
> *Thank you.*

Mind Power. Visualize your entire body shining golden light. Visualize this golden light connecting you with Heaven, Earth, and all universes.

Sound Power. This practice includes all applications in one sentence. Chant this sentence plus *thank you* repeatedly, silently or aloud:

Soul Tapping heals, prevents sickness, rejuvenates soul, heart, mind, and body, prolongs life, transforms relationships, finances, and every aspect of life, and enlightens soul, heart, mind, and body. Thank you all.

Soul Tapping heals, prevents sickness, rejuvenates soul, heart, mind, and body, prolongs life, transforms relationships, finances, and every aspect of life, and enlightens soul, heart, mind, and body. Thank you all.

Soul Tapping heals, prevents sickness, rejuvenates soul, heart, mind, and body, prolongs life, transforms relationships, finances, and every aspect of life, and enlightens soul, heart, mind, and body. Thank you all.

Soul Tapping heals, prevents sickness, rejuvenates soul, heart, mind, and body, prolongs life, transforms relationships, finances, and every aspect of life, and enlightens soul, heart, mind, and body. Thank you all.

Soul Tapping heals, prevents sickness, rejuvenates soul, heart, mind, and body, prolongs life, transforms relationships, finances, and every aspect of life, and enlightens soul, heart, mind, and body. Thank you all.

Soul Tapping heals, prevents sickness, rejuvenates soul, heart, mind, and body, prolongs life, transforms relationships, finances, and every aspect of life, and enlightens soul, heart, mind, and body. Thank you all.

*Soul Tapping heals, prevents sickness, rejuvenates soul,
    heart, mind, and body, prolongs life, transforms re-
    lationships, finances, and every aspect of life, and
    enlightens soul, heart, mind, and body. Thank
    you all . . .*

This mantra and practice have power beyond any words. You
are applying all powers from the Divine, Tao, Heaven, Earth, and
all universes, as well as the power of all of your inner souls to
heal, rejuvenate, and transform all life. You do not need to make
any specific requests. This practice covers everything you need
in your physical life and your soul life. This is *the* one-sentence
secret practice. This is an "aha!" moment. This is a "wow!" moment.

Practice more.

Let us chant a few times more:

*Soul Tapping heals, prevents sickness, rejuvenates soul,
    heart, mind, and body, prolongs life, transforms re-
    lationships, finances, and every aspect of life, and
    enlightens soul, heart, mind, and body. Thank
    you all.*
*Soul Tapping heals, prevents sickness, rejuvenates soul,
    heart, mind, and body, prolongs life, transforms re-
    lationships, finances, and every aspect of life, and
    enlightens soul, heart, mind, and body. Thank
    you all.*
*Soul Tapping heals, prevents sickness, rejuvenates soul,
    heart, mind, and body, prolongs life, transforms re-
    lationships, finances, and every aspect of life, and*

*enlightens soul, heart, mind, and body. Thank
you all.*

*Soul Tapping heals, prevents sickness, rejuvenates soul,
heart, mind, and body, prolongs life, transforms relationships, finances, and every aspect of life, and
enlightens soul, heart, mind, and body. Thank
you all.*

*Soul Tapping heals, prevents sickness, rejuvenates soul,
heart, mind, and body, prolongs life, transforms relationships, finances, and every aspect of life, and
enlightens soul, heart, mind, and body. Thank
you all.*

*Soul Tapping heals, prevents sickness, rejuvenates soul,
heart, mind, and body, prolongs life, transforms relationships, finances, and every aspect of life, and
enlightens soul, heart, mind, and body. Thank
you all.*

*Soul Tapping heals, prevents sickness, rejuvenates soul,
heart, mind, and body, prolongs life, transforms relationships, finances, and every aspect of life, and
enlightens soul, heart, mind, and body. Thank
you all.*

*Soul Tapping, Soul Tapping, Soul Tapping
Healing, healing, healing
Preventing sickness, preventing sickness, preventing
sickness
Rejuvenating, rejuvenating, rejuvenating
Transforming, transforming, transforming
Enlightening, enlightening, enlightening
Hao! Hao! Hao!
Thank you. Thank you. Thank you.*

This is the way to heal, prevent sickness, rejuvenate, transform, and enlighten all life. This is extremely simple. The extremely simple thing is the most difficult thing for human beings to believe. Therefore, for us to spread this teaching, the most difficult thing is to have people believe this simple teaching. People will believe it. If you are ready, as you read the last several pages, you will say, "Aha! I got it." and "Wow! I got it. I really understand Da Tao zhi jian."

Chant a little more with me:

Da Tao Zhi Jian
Da Tao Zhi Jian
Da Tao Zhi Jian

Da Tao Zhi Jian
Da Tao Zhi Jian
Da Tao Zhi Jian

Da Tao Zhi Jian
Da Tao Zhi Jian
Da Tao Zhi Jian . . .

Now sing with me:

Da Tao Zhi Jian
Da Tao Zhi Jian
Da Tao Zhi Jian

Da Tao Zhi Jian
Da Tao Zhi Jian
Da Tao Zhi Jian

Da Tao Zhi Jian
Da Tao Zhi Jian
Da Tao Zhi Jian . . .

Hao! Hao! Hao!
Thank you. Thank you. Thank you.

灵草药
Ling Cao Yao

Soul Herbs

"Ling" means *soul*. "Cao yao" (pronounced *tsow yow*, rhymes with *cow*) means *herbs*. For five thousand years the herbs of traditional Chinese medicine have served millions of people. Today, Chinese herbs are popular worldwide. They are used in almost every country. There are also Indian herbs, indigenous peoples' herbs, and many others. Almost every country and every culture has its own herbs.

Herbs come from nature. They carry the Five Elements of nature, which are Wood, Fire, Earth, Metal, and Water. Five Elements is a universal law. Everyone and everything consists of Five Elements. A human being has Five Elements. Herbs have Five Elements. An herb that has the nature of the Wood element can heal the disorders of the Wood element in a human being or in a pet.

The Wood element in a human being includes the liver, gallbladder, eyes, and tendons, and the emotional body of anger. If an herb carries the nature of the Wood element, it can serve all of these Wood element organs and tissues, as well as anger in the emotional body.

The Fire element in a human being includes the heart, small

intestine, tongue, and blood vessels, and the emotional body of depression and anxiety. If an herb carries the nature of the Fire element, it can serve these Fire element organs and tissues, as well as depression and anxiety in the emotional body.

The Earth element in a human being includes the spleen, stomach, teeth and gums, and muscles, and the emotional body of worry. If an herb carries the nature of the Earth element, it can serve these Earth element organs and tissues, as well as worry in the emotional body.

The Metal element in a human being includes the lungs, large intestine, nose, and skin, and the emotional body of grief. If an herb carries the nature of the Metal element, it can serve these Metal element organs and tissues, as well as grief in the emotional body.

The Water element in a human being includes the kidneys, urinary bladder, ears, and bones, and the emotional body of fear. If an herb carries the nature of the Water element, it can serve these Water element organs and tissues, as well as fear in the emotional body.

For example, the herb Bo He (pronounced *baw huh*), which is *peppermint,* can stimulate cellular vibration in the liver. Therefore, Bo He is a very important herb for liver conditions, including inflammation, bacterial and viral infections, cysts, tumors, and cancer. Bo He can dissipate energy blockages in the liver.

The important wisdom in this Tao teaching is that you can say *hello* to the soul, mind, and body of an herb to do soul healing using the *soul* of an herb. Drinking physical herb tea is very important, as has been proven by millions of people's experiences over thousands of years. However, there is a special ancient statement:

Shen xian yong ling yao

"Shen xian" means *saint*. "Yong" means *use*. "Ling yao" means *soul herbs*. Therefore, "Shen xian yong ling yao" (pronounced *shun shyen yawng ling yow*) means *a saint uses soul herbs*. This is a fairy-tale story for humanity. How do saints use soul herbs? They can create miracles without using physical herbs to offer healing. They can appear in front of a person, offer soul herbs, and the person receives remarkable healing. Many such "fairy-tale stories" are described in books about Buddhist and Taoist saints.

I am honored to tell you that anybody can apply the secrets of soul herbs to heal yourself, your loved ones, and others. The secret is so simple. It may be too simple to believe, but remember *Da Tao zhi jian*.

This is the way to do it. I will use a liver condition as an example. If a person has hepatitis A, B, or C, cirrhosis of the liver, liver cancer, other liver conditions, or anger in the emotional body, apply the Four Power Techniques:

Body Power. Sit up straight. Put the tip of your tongue as close as you can to the roof of your mouth without touching it. Put one palm over your liver. Do gentle Soul Tapping on your liver area. Do it now.

Soul Power. Say *hello:*

> *Dear soul mind body of Bo He* (peppermint),
> *I love you.*
> *You have the power to heal my* _____ (name
>   your liver conditions, including anger if applic-
>   able).

Do a good job.
Thank you.

Mind Power. Visualize beautiful green light (green is the color of the Wood element) radiating from the soul of Bo He to your entire liver. Your entire liver shines green light.

Sound Power. Chant repeatedly, silently or aloud:

Bo He heals my liver. Thank you.
Bo He heals my liver. Thank you.
Bo He heals my liver. Thank you.
Bo He heals my liver. Thank you.
Bo He heals my liver. Thank you.
Bo He heals my liver. Thank you.
Bo He heals my liver. Thank you . . .

Practice a lot. To practice three to five minutes to heal serious liver conditions is not enough. Generally speaking, for chronic and life-threatening conditions, practice two hours a day. Add up all of your practice time to total at least two hours each day. You could receive healing results that you cannot believe yourself.

Now I am going to offer Tao Soul Herb Bo He Soul Mind Body Transplants.

Prepare.

Sit up straight.

Totally relax.

Open your heart and soul to receive these permanent Tao treasures.

Tao Order: Tao Soul Herb Bo He Soul Transplant Transmission!

This treasure is a golden light soul of Bo He from the Tao realm. About seven hundred feet tall, it has come to your body.

Tao Order: Tao Soul Herb Bo He Mind Transplant Transmission!

This golden light being is also about seven hundred feet tall. It has come to you carrying the consciousness of the Tao soul herb Bo He.

Tao Order: Tao Soul Herb Bo He Body Transplant Transmission!

This golden light being carries the energy and tiny matter of the Tao soul herb Bo He. It has come to your body and will take a few days to shrink from its original size (about seven hundred feet tall) to adapt better to your body.

Tao Order: Tao Soul Herb Bo He Soul Mind Body Transplants join as one.

He Ya Ya Ya Ya You!

This Tao Order is for your Tao Soul Herbs Bo He Soul Mind Body Transplants to join as one to serve.

Now chant with me:

Tao Soul Herb Bo He Soul Mind Body Transplants
heal my liver. Thank you.
Tao Soul Herb Bo He Soul Mind Body Transplants
heal my liver. Thank you.
Tao Soul Herb Bo He Soul Mind Body Transplants
heal my liver. Thank you.
Tao Soul Herb Bo He Soul Mind Body Transplants
heal my liver. Thank you.
Tao Soul Herb Bo He Soul Mind Body Transplants
heal my liver. Thank you.
Tao Soul Herb Bo He Soul Mind Body Transplants
heal my liver. Thank you.
Tao Soul Herb Bo He Soul Mind Body Transplants
heal my liver. Thank you . . .

Chant three to five minutes per time. The longer you chant, the better. The Tao Soul Herb Bo He has power beyond comprehension because it is not the herb Bo He that we know on Mother Earth. The Tao Soul Herb Bo He has come to you directly from the Tao realm. There is no comparison between its power and the power of Mother Earth's herb Bo He. I wish you will chant the Tao Soul Herb Bo He Soul Mind Body Transplants more. To chant them is to invoke them and "turn them on." Otherwise, they will be resting. Chant more. You could receive remarkable healing and rejuvenation for your liver and the entire Wood element in your body beyond any words.

In summary, you have learmed how to apply *ling yao,* the soul of herbs, for healing. I am releasing this secret to tell you and humanity once again that soul has the power to heal.

You have also received Tao Soul Herb Bo He Soul Mind Body

Transplants and learned how to apply them. They carry divine and Tao Soul Power to heal.

Millions of people are on the spiritual journey. The Bible has shared many stories of the healing power of Jesus. There are many historical Buddhist books that explain the healing power of Guan Yin (the Compassion Buddha), the Medicine Buddha, Shi Jia Mo Ni Fuo (the founder of Buddhism), A Mi Tuo Fuo (the leader of the Pure Land), and other buddhas. Many other spiritual realms also have stories about their spiritual leaders who have offered miracle healings. All of these great spiritual leaders applied soul healing power to create miracles. The Divine is the leader of all souls. The Divine is our father and mother. The Divine has divine soul healing power beyond imagination.

The herb Bo He has a soul. Every herb has a soul. To boil herbs to make tea or to eat raw herbs is to use the matter and energy of the herbs to heal. To chant the names of herbs is to use the souls of the herbs to heal. The souls of herbs have power beyond words. To chant herbs is to apply *ling yao* for healing. Many people have extensive knowledge about all kinds of herbs. I will not teach you about very many herbs in this book. I am releasing the divine and Tao secret of soul herbs to you and humanity so that you can apply *ling yao* to heal yourself and others. To summarize, the one-sentence secret of soul herbs is:

To invoke the souls of herbs and chant them is to apply *ling yao* for healing.

There are many good books on Chinese and other herbs. Study them. Then, call the soul of the appropriate herbs for healing. You could receive results that totally surprise you.

So far, we have been talking about herbs in the human realm, which are the herbs on Mother Earth. There are also herb gardens in different realms of Heaven and Tao. Divine and Tao herbs may not exist on Mother Earth. You have received Soul Mind Body Transplants of the Tao Soul Herb Bo He from the Tao realm.

In 2003, the Divine gave me the honor and authority to transmit Divine Soul Herbs from the Divine's Soul Herbs Garden to humanity. In 2010, Tao gave me the honor to transmit Tao Soul Herbs from the Tao herb garden to humanity. The Divine and Tao have guided me to create Tao Soul Herbs Tea. This will be a historic, breakthrough treasure to serve humanity's healing and rejuvenation.

The Divine and Tao guided me that the Tao realm will download permanent Tao Soul Herbs to people's physical tea bags or loose tea leaves. When people drink the tea, the downloaded souls of Tao Soul Herbs will reside inside the person's body to offer healing and rejuvenation.

For example, to create Tao Soul Herbs Tea for Healing and Rejuvenation of the Wood Element, the Tao realm will download permanent soul herbs with the nature of the Wood element to physical tea. When people drink this tea, the downloaded Tao Soul Herbs will come into their bodies to balance everything with a Wood element character, including the liver, gallbladder, eyes, and tendons, and the emotion of anger. If you drink Tao Soul Herbs Tea, remember one secret. Chant silently or aloud:

> *Tao Soul Herbs Tea heals and rejuvenates my Wood element system. Thank you, Tao.*
> *Tao Soul Herbs Tea heals and rejuvenates my Wood element system. Thank you, Tao.*

Tao Soul Herbs Tea heals and rejuvenates my Wood el-
ement system. Thank you, Tao.
Tao Soul Herbs Tea heals and rejuvenates my Wood el-
ement system. Thank you, Tao.
Tao Soul Herbs Tea heals and rejuvenates my Wood el-
ement system. Thank you, Tao.
Tao Soul Herbs Tea heals and rejuvenates my Wood el-
ement system. Thank you, Tao.
Tao Soul Herbs Tea heals and rejuvenates my Wood el-
ement system. Thank you, Tao . . .

Chant a few minutes per time. The longer and the more often you chant, the better. These Tao Soul Herbs are different from Mother Earth's herbs. This is the first time in history that the Tao realm has released Tao Soul Herbs to humanity. Most of the Tao Soul Herbs do not exist in physical form on Mother Earth. I am honored to be the chosen servant to download Tao Soul Herbs to physical tea to serve humanity's healing in a special way.

I have created the Soul Power Series, of which this is the sixth book. I have offered karma cleansing for thousands of people worldwide with heart-touching and moving results. I have downloaded countless Divine Soul Mind Body Transplants. An ordinary being may not be able to fully understand this kind of service. A highly developed spiritual being can see the images of karma cleansing and Divine Soul Mind Body Transplants and also communicate directly with the Divine to learn the value and power of these divine treasures.

Now, as I am writing this *Tao I* book, Tao guided me to offer Tao Soul Herbs Tea. I am excited to be asked to offer this special Tao soul treasure to serve humanity from the Tao realm, but I do not have Tao Soul Herbs Tea yet. Let me do a slightly different live demonstration with the group of advanced teachers with me now. I will download Tao Soul Herbs directly to their soul, mind, and body.

I asked if anyone present had any significant health challenges in order to receive Tao Soul Herbs as a demonstration. One of my advanced teachers responded:

> *My name is Frances Anne Brown. The first night that we were here, you gave us such incredible treasures. I was sitting with my legs crossed. I tried to change positions and heard a crack and a pop on my side. Initially, I did not think my ribs were broken or cracked, but it has progressively hurt more and more. The intensity and depth of the pain are not as much as in the beginning, but I am still in incredible pain. I just reached over and picked up your latest book, Master Sha:* Divine Soul Mind Body Healing and Transmission System. *I need some support against my ribs and your book has been phenomenal of course with your specially blessed photo on the back cover. I am just assured that there has been great healing just because of this book's support that I am carrying around with me. It has also been incredible for me to realize how deep are my belief and mind-set that I don't need the kind of help that I offer to other people. It has been a challenge to let people help me. They are very loving, and yet it has been very emotional.*

Another one of my advanced teachers had been offering some healing to Frances Anne. Here is his evaluation:

> *My name is Dr. Brock Schwartz. I am a doctor of chiropractic with thirty years of experience. When Frances Anne came*

to me two days ago, she said that she had rib pain. I felt there and her ribs were really stuck. I first tried a technique to get the vertical and horizontal energy flowing. There were several vertebrae in back that were out of alignment. I was touching it and when I moved around to the front, she jumped. I touched it as you would touch an eyeball, with the lightest possible pressure. The first thought was that she cracked a rib. The pain was ten on a scale of one to ten. She was feeling better, but it was when I went to touch her that it showed me how tender and injured it was, even though several of you Worldwide Representatives have given her healing blessings.

I asked Dr. Schwartz, "Could you kindly check Frances Anne now and give us a report?"

Dr. Schwartz said, "I will be happy to." He examined Frances Anne, and suddenly she jumped in a painful response. Dr. Schwartz noted, "What we just saw is the classic jump sign. The pain is still that intense. It is still very sore. On a pain scale of zero to ten, the pain is still around seven."

Frances Anne had been injured five days earlier. She said that her pain was initially at a level of ten on a scale of zero to ten. After receiving several healing blessings from my Worldwide Representatives and other advanced teachers and healers over several days, Frances Anne said, "For the last day or two, my level of pain has ranged from five to seven on a scale from zero to ten. Now it is a seven."

Thank you, Frances Anne and Dr. Schwartz, for your explanation of the situation. I am honored to offer a permanent Tao Realm Soul Herbs Download to Frances Anne.

Prepare.

Ultimate Tao Order:
Ultimate Tao Soul Herbs Formula will be permanently
downloaded to Frances Anne for her condition.
Transmission!

You are very blessed. Now turn on these permanent Tao Soul Herbs to give her a short healing. We can all silently chant:

Tao Soul Herbs heal her condition. Thank you, Tao.
Tao Soul Herbs heal her condition. Thank you, Tao.
Tao Soul Herbs heal her condition. Thank you, Tao.
Tao Soul Herbs heal her condition. Thank you, Tao.
Tao Soul Herbs heal her condition. Thank you, Tao.
Tao Soul Herbs heal her condition. Thank you, Tao.
Tao Soul Herbs heal her condition. Thank you, Tao . . .

Hao! Thank you. Thank you. Thank you.

Now, who can share what they saw?

Worldwide Representative Peggy Werner:

Thank you, Master Sha. I saw the Tao herb garden. I saw a magnificent soul pick the particular herbs. There were seeds and four different leaves. They went into Frances Anne's ribs and also wrapped around her ribs. Her body is vibrating at the level of the Tao Soul Herbs. These herbs do not exist on Mother Earth. There was a lot of darkness and excess, blocked energy in her ribs. After the transmission, the Tao Soul Herbs were vibrating and connecting to Tao realm to bring much Tao light and Tao support to remove the blockages. At the same time, energy circles were being rotated to help clear the excess energy in the painful area, and golden and crystal light came in to give support on the soul level.

Worldwide Representative Francisco Quintero:

I saw the Tao realm open and then I saw the Tao herb garden. Frances Anne received at least five different types of herbs to heal the pain she has been experiencing. Herbs came from Tao realm to her rib area, filling it up. They then spread throughout her entire body. I have seen Master Sha transmit Divine Soul Herbs before. The difference between those and these Tao Soul Herbs is that the cells, bones, and whole area were being rejuvenated and renewed by the Tao Soul Herbs.

Frances Anne:

Initially what I experienced was a river of light coming around my back and then into my body and through my ribs. I immediately experienced light. The river was crystal. It contained colors that we do not see on Mother Earth. Immediately I started to feel some release. I felt my shoulders drop down and anxiety that I was not aware of dissipated. The pain at this point is maybe a two. I realize that I've put the book down and that is a sign to me that things are better. I am ever so grateful.

Dr. Schwartz:

I also felt a river of light coming through. It was healing me also. About mid-way through I could feel the field around Frances Anne relaxing. I feel very happy.

I then asked Dr. Schwartz to examine Frances Anne again.

Dr. Schwartz: "I am using the same pressure as before."

Frances Anne: "I am not experiencing difficulty."

Dr. Schwartz: "I am going to use a little stronger pressure."

Frances Anne: "I am not experiencing difficulty."

Dr. Schwartz: "I am using twice the pressure now."

Frances Anne: "I am still not experiencing difficulty."

I said again, "Dr. Schwartz, could you triple the pressure on the tender parts?"

Dr. Schwartz used three times more pressure.

Frances Anne: "I am still not experiencing difficulty."

Everybody is amazed and speechless at the power of Tao Soul Herbs.

Dr. Schwartz explained that Frances Anne's condition is different now: "Her ribs are moving properly, and when I touch the area that was so sore, I can palpate the whole area and she does not jump as she did originally. It is still quite tender, but before, it was exquisitely tender, to the point that she would jump at the slightest touch."

Thank you, Frances Anne and Dr. Schwartz. Thank you, Divine and Tao.

I am honored and very much looking forward to offering Tao Soul Herbs Tea to humanity.

>✹<

The Fire element in a human being is connected with the heart, small intestine, tongue, and blood vessels, and depression and anxiety in the emotional body. If an herb carries the nature of the Fire element, it can serve all of the Fire element organs and tissues as well as depression and anxiety in the emotional body.

Let me share with you one herb that is very important for increasing heart qi. It is Sheng Mai Ya (pronounced *shung mye yah*). "Sheng" means *raw*. "Mai ya" is *germinated barley*. One of Sheng Mai Ya's most significant powers is to boost liver qi. According to Five Elements theory, Wood produces Fire. Wood is the mother of Fire. Since the liver is the major Wood organ and the heart is the major Fire organ, liver qi is the mother of heart qi. Because Sheng Mai Ya boosts liver qi, the liver qi will in turn nourish the heart qi. It is like a mother nourishing her baby.

How can we apply soul herbs to increase heart qi? Use the Four Power Techniques:

Body Power. Sit up straight. Put your right palm over your liver. Put your left palm over your heart.

Soul Power. Say *hello:*

> *Dear soul mind body of Sheng Mai Ya,*
> *Dear soul mind body of my liver,*
> *Dear soul mind body of my heart,*
> *I love you all.*
> *Please boost my heart qi.*
> *Do a good job.*
> *Thank you.*

Mind Power. Visualize golden light shining in your liver and heart.

Sound Power. Chant silently or aloud:

> *Sheng Mai Ya boosts my heart qi. Thank you.*
> *Sheng Mai Ya boosts my heart qi. Thank you.*

Sheng Mai Ya boosts my heart qi. Thank you.
Sheng Mai Ya boosts my heart qi. Thank you.
Sheng Mai Ya boosts my heart qi. Thank you.
Sheng Mai Ya boosts my heart qi. Thank you.
Sheng Mai Ya boosts my heart qi. Thank you . . .

Chant at least three to five minutes per time. The longer you chant, the better. For life-threatening or chronic conditions, it is best to chant two hours a day. You can add together all of your chanting time to total at least two hours.

Now I am going to offer Tao Soul Herb Sheng Mai Ya Soul Mind Body Transplants.

Prepare.

Sit up straight.

Totally relax.

Open your heart and soul to receive these Tao treasures.

Tao Order: Tao Soul Herb Sheng Mai Ya Soul Transplant Transmission!

This golden light being is about seven hundred feet high.

Tao Order: Tao Soul Herb Sheng Mai Ya Mind Transplant Transmission!

Another golden light being about seven hundred feet high carries the Tao consciousness of Sheng Mai Ya to your body.

Tao Order: Tao Soul Herb Sheng Mai Ya Body Transplant Transmission!

This third golden light being carries the Tao energy and matter of Sheng Mai Ya to your body.

Tao Order: Tao Soul Herb Sheng Mai Ya Soul Mind Body Transplants join as one.

He Ya Ya Ya Ya You!

This Tao Order directs your Tao Soul Herbs Sheng Mai Ya Soul Mind Body Transplants to join as one to serve.

Now chant silently or aloud:

Tao Soul Herb Sheng Mai Ya Soul Mind Body Transplants boost my heart qi and heal my heart. Thank you, Tao.

Tao Soul Herb Sheng Mai Ya Soul Mind Body Transplants boost my heart qi and heal my heart. Thank you, Tao.

Tao Soul Herb Sheng Mai Ya Soul Mind Body Transplants boost my heart qi and heal my heart. Thank you, Tao.

Tao Soul Herb Sheng Mai Ya Soul Mind Body Transplants boost my heart qi and heal my heart. Thank you, Tao.

Tao Soul Herb Sheng Mai Ya Soul Mind Body Transplants boost my heart qi and heal my heart. Thank you, Tao.

Tao Soul Herb Sheng Mai Ya Soul Mind Body Transplants boost my heart qi and heal my heart. Thank you, Tao.

> *Tao Soul Herb Sheng Mai Ya Soul Mind Body Trans-*
> *plants boost my heart qi and heal my heart. Thank*
> *you, Tao . . .*

Chant three to five minutes per time. The longer and the more often you chant, the better. The Tao Soul Herb Sheng Mai Ya has power beyond imagination because it is not the Sheng Mai Ya on Mother Earth. This Tao Soul Herb Sheng Mai Ya comes from the Tao herb garden. There is no comparison between the power of the Tao Soul Herb Sheng Mai Ya and the Mother Earth herb Sheng Mai Ya. Please chant more. You could receive remarkable healing and rejuvenation for your heart beyond any words.

>≍

The Earth element connects with the spleen, stomach, gums and teeth, and muscles, and worry in the emotional body. If an herb carries the nature of the Earth element, it can serve all Earth element organs and tissues as well as worry in the emotional body. A common herb for strengthening the function of the spleen is Chao Bai Zhu (pronounced *chow bye joo*). "Chao" means *cooked*. "Bai zhu" is *Atractylodes macrocephala*. "Chao Bai Zhu" means *cooked Bai Zhu*. Use the Soul Herb Chao Bai Zhu to strengthen the function of the spleen with the Four Power Techniques:

Body Power. Sit up straight. Put your left palm over your spleen. Put your right palm on your lower abdomen.

Soul Power. Say *hello:*

> *Dear soul mind body of Chao Bai Zhu,*
> *Dear soul mind body of my spleen,*
> *I love you.*

You have the power to strengthen the functioning of my spleen.
Thank you.

Mind Power. Visualize golden light shining in your spleen.

Sound Power. Chant silently or aloud:

Chao Bai Zhu strengthens my spleen function. Thank you.
Chao Bai Zhu strengthens my spleen function. Thank you.
Chao Bai Zhu strengthens my spleen function. Thank you.
Chao Bai Zhu strengthens my spleen function. Thank you.
Chao Bai Zhu strengthens my spleen function. Thank you.
Chao Bai Zhu strengthens my spleen function. Thank you.
Chao Bai Zhu strengthens my spleen function. Thank you . . .

Chant at least three to five minutes; the longer, the better.

※

Now I am going to offer the Tao Soul Herb Chao Bai Zhu Soul Mind Body Transplants.
Prepare.
Sit up straight.
Totally relax.
Open your heart and soul to receive these Tao treasures.

Tao Order: Tao Soul Herb Chao Bai Zhu Soul Transplant Transmission!

Tao Order: Tao Soul Herb Chao Bai Zhu Mind Transplant Transmission!

Tao Order: Tao Soul Herb Chao Bai Zhu Body Transplant Transmission!

Tao Order: Tao Soul Herb Chao Bai Zhu Soul Mind Body Transplants join as one.

He Ya Ya Ya Ya You!

This last Tao Order directs your Tao Soul Herb Chao Bai Zhu Soul Mind Body Transplants to join as one to serve.

Now chant silently or aloud:

Tao Soul Herb Chao Bai Zhu Soul Mind Body Transplants heal my spleen. Thank you, Tao.
Tao Soul Herb Chao Bai Zhu Soul Mind Body Transplants heal my spleen. Thank you, Tao.
Tao Soul Herb Chao Bai Zhu Soul Mind Body Transplants heal my spleen. Thank you, Tao.
Tao Soul Herb Chao Bai Zhu Soul Mind Body Transplants heal my spleen. Thank you, Tao.
Tao Soul Herb Chao Bai Zhu Soul Mind Body Transplants heal my spleen. Thank you, Tao.
Tao Soul Herb Chao Bai Zhu Soul Mind Body Transplants heal my spleen. Thank you, Tao.
Tao Soul Herb Chao Bai Zhu Soul Mind Body Transplants heal my spleen. Thank you, Tao . . .

Chant for at least three to five minutes per time. The longer and the more often you chant, the better. The Tao Soul Herb Chao Bai Zhu has power beyond measurement because it is not Mother Earth's Chao Bai Zhu. It comes from the Tao realm. There is no comparison between the power of the Tao Soul Herb Chao Bai Zhu and the Mother Earth herb Chao Bai Zhu.

Please chant more. You could receive remarkable healing and rejuvenation for your spleen beyond any words.

⋇

The Metal element in a human being includes the lungs, large intestine, nose, and skin, and grief in the emotional body. If an herb carries the nature of the Metal element, it can serve all Metal element organs and tissues as well as grief in the emotional body.

Let me share a very important herb for the lungs, the Message Center, and the brain. This herb is named Shi Chang Pu (pronounced *shr chahng poo*). Shi Chang Pu is *rhizome of Acorus gramineus Soland*. This soul herb can clear energy and matter blockages in the lungs, Message Center, and brain. Shi Chang Pu is the key herb for healing the lungs, depression, anxiety, and Alzheimer's disease.

Let us practice using this soul herb to heal your lungs, Message Center, and brain. Use the Four Power Techniques:

Body Power. Sit up straight. Put one palm on your Message Center. Put the other palm on your lower abdomen.

Soul Power. Say *hello:*

> *Dear soul mind body of Shi Chang Pu,*
> *Dear soul mind body of my Message Center,*

Dear soul mind body of my lungs and brain,
I love you all.
You have the power to heal my lungs, Message Center,
   and brain.
Thank you.

Mind Power. Visualize golden light shining in your lungs, Message Center, and brain.

Sound Power. Chant silently or aloud:

Shi Chang Pu heals my lungs, Message Center, and
   brain. Thank you.
Shi Chang Pu heals my lungs, Message Center, and
   brain. Thank you.
Shi Chang Pu heals my lungs, Message Center, and
   brain. Thank you.
Shi Chang Pu heals my lungs, Message Center, and
   brain. Thank you.
Shi Chang Pu heals my lungs, Message Center, and
   brain. Thank you.
Shi Chang Pu heals my lungs, Message Center, and
   brain. Thank you.
Shi Chang Pu heals my lungs, Message Center, and
   brain. Thank you . . .

Chant three to five minutes; the longer, the better. There is no time limit for this practice.

※

Now I am going to offer the Tao Soul Herb Shi Chang Pu Soul Mind Body Transplants.

Prepare.
Sit up straight.
Totally relax.
Open your heart and soul to receive these Tao treasures.

Tao Order: Tao Soul Herb Shi Chang Pu Soul Transplant Transmission!

Tao Order: Tao Soul Herb Shi Chang Pu Mind Transplant Transmission!

Tao Order: Tao Soul Herb Shi Chang Pu Body Transplant Transmission!

Tao Order: Tao Soul Herb Shi Chang Pu Soul Mind Body Transplants join as one.

He Ya Ya Ya Ya You!

This Tao Order is for the Tao Soul Herb Shi Chang Pu Soul Mind Body Transplants to join as one to serve.

Now chant silently or aloud:

> *Tao Soul Herb Shi Chang Pu Soul Mind Body Transplants heal my lungs, Message Center, and brain. Thank you, Tao.*
> *Tao Soul Herb Shi Chang Pu Soul Mind Body Transplants heal my lungs, Message Center, and brain. Thank you, Tao.*
> *Tao Soul Herb Shi Chang Pu Soul Mind Body Transplants heal my lungs, Message Center, and brain. Thank you, Tao.*

Tao Soul Herb Shi Chang Pu Soul Mind Body Trans-
plants heal my lungs, Message Center, and brain.
Thank you, Tao.
Tao Soul Herb Shi Chang Pu Soul Mind Body Trans-
plants heal my lungs, Message Center, and brain.
Thank you, Tao.
Tao Soul Herb Shi Chang Pu Soul Mind Body Trans-
plants heal my lungs, Message Center, and brain.
Thank you, Tao.
Tao Soul Herb Shi Chang Pu Soul Mind Body Trans-
plants heal my lungs, Message Center, and brain.
Thank you, Tao . . .

Chant at least three to five minutes per time; the longer, the better. The Tao Soul Herb Shi Chang Pu has power beyond any thoughts because it is not Mother Earth's Shi Chang Pu. There is no comparison between the power of the Tao Soul Herb Shi Chang Pu and Mother Earth's herb Shi Chang Pu. Please chant more. You could receive remarkable healing and rejuvenation for your lungs, Message Center and brain, beyond any words.

☀

The Water element in a human being includes the kidneys, urinary bladder, ears, and bones, and fear in the emotional body. If an herb carries the nature of the Water element, it can serve the Water element organs and tissues as well as fear in the emotional body.

Let me share a very important herb for the kidneys. This herb is named Sheng Huai Shan (pronounced *shung hwye shahn*). Sheng Huai Shan is *dioscorea* or *Chinese wild yam*. This herb is one of the keys for nourishing kidney yin. This is a very important herb for strengthening weak kidney function and for healing menopausal symptoms, fatigue, and more.

Now let us use this soul herb to heal your kidneys, bones, menopausal symptoms, and fatigue. Use the Four Power Techniques:

Body Power. Sit up straight. Put your left palm on your left kidney. Put your right palm on your right kidney.

Soul Power. Say *hello:*

> *Dear soul mind body of Sheng Huai Shan,*
> *Dear soul mind body of my kidneys,*
> *Dear soul mind body of my bones,*
> *Dear soul mind body of my ears,*
> *I love you all.*
> *You have the power to heal my kidneys, bones, and ears.*
> *Thank you.*

Mind Power. Visualize the kidneys shining golden light.

Sound Power. Chant silently or aloud:

> *Sheng Huai Shan heals my kidneys, bones, ears,*
> *   fatigue, and fear. Thank you.*
> *Sheng Huai Shan heals my kidneys, bones, ears,*
> *   fatigue, and fear. Thank you.*
> *Sheng Huai Shan heals my kidneys, bones, ears,*
> *   fatigue, and fear. Thank you.*
> *Sheng Huai Shan heals my kidneys, bones, ears,*
> *   fatigue, and fear. Thank you.*
> *Sheng Huai Shan heals my kidneys, bones, ears,*
> *   fatigue, and fear. Thank you.*

Sheng Huai Shan heals my kidneys, bones, ears,
fatigue, and fear. Thank you.
Sheng Huai Shan heals my kidneys, bones, ears,
fatigue, and fear. Thank you . . .

Chant for at least three to five minutes. The longer and the more often you chant, the better.

※

Now I am going to offer Tao Soul Herb Sheng Huai Shan Soul Mind Body Transplants.

Prepare.

Sit up straight.

Totally relax.

Open your heart and soul to receive these Tao treasures.

Tao Order:
Tao Soul Herb Sheng Huai Shan Soul Transplant
Transmission!

Tao Order:
Tao Soul Herb Sheng Huai Shan Mind Transplant
Transmission!

Tao Order:
Tao Soul Herb Sheng Huai Shan Body Transplant
Transmission!

Tao Order: Tao Soul Herb Sheng Huai Shan
Soul Mind Body Transplants join as one.

He Ya Ya Ya Ya You!

This is the Tao Order to join Tao Soul Herb Sheng Huai Shan Soul Mind Body Transplants as one to serve.

Now chant silently or aloud:

> *Tao Soul Herb Sheng Huai Shan Soul Mind Body*
> *Transplants heal my kidneys, bones, ears, fatigue,*
> *and fear. Thank you, Tao.*
> *Tao Soul Herb Sheng Huai Shan Soul Mind Body*
> *Transplants heal my kidneys, bones, ears, fatigue,*
> *and fear. Thank you, Tao.*
> *Tao Soul Herb Sheng Huai Shan Soul Mind Body*
> *Transplants heal my kidneys, bones, ears, fatigue,*
> *and fear. Thank you, Tao.*
> *Tao Soul Herb Sheng Huai Shan Soul Mind Body*
> *Transplants heal my kidneys, bones, ears, fatigue,*
> *and fear. Thank you, Tao.*
> *Tao Soul Herb Sheng Huai Shan Soul Mind Body*
> *Transplants heal my kidneys, bones, ears, fatigue,*
> *and fear. Thank you, Tao.*
> *Tao Soul Herb Sheng Huai Shan Soul Mind Body*
> *Transplants heal my kidneys, bones, ears, fatigue,*
> *and fear. Thank you, Tao.*
> *Tao Soul Herb Sheng Huai Shan Soul Mind Body*
> *Transplants heal my kidneys, bones, ears, fatigue,*
> *and fear. Thank you, Tao . . .*

Chant for at least three to five minutes. The longer and the more often you chant, the better.

Tao Soul Herb Sheng Haui Shan has power beyond any thoughts because it is not Mother Earth's Sheng Haui Shan. The Tao Soul Herb Sheng Haui Shan comes from the Tao realm.

There is no comparison between the power of the Tao Soul Herb Sheng Haui Shan and Mother Earth's herb Sheng Haui Shan. Please chant more. You could receive remarkable healing and rejuvenation for your kidneys, bones, and fatigue, beyond any words.

※

I have just offered five Tao Soul Herb Soul Mind Body Transplants. They are Tao Soul Herb Bo He for healing and rejuvenating the liver, Tao Soul Herb Sheng Mai Ya for healing and rejuvenating the heart, Tao Soul Herb Chao Bai Zhu for healing and rejuvenating the spleen, Tao Soul Herb Shi Chang Pu for healing and rejuvenating the lungs, Message Center, and brain, and Tao Soul Herb Sheng Huai Shan for healing and rejuvenating the kidneys.

This is the way to practice with them together to benefit your Five Elements.

Body Power. Sit up straight. Put one palm on your Message Center. Put the other palm on your Snow Mountain Area. Do Soul Tapping of both areas simultaneously.

Soul Power. Say *hello:*

> *Dear soul mind body of Tao Soul Herb Bo He, Tao Soul Herb Sheng Mai Ya, Tao Soul Herb Chao Bai Zhu, Tao Soul Herb Shi Chang Pu, and Tao Soul Herb Sheng Huai Shan,*
> *Dear soul mind body of my Message Center,*
> *Dear soul mind body of my Snow Mountain Area,*
> *Dear soul mind body of my liver,*
> *Dear soul mind body of my heart,*

Dear soul mind body of my spleen,
Dear soul mind body of my lungs,
Dear soul mind body of my kidneys,
Dear soul mind body of my brain,
I love you all.
You have the power to heal and rejuvenate my liver,
  heart, spleen, lungs, kidneys, Message Center, and
  brain, as well as my whole body.
Do a good job!
I am extremely grateful.
Thank you.

Mind Power. Visualize golden light radiating in your entire body, from head to toe, skin to bone.

Sound Power. Chant silently or aloud:

Tao Soul Herbs Bo He, Sheng Mai Ya, Chao Bai Zhu,
  Shi Chang Pu, and Sheng Huai Shan heal and re-
  juvenate my liver, heart, spleen, lungs, kidneys, Mes-
  sage Center, brain, and whole body. Thank you.
Tao Soul Herbs Bo He, Sheng Mai Ya, Chao Bai Zhu,
  Shi Chang Pu, and Sheng Huai Shan heal and re-
  juvenate my liver, heart, spleen, lungs, kidneys, Mes-
  sage Center, brain, and whole body. Thank you.
Tao Soul Herbs Bo He, Sheng Mai Ya, Chao Bai Zhu,
  Shi Chang Pu, and Sheng Huai Shan heal and re-
  juvenate my liver, heart, spleen, lungs, kidneys, Mes-
  sage Center, brain, and whole body. Thank you.
Tao Soul Herbs Bo He, Sheng Mai Ya, Chao Bai Zhu,
  Shi Chang Pu, and Sheng Huai Shan, heal and re-

juvenate my liver, heart, spleen, lungs, kidneys, Message Center, brain, and whole body. Thank you.

Tao Soul Herbs Bo He, Sheng Mai Ya, Chao Bai Zhu, Shi Chang Pu, and Sheng Huai Shan, heal and rejuvenate my liver, heart, spleen, lungs, kidneys, Message Center, brain, and whole body. Thank you.

Tao Soul Herbs Bo He, Sheng Mai Ya, Chao Bai Zhu, Shi Chang Pu, and Sheng Huai Shan, heal and rejuvenate my liver, heart, spleen, lungs, kidneys, Message Center, brain, and whole body. Thank you.

Tao Soul Herbs Bo He, Sheng Mai Ya, Chao Bai Zhu, Shi Chang Pu, and Sheng Huai Shan, heal and rejuvenate my liver, heart, spleen, lungs, kidneys, Message Center, brain, and whole body. Thank you . . .

Chant for at least three to five minutes. The longer and more often you chant, the better. There is no time limit. These five Tao Soul Herbs carry Tao realm frequency. This is the first time that Tao has released them to humanity. We cannot honor enough how blessed we are that we can receive these five priceless permanent Tao Soul Herb treasures.

Remember to chant more and more. You will receive "aha!" moments and "wow!" moments again and again.

灵针灸
Ling Zhen Jiu

Soul Acupuncture

"Ling" means *soul*. "Zhen jiu" means *acupuncture*. So "Ling zhen jiu" (pronounced *ling jun jeo*) means *soul acupuncture*. Acupuncture has been one of the major practices in traditional Chinese medicine for five thousand years.

I am honored to share Soul Acupuncture with you and humanity. I am going to show you how to apply Soul Acupuncture for healing and rejuvenation. In fact, it is a one-sentence secret:

To apply Soul Acupuncture is to say
***hello* to the acupuncture point.**

Now I release further Soul Acupuncture secrets from the Divine and Tao to you and humanity. I will use back pain as the first example. There is an acupuncture point at the middle of the back of the lower part of the knee. It is named the Wei Zhong (pronounced *way jawng*) and is also called UB 40 (Urinary Bladder meridian 40). The anatomical description of its location is the midpoint of the transverse crease of the popliteal fossa, between the tendons of biceps femoris and semitendinosis. In traditional Chinese medicine, UB 40 is an excellent point for lower back conditions.

Use the Four Power Techniques:

Body Power. Sit up straight or stand. Put the tip of your tongue as close as you can to the roof of your mouth without touching it. Relax your whole body. Put one palm on your lower abdomen. Put the other palm on your lower back.

Soul Power. Say *hello:*

> *Dear soul mind body of my Wei Zhong acupuncture*
> *points,*
> *I love you, honor you and appreciate you.*

You have the power to heal the whole back side of my
*   body from the back of my head to the back of my feet.*
Do a good job.
Thank you.

Mind Power. Visualize golden light shining in your whole back.

Sound Power. Chant silently or aloud:

Wei Zhong heal and rejuvenate my whole back.
*   Thank you.*
Wei Zhong heal and rejuvenate my whole back.
*   Thank you.*
Wei Zhong heal and rejuvenate my whole back.
*   Thank you.*
Wei Zhong heal and rejuvenate my whole back.
*   Thank you.*
Wei Zhong heal and rejuvenate my whole back.
*   Thank you.*
Wei Zhong heal and rejuvenate my whole back.
*   Thank you.*
Wei Zhong heal and rejuvenate my whole back.
*   Thank you . . .*

Chant for at least three to five minutes. The longer you chant and the more you chant, the better.

⁂

The second example will apply Soul Acupuncture for the digestive system and for any part of the body. We will use the Zu San Li (pronounced *dzoo sahn lee*) acupuncture point, also called

ST 36 (Stomach meridian 36). It is located below the knee on the anterior aspect of the lower leg, one finger breadth (middle finger) from the anterior crest of the tibia. In traditional Chinese medicine, Zu San Li is a very important point for the abdomen, spleen, stomach, digestion, and general wellness.

Use the Four Power Techniques:

Body Power. Sit up straight or stand. Put the tip of your tongue as close as you can to the roof of your mouth without touching it. Relax your whole body. Put both palms on your lower abdomen.

Soul Power. Say *hello:*

> *Dear soul mind body of my Zu San Li acupuncture*
> *points,*
> *Dear soul mind body of my digestive system,*
> *Dear soul mind body of my whole body,*
> *I love you all.*
> *You have the power to heal yourselves.*
> *Do a good job.*
> *Thank you.*

Mind Power. Visualize golden light radiating in your digestive system and throughout your whole body.

Sound Power. Chant silently or aloud:

> *Zu San Li heal and rejuvenate my digestive system and*
> *whole body. Thank you.*
> *Zu San Li heal and rejuvenate my digestive system and*
> *whole body. Thank you.*

Zu San Li heal and rejuvenate my digestive system and
   whole body. Thank you.
Zu San Li heal and rejuvenate my digestive system and
   whole body. Thank you.
Zu San Li heal and rejuvenate my digestive system and
   whole body. Thank you.
Zu San Li heal and rejuvenate my digestive system and
   whole body. Thank you.
Zu San Li heal and rejuvenate my digestive system and
   whole body. Thank you . . .

Chant for at least three to five minutes. The longer and the more often you chant, the better.

※

Finally, let me share with you the most important secret of Soul Acupuncture. This is to say *hello* to the soul, mind, and body of *all* meridians and *all* acupuncture points. This is the top secret of Soul Acupuncture. Apply the Four Power Techniques:

Body Power. Sit up straight or stand. Put the tip of your tongue as close as you can to the roof of your mouth without touching it. Relax. Put one fist on your Message Center. Put the other fist on your Snow Mountain Area. Do Soul Tapping of both areas simultaneously.

Soul Power. Say *hello:*

Dear soul mind body of all my meridians and all my
   acupuncture points,
Dear soul mind body of my Message Center,

Dear soul mind body of my Snow Mountain Area,
I love you all.
You have the power to heal and rejuvenate my physi-
*   cal, emotional, mental, and spiritual bodies.*
Do a good job.
I am very grateful.
Thank you.

Mind Power. Visualize golden light radiating on all acupuncture points and all meridians from head to toe, skin to bone.

Sound Power. Chant silently or aloud:

Soul mind body of all my acupuncture points and all
*   my meridians heal and rejuvenate my physical,*
*   emotional, mental, and spiritual bodies. Thank you.*
Soul mind body of all my acupuncture points and all
*   my meridians heal and rejuvenate my physical,*
*   emotional, mental, and spiritual bodies. Thank you.*
Soul mind body of all my acupuncture points and all
*   my meridians heal and rejuvenate my physical,*
*   emotional, mental, and spiritual bodies. Thank you.*
Soul mind body of all my acupuncture points and all
*   my meridians heal and rejuvenate my physical,*
*   emotional, mental, and spiritual bodies. Thank you.*
Soul mind body of all my acupuncture points and all
*   my meridians heal and rejuvenate my physical,*
*   emotional, mental, and spiritual bodies. Thank you.*
Soul mind body of all my acupuncture points and all
*   my meridians heal and rejuvenate my physical,*
*   emotional, mental, and spiritual bodies. Thank you.*

Soul mind body of all my acupuncture points and all
my meridians heal and rejuvenate my physical,
emotional, mental, and spiritual bodies.
Thank you . . .

Chant for at least three to five minutes per time. The longer you chant and the more you chant, the better.

Soul Acupuncture has power beyond comprehension. This is the sacred wisdom and practical technique that the Divine and Tao asked me to share with humanity. I am very grateful that this wisdom and practical technique can serve millions of people.

Acupuncture has been practiced for five thousand years in history. To do acupuncture requires special training. Acupuncture has made great and important contributions to humanity. Acupuncture continues to be very important.

What I am sharing with you and humanity is Soul Acupuncture. Everyone and everything in the universe has a soul, mind, and body. Every acupuncture point and every meridian has a soul, mind, and body. In 2002, I introduced the essence of Say Hello Healing in my first major book, *Power Healing: The Four Keys to Energizing Your Body, Mind and Spirit.* This wisdom and techniques have benefited thousands of people worldwide. There are thousands of heart-touching and moving stories about Say Hello Healing and Say Hello Blessing.

In my 2006 book *Soul Mind Body Medicine: A Complete Soul Healing System for Optimum Health and Vitality,* I gave the complete Say Hello Healing and Say Hello Blessing formula. Say Hello Healing and Say Hello Blessing can be used to offer healing and blessing to every aspect of your life. They can also be used to offer healing and blessing to anyone and anything.

Say Hello Healing and Say Hello Blessing can be summarized in one sentence:

Say Hello Healing and Blessing is one of the highest secrets and practical techniques of soul healing and blessing for healing, prevention of sickness, rejuvenation, prolonging life, and transformation of every aspect of life, including relationships and finances, as well as for enlightenment of soul, heart, mind, and body in order to create love, peace, and harmony for humanity, Mother Earth, and all universes.

If you apply Soul Acupuncture to heal yourself and others, you could receive remarkable healing results that surprise and even shock you.

I wish you will receive great healing and life-transforming results by applying Soul Acupuncture.

灵按摩

Ling An Mo

Soul Massage

"Ling" means *soul*. "An mo" means *massage*. "Ling an mo" (pronounced *ling ahn maw*) means *soul massage*.

Massage is a wonderful experience that everyone should have. When you are a baby, your parents bathe you and gently massage your body. When you are an adult, you could ask your loved ones to massage you or you could receive a massage from a professional massage therapist.

Soul massage means that soul has the power to massage. Your

own soul has the power to massage you. I am releasing this Soul Massage secret now.

Apply the Four Power Techniques:

Body Power. Lie down comfortably. Cover yourself well to stay warm.

Soul Power. Say *hello*:

> *Dear my body soul,*
> *Dear souls of all of my systems, organs, cells, cell units,*
>   *DNA, RNA, smallest matter inside the cells, and*
>   *spaces between the cells,*
> *I love you, honor you, and appreciate you.*
> *You have the power to offer a massage to all of my sys-*
>   *tems, organs, cells, cell units, DNA, RNA, smallest*
>   *matter inside of the cells, and spaces between the*
>   *cells from skin to bone, head to toe.*
> *Do a good job.*
> *I am very grateful.*
> *Thank you.*

Mind Power. Visualize your whole body shining golden light from head to toe, skin to bone.

Sound Power. Chant silently:

> *My souls massage my whole body. Thank you.*
> *My souls massage my whole body. Thank you.*
> *My souls massage my whole body. Thank you.*
> *My souls massage my whole body. Thank you.*
> *My souls massage my whole body. Thank you.*

My souls massage my whole body. Thank you.
My souls massage my whole body. Thank you . . .

Chant silently for at least three to five minutes. The longer, the better.

Pause for a moment and ask yourself, "Can it really be so simple to do Soul Massage?" Remember my teaching. I have said it for many years. *If you want to know if a pear is sweet, taste it.* If you want to know if Soul Massage works, experience it.

After you experience Soul Massage for a few minutes, you could feel a little better. You could feel much better. If so, you will further understand Da Tao zhi jian, *The Big Way is extremely simple.* If you did not feel any improvement, practice the Soul Massage a little longer. In a short time, you could start to feel the healing results.

Imagine everyone doing Soul Massage for themselves.

Soul Massage can make people feel relaxed, calm, comforted, healed, and happy.

I wish Soul Massage will serve you well.

I wish Soul Massage will serve your loved ones well.

I wish Soul Massage will serve humanity well.

I wish Soul Massage will serve Mother Earth well.

I wish Soul Massage will serve all universes well.

灵治疗
Ling Zhi Liao

Soul Healing

"Ling" means *soul.* "Zhi liao" means *healing.* "Ling zhi liao" (pronounced *ling jr lee-yow*) means *soul healing.* Soul healing is the major teaching I offer to humanity. I teach soul healing in every book of my Soul Power Series. I am delighted to summarize the major types of soul healing for you and humanity.

Soul healing can be divided into four types:

- self-healing
- healing others
- group healing
- remote healing

We can invoke many souls to assist us in our healing: inner souls and outer souls, including the souls of human beings, nature, saints, other high-level spiritual beings, the Divine, and Tao.

Self-Healing

A human being has a body soul, system souls, organ souls, cell souls, cell unit souls, DNA and RNA souls, smallest matter souls, and space between cells souls. A soul is a golden light being. The souls in the body differ in size from body soul to cell soul, with the cell souls being much smaller, but all layers of souls are golden light beings.

We will use the Say Hello Healing formula and apply the Four Power Techniques for self-healing and for healing others.

To review, the Say Hello Healing formula is:

Say hello: *Dear soul mind body of my _____,*
Give love: *I love you.*
Make an affirmation: *You have the power to heal yourself.*
Give an order: *Do a good job!*
Express gratitude: *Thank you.*

Join me now to do a soul self-healing practice.

Body Power. Sit up straight. Put the tip of your tongue as close as you can to the roof of your mouth without touching it. Put one palm on the area of the body where you need healing, for example, the liver.

Soul Power. Say *hello:*

> *Dear soul mind body of my liver,*
> *I love you.*
> *You have the power to heal yourself.*
> *Do a good job!*
> *Thank you.*

Mind Power. Visualize golden light shining in your liver.

Sound Power. Chant silently or aloud:

> *Soul of my liver heals my liver. Thank you.*
> *Soul of my liver heals my liver. Thank you.*
> *Soul of my liver heals my liver. Thank you.*
> *Soul of my liver heals my liver. Thank you.*
> *Soul of my liver heals my liver. Thank you.*
> *Soul of my liver heals my liver. Thank you.*
> *Soul of my liver heals my liver. Thank you . . .*

> *Hao!*

Chant for at least three to five minutes per time. The longer and the more often you chant, the better. For chronic or life-threatening conditions, chant for two hours or more each day.

※

Many people worldwide suffer from lower back pain. Let us practice soul self-healing for the lower back now.

Body Power. Sit up straight. Put the tip of your tongue as close as you can to the roof of your mouth without touching it. Put one palm on your lower back.

Soul Power. Say *hello:*

> *Dear soul mind body of my lower back,*
> *I love you.*
> *You have the power to heal yourself.*
> *Do a good job!*
> *Thank you.*

Mind Power. Visualize golden light shining in your lower back.

Sound Power. Chant silently or aloud:

> *Soul of my lower back heals my lower back. Thank you.*
> *Soul of my lower back heals my lower back. Thank you.*
> *Soul of my lower back heals my lower back. Thank you.*
> *Soul of my lower back heals my lower back. Thank you.*
> *Soul of my lower back heals my lower back. Thank you.*
> *Soul of my lower back heals my lower back. Thank you.*
> *Soul of my lower back heals my lower back. Thank you . . .*

> *Hao!*

Chant for at least three to five minutes per time. The longer and the more often you chant, the better. For chronic or lifethreatening conditions, chant for two hours or more each day.

�֎

You may think soul healing is too simple to believe. Ancient wisdom says *the best teaching is the simplest teaching*. I have received thousands of heart-touching and moving stories in the last few years from people worldwide about the power of soul healing. The power of soul healing is beyond any words and comprehension. I encourage you to sincerely try soul healing to experience it for yourself.

You can apply the above soul healing wisdom for any system, any organ, any cell, any cell unit, any DNA, any RNA, or any part of body. You could find out for yourself how powerful soul self-healing is. Ancient teaching says *if you want to know if a pear is sweet, taste it*. If you want to know if soul self-healing works, experience it.

Remember that you *must* take time to practice if you want to experience soul healing. Remember also that if you have a chronic or life-threatening condition, do not expect to achieve significant results in three minutes of practice. For chronic and life-threatening conditions, it usually takes practicing two hours per day for a few weeks or even a few months to see significant improvement.

Have patience.

Have confidence.

Apply soul healing.

Benefit from it.

Healing Others

When your family member, loved one, friend, or client is sick, you can apply the Four Power Techniques to offer soul healing to them.

For example, to heal a person's knees:

Body Power. Sit up straight or stand. Point the fingers of one hand at the person's knees.

Soul Power. Say *hello:*

> *Dear soul mind body of your knees,*
> *I love you.*
> *You have the power to heal yourselves.*
> *Do a good job!*
> *Thank you.*

> *Dear my beloved soul,*
> *I love you.*
> *You have the power to heal this person's knees.*
> *Do a good job!*
> *Thank you.*

> *Dear Sha's Golden Healing Ball,*[9]
> *I love you.*
> *You have the power to heal this person's knees.*
> *Please come from Heaven to heal this person's knees.*
> *Thank you.*

Mind Power. Visualize golden light shining in the person's knees.

---

9 Dr. Sha received Sha's Golden Healing Ball, a spiritual gift for all humanity, on December 7, 1995. Everyone can call on Sha's Golden Healing Ball for healing, preventing sickness, rejuvenation, and transforming all aspects of life, including relationships and finances. See Zhi Gang Sha, *Sha's Golden Healing Ball: A Perfect Gift*, revised edition (Toronto, Canada: Heaven's Library, 2010).

Sound Power. Chant silently or aloud:

> *Souls of your knees heal your knees.*
> *My soul heals your knees.*
> *Sha's Golden Healing Ball heals your knees.*
> *Thank you all.*

> *Souls of your knees heal your knees.*
> *My soul heals your knees.*
> *Sha's Golden Healing Ball heals your knees.*
> *Thank you all.*

> *Souls of your knees heal your knees.*
> *My soul heals your knees.*
> *Sha's Golden Healing Ball heals your knees.*
> *Thank you all.*

> *Souls of your knees heal your knees.*
> *My soul heals your knees.*
> *Sha's Golden Healing Ball heals your knees.*
> *Thank you all.*

> *Souls of your knees heal your knees.*
> *My soul heals your knees.*
> *Sha's Golden Healing Ball heals your knees.*
> *Thank you all.*

> *Souls of your knees heal your knees.*
> *My soul heals your knees.*
> *Sha's Golden Healing Ball heals your knees.*
> *Thank you all.*

Souls of your knees heal your knees.
My soul heals your knees.
Sha's Golden Healing Ball heals your knees.
Thank you all . . .

Hao!
Thank you. Thank you. Thank you.

Chant for at least three to five minutes per time. The longer and the more often you chant, the more soul healing the person's knees will receive.

Group Healing

You can offer healing to a group of people, each with their individual requests. You can apply the same simple techniques to heal a few people, a room full of people, or a group of one thousand people at the same time. How? Say *hello* and apply the Four Power Techniques:

Body Power. Put your left palm over your Message Center (heart chakra) without touching your body. Put your right hand in the traditional prayer position in front of your left hand.

Soul Power. Say *hello:*

> *Dear everybody,*
> *Choose one part of the body where you need healing.*

Then silently say:

> *Dear souls of the parts of the body everybody requested*
> *   healing for,*

I love you.
You have the power to heal yourselves.
My soul has the power to help you.
Sha's Golden Healing Ball has the power to heal you.
Please come from Heaven to heal their requests as
    appropriate.
Thank you.

Mind Power. Visualize a huge golden light ball shining in the whole group.

Sound Power. Silently chant:

Your souls heal you. My soul heals you. Sha's Golden
    Healing Ball heals you. Thank you all.
Your souls heal you. My soul heals you. Sha's Golden
    Healing Ball heals you. Thank you all.
Your souls heal you. My soul heals you. Sha's Golden
    Healing Ball heals you. Thank you all.
Your souls heal you. My soul heals you. Sha's Golden
    Healing Ball heals you. Thank you all.
Your souls heal you. My soul heals you. Sha's Golden
    Healing Ball heals you. Thank you all.
Your souls heal you. My soul heals you. Sha's Golden
    Healing Ball heals you. Thank you all.
Your souls heal you. My soul heals you. Sha's Golden
    Healing Ball heals you. Thank you all . . .

Hao!
Thank you. Thank you. Thank you.

Chant silently for three to five minutes to offer group healing.

After three to five minutes of chanting with the assistance of Sha's Golden Healing Ball, you may hardly believe the results. Many people could receive instant benefits.

Remote Healing

You may be in North America, while the person you wish to offer healing to is in Europe. Or you could be at work and learn that a loved one is in the hospital across the country. Soul healing is not limited by time or space. You can offer soul healing to anyone remotely. Whatever soul healing you can offer to someone who is physically in front of you, you can also do remotely.

You can do remote soul healing for your friends and loved ones anywhere in the world. Because this healing is offered at the soul level, it makes no difference if the person is in front of you or halfway around the world.

Here is how to do remote soul healing. Apply the Four Power Techniques:

Body Power. Put your left palm over your Message Center (heart chakra) without touching your body. Put your right hand in the traditional prayer position in front of your left hand.

Soul Power. Say *hello:*

> *Dear soul mind body of* _____ (name the
>   person),
> *I love you.*
> *Your soul has the power to heal your* _____
>   (name the unhealthy condition).

My soul has the power to heal your _____
   (repeat the unhealthy condition).
Do a good job.
Thank you.

Dear Sha's Golden Healing Ball,
I love you.
You have the power to heal _____ (name
   the person).
Please come from Heaven to heal his/her _____
   (repeat the unhealthy condition).
Thank you.

Mind Power. Visualize a golden light ball shining in the person.

Sound Power. Chant silently or aloud:

Your soul heals you. My soul heals you. Sha's Golden
   Healing Ball heals you. Thank you.
Your soul heals you. My soul heals you. Sha's Golden
   Healing Ball heals you. Thank you.
Your soul heals you. My soul heals you. Sha's Golden
   Healing Ball heals you. Thank you.
Your soul heals you. My soul heals you. Sha's Golden
   Healing Ball heals you. Thank you.
Your soul heals you. My soul heals you. Sha's Golden
   Healing Ball heals you. Thank you.
Your soul heals you. My soul heals you. Sha's Golden
   Healing Ball heals you. Thank you.
Your soul heals you. My soul heals you. Sha's Golden
   Healing Ball heals you. Thank you . . .

Hao!
Thank you. Thank you. Thank you.

Chant for at least three to five minutes per time. The longer and the more often you chant, the better.

It is so simple to do remote healing like this. Some healers have studied other methods of remote healing for more than ten years and still are not clear on how to do it. I am honored to reveal this secret remote healing technique to you and to all humanity.

※

Now I am going to explain how to do soul healing by invoking the souls of nature. For example, if you have cold hands and feet, here is how to do soul healing by invoking the souls of nature. As with the other practices, say *hello* and apply the Four Power Techniques:

Body Power. Put your left palm over your Message Center (heart chakra) without touching your body. Put your right hand in the traditional prayer position in front of your left hand. This is the Soul Light Era Prayer Position.

Soul Power. Say *hello:*

> *Dear soul mind body of the sun,*
> *I love you.*
> *You have the power to heal me.*
> *Please heal my cold hands and feet.*
> *Thank you.*

Mind Power. Visualize the sun shining brightly *in* your hands and feet.

Sound Power. Chant silently or aloud:

> *The soul of the sun warms my hands and feet. Thank*
> *you.*
> *The soul of the sun warms my hands and feet. Thank*
> *you.*
> *The soul of the sun warms my hands and feet. Thank*
> *you.*
> *The soul of the sun warms my hands and feet. Thank*
> *you.*
> *The soul of the sun warms my hands and feet. Thank*
> *you.*
> *The soul of the sun warms my hands and feet. Thank*
> *you.*
> *The soul of the sun warms my hands and feet. Thank*
> *you . . .*

Hao!
Thank you. Thank you. Thank you.

Chant for at least three to five minutes per time. The longer and the more often you chant, the better.

The sun is a great unconditional universal servant. You can ask the soul, mind, and body of the sun to heal you in the daytime. You can also ask the sun for healing in the middle of the night. The soul of the sun is available twenty-four hours a day, seven days a week, rain or shine, day or night. Invoke the soul, mind, and body of the sun anytime, anywhere. You could receive great soul healing from the sun for any unhealthy condition.

※

Expanding this wisdom, you can invoke the souls of the moon, the Big Dipper, the Himalayas, the Great Wall of China, the Pacific Ocean, and the Amazon rain forest for healing. They would be delighted to serve you. It is very important to always express gratitude for their service.

You can also call on saints, angels, buddhas, ascended masters, and other high-level spiritual beings for healing. They are unconditional universal servants. Many of them were great servants in the physical form on Mother Earth. You may not realize that they continue to serve in soul form. You can call on them for healing and blessing. All you need to do is say *hello*. Then totally relax to receive their blessing.

You can follow the same general Say Hello Healing formula to ask for healing from these souls as we did with the souls of nature. Let us do another practice, this time for healing neck pain. Apply the Four Power Techniques:

Body Power. Sit up straight. Put the tip of your tongue as close as you can to the roof of your mouth without touching it. Place one hand on your neck.

Soul Power. Say *hello*:

> *Dear soul mind body of Ling Hui Sheng Shi* (pronounced *ling hway shung shr,* this is the new name of Guan Yin in the Soul Light Era),
> *I love you.*
> *You have the power to heal me.*
> *Please heal my neck pain.*
> *I am very grateful.*
> *Thank you.*

Mind Power. Visualize Ling Hui Sheng Shi healing your neck.

Sound Power. Chant silently or aloud:

Ling Hui Sheng Shi heals me. Thank you.
Ling Hui Sheng Shi heals me. Thank you.
Ling Hui Sheng Shi heals me. Thank you.
Ling Hui Sheng Shi heals me. Thank you.
Ling Hui Sheng Shi heals me. Thank you.
Ling Hui Sheng Shi heals me. Thank you.
Ling Hui Sheng Shi heals me. Thank you . . .

Hao!
Thank you. Thank you. Thank you.

Chant for at least three to five minutes per time. The longer and the more often you chant, the better.

You can ask any saint from your spiritual tradition or belief system to heal and bless you. For example, you can ask Saint Germain, Shi Jia Mo Ni Fuo, Nan Ji Xian Weng, Archangel Michael, Jesus, or Lord Krishna. Always remember to show your respect and gratitude for their service, regardless of your healing results.

Divine Healing

In many traditions, people pray to ask for special healing or blessing. They say a brief prayer and wait for healing results. My insight that I wish to share is that when you invoke the Divine to request healing and blessing for your life, do not be so quick. You will receive more blessing as long as you continue to chant. Better to keep chanting! You could receive great results from blessings of divine love and light.

You can directly invoke the Divine for healing. This is the way to do it:

Body Power. Put your hands in the Soul Light Era Prayer Position (left palm over your Message Center without touching it, right hand in the traditional prayer position).

Soul Power. Say *hello:*

> *Dear soul mind body of the Divine,*
> *I love you.*
> *You have the power to heal me.*
> *Please heal me.*
> *Thank you.*

Mind Power. Visualize the Divine healing you. Visualize pure, brilliant crystal light healing you.

Sound Power. Chant silently or aloud:

> *Divine heals me. Thank you, Divine.*
> *Divine heals me. Thank you, Divine.*
> *Divine heals me. Thank you, Divine.*
> *Divine heals me. Thank you, Divine.*
> *Divine heals me. Thank you, Divine.*
> *Divine heals me. Thank you, Divine.*
> *Divine heals me. Thank you, Divine . . .*
>
> *Hao!*
> *Thank you. Thank you. Thank you.*

Chant for at least three to five minutes per time. The longer and the more often you chant, the better.

Soul healing is simple, practical, effective, and very flexible. Everyone and everything has a soul. Every soul in the universe has its soul healing power. You can invoke the souls of nature, high spiritual beings, and the Divine to offer you healing. Very important wisdom is to send your greatest gratitude to the souls you invoke. They will be moved by your great love, sincerity, and gratitude.

灵预防

Ling Yu Fang

Soul Prevention of Illness

"Ling" means *soul*. "Yu fang" means *prevention*. "Ling yu fang" (pronounced *ling yü fahng*) means *soul prevention of all sicknesses*.

Preventing sickness is very important. In my book *The Power of Soul: The Way to Heal, Rejuvenate, Transform, and Enlighten All Life,* I released the one-sentence soul secret of prevention of sickness:

**Prevent sickness of the soul first;
then prevention of all sickness will follow.**

During this transition period on Mother Earth, millions of people are worried and even fearful of new strains of viruses and other illnesses. Many people suffer from chronic conditions that compromise their ability to prevent illness. The power and benefits of soul prevention of sickness are obvious. This is the way to do it:

Body Power. Put your left palm over your Message Center (heart chakra) without touching your body. Put your right hand in the traditional prayer position in front of your left hand.

Soul Power. Say *hello:*

> *Dear soul mind body of all my systems, organs, cells,*
>   *cell units, DNA, RNA, smallest matter, and spaces,*
> *I love you, honor you, and appreciate you.*
> *You have the power to prevent sickness.*
> *Do a good job!*
> *Thank you.*

Mind Power. Visualize golden light vibrating in your whole body, from head to toe, skin to bone.

Sound Power. Chant silently or aloud:

> *I have the power to prevent sickness. My souls have the*
>   *power to prevent sickness. Thank you.*
> *I have the power to prevent sickness. My souls have the*
>   *power to prevent sickness. Thank you.*
> *I have the power to prevent sickness. My souls have the*
>   *power to prevent sickness. Thank you.*
> *I have the power to prevent sickness. My souls have the*
>   *power to prevent sickness. Thank you.*
> *I have the power to prevent sickness. My souls have the*
>   *power to prevent sickness. Thank you.*
> *I have the power to prevent sickness. My souls have the*
>   *power to prevent sickness. Thank you.*
> *I have the power to prevent sickness. My souls have the*
>   *power to prevent sickness. Thank you . . .*

Chant for at least three to five minutes per time. The longer and the more often you chant, the better.

⁂

You can also invoke the souls of nature to help you prevent sickness. Here is an example:

Body Power. Put one fist on your Message Center (heart chakra) and the other fist on your Snow Mountain Area (lower back, above the tailbone). Do Soul Tapping of both areas.

Soul Power. Say *hello:*

> *Dear soul mind body of Heaven and Earth* (Heaven
>   represents yang, Mother Earth represents yin),
> *I love you, honor you, and appreciate you.*
> *You have the power to prevent all sicknesses.*
> *Please bless me.*
> *Thank you.*

Mind Power. Visualize golden light radiating and vibrating in your whole body, from head to toe, skin to bone.

Sound Power. Chant silently or aloud:

> *Souls of Heaven and Earth prevent sickness. Thank*
>   *you.*
> *Souls of Heaven and Earth prevent sickness. Thank*
>   *you.*
> *Souls of Heaven and Earth prevent sickness. Thank*
>   *you.*

Souls of Heaven and Earth prevent sickness. Thank
you.
Souls of Heaven and Earth prevent sickness. Thank
you.
Souls of Heaven and Earth prevent sickness. Thank
you.
Souls of Heaven and Earth prevent sickness. Thank
you . . .

Hao!
Thank you. Thank you. Thank you.

Chant for at least three to five minutes per time. The longer and the more often you chant, the better.

You can also invoke saints, other high-level spiritual beings, or the Divine for prevention of sickness by following the same formula. Let us ask Jesus to bless us for prevention of sickness. Use the Four Power Techniques:

Body Power. Place one fist on your Lower Dan Tian (lower abdomen) and the other fist on your Snow Mountain Area (lower back, above the tailbone). Do Soul Tapping of both areas.

Soul Power. Say *hello:*

Dear soul mind body of Jesus,
I love you, honor you, and appreciate you.
You have the power to prevent all sicknesses.
Please bless me.

I am very grateful.
Thank you.

Mind Power. Visualize Jesus's light filling your whole body, from head to toe, skin to bone.

Sound Power. Chant silently or aloud:

Jesus prevents sickness. Thank you.
Jesus prevents sickness. Thank you.
Jesus prevents sickness. Thank you.
Jesus prevents sickness. Thank you.
Jesus prevents sickness. Thank you.
Jesus prevents sickness. Thank you.
Jesus prevents sickness. Thank you . . .

Hao!

Chant for three to five minutes per time. The longer and the more often you chant, the better.

Remember to express your gratitude for Jesus's blessings: *Thank you. Thank you. Thank you.*

灵转化
Ling Zhuan Hua

Soul Transformation

"Ling" means *soul*. "Zhuan hua" means *transformation*. "Ling zhuan hua" (pronounced *ling jwahn hwah*) means *soul transformation*.

Transformation includes transformation of every aspect of life, including relationships and finances.

Transformation of Relationships

Let me explain to you how to transform a relationship. Apply the Four Power Techniques:

Body Power. Sit up straight. Put the tip of your tongue as close as you can to the roof of your mouth without touching it. Put your left palm over your Message Center (heart chakra) without touching your body. Put your right hand in the traditional prayer position in front of your left hand.

Soul Power. Say *hello*:

> *Dear soul mind body of* _____ (name the
>   person with whom you wish transform a relation-
>   ship),
> *I love you.*
> *We have some blockages in our relationship.*
> *I would like our relationship to be transformed.*
> *I would like to offer love and forgiveness to you.*
> *I wish you will offer love and forgiveness back to me.*
> *Thank you.*
>
> *Dear Divine,*
> *Please bless our relationship.*
> *Thank you so much.*

Mind Power. Visualize golden light shining between you and the soul of the other person in front of you.

Sound Power. Chant silently or aloud:

Soul of _____ (name the person) *and my soul bless our relationship. Divine blesses our relationship. Thank you.*

Soul of _____ (name the person) *and my soul bless our relationship. Divine blesses our relationship. Thank you.*

Soul of _____ (name the person) *and my soul bless our relationship. Divine blesses our relationship. Thank you.*

Soul of _____ (name the person) *and my soul bless our relationship. Divine blesses our relationship. Thank you.*

Soul of _____ (name the person) *and my soul bless our relationship. Divine blesses our relationship. Thank you.*

Soul of _____ (name the person) *and my soul bless our relationship. Divine blesses our relationship. Thank you.*

Soul of _____ (name the person) *and my soul bless our relationship. Divine blesses our relationship. Thank you . . .*

Hao! Thank you. Thank you. Thank you.

Chant for at least three to five minutes per time. The longer and the more often you chant, the faster your relationship could be transformed.

Forgiveness is very important for healing and life transformation. I have thousands of students who do spiritual practices of forgiveness, such as in this example. I have received many heart-touching and moving stories about the benefits received. The technique is extremely simple. Practice sincerely and diligently. Sometimes you may need to practice a lot. You could receive remarkable transformation of your relationships.

Transformation of Business

Now let's apply the Four Power Techniques to transform a business:

Body Power. Sit up straight. Put the tip of your tongue as close as you can to the roof of your mouth without touching it. Put your hands in the Soul Light Era Prayer Position (left palm over Message Center, right hand in traditional prayer position).

Soul Power. Say *hello:*

> *Dear soul mind body of* _____ (name your business or company), *my boss, managers, colleagues, and employees,*
> *I love you, honor you, and appreciate you.*
> *Let our souls apply love and forgiveness and join hearts and souls together to create better harmony and service in our business.*
> *Thank you.*
>
> *Dear soul mind body of all our associates,*
> *I love you, honor you, and appreciate you.*
> *Please join hearts and souls with us together to create a great business for us and for you.*
> *Thank you.*
>
> *Dear soul mind body of all our customers and potential customers,*

We love you, honor you, and appreciate you.
We want to present the highest quality of service
  to you.
Thank you for being our customers.

Mind Power. Visualize golden light shining everywhere in your business, business team, associates, and customers.

Sound Power. Chant silently or aloud:

Join hearts and souls together to create a better business.
Join hearts and souls together to create a better business.
Join hearts and souls together to create a better business.
Join hearts and souls together to create a better business.
Join hearts and souls together to create a better business.
Join hearts and souls together to create a better business.
Join hearts and souls together to create a better business . . .

Hao! Thank you. Thank you. Thank you.

Chant for at least three to five minutes per time. The longer and the more often you chant, the faster your business could be transformed.

You can adapt these examples to transform your personal finances and any aspect of your life. Soul transformation has no limits. I shared the one-sentence secret in my previous books:

**Transform the soul first; then transformation
of every aspect of life will follow.**

灵圆满
Ling Yuan Man

Soul Enlightenment

"Ling" means *soul*. "Yuan man" means *enlightenment*. "Ling yuan man" (pronounced *ling ywen mahn*) means *soul enlightenment*.

Since 2003, I have offered soul enlightenment to humanity. The Divine gave me the honor to send a Divine Order to enlighten the souls who attend my Soul Healing and Enlightenment Retreats. I have enlightened thousands of people worldwide. I continue to offer divine soul enlightenment to humanity. In addition, I have personally trained more than ten new divine servants, my Worldwide Representatives, who are also honored to be given the honor and the task to enlighten the souls of humanity.

To enlighten a soul is to uplift the soul's standing in Heaven to the enlightened realm. Generally speaking, it could take a person hundreds of lifetimes to be enlightened through their unconditional universal service. A Divine Order means the Divine opens the virtue bank in Heaven to give lots of virtue to the participants in the retreat to uplift their souls' standing in Heaven to the enlightened realm. My Soul Healing and Enlightenment Retreats are the first time the Divine has enlightened a group of hundreds of people together. Mother Earth is in a transition period. The Divine needs enlightened souls in the human realm to serve to help humanity to pass this difficult time. After Mother Earth's transition, the Divine may stop offering this extraordinary honor and opportunity to humanity.

You can enlighten your soul by yourself. As I shared earlier, the Divine guided me that it usually takes hundreds of lifetimes of unconditional universal service to be enlightened. To enlighten one's own soul is not easy at all. However, it can be done.

How can you enlighten your own soul? There is only one way: offer unconditional universal service. This means to serve humanity without asking for anything in return. To offer unconditional universal service is to make others happier and healthier and to bring love, peace, and harmony to humanity, Mother Earth, and all universes. It takes lots of effort for a person to do lots of service, including volunteer work, charitable donations, and creating and joining special events for the love, peace, and harmony movement.

I would like to share a very special way that the Divine told me you can use to purify your soul, heart, mind, and body and to serve unconditionally. This way is unique. Therefore, not so many people do it diligently. This way is to chant Divine Soul Songs, especially the Divine Soul Song *Love, Peace and Harmony,* which you can listen to me singing on the enclosed CD.

Lu La Lu La Li
Lu La Lu La La Li
Lu La Lu La Li Lu La
Lu La Li Lu La
Lu La Li Lu La

I love my heart and soul
I love all humanity

Join hearts and souls together
Love, peace and harmony
Love, peace and harmony

How does this technique work? I will explain line by line.

Lu La Lu La Li / I love my heart and soul: Love melts all blockages and transforms all life. This is the secret of healing all your issues in the physical, mental, emotional, and spiritual bodies.

Lu La Lu La La Li / I love all humanity is to offer your love to humanity, Mother Earth, and all universes. Chant this sentence a lot. Your love will go to the spaces in Mother Earth and the universes as a service to transform people's consciousness. The Divine counts this chanting. Every moment you are chanting this, Heaven records your chanting. Then, they give you virtue. Virtue is yin money in the Soul World. On Mother Earth, when you do work, you receive payment. In the spiritual world, when you offer service, you receive virtue. Virtue in the Soul World is just like a salary on Mother Earth. When you accumulate enough virtue, your soul will be uplifted to the enlightened realm.

Lu La Lu La Li Lu La / Join hearts and souls together is a divine calling.

Lu La Li Lu La / Love, peace and harmony: Love, peace, and harmony are the goals of Soul Light Era. You can chant this mantra in a meditative state. But remember, you can chant this every day when you drive, cook, walk, take a shower, exercise, and more. The secret is that at any moment, any chance you have, chant this mantra. If you sing *Love, Peace and Harmony* as much as you can, purification of your soul, heart, mind, and body could happen very fast. You could gain a lot of virtue. Your soul enlightenment journey could move very fast.

灵智慧

Ling Zhi Hui

Soul Intelligence

"Ling" means *soul*. "Zhi hui" means *intelligence*. "Ling zhi hui" (pronounced *ling jr hway*) means *soul intelligence*.

There are many ways to increase your soul's intelligence. Let me share with you two practical soul treasures that you can use to increase your soul's intelligence very quickly. The first is to apply Soul Language to increase soul intelligence. The second is to sing a Soul Song to increase soul intelligence.

Apply Soul Language to Increase Your Soul Intelligence
Use the Four Power Techniques:

Body Power. Sit up straight. Put the tip of your tongue as close as you can to the roof of your mouth without touching it. Put your left palm over your Message Center (heart chakra) without touching it. Put your right hand in the prayer position in front of your left hand. This is the Soul Light Era Prayer Position.

Soul Power. Say *hello:*

> *Dear soul mind body of my Soul Language,*
> *I love you, honor you, and appreciate you.*
> *You have the power to increase my soul intelligence.*
> *Do a good job.*
> *Thank you.*

Mind Power. Visualize golden light shining in your heart, brain, and soul.

Sound Power. Chant *San San Jiu Liu Ba Yao Wu* (3396815 in Chinese) to bring out your Soul Language. Then speak your Soul Language for three to five minutes. Soul Language can develop your soul intelligence because it connects with the Soul World, which includes the Divine, saints, and all kinds of spiritual fathers and mothers. They will deliver soul wisdom to you through Soul Language. Generally speaking, practice three to five minutes per time, three to five times per day. There are no time limits. The more you practice, the better.

Apply Soul Song to Increase Your Soul Intelligence
Use the Four Power Techniques:

Body Power. Sit up straight. Put the tip of your tongue as close as you can to the roof of your mouth without touching it. Put your hands in the Soul Light Era Prayer Position (left palm over your Message Center, right hand in the prayer position).

Soul Power. Say *hello:*

> *Dear soul mind body of my Soul Song,*
> *I love you, honor you, and appreciate you.*
> *You have the power to develop my soul intelligence.*
> *Do a good job.*
> *Thank you.*

Mind Power. Visualize golden light shining in your heart, brain, and soul.

Sound Power. Chant *San San Jiu Liu Ba Yao Wu* (pronounced *sahn sahn jeo leo bah yow woo*) to bring out your Soul Language. Then sing your Soul Language to bring out your Soul Song.

(This was explained earlier in this chapter.) Sing your Soul Song for three to five minutes. The longer you sing, the better.

You can also invoke the Divine and spiritual fathers and mothers in Heaven to bless your soul intelligence.

灵潜能

Ling Qian Neng

Soul Potential

"Ling" means *soul*. "Qian neng" means *potential power and abilities*. "Ling qian neng" (pronounced *ling chyen nung*) means *soul potential power and abilities*.

Your soul could have experienced hundreds or thousands of lifetimes with all kinds of professions and experiences. Therefore, your soul carries incredible wisdom, power, and abilities. The many potential powers of your soul have probably not been exposed in your life. They have remained hidden. These potential powers can be developed and brought out. The key to developing your soul's potential is to gain soul communication abilities. The second book in the Soul Power Series, *Soul Communication: Opening Your Spiritual Channels for Success and Fulfillment*, teaches how to open four major spiritual channels: Soul Language, Direct Soul Communication, Third Eye, and Direct Knowing. Study that book and join workshops worldwide with my teachers to open your spiritual channels and fully realize your soul potential.

Now let me share some simple techniques using Soul Language and Soul Song to bring out your soul's potential abilities and potential powers.

Apply Soul Language and Soul Song to bring out your soul's potential power and abilities. Use the Four Power Techniques:

Body Power. Sit up straight. Put the tip of your tongue as close as you can to the roof of your mouth without touching it. Do Soul Tapping of your Message Center and your Snow Mountain Area simultaneously.

Soul Power. Say *hello:*

> *Dear soul mind body of my Soul Language and Soul*
>   *Song,*
> *I love you, honor you, and appreciate you.*
> *You have the power to bring out my soul's potential*
>   *power and abilities.*
> *Do a good job.*
> *Thank you.*

Mind Power. Visualize golden light shining in your Message Center, heart, brain, and soul.

Sound Power. Chant *San San Jiu Liu Ba Yao Wu* (the sacred code 3396815 in Chinese, pronounced *sahn sahn jeo leo bah yow woo*) to bring out your Soul Language and Soul Song. Then sing your Soul Song for at least three to five minutes. The longer you sing, the better.

⛬

Since I started to teach Soul Language in 1996, I have taught Soul Language and Soul Song to thousands of people worldwide. I have some students who were not authors but who, after developing their soul potentials, became authors. Others were not singers but, after developing their soul potentials, became singers.

Still others did not know how to write a poem but, after developing their soul potentials, now write beautiful poems.

Many people have gained abilities that they could not show before. Their soul potentials have been brought out. Study more. Practice more. I wish you will enjoy the benefits of your soul potentials as quickly as possible.

换灵脑身
Huan Ling Nao Shen

Soul Mind Body Transplant

"Huan" means *change.* "Ling" means *soul.* "Nao" means *mind.* "Shen" means *body.* "Huan ling nao shen" (pronounced *hwahn ling now shun*) means *Soul Mind Body Transplant.*

In my writings, I introduced Soul Mind Body Transplants in the authority book of my Soul Power Series, *The Power of Soul,* in chapter 14 on "Divine Soul Downloads and Divine Soul Orders." The fifth book in the series, *Divine Soul Mind Body Healing and Transmission System,* focuses on Soul Mind Body Transplants. These two books explain the complete system of Soul Mind Body Transplants.

Let me give you the essence and history here. In July 2003, the Divine chose me to offer his Divine Soul Transplants. Divine Soul Transplant means to change the soul of the heart, kidneys, liver, or any system, organ, part of body, cells, cell units, DNA, RNA, smallest matter in the cells, and spaces between the cells. The original soul or souls go back to the Divine. A new divine soul or souls are created and transmitted or "downloaded" to reside in the recipient's system, organ, or part of the body.

In 2008, the Divine asked me to offer Divine Mind Transplants and Divine Body Transplants. Divine Mind Transplant means the Divine sends a golden light being to change the consciousness of a system, organ, or part of the body. Divine Body Transplant means the Divine sends another golden light being to change the energy and tiny matter of a system, organ, or part of the body.

Divine Soul Mind Body Transplants have resulted in thousands of heart-touching and moving stories of healing and life transformation. Earlier in this chapter, you and every reader received Soul Mind Body Transplants of several Tao Soul Herbs.

Now I will offer Divine Soul Mind Body Transplants of Kidneys to you and every reader.

Prepare!

Sit up straight. Totally relax as you read the next few paragraphs. Open your heart and soul to receive these permanent divine treasures that will remain with your soul throughout this lifetime and all of your future lifetimes.

Divine Order: Divine Soul Transplant of Kidneys Transmission!

This divine golden light being is more than two hundred feet high and thirty-four feet wide. It has come to your kidneys. Your original kidney souls have returned to the heart of the Divine.

Divine Order: Divine Mind Transplant of Kidneys Transmission!

Another golden light being of similar size has come to your kidneys. This light being carries divine consciousness of kidneys, which can transform the original consciousness of your kidneys.

Divine Order: Divine Body Transplant of Kidneys Transmission!

This is another golden light being of similar size that has come to your kidneys. It carries divine energy and tiny matter of the kidneys. This can transform the energy and tiny matter of your kidneys.

Divine Order: Join Divine Soul Transplant of Kidneys, Divine Mind Transplant of Kidneys, and Divine Body Transplant of Kidneys as one.

Hei Ya Ya Ya Ya Ya You!

This is the Divine Order to join your Divine Soul Transplant of Kidneys, Divine Mind Transplant of Kidneys, and Divine Body Transplant of Kidneys together now. They will serve your kidneys as one.

To receive Divine Soul Mind Body Transplants does not mean you are healed or transformed. Divine Soul Mind Body Transplants are just like lightbulbs. You have to turn on a switch to turn a lightbulb on. If you turn on the Divine Soul Mind Body Transplants, then you will receive their benefits. Otherwise, your Divine Soul Mind Body Transplants are resting.

This is the way to do it. Use the Four Power Techniques:

Body Power. Sit up straight. Put the tip of your tongue as close as you can to the roof of your mouth without touching it. Do Soul Tapping of your Lower Dan Tian (lower abdomen) and your Snow Mountain Area (lower back above the tailbone) simultaneously.

Soul Power. Say *hello:*

> *Dear my Divine Soul Mind Body Transplants of Kid-*
> *neys,*
> *I love you, honor you, and appreciate you.*
> *Please turn on to heal and rejuvenate my kidneys.*
> *I am very grateful.*
> *Thank you.*

Mind Power. Visualize golden light shining in your kidneys.

Sound Power. Chant silently or aloud:

> *Divine Soul Mind Body Transplants of Kidneys heal*
> *and rejuvenate my kidneys. Thank you, Divine.*
> *Divine Soul Mind Body Transplants of Kidneys heal*
> *and rejuvenate my kidneys. Thank you, Divine.*
> *Divine Soul Mind Body Transplants of Kidneys heal*
> *and rejuvenate my kidneys. Thank you, Divine.*
> *Divine Soul Mind Body Transplants of Kidneys heal*
> *and rejuvenate my kidneys. Thank you, Divine.*
> *Divine Soul Mind Body Transplants of Kidneys heal*
> *and rejuvenate my kidneys. Thank you, Divine.*
> *Divine Soul Mind Body Transplants of Kidneys heal*
> *and rejuvenate my kidneys. Thank you, Divine.*
> *Divine Soul Mind Body Transplants of Kidneys heal*
> *and rejuvenate my kidneys. Thank you, Divine . . .*

Practice for at least three to five minutes per time. The longer and the more you practice, the better. For chronic kidney conditions, practice for two hours or more each day. When you are finished, close the practice and let your Divine Soul Mind Body Transplants rest:

Hao! Thank you. Thank you. Thank you.
My Divine Soul Mind Body Transplants of Kidneys,
*   please rest.*
I am very grateful.

Many different Divine Soul Mind Body Transplants for healing, transforming relationships and finances, and much more are available. You can apply to receive Divine Soul Mind Body Transplants on my website (www.DrSha.com) or at events offered by my Worldwide Representatives and me.

服务三界
Fu Wu San Jie

Serve Heaven, Earth, and Human Being

"Fu wu" means *serve*. "San jie" means *three layers: Heaven, Earth, and human being*. "Fu wu san jie" (pronounced *foo woo sahn jyeh*) means *serve Heaven, Earth, and human being*.

There are two renowned ancient statements. One is *Tian ren he yi*. "Tian" means *Heaven*. "Ren" means *human being*. "He yi" means *join as one*. "Tian ren he yi" (pronounced *tyen wren huh yee*) means *Heaven and human being join as one*. Heaven is the big universe. A human being is a small universe. What happens in the big universe is what will happen in the small universe.

The other renowned statement is *Tian di ren he yi*. "Ren" means *human being*. "Tian di ren he yi" (pronounced *tyen dee wren huh yee*) means *Heaven, Earth, and human being join as one*.

Mother Earth is in transition now. Heaven is reconstructing

now. Human beings are going through major challenges. At this moment, the Divine calls humanity and all souls to serve human beings, Mother Earth, and Heaven.

The purpose of life is to serve. To serve San Jie is to serve Heaven, Earth, and human being. This is very important spiritual service. One of the most powerful ways to serve is to chant:

Fu Wu San Jie
Fu Wu San Jie
Fu Wu San Jie
Fu Wu San Jie
Fu Wu San Jie
Fu Wu San Jie
Fu Wu San Jie . . .

This is a very powerful mantra. The more you chant it, the more virtue you will receive. The more virtue you receive, the more transformation of every aspect of life will follow.

灵光普照
Ling Guang Pu Zhao

Shining Soul Light

"Ling" means *soul*. "Guang" means *light*. "Pu" means *widely*. "Zhao" means *shining*. "Ling Guang Pu Zhao" (pronounced *ling gwahng poo jow*) can be translated as *shining soul light*.

I explained this ancient mantra in my book *Power Healing*, published in 2002. This mantra is extremely powerful. Ling Guang Pu Zhao includes all souls in all universes. When you chant Ling Guang Pu Zhao, the Divine will come. All saints, all healing angels, all buddhas, and all layers of spiritual fathers and mothers in Heaven will come.

Apply Ling Guang Pu Zhao for healing and life transformation for your relationships, finances, and every aspect of your life. Use the Four Power Techniques:

Body Power. Sit up straight. Put the tip of your tongue as close as you can to the roof of your mouth without touching it. Do Soul Tapping of your Message Center and your Snow Mountain Area simultaneously.

Soul Power. Say *hello:*

> *Dear soul mind body of* Ling Guang Pu Zhao,
> *I love you, honor you, and appreciate you.*
> *You have the power to heal* _____ (make a
>   request).
> *You have the power to transform my relationship with*
>   _____ (name a person).
> *You have the power to transform my business*
>   _____ (name the business).
> *You have the power to transform my finances.*
> *I am very grateful.*
> *Thank you.*

Mind Power. Visualize golden light shining in your body from head to toe, skin to bone, and to the other person, to your business, and to your finances.

Sound Power. Sing or chant silently or aloud (you can listen to me on the enclosed CD):

Ling Guang Pu Zhao (pronounced *ling gwahng poo jow*)
Ling Guang Pu Zhao
Ling Guang Pu Zhao
Ling Guang Pu Zhao
Ling Guang Pu Zhao
Ling Guang Pu Zhao
Ling Guang Pu Zhao . . .

Shining Soul Light
Shining Soul Light
Shining Soul Light
Shining Soul Light
Shining Soul Light
Shining Soul Light
Shining Soul Light . . .

Chant for at least three to five minutes per time; the longer, the better.

We are in the Soul Light Era, which started on August 8, 2003. The Soul Light Era will last for fifteen thousand years. Ling Guang Pu Zhao is one of the major mantras for the entire Soul Light Era. It is also a divine and Tao treasure to transform health, relationships, and finances, and to increase intelligence and bring out the potential powers of the soul, mind, and body. Chant and practice more. Incredible blessings for every aspect of your life are waiting for you when you chant this mantra.

万物更新
Wan Wu Geng Xin

Everything is renewed

"Wan" means *ten thousand*. "Wu" means *things*. "Wan wu" means *all things* or *everything*. "Geng xin" means *renew*. "Wan wu geng xin" (pronounced *wahn woo gung sheen*) means *everything is renewed*.

In the Soul Light Era, this statement means we need to chant *Ling Guang Pu Zhao* (the previous line of the Tao text). We can apply Soul Power to transform every aspect of human beings' lives, including health, relationships, and finances. We can also apply Soul Power to transform science, society, and every aspect of all life. Then, everything will be renewed, including human beings, Mother Earth, Heaven, and all universes.

For example, the Divine guided me that soul self-healing will become a revolutionary healing system for humanity. Soul self-healing means that anyone can apply soul healing to heal his or her own soul, heart, mind, and body. Since I started to teach soul healing, I have received thousands of heart-touching and moving healing stories. Soul healing is not new. Jesus did soul healing. Guan Yin did soul healing. There are many spiritual books telling of miracle healings by special saints, buddhas, healing angels, archangels, ascended masters, and more. These are all examples of miracle soul healings throughout history.

The Divine wants me to share soul self-healing with you and humanity. I started to teach Say Hello Healing techniques in my workshops in 1997. I formally released them in my book *Power Healing* in 2002. I expanded the teaching further, presenting Say Hello Healing in my book *Soul Mind Body Medicine* in 2006. I give credit for Say Hello Healing to my beloved spiritual father,

Master Guo, because he demonstrated Say Hello Healing in a group healing for more than thirty seniors. He offered them a few minutes healing without doing anything visible. When I asked him what he had done, he said, "I just asked their souls to heal themselves." That is when I got the essence of Say Hello Healing. Therefore, I honor my spiritual father and give the credit to him as my teacher. Later, when I wrote *Power Healing* and *Soul Mind Body Medicine*, the Divine gave me the whole picture of Say Hello Healing. I cannot honor Master Guo and the Divine enough for giving me this wisdom that I can share with humanity.

As I explained earlier in the section, *Ling Zhi Liao* (soul healing), soul self-healing can be done with the assistance of healing from the souls of nature, from saints, and from the Divine. This can be summarized in one sentence:

Soul Healing is to say *hello* to the inner souls of your body and to the outer souls of nature, saints, and the Divine for healing.

In the future, soul self-healing could transform the health of millions and billions of people. When more and more people realize the power of soul self-healing, the health of humanity will be transformed. The health of human beings will be renewed.

I have joined a few major antiaging conferences. World-renowned speakers spoke of using herbs, vitamins, minerals, lotions, and more. However, I have not heard anyone speak about energy rejuvenation or soul rejuvenation in any of these conferences.

As I wrote, or rather flowed, the authoritative book in my Soul Power Series, *The Power of Soul: The Way to Heal, Rejuvenate, Transform, and Enlighten All Life,* the Divine guided me to include a chapter on soul rejuvenation. Soul rejuvenation can be summarized in one sentence:

Rejuvenate the soul first; then rejuvenation of the heart, mind, and body will follow.

Let me share with you and all humanity one of the simplest ways to rejuvenate. Earlier in this chapter, I discussed the Tao text, *Fan Lao Huan Tong*. This renowned ancient Tao term has been used to explain rejuvenation for thousands of years. Recall that this phrase means *transform and return old age to the health and purity of a baby*. The Divine guided me to chant *Fan Lao Huan Tong* and, even better, to sing it as a Tao Song.

Apply Fan Lao Huan Tong *to Rejuvenate Soul, Heart, Mind, and Body*

Body Power. Sit up straight. Put the tip of your tongue as close as you can to the roof of your mouth without touching it. Place both palms on the lower abdomen below the navel.

Soul Power. Say *hello:*

> *Dear soul mind body of* Fan Lao Huan Tong,
> *I love you, honor you, and appreciate you.*
> *You have the power to rejuvenate my soul, heart, mind, and body.*
> *You have the power to transform my age to the purity and health of a baby.*
> *I am very grateful.*
> *Thank you.*

Mind Power. Visualize golden light shining in your whole body, from head to toe, skin to bone.

Sound Power. Chant or sing silently or aloud. You can listen to me singing *Fan Lao Huan Tong* on the enclosed CD.

> *Fan Lao Huan Tong*
> *Fan Lao Huan Tong*
> *Fan Lao Huan Tong*
> *Fan Lao Huan Tong*
> *Fan Lao Huan Tong*
> *Fan Lao Huan Tong*
> *Fan Lao Huan Tong . . .*
>
> *Hao!*

Chant or sing for three to five minutes per time. The longer you chant or sing, the more benefits of rejuvenation you could receive.

How does Fan Lao Huan Tong work?

To chant or sing *Fan Lao Huan Tong* is to send a Soul Order to your soul, heart, mind, and body to rejuvenate. This Soul Order will rejuvenate your soul first, and then your systems, organs, cells, cell units, DNA, RNA, smallest matter inside the cells, and spaces between the cells. That is exactly the teaching I shared in *The Power of Soul*:

**Rejuvenate the soul first; then rejuvenation of
the heart, mind, and body will follow.**

I have also released one-sentence secrets for chanting. I will repeat this one-sentence secret:

What you chant or sing is what you become.

When I was in Australia in 2009, one of the students told me:

Thank you, Master Sha. I am so grateful for the teaching I received. I learned to sing Fan Lao Huan Tong *through one of your teleconferences. Since then, I have sung* Fan Lao Huan Tong *all the time, from morning to night. When I awaken every morning, I start to sing silently. When I brush my teeth, I sing silently. I sing while driving to work. During my break, I sing. While cooking, I sing. Before sleep, I sing* Fan Lao Huan Tong. *I practiced only this singing and nothing else. Within less than three months, I couldn't believe how beautiful my skin had become! My skin turned much smoother compared to before. I cannot believe the energy I have now. I only sang* Fan Lao Huan Tong. *I definitely feel younger inside after only three months of practicing* Fan Lao Huan Tong.

As I explained in chapter 1, the Divine and Tao guided me to offer a ten-year Tao training program. To turn old age to the health and purity of a baby does take lots of practice, but it is possible to reach this condition.

Let me share some important wisdom with you and humanity. Many people who are on the spiritual journey or in the energy healing journey think that they have to learn from many masters and teachers. They want to practice many different methods. They think the more techniques they know and the more wisdom they have, the better. But they do not understand the truth for the spiritual journey and the energy healing journey.

Lao Zi, the author of *Tao Te Jing,* said, "Wei xue ri zeng, wei tao ri sun." "Wei" means *for the field.* "Xue" means *study.* "Ri" means *daily*. "Zeng" means *increase*. Tao is The Way, the source of all universes. "Sun" means *reduce*. "Wei xue ri zeng, wei Tao ri sun" (pronounced *way shoo-eh rr dzung, way dow rr swun*) means: *Study every day to gain wisdom and knowledge in your field. Reduce wisdom and knowledge to reach Tao*. To reach Tao, every day we must eliminate unnecessary wisdom and knowledge to reveal the truth. This profound wisdom is to share and explain that *Da Tao zhi jian*, The Big Way is extremely simple. If you want to reach Tao, practice the *simplest* technique. Do not run around searching for more secrets, wisdom, knowledge, and techniques. In one sentence:

The simplest secrets, wisdom, knowledge, and practical techniques are the best ones.

Fan Lao Huan Tong is one of the simplest secrets, wisdom, knowledge, and practical techniques to make you younger. Millions of people are searching for ways to become younger. They do not know the simple rejuvenation technique of singing and chanting *Fan Lao Huan Tong*. Remember, of course, that this is not a five-minute job or even a few months' job. Like my student in Australia, chant or sing *Fan Lao Huan Tong* as much as you can every day. You can chant silently or aloud. Every moment you are chanting *Fan Lao Huan Tong,* you are giving a Soul Order to your soul, heart, mind, and body to rejuvenate. The moment you chant, your whole body goes to work. Your systems, organs, cells, cell units, DNA, RNA, smallest matter in the cells, and spaces between the cells are working to rejuvenate. Purification takes place. Energy flows. Yin and yang are balancing. Your whole body, from head to toe and skin to bone, is transforming and returning to the health and purity of a baby.

Remember the teaching *Da Tao zhi jian*. The Big Way is extremely simple. Do not continue to search for more and more secrets, wisdom, knowledge, and practical techniques. Remember, *Wei xue ri zeng, wei tao ri sun.* In one's advanced spiritual journey, the most important secret is to *believe the simplicity.* If you still think that more secrets, wisdom, knowledge, and practical techniques are better, then you are not in the advanced spiritual stage. You need to continue to practice and purify in order to realize *Da Tao zhi jian.*

Soul is the boss of a human being. The Divine and Tao are the bosses for all souls. Soul can transform all life. Apply Soul Power to transform health, relationships, finances, science, every occupation, and every aspect of life. Soul Power can accomplish Wan wu geng xin, *everything is renewed.*

We are looking forward to *Wan wu geng xin* for humanity, Mother Earth, and all universes.

誓为公仆
Shi Wei Gong Pú

Vow to be an unconditional universal servant

"Shi" means *vow.* "Wei" means *to be.* "Gong pu" means *servant.* "Shi wei gong pu" (pronounced *shr way gawng poo*) means *vow to be a servant.*

A human being has a physical life and soul life. The purpose of physical life is to serve the soul life. The purpose of both the soul life and the physical life is to serve others. When you study Buddhism, Taoism, Confuciansim, and other holy texts and teachings, you may realize that all of the major teachers in these realms made a huge vow to the Divine to be a servant.

As I have shared in all of my Soul Power Series books, the

Divine gave me the Universal Law of Universal Service in April 2003. When I heard that law, I instantly made a vow to the Divine to be a Total GOLD (gratitude, obedience, loyalty, devotion) universal servant to the Divine. I would like to share with you and everyone on the spiritual journey that to make a vow to the Divine is very important for one's spiritual journey. Some people are scared to make a vow. My teaching is if you are not ready, do not make a vow. When you are ready, you are honored to make a vow to the Divine. To make a vow is to tell the Divine that you will be a Total GOLD unconditional universal servant for humanity and all souls. You will accomplish divine tasks. You will give your life for the divine mission. What is the divine mission? It is to serve humanity and all souls to make them happier and healthier, as well as to improve the qualities of humanity and all souls, including their intelligence, wisdom, knowledge, health, and abilities to serve. It is to transform the consciousness of humanity and all souls, and enlighten them, to bring love, peace, and harmony to humanity, Mother Earth, and all universes.

Let me share a story about Guan Yin. Millions of people honor Guan Yin, the Bodhisattva of Compassion. Guan Yin's teacher taught her the Da Bei Zhou (pronounced *dah bay joe*), which means *Big Compassion Mantra*. ("Da" means *big*. "Bei" means *compassion*. "Zhou" means *mantra*.) Essentially, this mantra consists of the names of eighty-seven major buddhas. Guan Yin instantly vowed to spread Da Bei Zhou throughout her entire life. Because her vow was such a pure and complete expression of total GOLD, her teacher passed the Da Bei Zhou lineage power to Guan Yin, which is the spiritual power of a thousand hands and a thousand eyes. People in the spiritual realm understand that Guan Yin does have a thousand hands and a thousand eyes. Depictions of her in paintings and sculptures often show this. Each of these spiritual hands and spiritual eyes has incredible spiritual power and abilities to serve. Millions of peope have experienced their power.

Guan Yin also made a vow to humanity that she would serve anyone who called her when in danger. For example, if you are in a fire with no escape, if you fall into a river and don't know how to swim, or if you are in a dangerous wartime situation, call Guan Yin. She will be there instantly to serve you. There are countless stories in history of Guan Yin saving people's lives in all kinds of life-threatening situations. Therefore, Guan Yin is revered by millions of people. Her huge compassion has averted disasters and saved many people's lives. She has been fulfilling her vow to the Divine. She continues to serve in this way every day and every moment.

To make a vow to the Divine is to commit your life to being an unconditional servant. After making a vow, you are given divine tasks. Accomplish your divine tasks and your spiritual standing in Heaven will be uplifted further and further. But you must know that if you do not accomplish your divine tasks, if you make a vow and do not do the work, your spiritual standing will go down.

The purpose of the soul journey is to uplift your soul standing in Heaven in order finally to reach the divine realm. To reach the divine realm is to stop reincarnation. To reach the divine realm is to receive direct teaching and blessing from the Divine in Heaven. Why are buddhas, holy saints, lamas, gurus, and all kinds of spiritual fathers and mothers very committed to service? It is because the Divine made a law that if you serve a little, you receive little blessings. If you serve more, you receive more blessings. If you serve unconditionally, you can receive unlimited blessings. This is the Universal Law of Univeral Service.

The spiritual journey can be summarized in one sentence:

To serve is to be on the spiritual journey.

Be honored to make a vow when you are ready. Accomplish your vow and your soul will be uplifted faster. Making a vow and accomplishing it will save you lifetimes in your spiritual journey. Let me give you an example of how to make a vow. When you are ready, this is the way to make a vow. Sit quietly in a meditative state. Use the Four Power Techniques to make a vow:

Body Power. Sit up straight. Put the tip of your tongue as close as you can to the roof of your mouth without touching it. Put your hands in the Soul Light Era Prayer Position (left palm over the Message Center without touching your body, right hand in the traditional prayer position in front of your left hand).

Soul Power. Say *hello:*

> *Dear Divine, dear Tao,*
> *I love you, honor you, and appreciate you.*
> *My name is _____ (give your full name to the*
>   *Divine, Tao, and Heaven).*
> *I am very honored to make a vow to you that I want*
>   *to be a Total GOLD universal servant.*
> *I give my life to serve humanity and all souls.*
> *Please bless me and assist me to accomplish my vow.*
> *I am extremely honored and blessed.*
> *Thank you, Divine. Thank you, Tao.*

Mind Power. Visualize your whole body shining golden light, from head to toe, skin to bone.

Sound Power. Chant silently or aloud:

I am an unconditional universal servant.
I am an unconditional universal servant.
I am an unconditional universal servant.
I am an unconditional universal servant.
I am an unconditional universal servant.
I am an unconditional universal servant.
I am an unconditional universal servant . . .

Chant for three to five minutes; the longer, the better.

If your Third Eye is open, you may be surprised when you chant this mantra. Virtue in the form of Heaven's flowers falls down to you on the spot. You are extremely blessed.

I want to share some very important additional wisdom about making a vow to the Divine: *once you make a vow to the Divine, spiritual testing will come.* Spiritual testing tests your commitment and loyalty to the Divine and to the divine tasks you are given. You could experience doubt, health challenges, emotional imbalances, relationship challenges, financial challenges, and other challenges in any aspect of life.

A spiritual being must understand spiritual testing. You must understand *no pain, no gain.* There is no way that one's spiritual journey can always be peaceful, smooth, and happy. The spiritual journey could be very painful. All high-level spiritual beings in history have gone through serious spiritual testing. Jesus and Guan Yin did not have completely smooth roads and peaceful, easy lives.

All spiritual testing is part of one's purification process on the spiritual journey. Pass your spiritual tests and your bad karma is cleared little by little. Pass your spiritual tests and new spiritual tests will come to give you the opportunity to purify further and to be more truly unconditional and more totally total GOLD.

Let me share with you some teachings about spiritual testing. The Divine could test a spiritual being seriously for about half of his or her life. If you live for one hundred years, fifty years of your life could have deep spiritual tests for you.

How does one pass spiritual testing? First, be aware that you are in spiritual testing. Anytime you are struggling in your spiritual journey, it can be reflected in every aspect of your life. You must be aware in every moment that any difficulties in your life could be a form of spiritual testing.

One of the most powerful ways to pass spiritual testing is to chant or sing:

> *Divine love and light*
> *Divine love and light*
> *Divine love and light*
> *Divine love and light*
> *Divine love and light*
> *Divine love and light*
> *Divine love and light . . .*

Divine love and light is one of the most powerful mantras. When you sing or chant this mantra, you may ask the Divine to bless you to pass all kinds of difficulties and spiritual tests. Remember my teaching: what you chant is what you become. You are in the the divine condition. You *become* divine love and light. In this condition, every challenge can be transformed quickly.

世代服务
Shi Dai Fu Wu

Serve in all lives

"Shi dai" means *lifetimes*. "Fu wu" means *serve*. "Shi dai fu wu" (pronounced *shr dye foo woo*) means *serve in all lifetimes*.

In my book *Divine Soul Songs*, I shared the stories of the two top leaders of the last era in Jiu Tian (the nine layers of Heaven). One had spent about 40,000 lifetimes and the other about 55,000 lifetimes doing Xiu Lian (purification practice, which represents the totality of the spiritual journey) before being uplifted to the divine realm. At this moment, I am doing direct soul communication with the Divine to ask how many lifetimes of Xiu Lian A Mi Tuo Fuo (the leader of the Pure Land, also known as Amitabha), Shi Jia Mo Ni Fuo (Shakyamuni, the founder of Buddhism), Guan Yin, and Medicine Buddha had to do in order to reach the divine realm. The answer is that all of them devoted between 30,000 and 55,000 lifetimes to Xiu Lian.

If you do soul communication with these major buddhas and saints and ask them how many lifetimes they have served and how many lifetimes they want to continue to serve, they will answer: *We served in all our past lives. Some of us are in the divine realm. We no longer appear in human form anymore. We will continue to serve in soul form for all of our lifetimes.* When you realize this, you will understand that service has no ending.

Serve in all lifetimes. Gain higher and higher abilities to serve. The more one serves, the higher abilities the Divine gives. Major buddhas and holy saints are given divine abilities to serve. Because they are Total GOLD servants and have served in all their lifetimes, the Divine gives them the abilities to be divine servants for humanity and all souls.

Serve. Serve. Serve.

Uplift soul standing. Uplift soul standing. Uplift soul standing.

Serve better. Serve better. Serve better.

Gain soul abilities. Gain soul abilities. Gain soul abilities.

Serve even better. Serve even better. Serve even better.

Chant or sing with me now, silently or aloud:

Universal service
Universal service
Universal service
Universal service
Universal service
Universal service
Universal service

Universal love
Universal love
Universal love
Universal love
Universal love
Universal love
Universal love

Universal forgiveness
Universal forgiveness
Universal forgiveness
Universal forgiveness
Universal forgiveness
Universal forgiveness
Universal forgiveness

Universal peace
Universal peace
Universal peace
Universal peace
Universal peace
Universal peace
Universal peace

Universal healing
Universal healing
Universal healing
Universal healing
Universal healing
Universal healing
Universal healing

Universal blessing
Universal blessing
Universal blessing
Universal blessing
Universal blessing
Universal blessing
Universal blessing

Universal harmony
Universal harmony
Universal harmony
Universal harmony
Universal harmony
Universal harmony
Universal harmony

Universal enlightenment
Universal enlightenment
Universal enlightenment
Universal enlightenment
Universal enlightenment
Universal enlightenment
Universal enlightenment

The longer and the more often you chant or sing this mantra of universal service, the better. There are no time limits. This is an extremely powerful mantra. The benefits from chanting or singing this mantra cannot be explained by any words.

灵光圣世

Ling Guang Sheng Shi

Soul Light Era

创新纪元

Chuang Xin Ji Yuan

Create a new era

·I will explain these next two lines of the Tao text together.

"Ling" means *soul*. "Guang" means *light*. "Sheng" means *saints*. "Shi" means *generations*.

"Ling guang sheng shi" (pronounced *ling gwahng shung shr*) can be translated as *Soul Light Era*.

"Chuang" means *create*. "Xin" means *new*. "Ji yuan" means *era*. "Chuang xin ji yuan" (pronounced *chwahng sheen jee ywen*) means *create a new era*.

The Soul Light Era started on August 8, 2003. It will last fifteen thousand years. Ling Guang Sheng Shi, the Soul Light Era, is a soul-guided era. In this era, the soul will play the leading role in transforming and enlightening every aspect of life.

Ling Guang Sheng Shi will manifest soul evolution. Pregnant mothers will apply Soul Power to develop their unborn babies' intelligence, health, happiness, and success. High-level souls in Heaven will come to Mother Earth to become human beings again in order to help humanity and Mother Earth.

Newborn babies, infants, toddlers, preschoolers, elementary school students, middle school students, high school students, university students, adults, and seniors—every age group—will apply Soul Power to transform their intelligence, health, happiness, and success. In fact, the Divine and Tao guided me to write another series of books about soul transformation of intelligence, health, happiness, and success for all age groups.

Ling Guang Sheng Shi will emphasize soul self-healing. Millions and billions of people will learn and practice soul healing. They will realize that soul healing has power beyond words or comprehension.

Ling Guang Sheng Shi will pay great attention to soul prevention of sickness. *The Yellow Emperor's Internal Classic* explained that the best doctor is one who teaches people how to prevent sickness, not one who heals sickness after it occurs. Billions of people are suffering. Mother Earth and humanity have not emphasized prevention of sickness enough. Soul prevention of sickness will help humanity and Mother Earth a lot.

How can one do soul prevention of sickness? Soul Song and Soul Dance are two of the major divine treasures to prevent all kinds of sickness because Soul Song and Soul Dance carry divine frequency and vibration with divine love, forgiveness, compassion, and light.

Ling Guang Sheng Shi will shine *fan lao huan tong,* transforming old age to the health and purity of a baby. The Divine is telling me at this moment that there could be tens of millions of people in the Soul Light Era who will live for more than one hundred years. There could be more than one million people who will live more than two hundred years. Some people will live even longer. In the Soul Light Era, the Divine will create immortals for humanity. There will be more immortals in the Soul Light Era than in any other era in history.

Every major era for Mother Earth and the universe lasts for fifteen thousand years. This is not a huge number. The Divine said there is the possibility that about fifty to one hundred people will reach immortality in the Soul Light Era. When I hear this from the Divine, it is fascinating. Of course, we need to do lots of practice in order to achieve *fan lao huan tong.* If you maintain *fan lao huan tong* for a few hundred years, it would be possible for you to live for a few hundred years. If you can reach and maintain your soul, heart, mind, and body in the baby state forever, that *is* the immortal state.

Ling Guang Sheng Shi will transform science and technology because Soul Power will assume leadership. Many "impossible" things will become possible. The Divine will release higher and higher soul abilities to develop science and technology. There will be many breakthrough discoveries and developments. Soul guidance will play a major role in scientific and technological research and development.

Ling Guang Sheng Shi will see many souls reach the divine realm—more than in any other era. In this Soul Light Era, all souls in all layers of Heaven will be uplifted together. Unconditional Total GOLD servants will be uplifted beyond any comprehension.

I have taught another renowned ancient Chinese statement: *Luan shi chu ying xiong* (pronounced *lwahn shr choo ying shyawng*). "Luan" means *disorder*. "Shi" means *world*. "Chu" means *produce*. "Ying xiong" means *hero*. "Luan shi chu ying xiong" means *a disordered world produces heroes*.

Mother Earth is in transition now. Mother Earth is a disordered world now. The Divine is choosing Total GOLD servants to help humanity and Mother Earth pass through this difficult time. Therefore, the Divine has said that Total GOLD servants are to serve the divine mission. Accomplish divine tasks, and these Total GOLD servants will be uplifted much higher. Many Total GOLD servants will be uplifted to the divine realm.

The final goal of Ling Guang Sheng Shi, the Soul Light Era, is to join hearts and souls together to create love, peace, and harmony for humanity, Mother Earth, and all universes.

We are honored in this historic time to be unconditional Total GOLD universal servants.

> *I love my heart and soul*
> *I love all humanity*
> *Join hearts and souls together*
> *Love, peace and harmony*
> *Love, peace and harmony*

道道道
Tao Tao Tao

The Way, the Source of All Universes, the Universal Principles and Laws

Tao is the source of all universes. Tao is the universal principles and laws. Tao is emptiness, nothingness. Tao is The Way of all life.

"Tao Tao Tao" is one of the most important mantras to sing or to chant. Remember the one-sentence secret about chanting or singing mantras:

What you chant or sing is what you become.

Therefore, to chant or sing *Tao Tao Tao* is to go into the Tao condition. There are no words to explain the power of this mantra. It has the power to transform all life, including health, happiness, relationships, finances, and every aspect of life. Apply the Four Power Techniques:

Body Power. Sit up straight. Put the tip of your tongue as close as you can to the roof of your mouth without touching it. Put both palms on your lower abdomen below the navel.

Soul Power. Say *hello:*

> *Dear Divine, dear Tao,*
> *I love you, honor you, and appreciate you.*
> *Please boost my energy, stamina, vitality, and immunity.*
> *Please heal my physical, emotional, mental, and spiritual bodies.*
> *Please transform my relationships, finances, and every aspect of my life.*
> *Please increase my intelligence, wisdom, and knowledge.*
> *Please bless me to reach fan lao huan tong.*
> *Please enlighten my soul, heart, mind, and body.*
> *Please help humanity to pass this difficult time.*

Please bless humanity, Mother Earth, and all universes
to create love, peace, and harmony.
Please uplift my spiritual standing in Heaven.
Please help me to reach Tao sooner.
I am grateful beyond words and thought.
Thank you.

Mind Power. Visualize your whole body, your relationships, your finances, humanity, Mother Earth, and all souls in all universes shining golden light.

Sound Power. Sing or chant silently or aloud (you can listen to me sing on the enclosed CD):

Tao Tao Tao
Tao Tao Tao
Tao Tao Tao
Tao Tao Tao
Tao Tao Tao
Tao Tao Tao
Tao Tao Tao . . .

Sing or chant for at least three to five minutes. The longer and the more often you chant, the better.

In fact, *Tao Tao Tao* is one of the most powerful mantras in all universes. You can chant nonstop in your heart from morning to night. There are not enough words and not enough comprehension to appreciate this chanting.

Now I will reveal one of the most important secrets in Tao teaching and training. It can be summarized in one sentence:

To chant *Tao Tao Tao* is to reach Tao.

Chant a lot.

The more you chant, the more benefits you could receive for every aspect of life.

The more you chant, the more benefits humanity, Mother Earth, and all universes receive.

The more you chant, the more virtue you gain.

The more you chant, the more your soul is uplifted in Heaven.

The more you chant, the sooner you reach Tao.

The most important secret is to chant from the bottom of your heart and soul. Chant with total love and total GOLD. If you chant through your mouth, but your heart is in a different place, it won't work. You will waste your time. Chant with your heart. Chant with your soul. You will be extremely blessed.

道定得

Tao Ding De

Tao stillness

道慧明

Tao Hui Ming

Tao intelligence, Tao realization

Tao is The Way. "Ding" means *stillness*. "De" means *achieve*. "Tao ding de" (pronounced *dow ding duh*) means *reach Tao stillness*.

"Hui" means *intelligence*. "Ming" means *realization*. "Tao hui ming" (pronounced *dow hway ming*) means *reach Tao realization and intelligence*.

Stillness and intelligence are the process of spiritual development. In order to receive intelligence and wisdom, one must go into the stillness condition. When you reach stillness, your soul, heart, mind, and body completely open. Then, divine love and light, Tao love and light, universal love and light, and Heaven's love and light can pour into you from head to toe, skin to bone. This will increase the intelligence of your soul, heart, mind, and body.

Millions of spiritual beings in history have reached stillness and developed intelligence. But stillness and intelligence have layers. There are unlimited layers of stillness and intelligence. That means spiritual development is unlimited. Divine secrets, knowledge, wisdom, and practical techniques are unlimited. Divine power for healing, rejuvenation, life transformation, and enlightenment is unlimited. A human being's potential is unlimited because the potential of Soul Power is unlimited.

There are many practical techniques to reach stillness and gain intelligence. I will reveal a secret to reach Tao stillness and Tao intelligence by applying the Four Power Techniques:

Body Power. Sit up straight. Put the tip of your tongue as close as you can to the roof of your mouth without touching it. Put both palms on your lower abdomen below the navel.

Soul Power. Say *hello:*

> *Dear soul mind body of Tao Ding De and Tao Hui Ming,*
> *I love you, honor you, and appreciate you.*
> *You have the power to bring Tao stillness and Tao intelligence to me.*
> *I am extremely grateful.*
> *Thank you.*

Mind Power. Visualize your whole soul, heart, mind, and body shining golden light.

Sound Power. Chant or sing silently or aloud:

> *Tao Ding De, Tao Hui Ming* (pronounced *dow ding*
>   *duh, dow hway ming*)
> *Tao Ding De, Tao Hui Ming*
> *Tao Ding De, Tao Hui Ming*
> *Tao Ding De, Tao Hui Ming*
> *Tao Ding De, Tao Hui Ming*
> *Tao Ding De, Tao Hui Ming*
> *Tao Ding De, Tao Hui Ming . . .*

You may also chant or sing in English:

> *Tao stillness, Tao intelligence*
> *Tao stillness, Tao intelligence*
> *Tao stillness, Tao intelligence*
> *Tao stillness, Tao intelligence*
> *Tao stillness, Tao intelligence*
> *Tao stillness, Tao intelligence*
> *Tao stillness, Tao intelligence . . .*

Chant or sing for three to five minutes; the longer, the better. To chant or sing *Tao Ding De, Tao Hui Ming* or *Tao stillness, Tao intelligence* can bring you to stillness and intelligence much faster than doing many other spiritual practices. The reason is that Tao Ding De and Tao Hui Ming carry the soul, mind, and body of Tao stillness and Tao intelligence. To chant is to become what you chant. There are so many meditations. Chanting these lines of the Tao text can really help you reach stillness and gain intelligence. Chanting *Tao Ding De, Tao Hui Ming* and *Tao stillness, Tao intelligence* is one of the most powerful practices for reaching Tao stillness and Tao intelligence.

道喜在

Tao Xi Zai

Tao happiness and joy

Tao is The Way, the source of all universes. "Xi" means *happiness and joy.* "Zai" means *existence.* "Tao xi zai" (pronounced *dow shee dzye*) means *Tao happiness and joy.* When you study Tao, practice Tao, and especially when you apply Tao in your daily life, you will gain inner joy and happiness. There are no words that can explain or express this enough. In chapter 3, I will teach Tao practice in daily life. That practice will bring incredible Tao happiness and Tao joy to you.

To reach Tao happiness and joy, you must remove soul, mind, and body blockages in your health, relationships, and finances. If you have any of these kinds of blockages, it is very hard to reach Tao happiness and joy.

To reach Tao happiness and joy is to reach the highest happiness and joy. You are melded with Tao. One of the top secret practices is to directly chant *Tao Xi Zai.* Use the Four Power Techniques:

Body Power. Sit up straight. Put the tip of your tongue as close as you can to the roof of your mouth without touching it. Put both palms on your lower abdomen below the navel.

Soul Power. Say *hello:*

Dear soul mind body of Tao Xi Zai,
I love you, honor you, and appreciate you.
You have the power to bring Tao happiness and joy to
every aspect of my life.
I am very honored and grateful.
Thank you.

Mind Power. Visualize golden light shining from head to toe, skin to bone in you and in every aspect of your life.

Sound Power. Chant or sing silently or aloud:

Tao Xi Zai (pronounced *dow shee dzye*)
Tao Xi Zai
Tao Xi Zai
Tao Xi Zai
Tao Xi Zai
Tao Xi Zai
Tao Xi Zai . . .

Chant or sing for three to five minutes; the longer, the better.

It takes time to reach Tao happiness and joy. Continue to chant. Continue to purify. Continue to remove your soul, mind, and body blockages in every aspect of life. Then, Tao Xi Zai will come to you.

道体生
Tao Ti Sheng

Tao body is produced

Tao is The Way. "Ti" means *body*. "Sheng" means *create* or *produce*. "Tao ti sheng" (pronounced *dow tee sheng*) means *the Tao body is produced*.

It will take the greatest effort to build the Tao body. What is the Tao body? In order to understand the Tao body, you must first understand enlightenment of soul, heart, mind, and body.

Soul enlightenment is to uplift your soul standing in Heaven. Soul enlightenment means your soul reaches the saints' level. The Akashic Records has special departments for enlightened souls. When you reach soul enlightenment, your Akashic Record book will be moved to these special departments.

Heart enlightenment is to reach total purity of the heart. Pure love, forgiveness, compassion, grace, and light will then radiate constantly from your heart.

Mind enlightenment is to remove all negative mind-sets, attitudes, and behaviors, as well as ego, attachments, and more in order to reach purity, stillness, and peace in your mind.

Body enlightenment is to transform your whole body, from head to toe, skin to bone, to a light body. All sicknesses will be completely removed. Your body will be greatly rejuvenated.

Soul enlightenment, heart enlightenment, mind enlightenment, and body enlightenment are the steps in the enlightenment journey. Each step in the process is more difficult than the previous step. In fact, each step is unlimited. But you can do it.

Tao ti sheng means that one's body reaches the Tao body. To reach the Tao body is to reach the highest light body attainable for a human being. There are many layers of light beings. Many spiritual beings in history have achieved a light body, but the Tao body is the highest light body. In fact, it is the highest light being.

It could take a whole lifetime and more to reach the Tao body. One who reaches the Tao body must have served the Divine and Tao mission for hundreds or thousands of lifetimes as a Total GOLD servant. It takes very hard service and the greatest effort to transform the body to a light body, but I am extremely honored that the Divine chose me as a servant to download Divine Light Body Soul Mind Body Transplants. These Divine Light Body Soul Mind Body Transplants are very high-level divine treasures. They can be given only to the ready ones. If one is not ready, one could not handle the frequency of the divine light body downloads. In my ten-year Tao training program, ready ones could receive these priceless treasures at the proper time.

To receive Divine Light Body Soul Mind Body Transplants does not mean your body automatically becomes a divine light body. It could take many years to transform your soul, mind, and body to a divine soul, mind, and body.

The Tao body is the highest layer and frequency body that a Tao practitioner or saint can reach. The greatest one-sentence secret about the Tao body is:

To reach the Tao body is to reach immortality.

Understand that it is very hard to reach the Tao body, but it is possible. The Divine and Tao give every Tao practitioner and every spiritual being an equal opportunity to achieve the Tao body.

To start to build your Tao body, I will share an important practice with you. Use the Four Power Techniques:

Body Power. Sit up straight. Put the tip of your tongue as close as you can to the roof of your mouth without touching it. Put both palms on your lower abdomen below the navel.

Soul Power. Say *hello:*

> *Dear soul mind body of Tao Ti Sheng,*
> *I love you, honor you, and appreciate you.*
> *You have the power to create my Tao body.*
> *I am very honored.*
> *I am extremely grateful.*
> *Thank you.*

Mind Power. Visualize golden light shining in your entire body, from head to toe, skin to bone.

Sound Power. Chant or sing silently or aloud:

> *Tao Ti Sheng* (pronounced *dow tee shung*)
> *Tao Ti Sheng*
> *Tao Ti Sheng*
> *Tao Ti Sheng*
> *Tao Ti Sheng*
> *Tao Ti Sheng*
> *Tao Ti Sheng . . .*

Chant or sing for at least three to five minutes. The longer and the more often you chant or sing *Tao Ti Sheng,* the better.

Practice more.

Serve more.

Chant more.

Purify your body further and further.

Build your light body frequency higher and higher.

Reach the Tao body.

We are so honored that the Divine and Tao have released this secret and sacred Tao body teaching to humanity.

道圆满
Tao Yuan Man

Tao enlightenment

Tao is The Way. "Yuan man" means *enlightenment*. "Tao Yuan Man" (pronounced *dow ywen mahn*) means *Tao enlightenment*.

Tao enlightenment is the highest enlightenment that a person or a soul can achieve. To reach Tao enlightenment is to reach complete soul, heart, mind, and body enlightenment. To reach *Tao yuan man* is to reach immortality. It is not easy at all. Fundamental practice is very important. Practice with me now. Use the Four Power Techniques:

Body Power. Sit up straight. Put the tip of your tongue as close as you can to the roof of your mouth without touching it. Put both palms on your lower abdomen below the navel.

Soul Power. Say *hello:*

> *Dear soul mind body of Tao Yuan Man,*
> *I love you, honor you, and appreciate you.*
> *You have the power to bring me to complete soul,*
>   *heart, mind, and body Tao enlightenment.*
> *I am very honored.*
> *Thank you.*

Mind Power. Visualize golden light shining from head to toe, skin to bone.

Sound Power. Chant or sing silently or aloud:

> *Tao Yuan Man* (pronounced *dow ywen mahn*)
> *Tao Yuan Man*
> *Tao Yuan Man*
> *Tao Yuan Man*
> *Tao Yuan Man*
> *Tao Yuan Man*
> *Tao Yuan Man . . .*

Chant or sing for at least three to five minutes. The longer and the more often you practice, the better.

Tao yuan man is the biggest dream goal for a spiritual being's achievement. It is an honor and a blessing beyond words to reach Tao enlightenment.

道合真

Tao He Zhen

Meld with Tao and become a Tao saint (servant)

Tao is The Way. "He" means *meld with Tao*. "Zhen" means *Tao saint* (zhen ren). "Tao he zhen" (pronounced *dow huh jun*) means *meld with Tao and become a Tao saint*.

This is the highest stage a Tao practitioner can achieve. To reach this state of *zhen ren* is to gain Tao abilities. This layer of *zhen ren* is the Tao saint layer. Those who reach this layer of *zhen ren* are given Tao abilities to harmonize countless universes. There are not enough words to explain and comprehend this layer of *zhen ren*. What saints' abilities you can conceive, this layer of *zhen ren* has. What saints' abilities you cannot conceive, this layer of *zhen ren* has also.

The top secret is to practice. Go into the Tao condition. Experience the wisdom and power that you cannot explain. Use the Four Power Techniques:

Body Power. Sit up straight. Put the tip of your tongue as close as you can to the roof of your mouth without touching it. Put both palms on your lower abdomen below the navel.

Soul Power. Say *hello:*

> *Dear Tao He Zhen,*
> *I love you, honor you, and appreciate you.*
> *You have the power to bring me to the zhen ren condition.*
> *I am extremely honored.*
> *Thank you.*

Sound Power. Chant or sing silently or aloud:

> *Tao He Zhen* (pronounced *dow huh jun*)
> *Tao He Zhen*
> *Tao He Zhen*
> *Tao He Zhen*
> *Tao He Zhen*
> *Tao He Zhen*
> *Tao He Zhen . . .*

Chant or sing for three to five minutes; the longer, the better.

Mind Power. Visualize golden light shining from head to toe, skin to bone. This chanting or singing of *Tao He Zhen* is beyond words and comprehension. Go into the condition. You may experience things you have never experienced by chanting or singing this mantra.

Practice it.

Benefit from it.

Have "aha!" and "wow!" moments from it.

There are no words anymore to explain the power of this chanting.

道果成

Tao Guo Cheng

Tao harvest

Tao is The Way. "Guo" means *fruits*. "Cheng" means *achievement*. "Tao guo cheng" (pronounced *dow gwaw chung*) means *receive the Tao harvest*.

If you plant, at harvest time you receive the fruits or results of your hard work.

Tao guo cheng means that after you reach the Tao, meld with Tao, and become a Tao saint, then you will enjoy the Tao fruits and receive the Tao harvest. There are no words to explain, and also not enough comprehension to explain, Tao fruits and Tao harvest. Human beings cannot imagine what kind of condition one has achieved when one completely reaches the Tao and has complete Tao abilities. When a person reaches this kind of condition, whatever abilities you can think of, this Tao saint will have.

The secret and sacred practice is to use the Four Power Techniques:

Body Power. Sit up straight. Put the tip of your tongue as close as you can to the roof of your mouth without touching it. Put both palms on the lower abdomen below the navel.

Soul Power. Say *hello:*

> *Dear Tao Guo Cheng,*
> *I love you, honor you, and appreciate you.*
> *You have the power to bring me to completely reach the*
>   *Tao and to have the honor to enjoy the Tao fruits*
>   *and receive the Tao harvest.*
> *I am extremely honored.*
> *Thank you.*

Mind Power. Visualize golden light shining in your entire body, from head to toe, skin to bone.

Sound Power. Chant or sing silently or aloud:

> *Tao Guo Cheng* (pronounced *dow gwaw chung*)
> *Tao Guo Cheng*
> *Tao Guo Cheng*
> *Tao Guo Cheng*
> *Tao Guo Cheng*
> *Tao Guo Cheng*
> *Tao Guo Cheng . . .*

Chant or sing for three to five minutes; the longer, the better.

It is the greatest honor for a Tao practitioner or a spiritual being to reach the Tao saint level. Then, enjoy the Tao fruits and receive the Tao harvest. To enjoy the Tao fruits and receive the Tao harvest is to apply Tao saint abilities to serve all universes.

The creation and manifestation abilities of Tao saints are beyond words.

道神通
Tao Shen Tong

Complete Tao saint abilities

Tao is The Way. "Shen tong" means *complete saint abilities*. "Tao shen tong" (pronounced *dow shun tawng*) means *complete Tao saint abilities*.

There are fairy-tale stories about saints flying, disappearing, and displaying other abilities that are beyond a human's thoughts or words. *Tao shen tong* refers to the Tao saints who have gained such saint's abilities that what you can think is what is available to them.

I'll give one example. Earlier in this chapter, I explained a renowned statement from *The Yellow Emperor's Internal Classic*:

Ju zhe cheng xing, san zhe cheng feng

"Ju" means *accumulation*. "Zhe" means *the person*. "Cheng" means *become*. "Xing" means *shape*. "San" means *dissipate*. "Feng" means *wind*. "Ju zhe cheng xing, san zhe cheng feng" (pronounced *jü juh chung shing, sahn juh chung fung*) means *energy accumulates to become a person, energy dissipates and the person's shape can disappear*. This is hard to explain in human words. The Divine and Tao asked me to present this to tell you, every reader, and humanity that to completely reach Tao and to become a Tao saint is to have any abilities that one can think of. In fact, Tao saints have abilities that you cannot think of. This can be summarized in one sentence:

Tao is the creator and source of all universes; therefore, Tao saints can create and manifest anything in all universes.

To completely reach Tao and become a Tao saint, what you think is what you can achieve because you become Tao and you are completely melded with Tao. Tao saints are the highest saints in the spiritual realm. It is an honor to reach this state and to be a Tao servant. To have the highest power is to be a better servant.

Practice by using the Four Power Techniques:

Body Power. Sit up straight. Put the tip of your tongue as close as you can to the roof of your mouth without touching it. Put both palms on your lower abdomen below the navel.

Soul Power. Say *hello:*

> *Dear Tao Shen Tong,*
> *I love you, honor you, and appreciate you.*
> *You have the power to bring and enjoy the Tao saints'*
>   *abilities to serve all universes.*
> *I am extremely honored.*
> *Thank you.*

Mind Power. Visualize golden light shining in your entire body, from head to toe, skin to bone.

Sound Power. Chant or sing silently or aloud:

> *Tao Shen Tong* (pronounced *dow shun tawng*)
> *Tao Shen Tong*
> *Tao Shen Tong*

Tao Shen Tong
Tao Shen Tong
Tao Shen Tong
Tao Shen Tong . . .

Chant or sing for three to five minutes; the longer, the better.

To become a Tao saint and to have Tao saints' abilities is to serve humanity, Mother Earth, and all universes better.

Serve. Serve. Serve.

There is no ending for service.

Tao saints are the highest servants.

Be very honored to reach that layer to be a servant with Tao abilities.

道法自然
Tao Fa Zi Ran

Follow Nature's Way

Tao is The Way, the universal principles and laws. "Fa" means *the universal method*. "Zi ran" means *be natural*. "Tao fa zi ran" (pronounced *dow fah dz rahn*) means *follow nature's way*.

To reach the Tao saints is to reach a level that cannot be explained in words anymore. It is to reach the level that follows nature's way. It is to gain the ability to meld with all conditions in countless universes. It is simply to reach the condition of natural flow.

Tao saints will meld with themselves, with nature, with all universes, and with all conditions. They have reached the level to follow all universal principles, laws, and methods naturally. They harmonize all kinds of conditions.

Practice by using the Four Power Techniques:

Body Power. Sit up straight. Put the tip of your tongue as close as you can to the roof of your mouth without touching it. Put both palms on your lower abdomen below the navel.

Soul Power. Say *hello:*

> *Dear Tao Fa Zi Ran,*
> *I love you, honor you, and appreciate you.*
> *You have the power to meld me with Tao, all nature,*
>   *and all universes.*
> *I am extremely honored.*
> *Thank you.*

Mind Power. Visualize golden light shining in your entire body, from head to toe, skin to bone.

Sound Power. Chant or sing silently or aloud:

> *Tao Fa Zi Ran* (pronounced *dow fah dz rahn*)
> *Tao Fa Zi Ran*
> *Tao Fa Zi Ran*
> *Tao Fa Zi Ran*
> *Tao Fa Zi Ran*
> *Tao Fa Zi Ran*
> *Tao Fa Zi Ran . . .*

Chant or sing for three to five minutes; the longer, the better.

If one reaches Tao Fa Zi Ran, then every aspect of this person's life will be completely transformed and enlightened. Everything will be smooth, balanced, and harmonized. To reach this state is not easy at all, but it is possible. Lao Zi shared Tao Fa Zi

Ran in *Tao Te Jing*. In thousands of years of history, it has guided millions of Tao practitioners to do Xiu Lian in order to reach the condition of Tao Fa Zi Ran.

Remember, the first two sentences of the new Tao text that the Divine gave to me are exactly the same as in *Tao Te Jing*: **Tao Ke Tao, Fei Chang Tao**. This means that to use words and comprehension to explain Tao is not the true Tao. Tao cannot be truly explained. To reach the Tao condition, to completely meld with Tao, or to reach Tao Fa Zi Ran, cannot be explained because if it could be explained, then it would not be the true Tao nor the true Tao Fa Zi Ran condition.

I would like to share this insight with you and humanity. When you reach Tao, you will experience Tao creation and manifestation that no one has experienced.

When you reach Tao, you will gain Tao abilities for healing, rejuvenation, preventing sickness, and transforming and enlightening others beyond imagination.

When you reach Tao, you will be able to harmonize humanity, Mother Earth, Heaven, and all universes beyond explanation.

When you reach Tao, you will gain the abilities to create and manifest anything in countless universes.

What I am sharing here is not just for Taoists. I am not teaching Taoism. I have shared ancient Tao secrets, wisdom, knowledge, and practical techniques; but beyond that, I am sharing Divine and Tao direct teaching through my soul communication abilities. I am not writing this book; I am flowing it. The Divine and Tao are above my head and explain to me on the spot. More than sixty of my top teachers have watched and listened to me flowing this book. I connect with the Divine and Tao. I directly talk. My assistants type. During the flowing, many profound secrets, wisdom, knowledge, and practical techniques come out directly from the Divine and Tao.

What I am sharing here is how every spiritual being can achieve the Tao, the source of all universes. If a spiritual being completely reaches the Tao and becomes a Tao saint, that cannot be explained anymore. I repeat one more time: what you can think of or what you cannot think of, including the Tao saint abilities that you know about or have heard about, Tao saints will have much more.

Tao Fa Zi Ran
Tao Fa Zi Ran
Tao Fa Zi Ran

Conclusion

Now I will share with you and humanity that to chant or sing the whole Tao text is the sacred and secret Tao practice to reach Tao faster. Listen to me singing on the enclosed CD. You can chant or sing now:

道可道	*Tao Ke Tao*	*dow kuh dow*
非常道	*Fei Chang Tao*	*fay chahng dow*
大无外	*Da Wu Wai*	*dah woo wye*
小无内	*Xiao Wu Nei*	*shee-yow woo nay*
无方圆	*Wu Fang Yuan*	*woo fahng ywen*
无形象	*Wu Xing Xiang*	*woo shing shyahng*
无时空	*Wu Shi Kong*	*woo shr kawng*
顺道昌	*Shun Tao Chang*	*shun dow chahng*
逆道亡	*Ni Tao Wang*	*nee dow wahng*
道生一	*Tao Sheng Yi*	*dow shung yee*

天一真水	Tian Yi Zhen Shui	tyen yee jun shway
金津玉液	Jin Jin Yu Ye	jeen jeen yü yuh
咽入丹田	Yan Ru Dan Tian	yahn roo dahn tyen
一生二	Yi Sheng Er	yee shung ur
道丹道神	Tao Dan Tao Shen	dow dahn dow shun
服务人类	Fu Wu Ren Lei	foo woo wren lay
服务万灵	Fu Wu Wan Ling	foo woo wahn ling
服务地球	Fu Wu Di Qiu	foo woo dee cheo
服务宇宙	Fu Wu Yu Zhou	foo woo yü joe
治愈百病	Zhi Yu Bai Bing	zhr yü bye bing
预防百病	Yu Fang Bai Bing	yoo fahng bye bing
返老还童	Fan Lao Huan Tong	fahn lao hwahn tawng
长寿永生	Chang Shou Yong Sheng	chahng sho yawng shung
和谐人类	He Xie Ren Lei	huh shyeh wren lay
道业昌盛	Tao Ye Chang Sheng	dow yuh chahng shung
功德圆满	Gong De Yuan Man	gawng duh ywen mahn
万灵融合	Wan Ling Rong He	wahn ling rawng huh
丹神养肾	Dan Shen Yang Shen	dahn shun yahng shun
二生三	Er Sheng San	ur shung sahn
三万物	San Wan Wu	sahn wahn woo
天地人	Tian Di Ren	tyen dee wren
神气精	Shen Qi Jing	shun chee jing
肾生精	Shen Sheng Jing	shun shung jing
精生髓	Jing Sheng Sui	jing shung sway
髓充脑	Sui Chong Nao	sway chawng now
脑神明	Nao Shen Ming	now shun ming
炼精化气	Lian Jing Hua Qi	lyen jing hwah chee
炼气化神	Lian Qi Hua Shen	lyen chee hwah shun
炼神还虚	Lian Shen Huan Xu	lyen shun hwahn shü
炼虚还道	Lian Xu Huan Tao	lyen shü hwahn dow
合道中	He Tao Zhong	huh dow jawng

无穷尽	Wu Qiong Jin	woo chyawng jeen
道灵宫	Tao Ling Gong	dow ling gawng
信息雪山	Xin Xi Xue Shan	sheen shee shoo-eh shahn
灵语言	Ling Yu Yan	ling yü yahn
灵信通	Ling Xin Tong	ling sheen tawng
灵歌舞	Ling Ge Wu	ling guh woo
灵敲打	Ling Qiao Da	ling chee-yow dah
灵草药	Ling Cao Yao	ling tsow yow
灵针灸	Ling Zhen Jiu	ling jun jeo
灵按摩	Ling An Mo	ling ahn maw
灵治疗	Ling Zhi Liao	ling jr lee-ow
灵预防	Ling Yu Fang	ling yü fahng
灵转化	Ling Zhuan Hua	ling jwahn hwah
灵圆满	Ling Yuan Man	ling ywen mahn
灵智慧	Ling Zhi Hui	ling jr hway
灵潜能	Ling Qian Neng	ling chyen nung
换灵脑身	Huan Ling Nao Shen	hwahn ling now shun
服务三界	Fu Wu San Jie	foo woo sahn jyeh
灵光普照	Ling Guang Pu Zhao	ling gwahng poo jow
万物更新	Wan Wu Geng Xin	wahn woo gung sheen
誓为公仆	Shi Wei Gong Pu	shr way gawng poo
世代服务	Shi Dai Fu Wu	shr dye foo woo
灵光圣世	Ling Guang Sheng Shi	ling gwahng shung shr
创新纪元	Chuang Xin Ji Yuan	chwahng sheen jee ywen
道道道	Tao Tao Tao	dow dow dow
道定得	Tao Ding De	dow ding duh
道慧明	Tao Hui Ming	dow hway ming
道喜在	Tao Xi Zai	dow shee dzye
道体生	Tao Ti Sheng	dow tee shung
道圆满	Tao Yuan Man	dow ywen mahn
道合真	Tao He Zhen	dow huh jun

道果成	*Tao Guo Cheng*	*dow gwaw chung*
道神通	*Tao Shen Tong*	*dow shun tawng*
道法自然	*Tao Fa Zi Ran*	*dow fah dzi rahn*

To chant or sing is to boost energy, vitality, stamina, and immunity.

To chant or sing is to heal.

To chant or sing is to prevent sickness.

To chant or sing is to rejuvenate your soul, heart, mind, and body.

To chant or sing is to purify your soul, heart, mind, and body.

To chant or sing is to transform relationships, finances, and every aspect of your life.

To chant or sing is to enlighten your soul, heart, mind, and body.

To chant or sing is to create love, peace, and harmony for you, your loved ones, all humanity, Mother Earth, and all universes.

To chant or sing is to reach Tao.

3

Jin Dan—Tao Practice in Daily Life

ANCIENT TAO PRACTICE has many practical treasures. The Divine and Tao guided me to release one of the most important practical sacred Tao practices. This new practical treasure is named **Jin Dan practice**. Jin Dan practice is both Da Tao (Big Tao) practice and Xiao Tao (Small Tao) practice. Jin Dan practice includes practices for every Xiao Tao of every aspect of daily life. To reach Xiao Tao in every aspect of life is to reach Da Tao or, simply, Tao.

What Is Jin Dan?

Jin Dan is a golden light ball located in one's lower abdomen, just below the navel and in the center of the body. No one is born with a Jin Dan. Special Tao practice is required to create a Jin Dan.

Jin Dan has layers—different sizes and frequencies. A Tao practitioner can absolutely form a Jin Dan through his or her own efforts. Generally speaking, the Jin Dan developed by a Tao practitioner in this way is the size of a fist. This Jin Dan is created entirely through the practitioner's own efforts. We could call such a Jin Dan a human Jin Dan.

Remember that the Divine can create a new soul of anyone and anything. The Divine can download Jin Dan Soul Mind Body Transplants. Tao can also download Jin Dan Soul Mind Body Transplants. Divine Jin Dans and Tao Jin Dans can vary in size and frequency. The size of a Divine or Tao Jin Dan can be two, three, or five times bigger than a fist. It can be as big as one's body or bigger. It can be the size of a city, the size of a country, the size of Mother Earth, the size of all universes, and the size of Tao. If you have a highly developed Third Eye and other spiritual channels, you could be totally surprised by the high frequency and power of a Divine Jin Dan or a Tao Jin Dan. "Surprised" is not enough. "Shocked" is also not enough. "Aha!" would not be enough. "Wow!" would still not be enough.

At the end of 2008, the Divine and Tao gave me the Tao text revealed in this book. They are continuously giving me much more that I will share in *Tao II, Tao III,* and even more Tao books. This is all new divine Tao teaching in the Soul Light Era from the Divine and Tao.

When the Divine and Tao gave me the Tao text for this book, they told me:

> *Zhi Gang,*
> *The Tao teaching you are offering from us to humanity in the Soul Light Era is unique. You will share the highest secrets, wisdom, knowledge, and practical techniques of traditional Tao teaching, but you will also offer new Tao teaching directly from us. We have new teachings for hu-*

manity. *The most important Tao teachings we give to you are the simplest teachings—Da Tao zhi jian. You will teach extremely simple theory and practical techniques, which are the most powerful theory and practical techniques.*

I bowed down to the Divine and Tao and made a vow to them:

I am honored to be a chosen servant to offer Tao teaching directly from you. I am honored to be a vessel and vehicle to pass these sacred and secret Tao teachings to humanity. I am honored to reveal these simplest and most powerful teachings and practices to humanity. I will accomplish my task.

Jin Dan is one of the highest treasures of Tao teaching. Jin Dan is one of the highest treasures from the Divine and Tao. **To reach Tao, Jin Dan is the key.**

The Power and Significance of Jin Dan

Jin Dan has the following powers and abilities:

- Jin Dan is the source of message, energy, and matter.
- Jin Dan has the highest power for healing your physical, emotional, mental, and spiritual bodies.
- Jin Dan is the key to preventing sickness in your physical, emotional, mental, and spiritual bodies.
- Jin Dan is the highest treasure for purifying your soul, heart, mind, and body.
- Jin Dan has the highest abilities for rejuvenating your soul, heart, mind, and body.

- Jin Dan has the highest strength for transforming all of your relationships.
- Jin Dan has the highest potential for transforming your business.
- Jin Dan has the highest honor for enlightening your soul, heart, mind, and body.
- Jin Dan has the highest power and abilities for healing, blessing, and transforming others.
- Jin Dan has the highest power and abilities for offering service to humanity, Mother Earth, and all universes.

In one sentence:

Jin Dan is the greatest treasure for all life.

A human being's soul, mind, and body and a human being's message, energy, and matter are not enough to build a Jin Dan. Jin Dan gathers the soul, mind, and body of Heaven and Earth, as well as the message, energy, and matter of Heaven and Earth.

How to Build Your Jin Dan

Use the Four Power Techniques with a secret and sacred mantra:

Body Power. Sit up straight. Put the tip of your tongue as close as you can to the roof of your mouth without touching it. Put both palms on your lower abdomen below the navel.

Soul Power. Say *hello*:

Dear soul mind body of the Divine,
Dear soul mind body of Tao,
Dear soul mind body of all universes, galaxies, stars,
and planets,
Dear soul mind body of Heaven,
Dear soul mind body of Mother Earth,
Dear soul mind body of all my spiritual fathers and
mothers in all layers of Heaven,
Dear soul mind body of all my systems, organs, cells,
cell units, DNA, RNA, smallest matter in the cells,
and spaces between the cells,
I love you all, honor you all, and appreciate you all.
You have the power to create, form, and build my Jin
Dan.
I am extremely blessed.
I cannot honor you enough.
Thank you.

Mind Power. Visualize a beautiful, bright, and powerful golden light ball forming in your lower abdomen, just below your navel.

Sound Power. Chant or sing silently or aloud (listen to me on the enclosed CD):

Tao Sheng Yi	*dow shung yee*
Tian Yi Zhen Shui	*tyen yee jun shway*
Jin Jin Yu Ye	*jeen jeen yü yuh*
Yan Ru Dan Tian	*yahn roo dahn tyen*
Shen Qi Jing He Yi	*shun chee jing huh yee*
Tian Di Ren He Yi	*tyen dee wren huh yee*
Jin Dan Lian Cheng	*jeen dahn lyen chung*

Tao Sheng Yi   dow shung yee
Tian Yi Zhen Shui   tyen yee jun shway
Jin Jin Yu Ye   jeen jeen yü yuh
Yan Ru Dan Tian   yahn roo dahn tyen
Shen Qi Jing He Yi   shun chee jing huh yee
Tian Di Ren He Yi   tyen dee wren huh yee
Jin Dan Lian Cheng   jeen dahn lyen chung

Tao Sheng Yi   dow shung yee
Tian Yi Zhen Shui   tyen yee jun shway
Jin Jin Yu Ye   jeen jeen yü yuh
Yan Ru Dan Tian   yahn roo dahn tyen
Shen Qi Jing He Yi   shun chee jing huh yee
Tian Di Ren He Yi   tyen dee wren huh yee
Jin Dan Lian Cheng   jeen dahn lyen chung

Tao Sheng Yi   dow shung yee
Tian Yi Zhen Shui   tyen yee jun shway
Jin Jin Yu Ye   jeen jeen yü yuh
Yan Ru Dan Tian   yahn roo dahn tyen
Shen Qi Jing He Yi   shun chee jing huh yee
Tian Di Ren He Yi   tyen dee wren huh yee
Jin Dan Lian Cheng   jeen dahn lyen chung

Tao Sheng Yi   dow shung yee
Tian Yi Zhen Shui   tyen yee jun shway
Jin Jin Yu Ye   jeen jeen yü yuh
Yan Ru Dan Tian   yahn roo dahn tyen
Shen Qi Jing He Yi   shun chee jing huh yee
Tian Di Ren He Yi   tyen dee wren huh yee
Jin Dan Lian Cheng   jeen dahn lyen chung

Tao Sheng Yi	*dow shung yee*
Tian Yi Zhen Shui	*tyen yee jun shway*
Jin Jin Yu Ye	*jeen jeen yü yuh*
Yan Ru Dan Tian	*yahn roo dahn tyen*
Shen Qi Jing He Yi	*shun chee jing huh yee*
Tian Di Ren He Yi	*tyen dee wren huh yee*
Jin Dan Lian Cheng	*jeen dahn lyen chung*
Tao Sheng Yi	*dow shung yee*
Tian Yi Zhen Shui	*tyen yee jun shway*
Jin Jin Yu Ye	*jeen jeen yü yuh*
Yan Ru Dan Tian	*yahn roo dahn tyen*
Shen Qi Jing He Yi	*shun chee jing huh yee*
Tian Di Ren He Yi	*tyen dee wren huh yee*
Jin Dan Lian Cheng . . .	*jeen dahn lyen chung . . .*

Chant or sing for at least fifteen minutes. It is best to chant or sing for thirty minutes to one hour. Building a Jin Dan takes time and effort. This practice produces Tian Yi Zhen Shui and Jin Jin Yu Ye to build your Jin Dan. The more you chant or sing, the more quickly you will build your Jin Dan.

Let me explain each line of the seven-line mantra used as the Sound Power in this practice to build a Jin Dan.

TAO SHENG YI

Tao is The Way, the source of all universes. Tao is the creator of all things. "Sheng" means *creates*. "Yi" means *one*. "Tao sheng yi" means *Tao creates One*.

TIAN YI ZHEN SHUI

"Tian" means *Heaven*. "Yi" means *one* or *unique*. "Zhen" means *sacred*. "Shui" means *liquid* or *water*. "Tian yi zhen shui" means *Heaven's unique sacred liquid*. Heaven's sacred liquid gathers the message, energy, and matter of Heaven. *Tian yi zhen shui* falls down from Heaven through the crown chakra (just above the top of the head), and then goes through the brain and the palate into the mouth.

JIN JIN YU YE

The first "Jin" means *gold*. The second "jin" means *liquid*. "Yu" means *jade*. "Ye" means *liquid*. "Jin jin yu ye" means *gold liquid, jade liquid*. Gold and jade express the preciousness of this liquid. Jin Jin and Yu Ye are also two acupuncture points that are located under the tongue. Jin Jin Yu Ye is Mother Earth's sacred liquid. It gathers the message, energy, and matter of Mother Earth. *Jin jin yu ye* comes in through the Yong Quan acupuncture points (Kidney 1), which are located on the soles of the feet between the second and third metatarsal bones, one-third of the distance from the webs of the toes to the heel. It then goes up through the center of the legs to the Hui Yin acupuncture point in the perineum (between the genitals and the anus), and then up through the first five soul houses in the center of the body. From the fifth soul house in the throat, it moves to the Jin Jin and Yu Ye acupuncture points, where it then flows out into the mouth.

YAN RU DAN TIAN

"Yan" means *swallow*. "Ru" means *into*. "Dan" means *light ball*. "Tian" means *field*. This Dan Tian refers to the Lower Dan Tian, which is one of the most important energy centers in the body. The Jin Dan is located slightly above the Lower Dan Tian.

SHEN QI JING HE YI

"Shen" means *all of one's souls, including one's body soul, system souls, organ souls, cell souls, cell unit souls, DNA and RNA souls, smallest matter souls, and space souls.* "Qi" means *all of one's energies, including the energies of the body, systems, organs, cells, cell units, DNA and RNA, smallest matter, and spaces.* "Jing" means *all matter in one's body.* "He" means *join as.* "Yi" means *one.* "Shen qi jing he yi" means *all souls, energies, and matter join as one.* They all join as one in the Jin Dan.

TIAN DI REN HE YI

"Tian" means *Heaven.* "Di" means *Earth.* "Ren" means *human being.* "He" means *join as.* "Yi" means *one.* "Tian di ren he yi" means *Heaven, Mother Earth, and human being join as one.* They all join as one in the Jin Dan.

JIN DAN LIAN CHENG

"Jin" means *gold.* "Dan" means *light ball.* "Lian" means *cook.* "Cheng" means *done.* "Jin dan lian cheng" means *golden light ball is formed.*

Let me summarize the essence of the meaning and significance of each line in this sacred mantra:

Tao Sheng Yi. Tao creates One. One includes all universes, galaxies, stars, and planets. Chanting *Tao sheng yi* gathers message, energy, and matter from Tao and from all universes.

Tian Yi Zhen Shui. Chanting this line gathers Heaven's sacred liquid, which gathers the message, energy, and matter of Heaven.

Jin Jin Yu Ye. Chanting this line gathers Mother Earth's sacred liquid, which gathers the message, energy, and matter of Mother Earth.

Yan Ru Dan Tian. The message, energy, and matter from Tao and from all universes, are gathered in the mouth with Heaven's sacred liquid and Mother Earth's sacred liquid, and then swallowed into the lower abdomen to form the Jin Dan. From the Lower Dan Tian, the Jin Dan is formed and then it moves up a little, to just below the navel.

Shen Qi Jing He Yi. All the souls, energies, and matter of the whole body join as one in the Jin Dan.

Tian Di Ren He Yi. All the essences of Heaven, Mother Earth, and human being join as one in the Jin Dan.

Jin Dan Lian Cheng. From *Tao sheng yi, Tian yi zhen shui, Jin jin yu ye, Yan ru dan tian, Shen qi jing he yi,* and *Tian di ren he yi,* the Jin Dan is formed.

This is the simplest way to form a Jin Dan: by gathering message, energy, and matter from Tao, all universes, all galaxies, all stars, all planets, all layers of Heaven, Mother Earth, the human realm, and from your own soul, mind, and body.

For a new but dedicated practitioner who practices for one hour each day, it generally takes about four hundred hours to build a Jin Dan. It would take such a practitioner more than one year to build a Jin Dan through dedicated daily hour-long practice. Someone who practices two hours per day could form a Jin Dan in about two hundred days.

The Divine and Tao are guiding me at this moment that this sacred divine and Tao teaching could help you build your Jin Dan eight to ten times faster than traditional ways. The traditional way could even take decades with traditional practices.

This Jin Dan is still a human being's Jin Dan. Now let me explain to you Divine Jin Dan and Tao Jin Dan.

Divine Jin Dan and Tao Jin Dan

In my ten-year Tao training program, the Divine and Tao guided me that students who are ready could apply to receive Divine Jin Dan and Tao Jin Dan Soul Mind Body Transplants. If students are not ready, they are required to form their own Jin Dan first. Some students' bodies are not strong enough to handle Divine Jin Dan and Tao Jin Dan frequency. These students will need to practice building their own Jin Dan in order to raise their frequency before they can receive Divine Jin Dan or Tao Jin Dan.

Both Divine Jin Dan and Tao Jin Dan have their own layers of frequency. The Divine and Tao together plan to offer ten different layers of Jin Dan to Tao practitioners. Each successive layer of Divine Jin Dan and Tao Jin Dan carries a big increase in frequency, vibration, and power.

Every year for ten years, the Divine and Tao will release a higher layer of Jin Dan. However, the Divine and Tao are telling me at this moment not to announce the specific layers yet. Further details will be provided to students in my ten-year sacred Tao practitioner training program. To receive higher-layer frequencies and powers of Jin Dan, a Tao practitioner must join the ten-year Tao training program.

Earlier I explained the power and significance of Jin Dan and how to build your own Jin Dan. Divine Jin Dan and Tao Jin Dan have their own power. There is no comparison between a human being's Jin Dan and Divine Jin Dan or Tao Jin Dan.

The Divine and Tao will offer Divine Jin Dan Soul Mind Body Transplants and Tao Jin Dan Soul Mind Body Transplants to Tao practitioners. After receiving these priceless treasures, recipients will be taught how to apply their Divine Jin Dan and Tao Jin Dan to transform every aspect of their lives—including health, relationships, finances, purification, and rejuvenation of soul, heart, mind, and body—and to transform their frequency to the frequency of Divine Jin Dan and Tao Jin Dan.

The ten-year Tao training program is sacred divine and Tao training. As I explained in chapter 1, this Tao training has five major steps. Each step requires at least two years of training. There could be millions of people who complete the first two years of training. There will be very few people who will successfully complete all ten years of training.

Because this is sacred and secret divine and Tao training, participants must apply for admission to every major step of training. Applicants must be approved by Divine and Tao Guidance.

We are honored that the Divine and Tao are willing to download their Jin Dans to a group of Tao practitioners for the first time in history. Since ancient times, they have downloaded these permanent divine and Tao treasures only to the highest spiritual leaders. Now, hundreds, thousands, and perhaps even millions of people could have the opportunity to receive Divine Jin Dan and Tao Jin Dan through the Tao training program.

There are not enough words to explain the power of Divine Jin Dan and Tao Jin Dan. I am extremely honored. I cannot honor Divine Jin Dan and Tao Jin Dan enough. I cannot honor the Divine and Tao enough.

> *God gives his heart to me*
> *God gives his love to me*
> *My heart melds with his heart*
> *My love melds with his love*

> *Tao gives his heart to me*
> *Tao gives his love to me*
> *My heart melds with Tao's heart*
> *My love melds with Tao's love*

Sacred Jin Dan Mantras for Daily Practice

Earlier in this chapter, I revealed the secret and sacred practice to build your own Jin Dan. You need to spend as many hours as you can each day to build your Jin Dan by applying the sacred technique I shared with you. Generally speaking, it takes about four hundred hours of dedicated practice to build your own Jin Dan with this technique. Some highly developed spiritual beings could build a Jin Dan in much less time with this technique because they already have a great foundation.

In any case, practice the technique a lot to build your own Jin Dan. Jin Dan is built little by little. It can always be built further.

But you can always apply your Jin Dan to benefit every aspect of your life. I will show you several key Jin Dan practices for daily life. I ask you to do each of these practices. Each of these practices will also help you build your Jin Dan. The more you practice, the faster you will build your Jin Dan. These practices are to help you build your Jin Dan as quickly as possible. I sing each of these practice mantras for you on the enclosed CD, but I also suggest you use the audio version of this book. With it, you can practice directly with me. This will boost your practice and could greatly accelerate building your Jin Dan. I also offer additional blessings to listeners of the audio book. Do not think the print book and the audio book are the same. Each one carries its own frequency, vibration, and treasures. Each one could bring you different "aha!" moments and "wow!" moments. Serious students and practitioners, and anyone with a serious need or desire for healing and transformation, will appreciate the benefits of both the print book and the audio book.

Tao is in daily life. The Divine and Tao guided me to offer the following teachings and practices for daily life to you, to all Tao practitioners, and to humanity. These practices are extremely simple, but they are also extremely powerful for transforming your health, happiness, intelligence, relationships, finances, and success in every aspect of your life. Remember one line of the Tao text explained in chapter 2: Tao fa zi ran, which means *follow nature's way*. When you reach Tao, you will meld with Tao in every aspect of your life. You will follow the universal principles and laws naturally. Doing the following practices is very important to build your Jin Dan and to help you reach Tao in daily life.

金丹醒神
Jin Dan Xing Shen

1. Morning Practice Upon Waking Up

The sacred and secret mantra for this practice is *Jin Dan Xing Shen* (pronounced *jeen dahn shing shun*). "Jin" means *gold*. "Dan" means *light ball*. "Xing" means *awaken*. "Shen" means *your soul* and also *the highest energy*. "Jin dan xing shen" means *Jin Dan awakens your soul and boosts your highest energy for the day*.

Right after you wake up in the morning, apply the Four Power Techniques in this practice:

Body Power. After waking up, remain lying in bed on your back. Put both palms over your abdomen below the navel. Put the tip of your tongue as close as you can to the roof of your mouth without touching it.

Soul Power. Say *hello:*

> *Dear soul mind body of my Jin Dan* (even if you have only built your Jin Dan for one day, it does not matter; invoke and use the Soul Power of whatever Jin Dan you have),
> *I love you, honor you, and appreciate you.*
> *You have the power to awaken me fully and to boost my energy, stamina, vitality, and immunity for the whole day.*
> *I am very grateful.*
> *Thank you.*

Mind Power. Visualize your Jin Dan rotating and growing in your lower abdomen, just below your navel.

Sound Power. Chant or sing silently (listen to me on the enclosed CD):

> *Jin Dan Xing Shen* (pronounced *jeen dahn shing shun*)
> *Jin Dan Xing Shen*
> *Jin Dan Xing Shen*
> *Jin Dan Xing Shen*
> *Jin Dan Xing Shen*
> *Jin Dan Xing Shen*
> *Jin Dan Xing Shen . . .*

Chant or sing silently (never aloud when lying down because that drains energy) for at least five minutes. Practicing a little longer would be perfect.

This practice is extremely important:

- to awaken your soul, heart, mind, and body
- to receive the morning's energy from Heaven and Mother Earth
- to boost your highest energy for your entire day of activities

金丹进谷
Jin Dan Jin Gu

2. Practice Before Meals

The sacred and secret mantra for this practice is *Jin Dan Jin Gu* (pronounced *jeen dahn jeen goo*). The first "Jin" means *gold*.

"Dan" means *light ball*. The second "Jin" means *go into*. "Gu" means *food*. "Jin dan jin gu" means *Jin Dan prepares your entire digestive system for food intake.*

Five minutes before eating, apply the Four Power Techniques in this practice.

Body Power. Sit up straight with your feet flat on the floor. Put the tip of your tongue as close as you can to the roof of your mouth without touching it. Put your right palm just above your navel. Put your left palm just below your navel.

Soul Power. Say *hello:*

> *Dear soul mind and body of my Jin Dan* (after doing
>   the morning practice upon waking up, your Jin
>   Dan has already grown a little),
> *Dear soul mind body of my entire digestive system,*
> *I love you, honor you, and appreciate you.*
> *You have the power to prepare my entire digestive sys-*
>   *tem for food intake.*
> *I am very happy and grateful.*
> *Thank you.*

Mind Power. Visualize a golden light ball rotating in your entire digestive system, from mouth, teeth, tongue, and salivary glands, to esophagus, stomach, spleen, small intestine, and more, to prepare it well for your meal.

Sound Power. Chant or sing silently or aloud (listen to me on the enclosed CD):

Jin Dan Jin Gu (pronounced *jeen dahn jeen goo*)
Jin Dan Jin Gu
Jin Dan Jin Gu
Jin Dan Jin Gu
Jin Dan Jin Gu
Jin Dan Jin Gu
Jin Dan Jin Gu . . .

Chant or sing for at least five minutes. Practicing a little longer would be perfect.

This practice is extremely important:

- to prepare your entire digestive system, including all digestive liquids, enzymes, and more
- to boost the functioning of every organ and every cell in your digestive system

金丹化谷
Jin Dan Hua Gu

3. Practice After Meals

The sacred and secret mantra for this practice is *Jin Dan Hua Gu* (pronounced *jeen dahn hwah goo*). The first "Jin" means *gold*. "Dan" means *light ball*. "Hua" means *digest and absorb*. "Jin dan hua gu" means *Jin Dan assists your entire digestive system to digest and absorb food well.*

Right after eating, apply the Four Power Techniques in this practice:

Body Power. Sit up straight. Put the tip of your tongue as close as you can to the roof of your mouth without touching it. Put your right palm just above your navel. Put your left palm just below your navel.

Soul Power. Say *hello:*

> *Dear soul mind body of my Jin Dan,*
> *Dear soul mind body of my entire digestive system,*
> *I love you, honor you, and appreciate you.*
> *You have the power to help me digest and absorb food*
>   *well.*
> *I deeply appreciate it.*
> *Thank you.*

Sound Power. Chant or sing silently or aloud (listen to me on the enclosed CD):

> *Jin Dan Hua Gu* (pronounced *jeen dahn hwah goo*)
> *Jin Dan Hua Gu*
> *Jin Dan Hua Gu*
> *Jin Dan Hua Gu*
> *Jin Dan Hua Gu*
> *Jin Dan Hua Gu*
> *Jin Dan Hua Gu . . .*

Chant or sing for at least fifteen minutes. Practicing for a half hour would be best.

Mind Power. Visualize a golden light ball rotating in your whole digestive system to digest and absorb food well. This practice is extremely important:

- to help your entire digestive system digest and absorb food well
- to boost the functioning of every organ and every cell in your digestive system

金丹舒肝
Jin Dan Shu Gan

金丹治木
Jin Dan Zhi Mu

4. Practice to Heal Your Liver and Wood Element

The sacred and secret mantra for this practice is *Jin Dan Shu Gan* (pronounced *jeen dahn shoo gahn*). "Jin" means *gold.* "Dan" means *light ball.* "Shu" means *smooth.* "Gan" means *liver.* "Jin dan shu gan" means *Jin Dan smooths the liver function with healing and rejuvenation.*

Another sacred and secret mantra for this practice is *Jin Dan Zhi Mu* (pronounced *jeen dahn jr moo*). "Zhi" means *heal.* "Mu" means *Wood element,* which includes the gallbladder, eyes, tendons, and anger in the emotional body. "Jin dan zhi mu" means *Jin Dan heals Wood element, including gallbladder, eyes, and tendons, and anger in the emotional body.*

Apply the Four Power Techniques to do this practice at any time:

Body Power. Sit up straight. Put the tip of your tongue as close as you can to the roof of your mouth without touching it. Put your right palm on your liver. Put your left palm on your lower abdomen below your navel.

Soul Power. Say *hello:*

> *Dear soul mind body of my Jin Dan,*
> *Dear soul mind body of my liver and my Wood ele-*
> *ment,*
> *I love you, honor you, and appreciate you.*
> *You have the power to heal my liver and to heal my*
> *Wood element, including the gallbladder, eyes, ten-*
> *dons, and anger.*
> *I am very honored.*
> *Thank you.*

Mind Power. Visualize a golden light ball rotating in your liver, gallbladder, eyes, and tendons, and healing anger.

Sound Power. Chant or sing silently or aloud (listen to me on the enclosed CD):

> *Jin Dan Shu Gan* (pronounced *jeen dahn shoo gahn*)
> *Jin Dan Shu Gan*
> *Jin Dan Shu Gan*
> *Jin Dan Shu Gan*
> *Jin Dan Shu Gan*
> *Jin Dan Shu Gan*
> *Jin Dan Shu Gan*
>
> *Jin Dan Zhi Mu* (pronounced *jeen dahn jr moo*)
> *Jin Dan Zhi Mu*
> *Jin Dan Zhi Mu*
> *Jin Dan Zhi Mu*

Jin Dan Zhi Mu
Jin Dan Zhi Mu
Jin Dan Zhi Mu . . .

Chant or sing for at least three to five minutes; the longer, the better.

This practice is extremely important:

- to heal and rejuvenate the liver
- to heal and rejuvenate the Wood element, including gallbladder, eyes, and tendons, and to heal anger in the emotional body

金丹养心
Jin Dan Yang Xin

金丹治火
Jin Dan Zhi Huo

5. Practice to Heal Your Heart and Fire Element

The sacred and secret mantra for this practice is *Jin Dan Yang Xin* (pronounced *jeen dahn yahng sheen*). "Yang" means *nourish*. "Xin" means *heart*. "Jin dan yang xin" means *Jin Dan nourishes the heart with healing and rejuvenation.*

Another sacred and secret mantra for this practice is *Jin Dan Zhi Huo* (pronounced *jeen dahn jr hwaw*). "Zhi" means *heal*. "Huo" means *Fire element*, which includes the small intestine, tongue, and blood vessels, and depression and anxiety in the emotional body. "Jin dan zhi huo" means *Jin Dan heals Fire element, including small intestine, tongue, and blood vessels (including all arteries, veins, and capillaries), and depression and anxiety in the emotional body.*

Apply the Four Power Techniques to do this practice at any time:

Body Power. Sit up straight. Put the tip of your tongue as close as you can to the roof of your mouth without touching it. Put your right palm on your heart. Put your left palm on your lower abdomen below your navel.

Soul Power. Say *hello:*

> *Dear soul mind body of my Jin Dan,*
> *Dear soul mind body of my heart and my Fire element,*
> *I love you, honor you, and appreciate you.*
> *You have the power to heal my heart and to heal my*
>   *Fire element, including the small intestine, tongue,*
>   *blood vessels, and depression and anxiety.*
> *I am very grateful.*
> *Thank you.*

Mind Power. Visualize a golden light ball rotating in your heart, small intestine, tongue, and blood vessels, and healing depression and anxiety.

Sound Power. Chant or sing silently or aloud (listen to me on the enclosed CD):

> *Jin Dan Yang Xin* (pronounced *jeen dahn yahng*
>   *sheen)*
> *Jin Dan Yang Xin*
> *Jin Dan Yang Xin*
> *Jin Dan Yang Xin*

Jin Dan Yang Xin
Jin Dan Yang Xin
Jin Dan Yang Xin

Jin Dan Zhi Huo (pronounced *jeen dahn jr hwaw*)
Jin Dan Zhi Huo
Jin Dan Zhi Huo
Jin Dan Zhi Huo
Jin Dan Zhi Huo
Jin Dan Zhi Huo
Jin Dan Zhi Huo . . .

Chant or sing for at least three to five minutes; the longer, the better.

This practice is extremely important:

- to heal and rejuvenate the heart
- to heal and rejuvenate the Fire element, including small intestine, tongue, and blood vessels, and to heal depression and anxiety in the emotional body

金丹健脾
Jin Dan Jian Pi

金丹治土
Jin Dan Zhi Tu

6. Practice to Heal Your Spleen and Earth Element

The sacred and secret mantra for this practice is *Jin Dan Jian Pi* (pronounced *jeen dahn jyen pee*). "Jian" means *strengthen*. "Pi" means *spleen.* "Jin dan jian pi" means *Jin Dan strengthens the spleen function with healing and rejuvenation.*

Another sacred and secret mantra for this practice is *Jin Dan Zhi Tu* (pronounced *jeen dahn jr too*). "Zhi" means *heal.* "Tu" means *Earth element,* which includes the stomach, mouth, lips, gums and teeth, and muscles, and worry in the emotional body. "Jin dan zhi tu" means *Jin Dan heals Earth element, including stomach, mouth, lips, gums and teeth, and muscles, and worry in the emotional body.*

Apply the Four Power Techniques to do this practice at any time:

Body Power. Sit up straight. Put the tip of your tongue as close as you can to the roof of your mouth without touching it. Put your left palm on your spleen. Put your right palm on your lower abdomen below your navel.

Soul Power. Say *hello:*

> *Dear soul mind body of my Jin Dan,*
> *Dear soul mind body of my spleen and my Earth element,*
> *I love you, honor you, and appreciate you.*
> *You have the power to heal my spleen and to heal my*
>   *Earth element, including the stomach, mouth, lips,*
>   *gums and teeth, muscles, and worry.*
> *I am very pleased.*
> *Thank you.*

Mind Power. Visualize a golden light ball rotating in your spleen, stomach, mouth, lips, gums and teeth, and muscles, and healing worry.

Sound Power. Chant or sing silently or aloud (listen to me on the enclosed CD):

> *Jin Dan Jian Pi* (pronounced *jeen dahn jyen pee*)
> *Jin Dan Jian Pi*
> *Jin Dan Jian Pi*
> *Jin Dan Jian Pi*
> *Jin Dan Jian Pi*
> *Jin Dan Jian Pi*
> *Jin Dan Jian Pi*
>
> *Jin Dan Zhi Tu* (pronounced *jeen dahn jr too*)
> *Jin Dan Zhi Tu*
> *Jin Dan Zhi Tu*
> *Jin Dan Zhi Tu*
> *Jin Dan Zhi Tu*
> *Jin Dan Zhi Tu*
> *Jin Dan Zhi Tu* . . .

Chant or sing for at least three to five minutes; the longer, the better.

This practice is extremely important:

- to heal and rejuvenate the spleen
- to heal and rejuvenate the Earth element, including stomach, mouth, lips, gums and teeth, and muscles, and to heal worry in the emotional body

金丹宣肺
Jin Dan Xuan Fei

金丹治金
Jin Dan Zhi Jin

7. Practice to Heal Your Lungs and Metal Element

The sacred and secret mantra for this practice is Jin Dan Xuan Fei (pronounced *jeen dahn shwen fay*). "Xuan" means *spread the food essence.* In traditional Chinese medicine, the spleen has the function to spread the food essence (energy) from the stomach and small intestine to the chest. Then the lungs have the function to transfer the food essence to the heart. "Fei" means *lungs.* "Jin dan xuan fei" means *Jin Dan spreads the food essence to boost lung function with healing and rejuvenation.*

Another sacred and secret mantra for this practice is *Jin Dan Zhi Jin* (pronounced *jeen dahn jr jeen*). "Zhi" means *heal.* The second "Jin" means *Metal element,* which includes the large intestine, nose, and skin, and grief and sadness in the emotional body. "Jin dan zhi jin" means *Jin Dan heals Metal element, including the large intestine, nose, and skin, and grief and sadness in the emotional body.*

Apply the Four Power Techniques to do this practice at any time:

Body Power. Sit up straight. Put the tip of your tongue as close as you can to the roof of your mouth without touching it. Put your right palm on your upper chest. Put your left palm on your lower abdomen below your navel.

Soul Power. Say *hello:*

Dear soul mind body of my Jin Dan,
Dear soul mind body of my lungs and my Metal ele-
   ment,
I love you, honor you, and appreciate you.
You have the power to heal my lungs and to heal my
   Metal element, including the large intestine, nose,
   skin, and grief and sadness.
I am extremely honored.
Thank you.

Mind Power. Visualize a golden light ball rotating in your lungs, large intestine, nose, and skin, and healing grief and sadness.

Sound Power. Chant or sing silently or aloud (listen to me on the enclosed CD):

Jin Dan Xuan Fei (pronounced *jeen dahn shwen fay*)
Jin Dan Xuan Fei
Jin Dan Xuan Fei
Jin Dan Xuan Fei
Jin Dan Xuan Fei
Jin Dan Xuan Fei
Jin Dan Xuan Fei

Jin Dan Zhi Jin (pronounced *jeen dahn jr jeen*)
Jin Dan Zhi Jin
Jin Dan Zhi Jin
Jin Dan Zhi Jin
Jin Dan Zhi Jin
Jin Dan Zhi Jin
Jin Dan Zhi Jin . . .

Chant or sing for at least three to five minutes; the longer, the better.

This practice is extremely important:

- to heal and rejuvenate the lungs
- to heal and rejuvenate the Metal element, including the large intestine, nose, and skin, and to heal grief and sadness in the emotional body

金丹壮肾

Jin Dan Zhuang Shen

金丹治水

Jin Dan Zhi Shui

8. Practice to Heal Your Kidneys and Water Element

The sacred and secret mantra for this practice is *Jin Dan Zhuang Shen* (pronounced *jeen dahn jwahng shun*). "Zhuang" means *strengthen*. "Shen" means *kidneys*. "Jin dan zhuang shen" means *Jin Dan strengthens kidney function with healing and rejuvenation.*

Another sacred and secret mantra for this practice is *Jin Dan Zhi Shui* (pronounced *jeen dahn jr shway*). "Zhi" means *heal.* "Shui" means *Water element*, which includes the urinary bladder, ears, and bones, and fear and fright in the emotional body. "Jin dan zhi shui" means *Jin Dan heals Water element, including the urinary bladder, ears, and bones, and fear and fright in the emotional body.*

Apply the Four Power Techniques to do this practice at any time:

Body Power. Sit up straight. Put the tip of your tongue as close as you can to the roof of your mouth without touching it. Put your right palm on your right kidney. Put your left palm on your lower abdomen below your navel.

Soul Power. Say *hello:*

> *Dear soul mind and body of my Jin Dan,*
> *Dear soul mind body of my kidneys and my Water ele-*
>   *ment,*
> *I love you, honor you, and appreciate you.*
> *You have the power to heal my kidneys and to heal my*
>   *Water element, including the urinary bladder, ears,*
>   *bones, and fear and fright.*
> *I am extremely grateful.*
> *Thank you.*

Mind Power. Visualize a golden light ball rotating in your kidneys, urinary bladder, ears, and bones, and healing fear and fright.

Sound Power. Chant or sing silently or aloud (listen to me on the enclosed CD):

> *Jin Dan Zhuang Shen* (pronounced *jeen dahn*
>   *jwahng shun*)
> *Jin Dan Zhuang Shen*
> *Jin Dan Zhuang Shen*
> *Jin Dan Zhuang Shen*
> *Jin Dan Zhuang Shen*
> *Jin Dan Zhuang Shen*
> *Jin Dan Zhuang Shen*
>
> *Jin Dan Zhi Shui* (pronounced *jeen dahn jr shway*)
> *Jin Dan Zhi Shui*

Jin Dan Zhi Shui
Jin Dan Zhi Shui
Jin Dan Zhi Shui
Jin Dan Zhi Shui
Jin Dan Zhi Shui . . .

Chant or sing for at least three to five minutes; the longer, the better.

This practice is extremely important:

- to heal and rejuvenate the kidneys
- to heal and rejuvenate the Water element, including the urinary bladder, ears, and bones, and to heal fear and fright in the emotional body

金丹睡眠
Jin Dan Shui Mian

9. Evening Practice Before Going to Sleep

The sacred and secret mantra for this practice is *Jin Dan Shui Mian* (pronounced *jeen dahn shway myen*). "Shui mian" means *sleep*. "Jin dan shui mian" means *Jin Dan gives you high-quality sleep*.

As soon as you get in bed, apply the Four Power Techniques in this practice:

Body Power. After lying down, put your right palm just above your navel. Put your left palm just below your navel. Put the tip of your tongue as close as you can to the roof of your mouth without touching it.

Soul Power. Say *hello:*

> *Dear soul mind body of my Jin Dan,*
> *I love you, honor you, and appreciate you.*
> *You have the power to give me high-quality sleep.*
> *I am extremely blessed.*
> *Thank you.*

Mind Power. Visualize your Jin Dan rotating and growing in your lower abdomen.

Sound Power. Chant or sing silently (because you are lying down; listen to me on the enclosed CD):

> *Jin Dan Shui Mian* (pronounced *jeen dahn shway myen*)
> *Jin Dan Shui Mian*
> *Jin Dan Shui Mian*
> *Jin Dan Shui Mian*
> *Jin Dan Shui Mian*
> *Jin Dan Shui Mian*
> *Jin Dan Shui Mian . . .*

Continue until you fall asleep.

This practice is extremely important:

- to calm your soul, heart, mind, and body to prepare for high-quality sleep
- to heal and rejuvenate your soul, heart, mind, and body while you sleep

金丹能量

Jin Dan Neng Liang

10. Practice to Boost Energy Anytime

The sacred and secret mantra for this practice is *Jin Dan Neng Liang.* "Neng liang" means *energy.* "Jin dan neng liang" (pronounced *jeen dahn nung lyahng*) means *Jin Dan boosts energy in the whole body.*

Apply the Four Power Techniques to do this practice at any time.

Body Power. Sit up straight or stand. Put the tip of your tongue as close as you can to the roof of your mouth without touching it. Put both palms on your lower abdomen below your navel.

Soul Power. Say *hello:*

> *Dear soul mind body of my Jin Dan,*
> *I love you, honor you, and appreciate you.*
> *You have the power to boost energy, stamina, vitality,*
>   *and immunity in my whole body.*
> *I am extremely blessed.*
> *Thank you.*

Mind Power. Visualize a golden light ball rotating in your lower abdomen.

Sound Power. Chant or sing silently or aloud (listen to me on the enclosed CD):

Jin Dan Neng Liang (pronounced *jeen dahn nung lyahng*)
Jin Dan Neng Liang
Jin Dan Neng Liang
Jin Dan Neng Liang
Jin Dan Neng Liang
Jin Dan Neng Liang
Jin Dan Neng Liang . . .

Chant or sing for at least three to five minutes; the longer, the better.

This practice is extremely important:

- to boost energy in your whole body
- to boost stamina, vitality, and immunity

金丹治疗
Jin Dan Zhi Liao

11. Practice to Self-Heal Anytime

The sacred and secret mantra for this practice is Jin Dan Zhi Liao. "Zhi liao" means *healing*. "Jin dan zhi liao" (pronounced *jeen dahn jr lee-yow*) means *Jin Dan heals your soul, heart, mind, and body, as well as every aspect of life, including relationships and finances.*

Apply the Four Power Techniques to do this practice at any time:

Body Power. Sit up straight or stand. Put the tip of your tongue as close as you can to the roof of your mouth without touching it.

Put one palm on your lower abdomen below your navel. Put your other palm on any part of the body that needs healing.

Soul Power. Say *hello:*

> *Dear soul mind body of my Jin Dan,*
> *I love you, honor you, and appreciate you.*
> *You have the power to heal my soul, heart, mind, and*
>> *body, as well as every aspect of life, including rela-*
>> *tionships and finances.*
> *I am extremely appreciative.*
> *Thank you.*

Mind Power. Visualize a golden light ball rotating in any part of the body that needs healing or healing a relationship or your finances.

Sound Power. Chant or sing silently or aloud (listen to me on the enclosed CD):

> *Jin Dan Zhi Liao* (pronounced *jeen dahn jr lee-yow*)
> *Jin Dan Zhi Liao*
> *Jin Dan Zhi Liao*
> *Jin Dan Zhi Liao*
> *Jin Dan Zhi Liao*
> *Jin Dan Zhi Liao*
> *Jin Dan Zhi Liao . . .*

Chant or sing for at least three to five minutes; the longer, the better.

This practice is extremely important:

- to heal your soul, heart, mind, and body
- to heal your relationships, your finances, and every aspect of your life

金丹预防
Jin Dan Yu Fang

12. Practice to Prevent Sickness Anytime

The sacred and secret mantra for this practice is Jin Dan Yu Fang (pronounced *jeen dahn yü fahng*). "Yu fang" means *prevent all sicknesses*. "Jin dan yu fang" means *Jin Dan prevents all sicknesses in your physical, emotional, mental, and spiritual bodies, as well as prevents blockages in relationships, finances, and every aspect of life.*

Apply the Four Power Techniques to do this practice at any time:

Body Power. Sit up straight. Put the tip of your tongue as close as you can to the roof of your mouth without touching it. Put one palm on your lower abdomen below your navel. Put the other palm on any part of the body needing prevention of sickness.

Soul Power. Say *hello:*

> *Dear soul mind body of my Jin Dan,*
> *I love you, honor you, and appreciate you.*
> *You have the power to prevent all sicknesses in my*
> *physical, emotional, mental, and spiritual bodies, as*
> *well as to prevent blockages in relationships, fi-*
> *nances, and every aspect of life.*
> *I am extremely blessed.*
> *Thank you.*

Mind Power. Visualize a golden light ball rotating in any part of the body that needs prevention of sickness or visualize a golden light ball preventing blockages in relationships, finances, or any other aspect of life.

Sound Power. Chant or sing silently or aloud (listen to me on the enclosed CD):

> *Jin Dan Yu Fang* (pronounced *jeen dahn yü fahng*)
> *Jin Dan Yu Fang*
> *Jin Dan Yu Fang*
> *Jin Dan Yu Fang*
> *Jin Dan Yu Fang*
> *Jin Dan Yu Fang*
> *Jin Dan Yu Fang* . . .

Chant or sing for at least three to five minutes; the longer, the better.

This practice is extremely important:

- to prevent all sicknesses in your physical, emotional, mental, and spiritual bodies
- to prevent blockages in every aspect of life, including relationships and finances

金丹长寿
Jin Dan Chang Shou

13. Practice to Prolong Life Anytime

The sacred and secret mantra for this practice is *Jin Dan Chang Shou* (pronounced *jeen dahn chahng sho*). "Chang shou" means *long life.* "Jin dan chang shou" means *Jin Dan helps you prolong your life.*

Apply the Four Power Techniques to do this practice at any time:

Body Power. Sit up straight. Put the tip of your tongue as close as you can to the roof of your mouth without touching it. Put one palm on your lower abdomen below your navel. Put your other palm on your Message Center (heart chakra).

Soul Power. Say *hello:*

> *Dear soul mind body of my Jin Dan,*
> *I love you, honor you, and appreciate you.*
> *You have the power to prolong my life.*
> *I am extremely honored and grateful.*
> *Thank you.*

Mind Power. Visualize a golden light ball rotating in your lower abdomen.

Sound Power. Chant or sing silently or aloud (listen to me on the enclosed CD):

> *Jin Dan Chang Shou* (pronounced *jeen dahn chahng sho*)
> *Jin Dan Chang Shou*
> *Jin Dan Chang Shou*
> *Jin Dan Chang Shou*
> *Jin Dan Chang Shou*
> *Jin Dan Chang Shou*
> *Jin Dan Chang Shou . . .*

Chant or sing for at least three to five minutes; the longer, the better.

This practice is extremely important for prolonging your life.

金丹转化
Jin Dan Zhuan Hua

14. Practice to Transform Every Aspect of Your Life Anytime

The sacred and secret mantra for this practice is Jin Dan Zhuan Hua (pronounced *jeen dahn jwahn hwah*). "Zhuan hua" means *transformation*. "Jin dan zhuan hua" means *Jin Dan can transform your relationships, finances, and every aspect of your life.*

Apply the Four Power Techniques to do this practice any time:

Body Power. Sit up straight. Put the tip of your tongue as close as you can to the roof of your mouth without touching it. Put one palm on your lower abdomen below your navel. Put your other palm on your Message Center (heart chakra).

Soul Power. Say *hello:*

> *Dear soul mind body of my Jin Dan,*
> *I love you, honor you, and appreciate you.*
> *You have the power to transform my relationships, fi-*
> *nances, and every aspect of my life.*
> *I am extremely honored.*
> *Thank you.*

Mind Power. Visualize a golden light ball rotating in your lower abdomen and Message Center.

Sound Power. Chant or sing silently or aloud (listen to me on the enclosed CD):

> *Jin Dan Zhuan Hua* (pronounced *jeen dahn jwahn hwah*)
> *Jin Dan Zhuan Hua*
> *Jin Dan Zhuan Hua*
> *Jin Dan Zhuan Hua*
> *Jin Dan Zhuan Hua*
> *Jin Dan Zhuan Hua*
> *Jin Dan Zhuan Hua* . . .

Chant or sing for at least three to five minutes; the longer, the better.

This practice is extremely important for transforming your relationships, finances, and every aspect of life.

金丹圆满
Jin Dan Yuan Man

15. Practice to Enlighten Your Soul, Heart, Mind, and Body Anytime

The sacred and secret mantra for this practice is *Jin Dan Yuan Man* (pronounced *jeen dahn ywen mahn*). "Yuan man" means *enlightenment*. "Jin dan yuan man" means *Jin Dan can enlighten your soul, heart, mind, and body.*

Apply the Four Power Techniques to do this practice any time:

Body Power. Sit up straight. Put the tip of your tongue as close as you can to the roof of your mouth without touching it. Put one palm on your lower abdomen below your navel. Put your other palm on your Message Center (heart chakra).

Soul Power. Say *hello:*

> *Dear soul mind body of my Jin Dan,*
> *I love you, honor you, and appreciate you.*
> *You have the power to enlighten my soul, heart, mind,*
>   *and body.*
> *I am extremely grateful.*
> *Thank you.*

Mind Power. Visualize a golden light ball rotating in your lower abdomen and Message Center.

Sound Power. Chant or sing silently or aloud (listen to me on the enclosed CD):

> *Jin Dan Yuan Man* (pronounced *jeen dahn ywen*
>   *mahn*)
> *Jin Dan Yuan Man*
> *Jin Dan Yuan Man*
> *Jin Dan Yuan Man*
> *Jin Dan Yuan Man*
> *Jin Dan Yuan Man*
> *Jin Dan Yuan Man . . .*

Chant or sing for at least three to five minutes; the longer, the better.

This practice is extremely important to enlighten your soul, heart, mind, and body.

Jin Dan has power beyond words and comprehension.

Jin Dan can transform every aspect of life, including health, relationships, and finances.

Jin Dan can rejuvenate and prolong your life.

Jin Dan can purify your soul, heart, mind, and body.

Jin Dan can enlighten your soul, heart, mind, and body.

Jin Dan can transform the frequency and vibration of your whole body from head to toe, skin to bone.

In one sentence:

Jin Dan can bring you to reach Tao.

This chapter is the practical chapter of this book. It is vital to do these practices to transform every aspect of your life and to bring you to reach Tao. It takes a Tao practitioner's greatest effort to do Jin Dan practices as much as possible. Practice together with me on the audio version of this book. My frequency, vibration, and blessings will boost your practice.

⁕

After studying and doing the fifteen practices in this chapter, you can chant or sing these sacred and secret Tao mantras together to receive all of their benefits in order to reach Tao.

Jin Dan Jin Dan	*jeen dahn jeen dahn*
Jin Dan Xing Shen	*jeen dahn shing shun*
Jin Dan Jin Gu	*jeen dahn jeen goo*
Jin Dan Hua Gu	*jeen dahn hwah goo*
Jin Dan Shu Gan	*jeen dahn shoo gahn*
Jin Dan Zhi Mu	*jeen dahn jr moo*
Jin Dan Yang Xin	*jeen dahn yahng sheen*

Jin Dan Zhi Huo	*jeen dahn jr hwaw*
Jin Dan Jian Pi	*jeen dahn jyen pee*
Jin Dan Zhi Tu	*jeen dahn jr too*
Jin Dan Xuan Fei	*jeen dahn shwen fay*
Jin Dan Zhi Jin	*jeen dahn jr jeen*
Jin Dan Zhuang Shen	*jeen dahn jwahng shun*
Jin Dan Zhi Shui	*jeen dahn jr shway*
Jin Dan Shui Mian	*jeen dahn shway myen*
Jin Dan Neng Liang	*jeen dahn nung lyahng*
Jin Dan Zhi Liao	*jeen dahn jr lee-yow*
Jin Dan Yu Fang	*jeen dahn yü fahng*
Jin Dan Chang Shou	*jeen dahn chahng sho*
Jin Dan Zhuan Hua	*jeen dahn jwahn hwah*
Jin Dan Yuan Man	*jeen dahn ywen mahn*

The more you chant or sing, the better. There is no time limit. Chant or sing anytime, anywhere. Chant or sing silently or aloud. To chant or sing is to *go into the condition.*

Chant well.

Sing well.

Practice well.

Practice more.

Practice as much as possible.

Reach Tao as quickly as possible.

Conclusion

ꞮN THIS BOOK, I have revealed and explained divine and Tao secrets, wisdom, knowledge, and practical techniques. Let me summarize the essence for you and all humanity.

- Tao is the source. Tao is the creator. Tao is the universal laws and principles. Tao is emptiness and nothingness. Tao is The Way of all life.
- The normal creation of Tao is that Tao creates One. One creates Two. Two creates Three. Three creates all things.
- The reverse creation of Tao is that all things return to Three. Three returns to Two. Two returns to One. One returns to Tao.
- My ten-year Tao training program is divided into five major phases:
  - o The goal for the first phase is to remove all sicknesses. The Jin Dan practices in chapter 3 are essential to achieving this goal.

- o The goal for the second phase is to reach Fan Lao Huan Tong, which is to return to the health and purity of a baby. The highest secret practice to reach Fan Lao Huan Tong is to chant *Fan Lao Huan Tong* nonstop. To reach Fan Lao Huan Tong is to become a human saint. A human saint is a human servant who is given divine and Tao abilities to harmonize humanity.

- o The goal for the third phase is to become a Mother Earth saint. A Mother Earth saint is a Mother Earth servant who is given divine and Tao abilities to harmonize everything on Mother Earth.

- o The goal for the fourth phase is to become a Heaven saint. A Heaven saint is a Heaven servant who is given divine and Tao abilities to harmonize everything in Heaven.

- o The goal for the fifth phase is to become a Tao saint. A Tao saint is a Tao servant who is given divine and Tao abilities to harmonize all universes.

- o To reach the Tao saint level is to reach and meld with Tao.

- Jin Dan practices are the foundational Tao practice of Tao. They are the most important Tao practices. My next books on Tao will reveal further secrets, wisdom, knowledge, and practical techniques to you and humanity in order to reach Tao.

- Apply Jin Dan to chant or sing the fifteen Jin Dan sacred and secret mantras in your daily life in order to transform and enlighten all aspects of your life. Practice with me using the enclosed CD and the audio version of this book.

- Chant or sing the whole Tao text in order to reach Tao.

This book brings the secrets, wisdom, knowledge, and practical techniques of the Soul Power Series to a deeper and simpler level. This book teaches and practices that *Da Tao zhi jian*—The Big Way is extremely simple.

To study and practice Tao is to train yourself to be a better servant for humanity, Mother Earth, and all universes. The final goal of the Soul Light Era is to bring love, peace, and harmony to humanity, Mother Earth, and all universes. The Divine and Tao are preparing sacred and secret training to prepare divine servants to help humanity, Mother Earth, and all universes pass through this difficult time of transition and purification and also to bring the full flowering of the Soul Light Era for humanity, Mother Earth, and all universes.

> *I love my heart and soul*
> *I love all humanity*
> *Join hearts and souls together*
> *Love, peace and harmony*
> *Love, peace and harmony*
>
> *God gives his heart to me*
> *God gives his love to me*
> *My heart melds with his heart*
> *My love melds with his love*
>
> *Tao gives his heart to me*
> *Tao gives his love to me*

My heart melds with Tao's heart
My love melds with Tao's love

Thank you, Divine
Thank you, Divine
Thank you, Divine
Thank you, Divine
Thank you, Divine

Thank you, Tao
Thank you, Tao
Thank you, Tao
Thank you, Tao
Thank you, Tao

Thank you, Humanity
Thank you, Humanity
Thank you, Humanity
Thank you, Humanity
Thank you, Humanity

Thank you, All Souls
Thank you, All Souls
Thank you, All Souls
Thank you, All Souls
Thank you, All Souls

Thank you, All Universes
Thank you, All Universes
Thank you, All Universes
Thank you, All Universes
Thank you, All Universes

Acknowledgments

First, I thank the Divine and Tao for choosing me as a servant of humanity, all souls, the Divine, and Tao. I thank the Divine and Tao for giving me the sacred and secret wisdom, knowledge, and practical techniques of this book and all of my books. I thank the Divine and Tao for all of the blessings and honor they have given to me. I cannot honor the Divine and Tao enough. I am grateful beyond words, thoughts, and actions.

I thank my beloved spiritual father, Master and Dr. Zhi Chen Guo, for his teaching and training. I cannot honor him enough. I am grateful.

I thank Peng Zu and my Peng Zu Lineage Master, Dr. and Professor De Hua Liu, for his teaching and training. I thank Lao Zi for his teaching. I am grateful.

I thank my two Taoist masters who do not want to reveal their names to the public for their teaching and training. I am grateful.

I thank Shi Jia Mo Ni Fuo, A Mi Tuo Fuo, Guan Yin, and all of the buddhas, bodhisattvas, and beings in all heavenly realms, as well as all of my spiritual fathers and mothers in all of my lifetimes, for their teaching and training. I am grateful.

I thank Allan Chuck for his editing of this book and all of my books, as well as for his unconditional service to the Divine and Tao. His contribution of editing all of my books has deeply touched my heart and soul. I thank Elaine Ward for her assistance in editing this book. I thank Lynda Chaplin and Rick Riecker for their assistance with the figures and more. I am grateful for Allan, Elaine, Lynda, Rick, and other Divine Editors. I thank Pierre Grill for his recording of the CD enclosed with this book. I am grateful.

I thank my publisher Judith Curr, head of Atria Books, and my senior editor at Atria, Johanna Castillo. I thank all of the team at Atria, including Rachel Bostic, Deb Darrock, Lisa Keim, Chris Lloreda, Michael Noble, Kitt Reckord, Isolde Sauer, Christine Saunders, Tom Spain, and Amy Tannenbaum. I am grateful.

I thank Cynthia Deveraux and David Lusch for transcribing my flow of this book. Their fast typing really helped. I am grateful.

I thank my Worldwide Representatives, Marilyn Smith, Francisco Quintero, Patty Baker, Allan Chuck, Peter Hudoba, Petra Herz, David Lusch, Roger Givens, Patricia Smith, Peggy Werner, Lynne Nusyna, Joyce Brown, Shu Chin Hsu, Maria Sunukjian, Trevor Allen, and Hannah Stevens, for their great contribution to the mission. I am grateful.

I thank my one thousand Soul Healing Teachers and Healers worldwide for their great contribution to the mission. I am grateful.

I thank every member of my business team for their great contribution to the mission. I am grateful.

I thank my wife and my three children for their great support of my work. I am grateful.

I thank all of my students and friends for giving me the opportunity to share my teaching. I am grateful.

I thank all humanity and all souls for giving me opportunities to serve them. I am grateful.

I am the servant of all humanity, all souls, the Divine, and Tao. I am grateful.

I thank you all.

With love and blessing,

Zhi Gang Sha

A Special Gift

THE ENCLOSED CD is an integral part of this book, *Tao I: The Way of All Life.* In it, I sing the entire new Tao text that is a major focus of the book (chapter 2 especially). I also demonstrate individually many of the major powerful practice mantras so that you and every reader will be able to sing them correctly. Pay special attention to the Jin Dan (golden light ball) practices that are the subject of chapter 3.

The contents of the CD are as follows:

Track 1   Tao Song of Normal Creation, Tao Song of Reverse Creation

Track 2   *Love, Peace and Harmony*

Track 3   *Divine Healing; Thank You, Divine*

Track 4   *Tao Sheng Yi, Tian Yi Zhen Shui, Jin Jin Yu Ye, Yan Ru Dan Tian*

Track 5   Tao I text (each line repeated four times)

Track 6   *Universal Light*

Track 7   *Happy Happy Happy*

Track 8   *Ling Guang Pu Zhao—Shining Soul Light*

Track 9   Tao I text (sung once from start to finish)

Track 10   *Tao Sheng Yi, Tian Yi Zhen Shui, Jin Jin Yu Ye, Yan Ru Dan Tian, Shen Qi Jing He Yi, Tian Di Ren He Yi, Jin Dan Lian Cheng*

Track 11   Practice 1: Morning Practice Upon Waking Up— *Jin Dan Xing Shen*

Practice 2: Practice Before Meals—*Jin Dan Jin Gu*

Practice 3: Practice After Meals—*Jin Dan Hua Gu*

Track 12   Practice 4: Practice to Heal Your Liver and Wood Element—*Jin Dan Shu Gan* and *Jin Dan Zhi Mu*

Practice 5: Practice to Heal Your Heart and Fire Element—*Jin Dan Yang Xin* and *Jin Dan Zhi Huo*

Practice 6: Practice to Heal Your Spleen and Earth Element—*Jin Dan Jian Pi* and *Jin Dan Zhi Tu*

Track 13   Practice 7: Practice to Heal Your Lungs and Metal Element—*Jin Dan Xuan Fei* and *Jin Dan Zhi Jin*

Practice 8: Practice to Heal Your Kidneys and Water Element—*Jin Dan Zhuang Shen* and *Jin Dan Zhi Shui*

Practice 9: Evening Practice Before Going to Sleep—*Jin Dan Shui Mian*

Track 14   Practice 10: Practice to Boost Energy Anytime— *Jin Dan Neng Liang*

Practice 11: Practice to Self-Heal Anytime—*Jin Dan Zhi Liao*

Practice 12: Practice to Prevent Sickness Anytime—*Jin Dan Yu Fang*

Track 15 Practice 13: Practice to Prolong Life Anytime—*Jin Dan Chang Shou*

Practice 14: Practice to Transform Every Aspect of Your Life Anytime—*Jin Dan Zhuan Hua*

Practice 15: Practice to Enlighten Your Soul, Heart, Mind, and Body Anytime—*Jin Dan Yuan Man*

Use this full-length disc as a learning tool and guide for your own practice. Use this CD to practice with me, or simply listen to it. Enter a meditative state. Sing along silently or just relax and listen. Receive the divine frequency and vibration of these sacred texts and my singing as a gentle and soothing, yet dynamic and powerful blessing.

Serious students and practitioners will also want to practice with me using the audio version of this book. The audio version is also itself a healing and blessing tool to serve every aspect of your life.

May this CD and book assist you in healing, rejuvenating, and transforming every aspect of your life.

May this CD and book not only bring you to your Tao journey but also accelerate it.

May you reach Tao as quickly as possible.

Index

Acupuncture, 294–301
Acupuncture points, 31, 94, 394
  saying *hello* to, 298–301
Age, reversal of (*see also* Fan Lao Huan
    Tong), 17, 24, 30, 34, 37, 43, 49, 122
"Aha!" moments, 12, 13, 131
Akashic Records:
  access to information in, 132
  in Divine Karma Cleansing, 73–74, 89
  physical life is recorded in, 91, 126,
    132–33, 155, 190
  reincarnation and, 132
  virtue given by, 72, 73, 102, 154–155, 165
Allen, Trevor, 146
Amitabha (A Mi Tuo Fuo), 271, 355
Angels, healing power of, xiv, 228, 316
Anger:
  burns virtue, 90
  and Wood element, 123, 265, 406, 408
Anxiety:
  and Fire element, 266, 278
  healing, 285
A Mi Tuo Fuo (Amitabha), 271, 355

Back pain, healing, 294–95, 306
Bai Bing Xiao Chu (Remove all sicknesses),
  33
Balance, 55
  of Heaven and Earth, 95–97
  humanity, Mother Earth, and all
    universes, 70–71

Ba Wo Yin Yang (Mastered yin and yang),
  26
Bi Gu Jing Hua (Fasting to purify), 38, 47
Blessing:
  permanent, xxvi
  receive from all things in all universes,
    15, 17
  received through Soul Song and Soul
    Dance, 52
  Say Hello, 128
  in universal service, xv, xvi, 103, 130,
    151, 357
Blockages:
  apply normal creation and reverse
    creation to remove, 80–81
  and bad karma, 88, 133
  in the body, 114
  and sickness, 109–110
  in some aspect of life, 86, 127–28, 153,
    159
  from not following Tao, 9
  Jin Dan can remove soul, mind, and body
    blockages, 34, 114
  love melts all blockages, 106–7
  of soul, 34, 36, 114
  and Tao Shen, 100
  transformation of, 129
Blood vessels, and Fire element, 266, 278
Body:
  Earth's area of, 112
  enlightenment of, 29, 37, 160, 369

Body (*cont.*)
  Heaven's area of, 112
  light, 149
  soul system in, 209
  transforming sickness to health of, 30–34
  yin and yang of, 98
Body Power, 69, 227–28
  Lotus Hands position, *220,* 221
  One Hand Near, One Hand Far, 219
  saying *hello* to acupuncture points, 298
  Shen Mi, 220, 222, 223, 227
  Soul Light Era Prayer Position, 199, 313, 318, 332
  Soul Massage, 302
  Soul Tapping, 249, 250, 260, 321, 322
  see also Four Power Techniques
Body Space Medicine, xl
Body wisdom, 29
Bo He, 266, 268–72
Bones:
  healing, 289–90
  and Water element, 266, 288
Brain:
  blockages of, 285
  in Heaven's area, 112
  returning to Tao in, 186
  and spinal cord, 177
Brown, Frances Anne, 274–78
Buddha, 76*n,* 271, 316, 355
Buddhism, xiv, 102, 271
Business:
  karma of, 42
  Tao of, 9, 67, 86
  transformation of, 207–8, 240, 326–28

Cancer:
  healing through Divine Karma Cleansing, 74
  and normal and reverse creation, 10–11
Celis, Marcelo, 147–48
Chang Shou Yong Sheng (Long life, immortal), 61, 134–35
Chanting. *See also* Practices and Sound Power:
  and becoming, 177, 347, 366
  blessings received from, 107, 128
  duration of chant, 179, 186
  to go into the condition, 429
  importance of, 70, 108, 177
  for life-threatening conditions, 280
  mantras, *see* Mantras
  service in, 165

spiritual beings responding to, 129
to transform the consciousness of humanity and all souls, 109
Chao Bai Zhu, 282–84
Chao chu yin yang, tiao chu san jie, tuo chu wu xing (Go beyond the yin yang world, jump out from the control of Heaven, Earth, and human being, and escape the control of the Five Elements world), 22
Chi ba cheng bao (Eat until 80 percent full), 65
Chinese medicine, traditional:
  Five Elements in, 122–23
  and normal creation, 123
  prevention wisdom in, 144
  and reverse creation, 6–7, 123–24
  and yin and yang, 6
Chinese wild yam, 288
Chi su dan (Eat vegetables and less fat, oil, and salt), 65–66
Christianity, healing power in, xiv
Chuang Xin Ji Yuan (Create a new era), 64, 358–61
Compassion, 89, 107
  Da Bei Zhou (Big Compassion Mantra), 350
  Divine, xxi, 161–63, 164–66
  unconditional, 154, 156, 157
Condition:
  going into, 429
  reach fan lao huan tong condition, 35
  reach Tao condition, 23, 25
Confucius (Kong Zi), 91, 126
Crown chakra, 394

Da Bei Zhou (Big Compassion Mantra), 350
Dan Shen Yang Shen (Tao Dan, Tao Shen nourish kidneys), 61, 167–68
Da Tao (Big Tao), 7, 14, 133, 137, 216
Da Tao zhi jian (The Big Way is extremely simple), 11–12, 51, 107, 215, 231–32, 259, 264–65, 267, 348, 349
Da Wu Wai (Bigger than biggest), 18–19, 60, 76–77
De Hua Liu, 120
Demons, 160
Depression:
  and Fire element, 266, 278
  healing, 285
Devotion to the Divine, in total GOLD, xxiii, 43, 350

Digestive system:
    digestion after eating, 144–49, 404–6
    eat only until you are eighty percent full,
        65
    preparing for intake of food, 119–20,
        138–44, 403–4
    Soul Acupuncture for, 296–98
    Tao of, 153
Di qi shang sheng (Mother Earth's qi rises),
    95–96
Direct Knowing Channel, 254
Direct Soul Communication Channel, 254
Divine:
    author chosen as direct servant, vehicle,
        and channel of, xvii–xl, 370
    author's vows to, xvi, xviii–xix, 389
    as the boss of all souls, xiv, 349
    communication with, 252–53, 273
    healing techniques from, 227, 271,
        317–19
    honor to, xv, 399
    invoking the soul of, 228
    permanent healing and blessing treasures
        of, xvii, xxiv
    present in author's workshops, xv–xxiv
    service of, 156
    Soul Baby created by, 37–38
    soul treasures transmitted by, xiv–xv,
        xxvii, 51, 165
    Tao teaching given to author by, xl–xlii,
        59–65
    total GOLD to, 23, 43, 121, 126, 129,
        131, 350
Divine Body Transplants, xxi, 162–63, 173,
    269, 284, 287, 290, 337
Divine compassion, xxi, 161–63, 164–66
Divine forgiveness, xxi, 89, 126–27, 161–63,
    164–66
Divine frequency, xx, xxi, xxviii, 38, 51,
    173, 244
Divine healing, 317–19
Divine Jin Dan, 46, 115, 121, 388, 397–99
Divine Karma Cleansing, 42, 44, 73–74,
    89, 115, 132–33
Divine light, xxi, 161–63, 164–66
Divine love, xxi, 149, 161–63, 164–66, 254
Divine Master Teachers and Healers, 53,
    203
Divine Mind Transplants, xxi, 162–63, 173,
    269, 280, 284, 287, 290, 336
Divine mission, 152, 159, 350, 361
Divine oneness, 107
Divine Order, 160, 163

Divine realm, 105, 155–56, 158–59
Divine Soul Acupuncture, xxi
Divine Soul Downloads:
    Divine Body Transplant of Divine
        Compassion, 163
    Divine Body Transplant of Divine
        Forgiveness, 163
    Divine Body Transplant of Divine Light,
        163
    Divine Body Transplant of Divine Love,
        162
    Divine Body Transplant of Kidneys, 337
    Divine Mind Transplant of Divine
        Compassion, 163
    Divine Mind Transplant of Divine
        Forgiveness, 162
    Divine Mind Transplant of Divine Light,
        163
    Divine Mind Transplant of Divine Love,
        162
    Divine Mind Transplant of Kidneys, 336
    Divine Soul Transplant of Divine
        Compassion, 163
    Divine Soul Transplant of Divine
        Forgiveness, 162
    Divine Soul Transplant of Divine Light,
        163
    Divine Soul Transplant of Divine Love,
        162
    Divine Soul Transplant of Kidneys, 336
    leaving to history, xxv–xxvi
    list of, xxxv–xxxvi
    power of divine transmissions, xix, xxii,
        xxiii, 115, 162–63
    preprogrammed, xxv, xxvi
    to reach *fan lao huan tong,* 54
    readiness for, xxvi, 370
    Tao Soul Herb Bo He Body Transplant,
        269
    Tao Soul Herb Bo He Mind Transplant,
        269
    Tao Soul Herb Bo He Soul Transplant,
        269
    Tao Soul Herb Chao Bai Zhu Body
        Transplant, 284
    Tao Soul Herb Chao Bai Zhu Mind
        Transplant, 284
    Tao Soul Herb Chao Bai Zhu Soul
        Transplant, 284
    Tao Soul Herb Sheng Huai Shan Body
        Transplant, 290
    Tao Soul Herb Sheng Huai Shan Mind
        Transplant, 290

Divine Soul Downloads (*cont.*)
    Tao Soul Herb Sheng Huai Shan Soul
        Transplant, 290
    Tao Soul Herb Sheng Mai Ya Body
        Transplant, 280
    Tao Soul Herb Sheng Mai Ya Mind
        Transplant, 280
    Tao Soul Herb Sheng Mai Ya Soul
        Transplant, 280
    Tao Soul Herb Shi Chang Pu Body
        Transplant, 287
    Tao Soul Herb Shi Chang Pu Mind
        Transplant, 287
    Tao Soul Herb Shi Chang Pu Soul
        Transplant, 287
    unlimited, xxvii
    what to expect afterward, xxvii–xxviii
    yin companions, xxviii
Divine Soul Herbs, xxi, 272
*Divine Soul Mind Body Healing and
    Transmission System* (Sha), 5, 67, 110,
    274, 335
Divine Soul Mind Body Transplants:
    available, 44–52, 173, 273, 370
    Bi Gu, 47
    description of, xxi
    Fan Lao Huan Tong, 49
    Jin Dan, 46, 388, 397–99
    Jin Jin Yu Ye, 44–45
    of kidneys, 336–39
    resting, 339
    Shen Qi Jing He Yi, 45
    for Soul Song and Dance Healers, 53
    Tao Baby, 48
    Tao Nectar, 49
    Tian Di Ren He Yi, 46
    Tian Yi Zhen Shui, 44
    Tuo Tai Huan Gu, 47–48
Divine Soul Operation, xxi
Divine Soul Power, xiv, xxii
Divine Soul Songs, 51, 157–58
    Divine Healing; Thank You, Divine,
        56–57
    Happy Happy Happy, 243–44
    Love, Peace and Harmony, 56, 329–30
Divine Soul Songs (Sha), 5, 67, 232,
    355
Divine Soul Transplants, xxi, xxii, 162,
    163, 173, 269, 280, 284, 287, 290,
    336
Divine Tao teaching, xl–xli, 40–41
Drinking, Tao of, 87
Du Li Shou Shen, 26

Ears, and Water element, 266, 288
Earth element:
    balancing, 98
    and Soul Herbs, 266, 282
    yin-yang organs of, 98, 122
Eating:
    preparing the digestive system for,
        138–44
    Xiao Tao of, 8, 65–66, 86, 87, 133,
        137–38, 153
Emotions, 87, 90–91
    Divine and Tao Jin Dan to heal, 46
Emptiness, layers of, 186
    planets, stars, galaxies turning to, 21
    Tao servant returns to, 25
Energy, 172, 224, 258, 419–20
Enlightenment:
    advanced soul enlightenment, 38, 49
    Jin Dan practice, 426–28
    of one's soul, 37, 328–30
    reaching, 159–60, 178–80
    and rejuvenation, 37
    of soul, mind, and body 32, 37
    as unconditional universal service, 23
    in universal service, xv, 158, 159, 329,
        358
Er Sheng San (Two creates Three), 3, 9, 15,
    17, 21, 35, 62, 67, 168
Eyes, in Wood element, 265, 406, 408

Facebook, author's page, 52, 210, 232
Fan Lao Huan Tong, 4–5, 24, 29, 30, 33,
    34–39, 41, 61, 81, 122–33
    and becoming human saint, 34
    and building a light body, 43
    chanting to reach, 347
    difficult to reach, 150
    and Divine and Tao *Shen Qi Jing He Yi*
        Soul Mind Body Transplants, 45
    and gaining saint abilities, 47
    and immortality, 118
    Jin Dan and, 33
    and karma, 44
    key steps to, 35–37, 133
    and Ling Guang Sheng Shi, 360
    reaching, 41, 43, 54–55, 133, 135
    as signal of human saint, 38
    Soul Mind Body Transplants, 49–51
    as step to reach Tao, 30
    striving for, 44, 121, 136, 149
    and Tao *Fan Lao Huan Tong* Soul Mind
        Body Transplants, 49–50
    in Tao training, 41

total rejuvenation in, 124–25, 345–48
transmission of, 345–49
Fasting, 38, 47
Fatigue, healing, 289–90
Fear, and Water element, 266, 288
Fei Chang Tao, 60, 381
Finances, transformation of, 29, 207–9, 240
Financial karma, 42
Fire element:
  balancing, 98
  Jin Dan healing, 408–10
  and Soul Herbs, 265–66, 278–82
  yin-yang organs of, 98, 122
Five Elements:
  balancing, 98, 123
  escape control of, 22–23
  further division of, 123
  out of the control of, 23
  and Soul Herbs, 265–66
  strengthening, 292–94
  theory of, 122–23, 279
  in traditional Chinese medicine, 122–23
  in *Yellow Emperor's Internal Classic,* 98
Flowers, as spiritual currency, 89, 102, 155,
  165, 353
Forgiveness, 107, 325–26
  clearing karma, 72
  Divine, xxi, 89, 126–27, 161–63, 164–66
  Tao of, 91–92
  unconditional, 154, 156, 157
  in universal service, xv, 89, 356
Four Power Techniques, 68–70, 227–28,
  230, 234
  to benefit Five Elements, 292–94
  to boost energy, 419–20
  bringing out Soul Dance, 242–44
  bringing out Soul Song, 235–36
  to bring out soul potential, 333–34
  to build Jin Dan, 390–93
  to build Tao body, 370–72
  digestion after eating, 144–49, 404–6
  for divine healing, 318
  Divine Soul Mind Body Transplants, 44,
  337–39
  for enlightenment, 426–28
  evening practice, 417–18
  follow nature's way, 379–81
  in group healing, 310–12
  healing all sickness, 216–17, 224–26,
  229–30
  healing invoking souls of nature, 314–15
  healing neck pain, 316–17
  healing others, 307–10

increase soul intelligence, 331–32
invoking souls of nature, 314–17
Jin Dan to heal heart and Fire element,
  408–10
Jin Dan to heal kidneys and Water
  element, 415–17
Jin Dan to heal liver and Wood element,
  406–8
Jin Dan to heal lungs and Metal element,
  413–15
Jin Dan to heal spleen and Earth element,
  410–13
Lian Jing Hua Qi, 181–82
Lian Qi Hua Shen, 182–83
Ling Gong for healing, 191–92
Ling Gong for life transformation, 193–94
for lower back pain, 294–95
making a vow, 352–53
to meld with Tao, 374–75
for Ming Gong and Xing Gong, 195–96
morning practice, 401–2
preparing the digestive system, 138–44,
  296–98, 403–6
to prevent sickness, 237–38, 321–23,
  422–23
to prolong life, 423–25
for rejuvenation, 203–5, 238–39,
  247–48, 345–49
in remote healing, 312–14
Say Hello Healing, 304–7
saying *hello* to acupuncture points,
  298–301
self-healing, 236–37, 246, 304–6
for self-healing, 420–22
Shi Chang Pu for healing, 285–86
Shining Soul Light, 341–42
for soul communication, 212–14
soul herbs for Five Elements, 292–94; for
  heart qi, 279–80; for kidneys, 288–90;
  for liver, 267–68; for lungs, 285–86;
  for spleen, 282–83
for Soul Language, 198–99
Soul Language for healing, 203–4
for Soul Massage, 302–3
for Soul Tapping, 249–50
Soul Tapping for healing, 260–63
for Tao enlightenment, 372–73
for Tao happiness and joy, 367–68
Tao harvest, 375–76
Tao Shen Tong (Complete Tao saint
  abilities), 378–79
for Tao stillness and intelligence, 365–66
Tao Tao Tao, 362–64

Four Power Techniques (*cont.*)
   Tian Di Ren He Yi (Heaven, Earth, and
      human being join as one), 46, 71–72
   to transform a business, 326–28
   to transform every aspect of your life,
      425–26
   to transform finances or business, 207–9,
      240, 326–28
   to transform relationships, 205–6,
      239–40, 324–26
   Zhi Yu Bai Bing, 109–15
   for Zu San Li acupuncture point,
      297–98
Free will, xxvi
Fu Wu Di Qiu (Serve Mother Earth), 61,
   106–7
Fu Wu Ren Lei (Serve all humanity), 61,
   101–4
Fu Wu San Jie (Serve Heaven, Earth, and
   Human Beings), 64, 339–40
Fu Wu Wan Ling (Serve all souls), 61,
   105–6
Fu Wu Yu Zhou (Serve all universes), 61,
   108–9

Gallbladder:
   healing, 406–8
   in human being's area, 112
   in Wood element, 98, 122, 265
   and Zi time, 171
Gate of Life, 194
Ghosts, 160
God's Light, 219
GOLD (gratitude, obedience, loyalty,
   devotion), xvi, xxiii, 23, 30, 34, 43,
   126, 129, 131, 350
Golden Healing Ball, Sha's, 308, 312
Golden light ball:
   building Jin Dan, 222
   in Jin Dan Soul Mind Body Transplants,
     46
   in Mind Power, 69
   in Walter's liver, xvii, xix
Golden light beings, 211, 303
Golden light shines, 215, 238
Golden Urn, 194
Gong De Yuan Man (Serve unconditionally
   and gain complete virtue to reach full
   enlightenment), 61, 154–60
Gratitude:
   to the Divine, xvii
   expressing, 227, 316, 323, 433–34
   in total GOLD, xxiii, 350

Grief, and Metal element, 266, 285
Guan Yin, xiv, 141, 350–51, 355
   healing power of, xiii, xiv, 271,
     343

Hamilton, Jaylene, 142–43
Hand secrets, 219
Happy Happy Happy, 243–44
Harmonize humanity, Mother Earth,
   heaven, and all universes, 54
Harmony, xv, xxiv, 54, 357
Healing:
   all sickness, 224–27, 229–30
   approaches of conventional medicine, 11
   Divine, 317–19
   empowerment of, xi
   group, 310–12
   joining as one, 93
   message of, xi–xii, 67
   miracle, 271, 343
   One Hand Healing method, 219
   others, 307–10
   and practice, 54–55
   remote, 227, 312–15
   Say Hello, 128, 304–7
   self-healing, 33, 210, 227, 236–37, 246,
     304–7, 420–22
   and Shen Qi Jing He Yi, 68
   Soul healing, 303–19
   Soul Language for, 203–4
   Soul Tapping for, 260–63
   Tao of, 6, 12, 14, 29, 66, 67–68, 110
   Tian di ren he yi, 107
   in universal service, xv, 23, 357
   and Xiu Tao practice, 44
   yin-yang balance in, 12
   Zhi Yu Bai Bing (Heal all sickness), 61,
     109–15
Heart:
   connection with, 127
   enlightenment of, 34, 35, 37, 369
   of Fire element, 98, 122, 265–66, 278
   focus on, 27
   healing, 408–10
   in Heaven's area, 112
   intelligence in, 250–51
   Lian Shen Huan Xu (Transform
     and return Shen to Xu) in, 184,
     185
   and purification practice, 44
   reaching emptiness in, 186
   and Wu time, 171
Heart chakra, 190, 213

Heaven:
  area above the diaphragm belongs to, 112
  chant *Tian Di Ren He Yi* to offer service
    to, 127
  flowers from, 353
  gather energy and light from, 112
  gives you virtue, 114
  guidance from, 191
  layers of, 355
  reconstruction of, 339
  records, 126
  saint (servant), 125, 136
  and Universal Law of Universal Service,
    130
  unlimited realms in, 156
Heaven and Earth, 18, 20, 23, 54, 67
  balance of, 95–97
  chant *Tian Di Ren He Yi* to offer service
    to, 127
  energy gathers in lower abdomen, 113
  service of, 339–40
  yin and yang of, 97–98
Heaven saints/servants, 30, 39, 41, 55, 81,
    125, 136
Heaven's area, 112
Heaven's books, 151
Heaven's Library, xiii
Heaven's unique sacred liquid, 95
  swallow into Lower Dan Tian, 95–97
  Tian Yi Zhen Shui, 94
Herb gardens, 272, 277
Herbs, souls of, 266, 270–74
Herb tea, 266, 272–73
Herz, Petra, 141–42, 255
He Tao Zhong (Meld with Tao), 62, 188
He Xie Ren Lei (Harmonize all humanity),
    61, 135–36
Hinduism, healing power in, xiv
Huan Ling Nao Shen (Soul Mind Body
    Transplant), 63, 335–39
Hudoba, Peter, 120
Human beings:
  evolution of, 29
  physical and soul journey of, 136
Humanity:
  chanting Divine Soul Songs to serve,
    157
  chanting to transform the consciousness
    of, 109
  Divine mission and, 152
  Tao of, 13
  Tao of all professions is to serve, 154
  unconditional service to, 151

Huo shao gong te lin (Anger burns virtue),
    90–91
Hu Xi Jing Qi (Breathed and received
    nourishment from the essence of the
    universe), 26

Illness, prevention of, 29, 212, 215
  San mi and, 227
  Soul Song and, 234, 236–37
Immortality:
  attainable, 23, 24, 81, 135, 360, 372
  Chang Shou Yong Sheng (Long life,
    immortal), 134–35
  highest philosophy for, 25
  meaning of, 55
  qualities of, 27
  and Tao body, 370
  Tao of, 29, 259
  training for, 258
Immunity, building, 224
  and chanting *Weng Ma Ni Ba Ma Hong*,
    223
  San mi and, 222
  Snow Mountain Area and, 251
  Soul Dance and, 241
  Soul Song and, 233
Intelligence, 250–51, 364–67
Intercourse, 2, 35
Islam, healing power in, xiv

Jesus:
  blessing for prevention of sickness,
    322–23
  healing power of, xiii, xiv, 271, 343
  spiritual standing of, xiv
Jin Dan (Golden Dan):
  building, 113, 114–15, 118, 121, 169,
    222, 223, 390–93, 396–97
  Divine and Tao, 397–99
  Divine and Tao Soul Mind Body
    Transplants, 46, 121, 398
  and flow of qi, 34
  Human, 388
  importance of, 114, 222
  layers of, 33–34
  in lower abdomen, 32, 33, 114
  mantras for daily practice, 399–400
  and Mind Power, 69
  power and significance of, 389–90, 428
  to reach Tao, 389
  rotating, 120
  summary of, 121, 387–89
  what is, 387

Jin Dan Chang Shou, 423–25
Jin Dan Hua Gu, 145–46, 149, 153, 404–6
Jin Dan Jian Pi, 410–13
Jin Dan Jin Gu, 139–40, 146, 149, 153, 402–4
Jin Dan Lian Cheng (Form the Golden Dan), 33, 395, 396
Jin Dan Neng Liang, 419–20
Jin Dan Shu Gan, 406–8
Jin Dan Shui Mian (evening practice), 417–18
Jin Dan Xing Shen (morning practice), 401–2
Jin Dan Xuan Fei, 413–15
Jin Dan Yang Xin, 408–10
Jin Dan Yuan Man, 426–28
Jin Dan Yu Fang, 422–23
Jin Dan Zhi Huo, 408–10
Jin Dan Zhi Jin, 413–15
Jin Dan Zhi Liao, 420–22
Jin Dan Zhi Mu, 406–8
Jin Dan Zhi Shui, 415–17
Jin Dan Zhi Tu, 410–13
Jin Dan Zhuang Shen, 415–17
Jin Dan Zhuan Hua, 425–26
Jing, 168, 170, 171, 172, 251
Jing Qi Shen, 172–73
Jing Qi Shen Xu Tao, 188
Jing Sheng Sui (Jing creates spinal cord), 62, 176–77, 179–80
Jing Shen Nei Shou, 26
Jin guang zhao ti, bai bing xiao chu (Golden light shines; all sicknesses are removed), 69, 214–17
Jin Jin Yu Ye (Golden liquid, jade liquid), 31–32, 33, 44–45, 60, 94–95, 394, 396
Ji Rou Ruo Yi, 26–27
Jiu Tian, 355
Judaism, healing power in, xiv
Ju zhe cheng xing, san zhe cheng feng, 257–58, 377

Kaiser, Susanne, 147
Karma:
    bad, 42–43, 44, 88, 89, 92, 114–15, 130, 133, 158
    clearing, 72, 115, 130–31, 273
    Divine cleansing of, 41–42, 44, 89
    importance of, 74–75
    and life expectancy, 132
    as root cause of success and failure, 42–43, 73, 88
    self-clearing, 89, 92, 103, 114, 115, 157
    Tao of, 73
    and unconditional universal service, 158
    and *yang shou,* 132
Keehn, Christopher, 147
Khoe, G. K., 146–47
Kidneys:
    Dan Shen Yang Shen, 167–68
    Divine Soul Mind Body Transplant, 336–39
    Jin Dan healing, 415–17
    Lian Jing Hua Qi in, 184, 185
    in Mother Earth's area, 112
    Sheng Huai Shan for, 288–91
    Shen Sheng Jing, 175–76
    Soul Tapping on Snow Mountain Area, 251
    of Water element, 98, 122, 266, 288–289
    and water metabolism, 172
    Yong Quan acupuncture points, 394
    and You time, 171–72
Kindness, 89, 154, 156
Knee pain, healing, 225–26, 307–10
Kong Zi (Confucius), 91, 126
Kou Mi, 217–18, 221, 222, 223, 228
Kundalini, 194

Lao Zi:
    Peng Zu as teacher of, xl, 120, 251
    Tao Te Jing, xxxix, 2, 347–48, 380–81
Large intestine:
    and Mao time, 171
    of Metal element, 98, 122, 266, 285
    in Mother Earth's area, 112
Leadership, Tao of, 86
Lian Jing Hua Qi (Transform Jing to Qi), 62, 180–82, 184, 186–87
Lian Qi Hua Shen (Return Qi to Shen), 62, 182–83, 184, 186–87
Lian Shen Huan Xu (Return Shen to Xu), 62, 183–85, 186–87
Lian Xu Huan Tao (Return Xu emptiness to Tao), 62, 184, 185–88
Life:
    limited, 21
    physical vs. soul, 251, 349
    prolonging, 423–25
    purpose of, 156
Life expectancy, 251–52
Light, 107, 108, 129, 157
    divine, xxi, 149, 161–63, 164–66, 254

Light body:
  and body enlightenment, 369
  chant *Jin Dan Jin Gu* and *Jin Dan
    Hua Gu* to build, 149
  Divine Light Body Soul Mind Body
    Transplants, 370
  Tao body and, 369
Ling An Mo (Soul Massage), 63, 301–3
Ling Cao Yao (Soul Herbs), 63, 265–93
Ling Ge Wu (Soul Song, Soul Dance), 63,
  232–48
Ling Gong (soul temple), 190–94
  for healing, 191–92
  for life transformation, 193–94
Ling Guang Pu Zhao (Shining Soul Light),
  64, 218, 340–42
Ling Guang Sheng Shi (Soul Light Era),
  64, 358–61
Ling Qian Neng (Soul Potential), 63,
  333–34
Ling Qiao Da (Soul Tapping), 63, 248–
  265
Ling Xin Tong (Soul Communication), 63,
  209–32
Ling yao (soul herbs), 270, 271
Ling Yuan Man (Soul Enlightenment), 63,
  328–30
Ling Yu Fang (Soul Prevention of Illness),
  63, 319–23
Ling Yu Yan (Soul Language), 63, 196–209,
  234
Ling Zhen Jiu (Soul Acupuncture), 63,
  294–301
Ling Zhi Hui (Soul Intelligence), 63,
  331–33
Ling Zhi Liao (Soul Healing), 63, 303–19,
  344
Ling Zhuan Hua (Soul Transformation),
  63, 323–28
Liver:
  cells of, 123
  healing of, xix, 267–68, 305, 406–8
  in human being's area, 112
  and peppermint, 266
  Soul Software for, xviii
  in Wood element, 98, 122, 265
Logan, Ellen, 257
Longevity, 251–52
Lotus Hands Body Power position, *220,* 221
Love:
  Divine, xxi, xxiv, 161–63, 164–66
  melts all blockages, 106–7
  to Mother Earth, 106

unconditional, 154, 156, 157
universal, 356
  in universal service, xv, 89
Love Peace Harmony Center, Boulder,
  Colorado, 139–40
Lower Dan Tian, energy center, 32, 69,
  95, 100, 112, 114, 119–20, 251,
  395
Loyalty, in total GOLD, xxiii, 350
Luan shi chu ying xiong, 361
Lungs:
  in Heaven's area, 112
  Jin Dan healing, 413–15
  of Metal element, 98, 122, 266, 285
Lusch, David, 140–41, 149, 255–56

Mantras, 382–85
  All San Mi heal (request), 225, 226
  Bo He heals my liver, 268, 270
  to build Jin Dan, 391–93
  Chanting, singing, 245
  Chao Bai Zhu strengthens my spleen
    function, 283, 284–85
  Da Tao Zhi Jian, 264–65
  Develop Snow Mountain Area and
    Message Center, 195–96
  Divine heal me, 318
  Divine love, divine forgiveness, divine
    compassion, divine light, 161–62,
    164–66
  Divine love and light, 354
  Divine Soul Mind Body Transplants,
    338–39
  Fan Lao Huan Tong, 346
  Four Power Techniques heal all my
    sicknesses, 229
  Fu Wu San Jie, 340
  God's Light, 219
  Happy Happy Happy, 243–44
  I am an unconditional universal servant,
    353
  I have the power to prevent sickness, 320
  I love my heart and soul, 433–34
  Jesus prevents sickness, 323
  for Jin Dan daily practice, 399–400, 402,
    404, 405, 407–8, 409–10, 412, 414,
    416–17, 418, 420, 421, 423, 424, 426,
    427, 428–29
  Jing Sheng Sui, 176, 179–80
  Jin Guang Zhao Ti, Bai Bing Xiao Chu,
    216–17
  Join hearts and souls together to create a
    better business, 327

Mantras (*cont.*)
  Lian Jing Hua Qi, 182, 184–85, 186–87
  Lian Qi Hua Shen, 183, 184–85, 186–87
  Lian Shen Huan Xu, 184–85, 186–87
  Lian Xu Huan Tao, 186–87
  Ling Guang Pu Zhao, 218, 342
  Ling Hui Sheng Shi heals me, 317
  Love, Peace and Harmony, 329–30
  My souls massage my whole body, 302–3
  Na Mo A Mi Tuo Fuo, 218
  Nao Sheng Ming, 178, 179–80
  to reach Tao, 428–29
  San San Jiu Liu Ba Yao Wu, 198, 199,
    204, 205, 206, 208, 235–36
  serve—divine blessings, 104
  Sheng Huai Shan heal my kidneys, bones,
    ears, fatigue, and fear, 289–90, 291
  Sheng Mai Ya boosts my heart qi, 279–80
  Shen Qi Jing He Yi, 70
  Shen Sheng Jing, 175–76, 179–80
  Shi Chang Pu heal my lungs, Message
    Center, and brain, 286, 287–88
  for soul communication, 213–14
  Soul Herbs to benefit Five Elements,
    293–94
  Soul of my liver heal my liver, 305
  Soul of my lower back heal my lower
    back, 306
  Soul of . . . and my soul bless our
    relationship, 325
  The soul of the sun warms my hands and
    feet, 315
  Souls of Heaven and Earth prevent
    sickness, 321–22
  Souls of your knees heal your knees,
    309–10
  Soul Tapping heals, 250, 261–63
  Sui Chong Nao, 177–78, 179–80
  Tao Dan Tao Shen, 167
  Tao Ding De, Tao Hui Ming, 366
  Tao Fa Zi Ran, 380
  Tao Guo Cheng, 376
  Tao He Zhen, 374
  Tao Shen Tong, 378–79
  Tao Shen Yang Shen, 167–68
  Tao Soul Herb Sheng Mai Ya Soul Mind
    Body Transplants, 281
  Tao Soul Herbs Tea heals and rejuvenates,
    272–73, 276
  Tao Tao Tao, 362
  Tao Ti Sheng, 371
  Tao Xi Zai, 368
  Tao Yuan Man, 373

3396815 (San San Jiu Liu Ba Yao Wu),
    218–19
Tian Di Ren He Yi, 113, 128, 169
Tian Ming heals me, 192
Tian Ming transforms, 193–94
Universal Light, 108, 439
Universal service, 356–57
Wei Zhong heal and rejuvenate my whole
    back, 296
Weng Ar Hong, 218
Weng Ma Ni Ba Ma Hong, 218, 221,
    222–23
you are the mantra, 177
Your souls heal you (group healing),
    311–12; (remote healing), 313–14
Zu San Li heal and rejuvenate my
    digestive system and whole body,
    297–98
Mao time, 170, 171
Mary, Mother, xiii–xiv
Massage, 301
Masters, ascended, healing power of, xiv,
    228, 316
Master Teachers and Healers, 53, 253
Matter, 172
  to chant *Tian Di Ren He Yi* and, 112
  Jing and, 117
  Shen Qi Jing He Yi, 68, 93, 117
  smallest matter inside the cells, 123
Menopausal symptoms, healing, 289–90
Message Center, 190, 213
  blockages of, 285
  develop Snow Mountain Area and,
    194–96
  Soul Tapping, 250
Metal element:
  balancing, 98
  and grief, 266
  Jin Dan healing, 413–15
  and Soul Herbs, 266, 285
  yin-yang organs of, 98, 122
Mind:
  enlightenment of, 29, 37, 159–60,
    178–80, 369
  focus on, 27, 223–24
  intelligence of, 251
  misleading, 127
Mind over matter, xiii
Mind Power, 69, 227
  visualizing acupuncture points, 299
  Yi Mi, 220, 222, 223, 228
  see also Four Power Techniques
Mind wisdom, 29

Ming Gong, 194–96
Ming Men Area, 194
Ming Xin Jian Xing (Enlighten your heart to see your true self), 35–37
Monsters, 160
Moon, soul of, 316
Mother Earth:
  body areas of, 112
  harmony of, 54, 106
  and Jin Jin Yu Ye (Earth's sacred liquid), 32
  lessons learned in, 92
  natural disasters and Soul Light Era, xiii
  qi of, 95
  serving, 106–7
  Tian Di Ren He Yi, 106
  in transition period, 55–56, 106, 339, 361
  in yin yang world, 22
Mother Earth saint, becoming, 30, 39, 41, 55, 81, 125, 135
Mother Earth's sacred liquid, 94–95
Mudras, 219
Muscles, and Earth element, 266, 282

Na Mo A Mi Tuo Fuo, 218
Nao Shen Ming (Mind reaches enlightenment), 62, 178–80
Natural disasters, xi–xii
Nature, souls of, 314–16, 321–22
Nature's way, following, 379–82, 400
Neck pain, healing, 316–17
Ni Sheng (reverse creation), 6
Ni Tao Zhe Wang (Go against Tao, end), 7, 60, 85, 87–92
Normal creation:
  benefits of, 27–28
  constant, 19
  importance of, 6, 80
  from macro to micro, 10
  process of, 3–4, 9, 14, *19*, 21, 80, 92–93, 168, 257
  significance and power of, 18–19
  Tao Song of, 14–16
  and traditional Chinese medicine, 123
  and Western medicine, 6, 123–24
Nose, and Metal element, 266, 285
Nothingness, 78–79
Nusyna, Lynne, 256

Obedience, in total GOLD, xxiii, 350
One Hand Healing method, 219
One Hand Near, One Hand Far Body Power secret, 219

One-sentence secrets:
  Best spiritual practice is to offer total GOLD service, 43
  Best Xiu Lian is service, 102, 104
  Da Tao zhi jian (The Big Way is extremely simple), 215, 231–32, 259
  Direction for all souls of all universes is to reach *wan ling rong he,* 106
  Divine Jin Dan and Tao Jin Dan are treasures to heal all sicknesses, 115, 121
  For good karma, receive blessings; for bad karma, learn lessons, 89
  Four Power Techniques heal all of my sicknesses, 230
  Heal the soul first, 36, 128, 210, 212, 249, 319
  If the soul of a person becomes sick, then sickness of the mind and body will follow, 210–12
  Jin Dan can bring you to reach Tao, 428
  Jin Dan is the greatest treasure for all life, 390
  Jin guang zhao ti, bai bing xiao chu, 214–17
  Karma is the root cause of success and failure, 42, 73, 88
  Normal and reverse creation of Tao, 19
  Offer unconditional universal service, 151–52
  Only serve without asking, 128–29
  The purpose of one's physical journey and spiritual journey, 23
  Rejuvenate the soul first, 345, 346
  Return to Tao is the way of all life, 71
  Return to Tao as solution for healing, 68
  San Mi heals me, 227
  Say Hello Healing and Blessing is important soul secret, 128, 301
  Service is the fastest way to uplift one's soul, 103
  Shen Qi Jing He Yi is one of the major treasures, 118
  Simplest secrets, wisdom, knowledge, and practical techniques are best, 347
  Soul can heal, prevent sickness, rejuvenate, prolong life, 137
  Soul Healing is to say *hello* to the inner and outer souls, 344
  The spiritual journey is to serve others, 158
  Tao creates all things and all things return to Tao, 14, 21

One-sentence secrets (*cont.*)
  Tao is the creator and source of all universes, 378
  Tao of all souls in all universes, 13–14
  Tao of humanity, 13
  Tao of one's physical journey, 12–13
  Tao of one's soul journey, 13
  The higher the power, the more humble, 84
  To apply Soul Acupuncture is to say *hello* to the acupuncture point, 295
  To chant *Tao Tao Tao* is to reach Tao, 364
  To communicate with your souls is to prevent sickness, 212
  To invoke the souls of herbs and chant them is to apply *ling yao* for healing, 271
  To meld with Tao is to reach immortality, 259
  To reach Tao body is to reach immortality, 370
  To serve is to be on the spiritual journey, 352
  To serve is to transform all life, 130
  To serve unconditionally is to develop highest spiritual abilities, 153
  Total GOLD servant, 23, 43
  Transform the soul first, 328
  Unconditional universal service with total GOLD is the best way to fulfill one's spiritual journey, 126
  What you chant or sing is what you become, 347, 361
  Where you focus your mind is where you boost energy and heal, 223–24
  Where you put your hands is where energy goes, 222
  Yin and yang are two, 80
  You are the mantra, 177
Open Spiritual Channels classes, 202–3
Ovaries, in Mother Earth's area, 112

Pancreas, in human being's area, 112
Peace, in universal service, xv, 357
Peng Zu, xl, 120, 141, 251
Pollution, removal of, 109
Power, unlimited, 81
Power Healing (Sha), 68, 128, 217–18, 224, 227, 228, 300, 340, 343–44
Power of Soul, The (Sha), 5, 35, 42, 67, 72–73, 88, 136, 160, 211, 319, 335, 346

Practice:
  audio version as an essential companion, xxxii
  Evening Practice Before Going to Sleep, 417
  expressing gratitude in, 227
  importance of, xxxi–xxxiv, 54, 70, 119, 231
  important times for, 170–72
  Morning Practice Upon Waking Up, 401
  Practice After Meals, 404
  Practice Before Meals, 402
  Practice to Boost Energy Anytime, 419
  Practice to Enlighten Your Soul, Heart, Mind, and Body Anytime, 426
  Practice to Heal Your Heart and Fire Element, 408
  Practice to Heal Your Kidneys and Water Element, 415
  Practice to Heal Your Liver and Wood Element, 406
  Practice to Heal Your Lungs and Metal Element, 413
  Practice to Heal Your Spleen and Earth Element, 410
  Practice to Prevent Sickness Anytime, 422
  Practice to Prolong Life Anytime, 423
  Practice to Self-Heal Anytime, 420
  Practice to Transform Every Aspect of Your Life Anytime, 425
Pure Land, leader of, 271
Purification, xxxi, 126, 159, 329, 348
  of Mother Earth, 56
  Xiu Lian, 22, 37, 355
Purity, unconditional, 154

Qi, 32, 34, 68, 117, 170, 171
Qi gong, 173
Qi ju zhe cheng xing, qi san zhe cheng feng (energy accumulation and dissipation), 78
Quintero, Francisco, 253–55, 277

Red dots, receiving, 155
Reflection, 126–27
Reincarnation:
  and Akashic Records, 132
  stopping, 13, 105, 155, 156, 351
  universal law of, 19
Rejuvenation:
  Fan lao huan tong, 124–25, 345–49
  one-sentence secret, 345

Say Hello Healing and Blessing for, 128
Soul Dance for, 247–48
Soul Language for, 204–5
Soul Song for, 238–39
Tao of, 12, 14, 29, 37
Relationship karma, 42
Relationships:
Tao of, 86
transformation of, 29, 205–6, 239–40, 324–26
Religion, xiv
Renewal, 343–48
Residential karma, 42
Reverse creation:
benefits of, 27–28
in cancer, 11
constant, 19
and *fan lao huan tong,* 122
importance of, 6, 80
from micro to macro, 10
process of, 3, 4, 14, *19,* 68, 80, 93, 98, 122, 124, 257
significance and power of, 18–19, 258–259
Tao Song of, 16–17
and traditional Chinese medicine, 6–7, 123–24
Rice, Robyn, 148

Saints:
becoming, 30, 34, 38, 55, 81, 135, 373–75
four layers of, 125
healing power of, xiv, 228, 316
as high-level servants, 38, 135
humility of, 125
melded with Tao, 27
preventing sickness, 322
service of, 156, 355
and steps to reach Tao, 30
summary of Tao training, 41, 81
San mi he yi, 219, 224
"All San Mi," 226
to boost foundational energy, 222
San Mi heals me, 227
San San Jiu Liu Ba Yao Wu (3396815), 197–98, *198,* 204, 205, 206, 208, 218–19, 235–36, 332, 334
San Sheng Wan Wu (Three creates all things), 3, 15, 17, 21, 35, 62, 168
Say hello, *see* Four Power Techniques
Say Hello Blessing, 128, 300–301

Say Hello Healing, 128, 210, 300–301, 304–7, 316–17, 343–44
Schwartz, Brock, 274–78
Seasons, four, 7–8
Service:
in all lives, 355–58
and blessing, xvi, 103, 128, 130, 151
clearing karma in, 72, 130–31
endless, 355
Fu Wu Di Qiu, 61, 106–7
Fu Wu Ren Lei, 61, 101–4
Fu Wu San Jie, 64
Fu Wu Wan Ling, 61, 105–6
Fu Wu Yu Zhou, 61, 108–9
lessons learned from, xvi
as life mission, xi, xxiii, 41, 136, 156
total GOLD, 126
unconditional, 89, 92, 129, 133, 151–53, 154–60, 349–54
unpleasant, xvi
and virtue, 132, 158
without asking, 128–29
as Xiu Lian, 102–4
Sexual organs, in Mother Earth's area, 112
Shakyamuni, 76*n,* 355
Shang gong zhi wei bing, bu zhi yi bing (The best doctor prevents sickness instead of treating sickness), 116–17, 143–44
Shang Gu Zhen Ren, 25
Sha's Golden Healing Ball, 308, 312
Shen, 172
Sheng Huai Shan, 288–92
Sheng Mai Ya, 279–82
Shen Mi, 219, 220, 222, 223, 227
Shen Qi Jing (Soul Energy Matter), 62, 68, 93, 170–75
Shen Qi Jing He Yi (Soul, energy, matter join as one), 32–33, 45, 54, 68, 93, 116–20, 121, 395, 396
Shen Sheng Jing (Kidneys create jing), 62, 175–76, 179–80
Shen xian yong ling yao (A saint uses soul herbs), 267
Shi Chang Pu, 285–88
Shi Dai Fu Wu (Serve in all lives), 64, 355–58
Shi Jia Mo Ni Fuo (Buddha), 76, 102, 271, 355
Shi Wei Gong Pu (Vow to be an unconditional universal servant), 64, 349–54

Shi wei zhong (A beginning is an ending), 20

Shou Bi Tian Di (Life is as long as Heaven's and Earth's), 27

Shu Chin Hsu, 120

Shun Sheng (Normal creation), 6

Shun Tao Zhe Chang (Follow Tao, flourish), 7, 60, 80, 85–87

Sickness:
  disunity of Shen Qi Jing in, 33
  preventing, 116–18, 237–38, 319–23, 422–23
  removing, 30, 30–34, 41, 81
  as yin-yang imbalance, 6
  Yu Fang Bai Bing (Prevent all sickness), 116–21

Sickness karma, 42

Siddhartha Gautama, 76*n*

Simplicity, 348, 349

Singing:
  and becoming what you sing, 347
  blessings received from, 107
  and giving a Soul Order, 347
  to go into the condition, 429
  importance of, 70, 108, 157–58

Skin, and Metal element, 266, 285

Sleeping, Xiao Tao of, 8, 66, 86, 133

Small intestine:
  of Fire element, 98, 122, 266, 278
  in Mother Earth's area, 112

Smith, Marilyn, 201–2, 252–53, 254

Smith, Patricia, 148–49, 256

Snow Mountain Area, 194–96, 251

Soul Acupuncture, 294–301
  for digestive system, 296–98
  for lower back pain, 295–96
  power of, 300, 301
  saying *hello* to acupuncture points, 298–301

Soul Baby, 37–38, 48

Soul Communication (Sha), 5, 67, 202, 254

Soul Dance, 51–53, 232, 241–44
  applying Four Power Techniques to, 242–44, 245–46
  benefits of, 241–42, 244–45
  Certification Training Program, 53, 244
  healers, 53, 210, 244
  how they work, 242
  Ling Ge Wu, 232–48
  moving stories about, 53
  to prevent sickness, 359
  for rejuvenation, 247–48

for self-healing, 246
  what is, 241
  why we need to learn, 241
  Yin Yang Tao practice of, 133

Soul Enlightenment, 328–30, 368

Soul Healing, 66, 67, 210–12, 303–19
  group healing, 310–12
  healing others, 307–10
  remote healing, 312–15
  self-healing, 304–7

Soul Healing and Enlightenment Retreats, 160, 328

Soul Herbs, 265–93
  Bo He, 266–72
  Chao Bai Zhu, 282–84
  Sheng Huai Shan, 288–92
  Sheng Mai Ya, 279–82
  Shi Chang Pu, 285–88

Soul Intelligence, 331–33

Soul knowledge, in Soul Power, xiv, xxii, xxiii, xxxi, 128

Soul Language, 163, 196–209
  and divine code, 197–98, *198*
  for healing, 203–4
  how to develop, 197–98
  importance of, 197
  to increase soul intelligence, 331–32
  practicing, 203, 208–9
  as pure soul voice, 202
  for rejuvenation, 204–5
  and Soul Song, 234, 236
  special voice of, 199–200
  to transform a relationship, 205–6
  to transform your finances, 207–9
  as universal language, 200–202

Soul Language Channel, 254

Soul life, 103

Soul Light Era:
  beginning of, xii–xiii, xx, xl, 160, 342, 358
  Divine Downloads offered in, 115
  divine teachings for, xl
  evolution of humanity in, xxii
  final goal of, xxiii–xxiv, 105–6, 161
  Ling Guang Sheng Shi, 358–61
  Mother Earth saints in, 39
  and natural disasters, xi–xiii
  Prayer Position, 199, 313
  renewal in, 343
  singing and chanting in, 109
  Soul Language in, 208
  soul over matter, xiii, xxxiii, 212
  and Soul Power, xiv, xxiii

Tao Downloads offered in, 115, 388
time required to reach Tao in, 41–42
Soul Massage, 301–3
Soul Mind Body Medicine (Sha), xx, xxix,
110, 300, 343–44
Soul Mind Body Transplant, 335–39
Soul Operation, xxi, 210
Soul Order, 181, 335, 346, 348
Soul over matter, xiii, xxxiii, 212
Soul Potential, 333–34
Soul Power, 69, 227, 228
author's life mission in teaching of, xii
empowerment of, xii, 5
layers of, xiv
message of, xii, xxxi, xli
and Soul Light Era, xiii
Soul Mind Body Transplants, 164, 174
transformation of humanity in, xxii, 353
see also Four Power Techniques
Soul Power Series:
books in, 5, 66–67, 210
Divine Soul Downloads offered in every
book, xx
as a servant of humanity and all souls,
xxiii
summary of, 137
Xiao Tao of, 137
Soul practices, in Soul Power, xiv, xxii, xxiii,
xxxi
Souls:
aligned with divine consciousness, xxiv
blockages of, 34, 36
as the boss, xxii, 36, 128, 349
communication with, 190, 212–14
connection with, 127
countless, 172
created in Divine Soul Downloads, xxi,
xxviii
Divine Order for Enlightenment, 328
enlightenment of, 29, 37, 160, 369
focus on, 27
as golden light beings, 211, 303
healing power of, xiv
healing the soul first, 26, 128, 210, 319
inner, 228
intelligence of, 251
joining as one, 160–66, 395
layers of, 211
next life of, 20
outer, 228
production of, 36
purpose of, 105
replacement of, xxi

self-healing, 304–5
spiritual standing of, xiv
Tao of, 13–14
universality of, xiii, xxii, xxvii, 36, 128,
228
Soul secrets, in Soul Power, xiv, xxii, xxiii,
xxxi, 128
Soul Software, golden healing ball in, xix
Soul Song, 51–53, 109, 233–41
Apply to increase soul intelligence,
332–33
Apply to prevent sickness, 241
Apply to rejuvenate soul, mind, and body,
238
Apply to self-heal, 236
Certification Training Program, 53
channel, 235
healers, 53, 210
how to bring your Soul Song, 234–36
how Soul Song works, 233–34
Ling Ge Wu (Soul Song, Soul Dance),
232–48
moving stories about, 53
opening your Soul Song channel, 241
to prevent sickness, 237–38, 359
for rejuvenation, 238–39
for self-healing, 236–37
singers, 241, 244
to transform finances or business, 240
to transform relationships, 239–40
what is, 233
why we need to learn, 233
yin and yang, 52, 133
Soul standing, layers of, xiv
Soul system, 209
Soul Tapping, 248–65
Apply to self-heal, 249
benefits of, 249
Four Power Techniques, 249–50, 260–63
of Message Center, 250
of others, 248
to prevent sickness, 321
of Snow Mountain Area, 251
Soul Self-Tapping, 248
Soul temple, 190
Soul transformation, 323–28
Soul treasures, transmission of, xiv–xv
Soul Wisdom (Sha), xx, 5, 66, 196, 202,
232
Soul wisdom, in Soul Power, xiv, xxii, xxiii,
xxxi, 29, 128
Soul World, Light and Dark sides of,
160–61

Sound Power, 69, 227
for developing Snow Mountain Area and Message Center, 195–96
Kou Mi, 221, 222, 223, 228
Love Soul Mind Body Transplants, 164–66, 174–75, 338
mantras, *see* Mantras
saying *hello* to acupuncture points, 299–300
see also Four Power Techniques and Practices
Spinal cord, 77, 176–79
Spiritual channels, opening, 191, 194, 252
Spiritual development is unlimited, 365
Spiritual journey, 155
Spiritual laws, Universal Law of Universal Service, xv–xvi
Spiritual standing, layers of, xiv
Spiritual teaching, 158
Spiritual testing, 353–54
Spleen:
of Earth element, 98, 122, 266, 282
in human being's area, 112
Jin Dan healing, 410–13
and Soul Herb Chao Bai Zhu, 282–84
Stamina:
building, 113, 174–75, 195, 222, 224, 362, 401, 419
and chanting, 385
and compassion, 107, 161, 207
Lower Dan Tian and, 114
San Mi and, 222
Snow Mountain Area and, 194
Tao Dan and Tao Shen, 167
Stars, creation of, 20, 21
Stillness, 364–67
Stomach:
of Earth element, 98, 122, 266, 282
in human being's area, 112
Sui Chong Nao (Spinal cord fills brain), 62, 177–78, 179–80
Sunday Divine Blessings teleconferences, 51–52

Tai chi, 79, 173, 251
Tao:
of all souls in all universes, 13–14
author's vows to, 389
balance in, 56
as the boss of all souls, 349
communication with, 253–55, 257–59
creates One (Tao Sheng Yi), 2
as creator, 54, 431

Da Tao (Big Tao), 7, 14, 133, 137, 216
emptiness of, 21, 25, 76, 77, 78–79, 81, 85, 93, 124, 186
endlessness of, 77, 81
Er Sheng San (Two creates Three), 3
Escape control of the Five Elements world, 22–23
happiness and joy, 367
healing, 6, 12, 14, 29, 34, 66, 67–68, 110, 271
honor to, 399
of humanity, 13
for immortality, 29, 81
invoking the soul of, 228
of karma, 73
of life purpose, 153–54
micro and macro in, 10
miraculous and profound, 82
mission of, 54, 55
and normal creation, 3–4, 9, 14, 80, 92–93
oneness with, 1
of one's physical journey, 12–13, 14
of one's soul journey, 13, 14
permanence of, 23, 25
practice of, 118, 150
for prevention of illness, 29
for prolonging life, 29
of rejuvenation, 12, 14, 29
return to, 24–25, 68, 71, 98, 123, 124
and reverse creation, 4, 14, 68, 80, 93, 124
San Sheng Wan Wu (Three creates all things), 3
significance of studying and practicing, 28–30, 67, 105
sons and daughters of, 54
as source of universe, 67, 431
steps to reach, 30
striving to reach, 1, 23, 30, 42, 43, 348
study of, xxxix–xl, 28–29, 34, 41, 65
Tao is One, 2, 67
Tao Sheng Yi, 2, 67
techniques and practices released by, 51
The Way of, 2, 28, 65, 137, 348, 361, 431
total GOLD to, 23, 30, 43, 121
two creations of, 11
two ways to return to Tao, 24–25
universal principles and laws, 18, 28, 133
unlimited, 19, 81
what is, 2
Xiao Tao (Small Tao), 7, 14, 66, 133, 137, 215–16

Yi Sheng Er (One creates Two), 2
  of your entire life, 12
Tao Baby, 48–49
  and advanced soul enlightenment, 49
Tao Committee, 50
Tao Dan Tao Shen (Tao Golden Light Ball,
    Tao Heart Soul), 60, 99–101, 167
Tao Ding De (Tao stillness), 64, 364–67
Tao Downloads, power of, 115
Tao Fa Zi Ran (Follow Nature's Way),
    16–17, 18, 65, 379–82, 400
Tao frequency, 54
Tao Guo Cheng (Tao harvest), 65, 375–77
Tao herb garden, 282
Tao He Zhen (Meld with Tao and become a
    Tao saint), 65, 373–75
Tao Hui Ming (Tao intelligence), 64,
    364–67
Taoism:
  healing power in, xiv
  Lao Zi as founder of, xxxix
Tao I Text, 59–65
  as new divine teaching, xl–xlii
  Chang Shou Yong Sheng, 61
  Chuang Xin Ji Yuan, 64
  Dan Shen Yang Shen, 61
  Da Wu Wai, 60
  Er Sheng San, 62
  Fan Lao Huan Tong, 61
  Fei Chang Tao, 60
  Fu Wu Di Qiu, 61
  Fu Wu Ren Lei, 61
  Fu Wu San Jie, 64
  Fu Wu Wan Ling, 61
  Fu Wu Yu Zhou, 61
  Gong De Yuan Man, 61
  He Tao Zhong, 62
  He Xie Ren Lei, 61
  Huan Ling Nao Shen, 63
  Jing Sheng Sui, 62
  Jin Jin Yu Ye, 60
  Lian Jing Hua Qi, 62
  Lian Qi Hua Shen, 62
  Lian Shen Huan Xu, 62
  Lian Xu Huan Tao, 62
  Ling An Mo, 63
  Ling Cao Yao, 63
  Ling Ge Wu, 63
  Ling Guang Pu Zhao, 64
  Ling Guang Sheng Shi, 64
  Ling Qian Neng, 63
  Ling Qiao Da, 63
  Ling Xin Tong, 63

Ling Yuan Man, 63
Ling Yu Fang, 63
Ling Yu Yan, 63
Ling Zhen Jiu, 63
Ling Zhi Hui, 63
Ling Zhi Liao, 63
Ling Zhuan Hua, 63
Nao Shen Ming, 62
Ni Tao Wang, 60
San Wan Wu, 62
Shen Qi Jing, 62
Shen Sheng Jing, 62
Shi Dai Fu Wu, 64
Shi Wei Gong Pu, 64
Shun Tao Chang, 60
Sui Chong Nao, 62
Tao Dan Tao Shen, 60
Tao Ding De, 64
Tao Fa Zi Ran, 65
Tao Guo Cheng, 65
Tao He Zhen, 65
Tao Hui Ming, 64
Tao Ke Tao, 59
Tao Ling Gong, 62
Tao Shen Tong, 65
Tao Sheng Yi, 60
Tao Tao Tao, 64
Tao Ti Sheng, 64
Tao Xi Zai, 64
Tao Ye Chang Sheng, 61
Tao Yuan Man, 64
Tian Di Ren, 62
Tian Yi Zhen Shui, 60
Wan Ling Rong He, 61
Wan Wu Geng Xin, 64
Wu Fang Yuan, 60
Wu Qiong Jin, 62
Wu Shi Kong, 60
Wu Xing Xiang, 60
Xiao Wu Nei, 60
Xin Xi Xue Shan, 63
Yan Ru Dan Tian, 60
Yi Sheng Er, 60
Yu Fang Bai Bing, 61
Zhi Yu Bai Bing, 61
Tao Jin Dan, 121, 397–99
Tao Ke Tao, Fei Chang Tao (Tao that can be
    explained by words or comprehended
    by thoughts is not the eternal Tao or
    true Tao), 59, 65–75, 381
Tao Ling Gong (Tao Soul Temple), 62,
    190–94
Tao Nectar, 49

Tao saints/servants, 23, 25, 30, 40, 41, 55, 81, 84, 125, 136, 228
  abilities of, 23, 136, 375, 377–78, 382
  in ancient Tao books, 188
  becoming, 40
  description of, 188
  and four layers of saints, 125
  and immortality, 55
  last step in Tao training, 25
  longevity of, 257
  meld with Tao and become (Tao He Zhen), 373, 432
  and steps to reach Tao, 30
  and summary of Tao training, 41, 81
  and Tao light body, 47
  Tao Shen Tong, 377–79
Tao Sheng Yi (Tao creates One), 2, 9, 15, 17, 21, 35, 60, 67, 92–93, 393, 396
Tao Shen Tong (Complete Tao saint abilities), 65, 377–79
Tao Shen Yang Shen (Tao Dan and Tao Shen nourish kidneys), 167–68
Tao Songs, 51
  Fan Lao Huan Tong, 344
  of Normal Creation, 14–16
  of Normal Creation and Reverse Creation, 17–18
  of Reverse Creation, 16–17
  Tao sheng yi (Tao creates One), 97
Tao Soul Herbs Tea, 272–73, 278
Tao Soul Mind Body Transplants:
  available, 44–51, 173
  Baby, 48–49
  Bi Gu, 47
  Fan Lao Huan Tong, 49–51
  Herb Bo He, 268–71, 272
  Herb Chao Bai Zhu, 283–84
  Herb Sheng Huai Shan, 290–92
  Herb Sheng Mai Ya, 280–82
  Herb Shi Chang Pu, 286–88
  Jin Dan, 46
  Jin Jin Yu Ye, 44–45
  Nectar, 49
  Shen Qi Jing He Yi, 45
  Tao organs, 99
  Tian Di Ren He Yi, 46
  Tian Yi Zhen Shui, 44
  Tuo Tai Huan Gu, 47–48
Tao Tao Tao, 64, 361–64
  Go into the Tao condition, 362
  To chant *Tao Tao Tao* is to reach Tao, 363–64

Tao teaching:
  as advanced soul teaching, 5–6
  complicated techniques of, 150
  secret, 150
Tao Te Jing (Lao Zi), xxxix, 2, 347–48, 380–81
Tao Ti Sheng (Tao body is produced), 64, 369–71
Tao training:
  achievements in, 55
  applications for, 398–99
  author as servant to offer training, 258
  for four layers of saints, 125, 189
  Jin Dan and, 112
  offering of, 120–21, 134, 398
  opportunities, 189
  purpose of, 136
  purpose of energy and spiritual practices in, 172
  steps of, 41, 81, 134, 135, 431–32
  summary of, 41
  Xiu Tao (Practice Tao and reach Tao), 22, 23, 24–25
Tao Xi Zai (Tao happiness and joy), 64, 367–68
Tao Ye Chang Sheng (Tao career flourishes), 61, 137–54
Tao Yuan Man (Tao enlightenment), 64, 372–73
Teeth and gums, and Earth element, 266, 282
Tendons, in Wood element, 265, 406, 408
Third Eye, xxviii, 152, 211, 219, 388
  location of, 220
  moving energy toward, 223
  opening, 219–22, 223, 353
Third Eye Channel, 254–55
3396815 (divine code), 197–98, *198,* 218–19, 235, 334
Thyroid, in Heaven's area, 112
Tian Di Ren He Yi (Heaven, Earth, Human Being join as one), 46, 62, 71–75, 93, 96–97, 106–7, 111–14, 118, 119, 121, 127, 128, 129, 169, 395, 396
Tian Ming (special soul), 190–92, 193–94
  communicate with, 191, 252
Tian qi xia jiang (Heaven's qi falls), 95–96
Tian shu (Heaven's books), 151
Tian Yi Zhen Shui (Heaven's sacred liquid), 30–31, 33, 44, 60, 94–96, 394, 396
Ti Xie Tian Di (Completely connected and melded with Heaven and Earth), 26
Tongue, of Fire element, 266, 278

total GOLD service:
offering of, 43, 350
of saints, 355
unconditional, 360
vow to, 352–53
what is, 126
Transform old age to health and purity of
a baby (*See also* Fan Lao Huan Tong),
4–5, 24, 30, 34–39, 49–51, 122–33,
345, 347, 360
Tuo Tai Huan Gu (Completely transform
from human to saint), 47–48

Unity, 77
Universal Law of Universal Service, xv–xvi,
103, 130, 151, 350, 351
Universal Light, 108
Universal natural laws, principles, and
rules, 21
Universal service:
empowerment of, xi
key for spiritual development, 151–52
mantra of, 356
message of, xi, 130
with total GOLD, 126
Total GOLD servant and, 23
unconditional, 158, 316, 329, 349–56
Universal Law of, xv–xvi, 103, 130,
151, 350, 351
universal servant and, xv
Universes:
countless, 2, 40, 93, 373, 379, 381
create love, peace, and harmony for,
104
creation of, 18
harmony of, 54
return to Tao, 18, 19
soul, mind, and body enlightenment of,
100
Urinary bladder:
in Mother Earth's area, 112
of Water element, 98, 122, 266, 288–89
Uterus, in Mother Earth's area, 112

Vibrations, xxviii, 54, 100
Virtue, 87–88, 89, 90–91, 102–3, 114, 128,
154–55, 157
from Akashic Records, 73, 102,
165
and Divine Order for Soul
Enlightenment, 328
and service, 132, 158
uplifting soul standing by, 158–59

Vitality, 113, 224
and compassion, 161
Dan Shen Yang Shen and, 167
Four Power Techniques to boost, 195
Message Center and Snow Mountain
Area, 194
Ming Gong and Xing Gong, 196
Shen Qi Jing He Yi and, 175
strengthen kidneys to boost, 175

Walter:
Divine blessings bestowed on, xvii–xviii
Soul Software for Liver delivered to, xviii,
xix–xx, xxi
Wan Ling Rong He (All souls join as one),
13–14, 61, 106, 136, 160–66
Wan Wu Geng Xin (Everything is
renewed), 64, 343–49
Water element:
balancing, 98
Jin Dan healing, 415–17
and Soul Herbs, 266, 288–89
yin-yang organs of, 98, 122
Weather, Xiao Tao of, 7–8
Website www.DrSha.com, 210, 232
Wei Zhong acupuncture point (UB 40), 294
Weng Ar Hong, 218
Weng Ma Ni Ba Ma Hong, 218, 221, 222
Werner, Peggy, 276–77
Wisdom, unlimited, 81
Wood element:
balancing, 98
Jin Dan healing, 406–8
and Soul Herbs, 265
yin-yang organs of, 98, 122
Work, Xiao Tao of, 9, 86
Worldwide Representatives, 42, 51, 53, 120,
160, 203, 253, 328
Worry, and Earth element, 266, 282
"Wow!" moments, 231
Wu Fang Yuan (No square, no circle), 60,
82
Wu Qiong Jin (Benefits for all life are
endless), 62, 188–89
Wu Shi Kong (No time, no space), 60, 85
Wu time, 171
Wu Xing Xiang (No shape, no image), 60,
82–84
Wu You Zhong Shi (Physical life has no
ending), 27

Xiao Tao (Small Tao), 7, 14, 66, 133, 137,
215–16

Xiao Wu Nei (Smaller than smallest), 9, 60, 77–82
Xing Gong, 194–96
Xin Xi Xue Shan (Message Center, Snow Mountain), 63, 194–96
Xiu Lian (purification practice), 22, 37, 355
    service, 102–4
    and Tao Fa Zi Ran, 381
Xiu Lian A Mi Tuo Fuo, 355
Xiu Lian Ying Er (Xiu Lian Baby), 37–38
Xiu Tao (practice Tao and reach Tao), 22, 23, 24, 34, 37, 41, 44, 49

Yang companions, xxviii
Yang shou you xian, ji de zeng shou (Physical life is limited, accumulating virtue through service prolongs physical life), 131–33
Yan Ru Dan Tian (Swallow Heaven's sacred liquid), 32, 60, 95–97, 395, 396
Yellow Emperor's Internal Classic, The:
    Ba Wo Yin Yang, 26, 124
    Du Li Shou Shen, 26
    Five Elements in, 98
    Hu Xi Jing Qi, 26, 124
    Jing Shen Nei Shou, 26, 124
    Ji Rou Rou Yi, 26–27
    Ju zhe cheng xing, san zhe cheng feng, 257–58, 377
    on prevention of sickness, 359
    Qi ju zhe cheng xing, qi san zhe cheng feng, 78–79
    qualities of an immortal being, 27–28
    Shang gong zhi wei bing, bu zhi yi bing, 116–17, 143–44
    Shang Gu Zhen Ren, 25, 124
    Shou Bi Tian Di, 27, 124
    Ti Xie Tian Di, 26, 124
    Wu You Zhong Shi, 27, 124
Yi Mi (Thinking secret), 219, 220, 222, 223, 228
Yin and yang:
    balancing, 6, 12, 96–97, 98–99, 123, 124
    combine to produce a baby, 2
    go beyond, 22
    and Heaven and Earth, 2
    imbalance of, 6, 12, 123
    and intercourse, 35

and purification, 348
sickness due to imbalance of, 6
Soul Song and Soul Dance, 52
subdivisions of, 52
symbol of, *79*
Tao created, 22
Tao plus yin and yang, 168
Tao saints mastered, 27
Tao, yin, and yang create all things, 168
two (limited), 80
wisdom and practices, 54
Yuan Qi and Yuan Jing and, 35
Yin companions, xxviii
Yin-yang exchange, 96, 171
Yin yang Tao practice of Soul Song and Soul Dance, 133
Yin yang world:
    Heaven and Earth, 96–98
    human beings in, 21–22,
    is limited, 25
    in normal creation of Tao, 21, 24, 25, 67
    out of the control of, 22–23
    and reaching Tao, 22
    somethingness in, 79
    two is, 97
Yi Sheng Er (One creates Two), 2, 9, 15, 17, 21, 35, 60, 67, 97–99
Yong Quan acupuncture points (Kidney Meridian 1), 31, 394
You time, 171–72
Yuan Jing, 35, 36
Yuan Qi, 35, 36
Yuan Shen, 35, 36–37
Yu Fang Bai Bing (Prevent all sickness), 61, 116–21

Zhi Chen Guo, xxx, xl, 197, 219, 344
Zhi Neng Medicine, xl
Zhi Yu Bai Bing (Heal all sickness), 61, 109–15
Zhong Gong, Lian Jing Hua Qi in, 184, 185
Zhong wei shi, shi wei zhong (Ending is beginning; beginning is ending), 20
Zhu, Linhu, 142
Zi sheng zi mie (Your creation produces your own ending), 21–22, 24
Zi time, 170, 171
Zu San Li acupuncture point (ST 36), 296

Other Books of the Soul Power Series

Soul Wisdom: Practical Soul Treasures to Transform Your Life (revised trade paperback edition). Heaven's Library/Atria Books, 2008. Also available as an audio book.

The first book of the Soul Power Series is an important foundation for the entire series. It teaches five of the most important practical soul treasures: Soul Language, Soul Song, Soul Tapping, Soul Movement, Soul Dance.

Soul Language empowers you to communicate with the Soul World, including your own soul, all spiritual fathers and mothers, souls of nature, and more to access direct guidance.

Soul Song empowers you to sing your own Soul Song, the

song of your Soul Language. Soul Song carries soul frequency and vibration for soul healing, soul rejuvenation, and soul prolongation of life.

Soul Tapping empowers you to do advanced soul healing for yourself and others effectively and quickly.

Soul Movement empowers you to learn ancient secret wisdom and practices to rejuvenate your soul, heart, mind, and body and prolong life.

Soul Dance empowers you to balance your soul, heart, mind, and body for healing, rejuvenation, and prolonging life.

This book offers two permanent Divine Soul Transplants as gifts to every reader. Includes bonus Soul Song for Healing and Rejuvenation of Brain and Spinal Column MP3 download.

Soul Communication: Opening Your Spiritual Channels for Success and Fulfillment (revised trade paperback edition). Heaven's Library/Atria Books, 2008. Also available as an audio book.

The second book in the Soul Power Series empowers you to open four major spiritual channels: Soul Language Channel, Direct Soul Communication Channel, Third Eye Channel, Direct Knowing Channel.

The Soul Language Channel empowers you to apply Soul Language to communicate with the Soul World, including your own soul, all kinds of spiritual fathers and mothers, nature, and the Divine. Then, receive teaching, healing, rejuvenation, and prolongation of life from the Soul World.

The Direct Soul Communication Channel empowers you to

converse directly with the Divine and the entire Soul World. Receive guidance for every aspect of life directly from the Divine.

The Third Eye Channel empowers you to receive guidance and teaching through spiritual images. It teaches you how to develop the Third Eye and key principles for interpreting Third Eye images.

The Direct Knowing Channel empowers you to gain the highest spiritual abilities. If your heart melds with the Divine's heart or your soul melds with the Divine's soul completely, you do not need to ask for spiritual guidance. You know the truth because your heart and soul are in complete alignment with the Divine.

This book also offers two permanent Divine Soul Transplants as gifts to every reader. Includes bonus Soul Song for Weight Loss MP3 download.

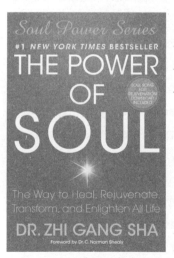

The Power of Soul: The Way to Heal, Rejuvenate, Transform, and Enlighten All Life. Heaven's Library/ Atria Books, 2009. Also available as an audio book.

The third book of the Soul Power Series is the flagship of the entire series.

The Power of Soul empowers you to understand, develop, and apply the power of soul for healing, prevention of sickness, rejuvenation, transformation of every aspect of life (including relationships and finances), and soul enlightenment. It also empowers you to develop soul wisdom and soul intelligence, and to apply Soul Orders for healing and transformation of every aspect of life.

This book teaches Divine Soul Downloads (specifically, Divine Soul Transplants) for the first time in history. A Divine Soul Transplant is the divine way to heal, rejuvenate, and transform every aspect of a human being's life and the life of all universes.

This book offers eleven permanent Divine Soul Transplants as gifts to every reader. Includes bonus Soul Song for Rejuvenation MP3 download.

Divine Soul Songs: Sacred Practical Treasures to Heal, Rejuvenate, and Transform You, Humanity, Mother Earth, and All Universes. Heaven's Library/Atria Books, 2009. Also available as an audio book.

The fourth book in the Soul Power Series empowers you to apply Divine Soul Songs for healing, rejuvenation, and transformation of every aspect of life, including relationships and finances.

Divine Soul Songs carry divine frequency and vibration, with divine love, forgiveness, compassion, and light, that can transform the frequency and vibration of all aspects of life.

This book offers nineteen Divine Soul Transplants as gifts to every reader. Includes bonus Soul Songs CD with seven samples of the Divine Soul Songs that are the main subjects of this book.

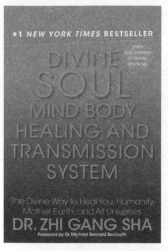

Divine Soul Mind Body Healing and Transmission System: The Divine Way to Heal You, Humanity, Mother Earth, and All Universes. Heaven's Library/Atria Books, 2009. Also available as an audio book.

The fifth book in the Soul Power Series empowers you to receive Divine Soul Mind Body Transplants and to apply Divine Soul Mind Body Transplants to heal and transform soul, heart, mind, and body.

Divine Soul Mind Body Transplants carry divine love, forgiveness, compassion, and light. Divine love melts all blockages and transforms all life. Divine forgiveness brings inner peace and inner joy. Divine compassion boosts energy, stamina, vitality, and immunity. Divine light heals, rejuvenates, and transforms every aspect of life, including relationships and finances.

This book offers forty-six permanent divine treasures, including Divine Soul Transplants, Divine Mind Transplants, and Divine Body Transplants, as gifts to every reader. Includes bonus Soul Symphony of Yin Yang excerpt MP3 download.

www.DrSha.com
www.HeavensLibrary.com
Telephone: 1-888-3396815
DrSha@DrSha.com

"This inspiring documentary has masterfully captured the vital healing work and global mission of Dr. Guo and Dr. Sha."
– Dr. Michael Bernard Beckwith – Founder, Agape International Spiritual Center

This film reveals profound soul secrets and shares the wisdom, knowledge, and practices of Dr. Guo's Body Space Medicine and Dr. Sha's Soul Mind Body Medicine. Millions of people in China have studied with Dr. Guo, who is Dr. Sha's most beloved spiritual father. Dr. Guo is "the master who can cure the incurable." After Dr. Sha heals her ailing father, American filmmaker Sande Zeig accompanies Dr. Sha to China to visit his mentor. At Dr. Guo's clinic, she captures first-ever footage of breakthrough healing practices involving special herbs, unique fire massage, and revolutionary self-healing techniques. These two Soul Masters have a special bond. They are united in their commitment to serve others. As you see them heal and teach, your heart and soul will be touched. Experience the delight, inspiration, wonder, and gratitude that *Soul Masters* brings.

PPV Video Streaming and DVD at
www.soulmastersmovie.com